2121

FUNNY STORIES

AND HOW TO TELL THEM

WINSTON K. PENDLETON

2121

Funny Stories

and how to tell them

THE BETHANY PRESS · St. Louis, Missouri

MANUFACTURED IN THE UNITED STATES OF AMERICA

TO

darling Gladys
who always laughed at these stories
no matter how many times she
heard me tell them
and with a special word of appreciation
to Bess who took this whole project so
seriously

The stories in this book are grouped for easy reference under 727 different categories. Other related stories are cross-referenced by number following each category.

WHY DO SOME FOLKS SEEM TO HAVE A KNACK FOR TELLING stories that bring down the house while somebody else—telling the same story—can't raise the slightest murmur?

The answer is simple—how.

How a story is told is more important than the story itself. I have heard brilliant stories go "thud" like a ball of dough hitting the floor and I have heard a banal remark start a wave of hysteria.

Some people say storytelling is a gift—something one is born with. One either has it or he doesn't. Others insist it is a skill that can be developed.

From my observations in the business over the years, I do not think the answer is clear-cut. Certainly, there are those who appear to be born funny. We call them naturals. Yet, even they improve with experience and practice. And the truly great performers work at it—and hard.

I have seen a few determined individuals who have developed into good storytellers from what could be described as "nothing." And, too, I have seen a few speakers try to be funny who couldn't make it if they spoke every night for a thousand years.

Maybe it is like music. Some take to it early and easily. Others have to work at it. Still others can never learn to carry the simplest tune.

In one way humor is like music. Study and practice according to careful plan and a few well-defined rules can help improve anyone's storytelling ability.

The temptation here is to list ten or twenty "dos" and "don'ts" or to launch into a learned treatise on how to stand, or what to say and when to say it, or how to wave the arms and ending with "don't put your hands in your pockets."

The result would be a lot of silly details that probably would make the reader self-conscious every time he started to tell a story. In the end they would keep him from freeing his own true personality for the audience to see and hear and enjoy.

I am suggesting two basic rules. If you will learn these two fundamentals about being funny, you can go as far as you like up the ladder of humor. (You might be thrown out of a few respectable parties and hissed off the speaking platform in the process, but you'll make it if you stick to the rules—long enough.)

Here they are:

1. Learn your story.
2. Believe what you are saying.

First, learn the laugh-getting part of your story and learn it perfectly. You must know it so well that you do not have to think about the words. You can then concentrate on something more important—how you are telling it.

Suppose you think story number 1832 is funny. The laugh-provoking words in that story are: "How do I get the chewing gum out of my ears?" Learn that line so well that if you woke up in the middle of the night out of a deep sleep, you could give it instantly and flawlessly.

If you know your story, most of the risk of ruining it will be gone. Once you learn it, you also will learn not to throw it away by saying to your audience: "Have you heard about the little man who stuck chewing gum in his ears? No? Then, I'll tell you. It sure is funny. You'll die laughing. (You're sure you haven't heard it?) It almost kills me even to think about it. Anyway, he was flying. . . . ."

Instead, you can concentrate on how to tell that punch line so that everyone in the audience will understand the story, so that they won't have to figure out what is funny, so that they will laugh automatically, even though they have heard it before. One good way to put that line across is to throw your elbows out and stick your fingers in your ears as you say it.

The point can be made more graphically, maybe, by asking how well you think you could tell story number 682 if you did not know it well. If you think you can do it, try telling it to your wife one minute after reading it over only one time. See how much of a laugh you won't get.

A good way to begin is to pick out a dozen stories that you think are funny and learn to tell them well. Many a funny man has risen to fame on a simple routine told over and over again. Witness Abbott and Costello and their age-old laugh-getter "Who's on first base?"

After you have picked your dozen funny stories, weave them together into a smooth-flowing routine. Learn the stories so well that the actual telling will sound easy and natural. That is rule number one.

Rule number two has to do with the most important ingredient in any public speech—sincerity. A sincere man who stutters will make a more persuasive speech than the eloquent hypocrite.

Since you can't fake sincerity, you must develop a belief in the stories you tell. Think of them as fact. Something that happened. Something that you are eager to tell your friends about. If a story doesn't ring true enough for you to believe, how do you expect your listeners to believe it?

Here is where your imagination comes in. With a funny punch line on the tip of your tongue you can make the "build-up" fit almost any occasion. Don't try to pass off an old Hitler-Goebbels story on an up-to-date audience. There will be people there who never heard of Goebbels. If the punch line is funny, build the story around two modern-day figures.

Use your imagination to make a story move from Milwaukee to Tampa to Tucson effortlessly—to fit the occasion.

Then, too, the moment you warn your audience you are going to tell a joke, they know that this part of your speech is fiction. You declare yourself to be a phony. They also begin to compare you with some highly skilled storyteller that they have heard and liked. This stacks the odds against you. Don't do it. Instead, slip into your stories unnoticed, and before anybody knows what you are doing.

Telling a story as though it were the truth will give it one of the richest elements of humor—surprise. The oldest funny joke in the circus, where a clown rushes toward the children with a bucket of water that turns out to be confetti, provokes screams of amusement because of surprise. If the clown had told the children what he was going to do, it would not have been funny.

This is such a basic component of humor that it is a wonder all speakers don't recognize it. And yet, they don't. For some reason, you still hear men standing before an audience saying, "I want to tell you a funny story I heard the other day."

At a banquet in West Virginia once, I heard a toastmaster begin his part of the program like this: "As toastmaster tonight I know part of my job is to tell some funny jokes. I'm not very good at telling jokes, and I spent several hours trying to think of some and couldn't remember any, so I went over to the library and got a book of jokes and picked out two or three for tonight. I know you probably have heard them before, and maybe you won't think they are funny, but I am going to read them anyway because, as I said, I am supposed to be funny. Maybe you won't think they are funny and maybe you already have heard them before and besides I'm not a very good storyteller, but here they are. As I said, maybe you won't think they are very funny." And they didn't. Nobody laughed—not even a ripple.

The master storyteller will move into his story as though he were telling an actual happening. Even though his audience discovers he is leading them on, they do have the thrill of making the discovery themselves. The element of surprise is still there. The story will always get a better laugh.

It is easy to make a story sound like the truth when it is told in the first person. If you want to get the crowd warmed up and ready to listen when you start a speech, tell a story on yourself. This is a good way to begin. Everybody seems to enjoy laughing at the speaker.

If you are called on to make a speech and you do not have your opening ready, turn to the book and select several stories that you think are funny. Suppose you select numbers 1094, 1784, and 521. Don't tell them word-for-word as they are written. Instead, blend them together and make them sound like a real experience. If you do, your three stories might go like this: "I want to thank Mr. Smith for that gracious introduction. The truth is, he read it exactly as I wrote it. (*Laugh*)

"That's important. Sometimes when a program chairman like Mr. Smith introduces a speaker, he takes that opportunity to make a long-winded speech. (*Laugh*) Several weeks ago I was invited to speak at an oil dealers' convention out in Pittsburgh.

The man who introduced me took thirty minutes. He forgot I was sitting there. (*Laugh*) Then, to make it up to me he really spread it on. He ended up introducing me as the fellow who had just made $800,000 in an oil deal down in Oklahoma. And that wasn't exactly true. It wasn't an oil deal, it was a real estate deal. (*Laugh*) And besides, it wasn't in Oklahoma, it was in Virginia. (*Laugh*) And he got his figures all mixed up. It wasn't $800,000, it was $800. And besides that, it wasn't a profit, it was a loss. (*Laugh*)

"I must say, I enjoyed that oil dealers' convention. After my speech that night I was standing with the president of the association at the door shaking hands with the people. They certainly were nice to me. I never had so many compliments in my life.

"One man even called it an address. 'That was the greatest address I ever heard,' he said. Another man said: 'That was great. I could have listened to you for another hour and a half.' (*Laugh*)

"And then the last man in the dining room came up to me and shook my hand and said: 'I thought it stunk. (*Laugh*) That was the worst speech anybody ever gave around here and whoever invited you to the meeting ought to be put out of the association. It was a disgrace.' And then he went on out.

"Of course, my feelings were hurt a little. But, the president of the association was the one who was embarrassed. He was upset about it and began to apologize.

" 'Don't pay any attention to what that fellow says,' he told me. 'Why, he's a half-wit. That man never had an original thought in his life. All he does is listen to what other people say and then he goes around repeating it.' (*Laugh*)

"I appreciate that noise. I don't like to stand in front of a quiet audience. I do that now and then—but I don't like it. The quietest audience I ever had was two weeks ago. I spoke to the State college for the deaf and dumb. (*Laugh*) Of course, I didn't speak to them. It was a talk on slides. It was a Sunday afternoon lecture and I drove down on Saturday so I would be there on time. Saturday night I was a guest of the president of the college for dinner. He told me that after dinner they were going to move the tables out of the cafeteria and have a dance and that I was invited. I told him that I was sorry but that I didn't know how to talk to any of those people. He said to me, you don't have to know how to talk to them. All you need to know is how to ask a girl to dance with you. All you have to do is walk up to the girl you want to dance with and point to her and then point to yourself and then make a dancing motion. And she will understand.

"Well, I stayed for the dance. Most of the time I was a wall-flower, but after a while I saw the cutest little girl in the world coming down the hall. I rushed to open the door for her and tried out this sign language I had just learned. And it worked.

"She danced with me that dance and then the next. After that, we ended up down by the orchestra. When the music stopped, the saxophone player leaned over and said, 'Edith, how about having the next dance with you.' And this little girl I was dancing with turned to him and said, 'I'd like to, Harry, but I can't. I'm stuck with this dummy.' *(Laugh)*

"And so, tonight, I am afraid that you are going to be stuck with me while I talk to you about. . . ." And they will listen to what you have to say.

Stories that seem to be tailored to fit the occasion are more apt to result in laughter than those told about somebody else—some-where else. At a furniture dealers' convention, tell story 873 and at a church supper tell 1871. At a fund-raising banquet, story 471 will make folks roar with laughter.

At an interclub meeting of Rotarians, Kiwanians, and Lions, tell story 1484. If you use this one, make it sound like the truth, not something you read out of a book. Tell it like this: "It is good to see the spirit of cooperation between these great civic organizations. It is good to see that you can get together and en-joy such warm fellowship. I like to attend meetings like this. Not long ago I spoke at a similar meeting, with Rotarians, Kiwanians, and Lions present. After the dinner was over, the presidents of the three clubs invited me to stick around for a cup of coffee.

"As we sat at the table chatting, the president of the Rotary Club said to the president of the Kiwanis Club: 'You know, I admire the work that you fellows do in this town. If I weren't a Rotarian, I would be a Kiwanian.' And the Kiwanian said the same thing. He said: 'I feel the same way and if I were not a Kiwanian, I would be a Rotarian.' And, of course, me and my big mouth. I saw the president of the Lions sitting there rather forlorn looking and I said to him: 'You are a Lion. Tell me, if you weren't a Lion what would you be?' And he raised his head up real proudly and said: 'Yes, I'm a Lion. And if I weren't a Lion, I'd be ashamed of myself.' "

With a little thought and experience, you will have no trouble finding stories to fit any occasion. Suppose you are invited to speak at a banquet and after you have been seated at the head table, you discover from the printed program that this is the 42nd anniversary dinner of the association. Change your opening to make it tie in with their anniversary. This is easy. Take two stories: 101 and 102.

Again, don't stand up there and read them as they are printed in the book. Tell them something like this: "I am especially honored to be invited to speak on the occasion of your 42nd anniversary. Anniversaries are wonderful days. They are days when you can be sentimental. Like the farmer's wife who woke him up one morning and said: 'Honey, wake up. Today is our 42nd wedding anniversary. I think we ought to celebrate. What do you say we kill a chicken?' Her husband looked at her and said: 'Why in the world do you want to punish a poor chicken for something that happened 42 years ago?'

"Of course, I like anniversaries—that is, when I can remember them. *(Laugh)* Not long ago, I put on my hat and coat to leave the house and as I was going out the front door, my wife gave me a big kiss and then looked up at me and said: 'Don't you know what day this is?' And there I was, caught again. *(Laugh)*

"I didn't remember what day it was, so I just pretended I didn't hear her and I hurried off to work. But, just to make things right at home, I called the drugstore and had them send around a two-pound box of candy. As the day wore on and I couldn't remember what day it was, I figured I'd better do more than a two-pound box of candy. So, at lunch time, I ordered four dozen roses sent over to the house. But the more I thought about it during the day, the more I was afraid I hadn't done enough. To make sure I wasn't in the doghouse, I stopped on the way home and bought her a fancy present at the shopping center.

"As I walked in the front door, I said: 'Look, honey, what I brought you.' She was so excited. She ran up and threw her arms around me and kissed me and said: 'This is wonderful. This is the happiest Groundhog Day I've ever known.' "

A funny story is not funny if it is offensive.

Determining whether or not a story is offensive is not always easy. There are times when it is impossible to know that a certain story might make a member of your audience cringe deep down inside. Let us take an extreme example. You think story number 573 is suitable for the occasion and you tell it. Suppose there is a bank cashier in the audience who is doing a bit of embezzling. The chances are he won't enjoy the story. (Also, the chances are, he will laugh louder than anybody there.)

Selecting and changing stories so they won't offend takes careful judgment, because what is offensive to one person may not be offensive to another. Maybe you have been invited to speak to a convention in Atlantic City and you want a story that will get you off to a good start. No story will make your audience feel warmer and closer to you than number 1013.

This is the old "Gideon Bible" story. For years, speakers up and down the land have been telling about picking up a copy of the Gideon Bible in their hotel room—and the story then unfolds. Telling this story can be dangerous because there are sure to be a few people present who think you shouldn't kid and joke about the Bible. (I'm sensitive to that myself.)

So, either throw the story away—or change it. Since it is a sure-fire laugh-getter (it has stood the test of time), change it and use it. All you need to do is tell it about some other book. It will come out just as funny. When you tell it, don't read it as it is printed in the book, but make it fit the occasion.

This is the way to tell it in Atlantic City. ". . . . . as I said, I am happy to be in Atlantic City. I have never been shown greater hospitality than I have enjoyed here. The people in the hotel have treated me like royalty. They have done everything to make me feel comfortable. In my room they had books and magazines for me to read.

"Right by my bed they had a little book called *The Bedside Reader*. I wanted to relax a bit after my drive, so I picked it up. It had all sorts of articles in it. Inside the front cover it said: Suggested things to read before you go to sleep at night. If you are down in the dumps and discouraged, read a certain page. I turned to that page and read it. That was an inspirational piece. This was interesting and I looked in the front of the book again. It said if you are lonesome and restless, read page number 96. I turned to page 96 and read it. That was a poem. And then I noticed at the bottom where some hospitable-minded person had written with a ball-point pen, 'If you are still lonesome and restless, call Atlantic 8-04792.' "

The story is just as funny that way as if it were told about the Gideon Bible—and you have removed the offensiveness.

Even though you never want to offend with your humor, it is impossible to please everybody. Once, following a speech at a civic club conference, a man upbraided me severely for being what he called "completely out of taste." Because this is the way I earn my living, I tried to draw him out and find exactly what I had said that bothered him. And because he was rather sore, he was willing to talk about it. I began to go over the stories I had told, one by one. "Oh, that's not it," he said. "I drove forty miles to hear an inspirational talk about my civic group—and all you did was make the audience roar with laughter. This organization is like a religion to me. I resent your wasting my time and I'm going to write to National Headquarters about it." You can't win them all.

A question that is asked me over and over concerns risqué stories. Once I was speaking at a large gathering of men. This was a well-known veterans' group and there were no women present. As I was sitting at the head table, the president of the organization said to me, "You can say anything you want tonight. This crowd doesn't mind a few rough stories—in fact, they love them." I said I appreciated his help and advice. Then he asked the question, "When do you know how far to go when you are telling stories? When can you be risqué?"

The answer, of course, is "never." If you can't be funny with clean humor—you won't be funny with risqué humor. And there is bound to be somebody in the audience who will wish you or he had stayed at home.

Don't let the fear of offending keep you from telling stories. If you censored them all, you would never tell a story about a minister or a bald man or a doctor or a mother-in-law or the weather in Maine or even a donkey.

The best rule to follow is to keep your stories clean, even to the point of never saying "hell" or "damn." A drawled out "aw" or "shucks" will do just as well. Generally, if you let the people know you mean no offense—no offense will be taken.

A stranger in New York, out for a stroll, stepped up to a beatnik loafing on the street corner and said, "Excuse me, but would you tell me how to get to Carnegie Hall?"

The beatnik said, "Practice, Daddy-O, practice."

That is the real answer to the question of how to tell a funny story—practice.

First, you must have your story in perfect shape—so you can't possibly ruin the punch line. Next, you must learn to tell the story as though it were the truth—to project an air of sincerity. After that it takes practice. Practice. Practice. Practice.

Practice in the privacy of your den or office. Practice before a mirror. Practice your stories on a recorder and play them back. Be your own critic. Then, practice some more.

When you think you are getting pretty good, start practicing at the breakfast table. That is undoubtedly the greatest test for any storyteller. Any time you can make your wife and children choke with laughter on their oatmeal, brother, you've got a gem of a story—and what is more, you have learned how to tell it.

Ability

1.   The schoolteacher was taking his class through the art gallery.

"With a single stroke of the brush," he said, "Leonardo da Vinci could change a smiling face into a frowning one."

A little boy spoke up and said, "That's nothing, so can my mother."

2.   "I hear Joe was the life of the party last night."

"Yes, he was the only one who could talk louder than the hi-fi."

3.   The young high school graduate applied for his first job at the electric computer department of an engineering firm. The application blank asked: "What machines can you operate?"

The young man studied a moment, then wrote, "Slot and pinball."

Ability

4. The personnel director was interviewing the applicant for the job of bookkeeper. "Your references show that you are an accountant," the personnel director said. "Why did you decide to be a bookkeeper?"

"Well, sir," said the applicant, "my wife used to keep a budget and also managed our money. Once when it wouldn't balance, I sat down with it and within an hour had it all straightened out."

"You'll do," said the personnel man. "Start work tomorrow."

165, 183, 206, 271, 297, 374, 412, 468, 531, 626, 781, 1425, 1546

Absence

5. A young fellow had been gone from his home town for eight years. Then, one day he came home. As he got off the bus, he was surprised not to see anyone he knew.

Looking for a friend, he went into the bus station and found the ticket agent who had gone to school with him. He was all set to give the ticket agent a big hello, when the ticket agent said to him, "Hi, Henry, you going away for a trip?"

6. A man woke up with a sore throat, but decided to go to work anyway. His throat gradually became worse during the day until he could hardly talk. On his way home from work that evening, he decided to stop in at the doctor's house between the bus stop and his home.

Walking up to the doctor's front door, he pushed the doorbell. When the doctor's wife opened the door, the man whispered, "Is the doctor at home?"

"No, he isn't," whispered the doctor's wife. "Come on in."

7. The teacher was giving a talk on science. "Can anyone tell me," she asked, "why lightning never strikes the same place twice?"

"That's because the same place isn't there after lightning strikes it," a little girl said.

93, 153, 411, 451, 573

Absentmindedness

8.　　An absentminded professor went to the drugstore and said to the druggist, "I would like a box of prepared tablets of the monacetic-acidester of salicyclic acid."

"Do you mean aspirin?" asked the druggist.

"That's it," said the professor, "I never can remember that name."

9.　　The saddest man in the nudist colony was the absentminded professor who wandered around all day with his clothes on.

10.　　Two fellows were talking about an absentminded friend of theirs.

"He's getting worse," one said. "Just the other day he kissed a woman by mistake."

"Thought it was his wife?" asked the other.

"No, it was his wife," said the first.

11.　　The absentminded professor dropped in on his long-time doctor friend one evening. They had a pleasant visit together and before they noticed, a couple of hours had slipped by. As the professor put on his coat to leave, the doctor said, "Family's all well, I suppose?"

"Good heavens," the professor said, "That reminds me why I came to see you. My wife's having a fit!"

12.　　"What are you in jail for?" asked the visitor.

"Nothing but absentmindedness," the prisoner said.

"Absentmindedness," said the visitor. "How could that be?"

"I forgot to change the engine number of the car before I sold it," the prisoner said.

395

Abstinence

13.　　The drunk was picked up and brought before the judge. "I got into bad company," he told the judge. "I had a quart of whiskey and the three fellows I was with didn't drink."

Abstinence

14.   Two young women were having lunch together, when one said to the other, "I can't figure out that man over there. He was trying to flirt with me a few minutes ago and now he won't even look at me."

"Maybe he saw me come in," said her friend. "He happens to be my husband."

286, 347, 408, 650, 669

Accident

15.   The one-armed customer winced each time the barber nicked him. But the barber kept talking and paid no attention.

"Have you been in here before?" he asked.

"No," said the customer, "I lost this arm in a sawmill."

16.   The minister was telling how Lot's wife looked back and turned into a pillar of salt.

A member of the congregation said, "That's nothing, my wife looked back once while she was driving, and she turned into a telephone pole!"

17.   "I wonder," said a man's wife, "why there are more automobile accidents than railway wrecks?"

"That's easy," her husband said, "Did you ever hear of the fireman hugging the engineer?"

18.   A man was lying beside the wrecked car with a broken leg. He was being questioned by the highway patrolman.

"Married?" asked the patrolman.

"No," the man said. "This is the worst mess I've ever been in."

19.   "How did the accident happen?" the policeman asked.

"My wife fell asleep in the back seat," the driver said.

20.   The driver was just regaining consciousness from a bad accident.

"I had the right of way, didn't I?" he asked.

"Yes," said his wife, "but the other fellow had the truck."

Accident

21.   The worried barber said to the man in his chair, "Excuse me, sir, was your tie red when you came in?"

"Of course not, it was blue," the man said.

"Gosh," said the barber.

108, 181, 204, 239, 324, 391, 440, 474, 492, 528, 603, 1654, 1732, 1851

Accommodate

22.   The man in the sick bed lived several miles out of town. "Doctor," he said, "isn't it pretty far out of your way to visit me here?"

"It's not too bad," the doctor said. "I have another patient right down the road, so I'm able to kill two birds with one stone."

23.   A young lady called a girl friend and said, "I am giving a party tonight. Can you come?"

"I wish I could," said her friend, "but I haven't a thing to wear."

"That's all right," said the young lady. "I'll get you a blind date."

179, 334, 1009, 1372

Accuracy

24.   A smart aleck student asked his teacher: "Do the Canadians have a Fourth of July?"

Professor: "Certainly not!"

Smart Aleck: "What do they do with their calendar? Go from the third to the fifth?"

25.   Two traveling salesmen were talking on the airplane.

"Does your wife miss you much?" asked the first.

"No," said the other. "She throws pretty straight for a woman."

26.   The judge said to the dairyman, "You are charged with selling adulterated milk. Guilty or not guilty?"

"Not guilty, your Honor," said the man.

Accuracy

"But the testimony shows that the milk you sold was 25% water," said the judge.

"Then it must be high-grade milk," said the dairyman. "The dictionary says that milk contains from 80 to 90 percent water. According to your figures, I should have sold it for cream!"

189, 235, 312, 363, 448, 487, 618, 1023, 1094, 1260, 2011

Acquaintance

27. A farmer bought a pig and fed him all year. At the end of that time he sold him for exactly what the pig and the feed had cost—making no profit. A friend asked why he did it. The farmer said, "I had the pleasure of his acquaintance and fellowship for a year, didn't I?"

28. The wedding had begun, the bride was walking down the aisle. A lady whispered to the man next to her, "Can you imagine, they've known each other only three weeks, and they are getting married!"

"Well," said her friend, "it's one way of getting acquainted."

29. A man at a seaside resort said to his new acquaintance, "I see two cocktails carried to your room every morning, as if you had someone to drink with."

"Yes, sir," said the man, "I do. One cocktail makes me feel like another man, and, of course, I have to buy a drink for the other man."

30. A man was seated at a lunch counter when a pretty girl, followed by a young man, came in. They took the only vacant stools, which happened to be on either side of the man. Wanting to be gracious, he offered to change seats with the young man so they might sit together.

"Oh, that isn't necessary," he said.

But the man insisted, and they changed seats.

The young man then said to the pretty girl, "Since the seating arrangements suit this polite gentleman, we might as well make him real happy and get acquainted."

Acquaintance

31.   One night, a man came home to his wife with lipstick on his collar.

"Where did you get that?" she asked. "From my maid?"

"No," her husband said.

"From my dressmaker?" snapped his wife.

"No," the man said indignantly. "Don't you think I have any friends of my own?"

32.   A woman was taking a Caribbean cruise. She liked everything about the plush ship except the seating arrangements in the dining room, where she was seated at a table with women only.

On the second day out, she said to the captain, "Everything about your ship is wonderful except that I'm at a table with women only. Would it be possible for you to put me at a table with some nice bachelors?"

The captain said he would be happy to arrange it.

That evening, when she went to dinner, she discovered that the captain had moved her to another table. This time she was seated with seven young priests.

84, 262, 273, 382, 403, 428, 625, 771, 1307

Actor

33.   Two strangers seated beside each other at a dinner struck up a conversation. "Well, well, so you're an actor," said one. "I'm a banker and I'm kept pretty busy, but I'm ashamed to admit that I haven't been in a theater in over ten years."

"Oh, don't let it worry you," said the actor, "I haven't been in a bank for a lot longer than that."

34.   A famous actor's wife died. There had been rumors of a pending divorce and it was common knowledge that he didn't care much for her. Yet, at the graveside he wept and carried on as if his heart were broken forever. Afterwards, a friend spoke to him about it. "I didn't know you cared that much for her," he said, "I never saw you show such emotion."

Actor

"If you think that was showing emotion," said the actor, "you should have caught me earlier at the funeral parlor."

35.   A budding young actor came home enthused about an assignment in a new play. "Dad, guess what?" he said. "I got my first part. I play the part of a man who's been married for 25 years."

"That's a good start, son," said his father. "Just keep at it and one of these days you'll get a speaking part."

36.   The Broadway actor was unbearable. His bragging became worse and worse. "Do you know," he said, "that I was just offered $5,000 a week to remain in New York?"

"Is that so?" asked his friend. "Did the offer come from Hollywood?"

37.   It was amateur night at the big dance hall. Often, some of the entertainers and producers from the television stations would catch the show to see if there were any promising stars to be discovered.

One night a promising young impersonator was doing his act when he noticed a famous movie star in the audience. He at once slipped an imitation of the visitor into his act. After the show was over, the amateur rushed up to the star and said, "You saw my act. You saw my imitation of you. What do you think?"

"Well," said the star, "all I can say is that one of us is pretty lousy."

110, 224, 427, 515, 890, 1667, 1921

Advertising

38.   A pawnbroker filled his show window with saxophones, trumpets, bongo drums—and shotguns.

"This is interesting," said a friend, "but does it sell merchandise?"

"Does it!" said the pawnbroker. "One day a fellow buys bongo drums. The next day his neighbors buy the shotguns."

Advertising

39. A young lady from a small town was visiting the city for the first time. At a street crossing she completely ignored the light which read, "Don't Walk."

She was halfway across the street, when a policeman stopped her and said, "What's the matter, lady, can't you read?"

"Why, yes," she said.

"Well, then, why did you walk across this street when the light up there said 'Don't Walk'?"

"Oh," she said, "I thought that was an advertisement for the bus company."

40. An American, who was a manufacturer of neon signs, was traveling in England and was describing his latest work of art. "It has over 300 feet of red tubing, about 600 feet of blue, almost 1,000 feet of green, all of which flash and form the image of a bathing beauty."

"It sounds very colorful," said the Englishman, "but isn't it a trifle conspicuous?"

41. The editor of a small-town newspaper in New England was trying to sell advertising.

"Don't need to advertise," said the owner of the store. "Been in business nigh on 40 years and never advertised."

"Could you tell me what that building is on the hill?" asked the editor.

"That's the village church," the man said.

"Been there long?" the editor asked.

"Oh, about 150 years," said the storekeeper.

"Well," said the editor, "they still ring the bell every Sunday, don't they?"

545, 1016, 1201, 1212, 1560

Advice

42. One farmer met another on the road and yelled at him, "Hey, Jed, got a mule with distemper. What'd you give that'n o'yourn when he had it?" "Give him turpentine," Jed said. A week later they met again and the first farmer shouted, "Say,

Advice

Jed, I give my mule some turpentine like you said, and it killed him." "Killed mine, too," said Jed.

43. A bum approached a genteel-appearing, elderly man with his tale of woe and a request for assistance. The old gentleman refused him, saying, "I'm sorry, my friend, I have no money, but I can give you some good advice." The bum said in a disgusted tone, "No, thanks, if you ain't got no money, I don't guess your advice is worth anything."

44. A client was telephoning his lawyer from the penitentiary:
"They've shaved my head, cut a slit in my pants, and rolled up my sleeves," he said. "Now what should I do?"
"My advice to you," said the lawyer, "is, don't sit down."

45. A man rushed into a lawyer's office and said, "I want your advice. That so-and-so across the street not only overcharged me, he didn't have the work ready on time, and when I objected, he told me to go to hell. What should I do? Here's five dollars."
"Is this a retainer?" the lawyer asked.
"Yes, that's right," the man said.
"Let's see," the lawyer told him, "he told you to go to hell, and you want my advice. My advice is—don't do it."

46. "Wonder drugs won't help you," the doctor told his elderly patient. "What you need is complete rest and a change of living. Go to a quiet country place for a month. Go to bed early, eat lots of vegetables, drink plenty of good rich milk, and smoke just one cigar a day."
A month later the man returned to the doctor's office. He looked like a new man.
"Yes, doctor," the man said, "your advice certainly did me a world of good. I went to bed early and did all the other things you told me. But that one cigar a day almost killed me at first. It's not easy to start smoking at my age."

Advice

47.   A young lady auditioned before a famous concert pianist, who had consented to listen to her play. After the audition, she said: "What do you think I should do now?"

"Get married," the pianist said.

48.   The young girl was worried about the amount of money her boy friend was spending on her whenever they had a date.

"Mother," she said, "how is the best way to stop him from spending too much money on me?"

"The only sure way is to marry him," her mother said.

49.   A judge was questioning the witness directly.

"I understand that your wife is scared to death of you?" he said.

"That's right, your Honor," said the witness.

The judge leaned over and whispered in his ear, "Man to man," he said, "how do you do it?"

50.   This item appeared in the advice column of the local paper:

"Is it ever permissible for a young woman to ask a man she has never met to call at her home?"

"Yes," said the advice columnist, "if she asks him to call for the laundry."

51.   "Has your wife learned to drive the car yet?" a man asked his friend.

"Yes, in an advisory capacity," the friend answered.

52.   A minister was given a parking ticket. In police court, the judge asked if he had anything to say.

"Yes," the minister said. "Blessed are the merciful for they shall obtain mercy."

The judge gave him a suspended sentence, but said to him, "Go thou and sin no more."

53.   The young agricultural agent was traveling through his new territory helping the farmers and giving them advice.

Advice

"Your methods are out of date," he said to a farmer. "I'd be surprised if you got even ten pounds of apples from that tree this season."

"So would I," said the farmer. "It's a pear tree."

54. An old hen said to the young pullet, "Let me give you some good advice."

"What is it?" asked the pullet.

"An egg a day keeps the ax away," said the voice of experience.

55. A young lady was talking to her grandmother about things in general.

"What kind of husband would you advise me to look for, Grandmother?" she asked.

"You just leave husbands alone," her grandmother said, "and find yourself a single man."

56. A man who had a reputation for never getting home before two or three o'clock in the morning, went to see his doctor.

"It's about my wife, doctor," he said. "She suffers from insomnia so badly that sometimes she stays awake until after two in the morning. What can I do for her?"

The doctor, who knew the man, said, "Start getting home earlier."

57. The county agricultural agent had told the old farmer he should collect all of his stock and have them branded.

"I suppose that's all right," said the farmer, "but I'm shore gonna have an awful time with them bees."

58. A woman wrote to her favorite magazine, the weekly farm journal, and asked for some advice about her twins who were teething. In the same mail, the editor received a request from a farmer asking what he should do about a horde of grasshoppers.

The farmer received this reply: "Wrap flannel cloths around their throats, rub their gums with oil, and massage their stomachs twice a day."

Advice

This is the advice the mother received about her twins: "Cover them with straw. Soak thoroughly with oil, and apply a match. The little pests will soon stop bothering you."

59.　　The neighborhood nurse had been conducting a class for prospective fathers. She felt that somehow or other she had not reached them as she should. As she wound up her final lesson, she said, "For five weeks I have been trying to teach you how to help your wives care for the new baby that is coming to live with you. If you forget everything else I have tried to teach you, remember this: When it's your turn to look after the baby, keep one end full and the other end dry, and you'll be all right."

112, 166, 174, 209, 246, 310, 369, 435, 465, 555, 564, 640, 737, 1355, 1696, 1866

Affectionate

60.　　It was their anniversary dinner and the man's wife was recalling the early days of their marriage. Suddenly she turned to her husband and said: "You know, dear, when we were first married you used to catch me in your arms."

"Yes, I know," her husband said. "Now I catch you in my pockets."

61.　　Word had leaked out around town that a certain fellow had been having trouble with his wife. In fact, so the story went, he had actually given her a punch in the face.

A friend of his asked him about it. "Did you really hit her?" he asked.

"Yes, I did," the fellow said. "I got tired of her nagging and popped her a good one right in the kisser. It taught her a lesson, too. I didn't see her for five days. Then, on the sixth day I could see her a little out of the corner of one eye."

62.　　It was their twenty-fifth wedding anniversary. They were having drinks and dinner at one of the fanciest restaurants in town. Both were feeling sentimental.

"Darling," said the husband, "what would you do if something happened to me?"

Affectionate

"I'd go absolutely out of my mind," his wife said.

"Aw, go on," he said. "I'll bet you would turn right around and get married again."

"Oh, no I wouldn't," his wife said. "I wouldn't go that far out of my mind."

485, 496, 514, 1827

Age

63.　Two club members were chatting.

"How old are you?" the first asked.

"Oh," said her friend, "I just turned twenty-three."

"I get it," said the first. "You're thirty-two."

64.　An old man was sitting in the park watching some boys at play.

"How old are you, sonny?" he asked one of them.

"I'm six," said the boy.

"Six?" said the man. "Why, you're not even as tall as my cane."

"Well," asked the boy, "how old is your cane?"

65.　The old man was celebrating his hundredth birthday and the reporter was interviewing him.

"To what do you attribute your longevity?" the reporter asked.

The old man thought a moment and then said, "I never smoked, drank whiskey, or stayed out late. And I always walked two miles a day."

"But," said the reporter, "I had an uncle who lived that way, yet he only lived to be eighty. How do you account for that?"

"He just didn't keep it up long enough," the man said.

66.　The patrolman said to the lady driver, "As soon as I saw you come around the bend, I said to myself, forty-five at least."

"That's silly," she said. "It's just that this hat makes me look that old."

Age

67. "That pain in your leg is caused by old age," the doctor told his elderly patient.

"That can't be," said the man. "The other leg is the same age and doesn't hurt a bit."

68. A teacher asked her class in ancient history, "What do you think Alexander the Great would be doing if he were alive today?"

"He'd be drawing an old-age pension," said the smart aleck.

69. There's really only one thing wrong with the younger generation. We just don't belong to it any more.

70. An eighty-year-old in St. Petersburg, Florida, wanted to be a centenarian. He was told by his doctor that we would have to give up drinking and smoking.

"Will I then live to be 100?" asked the man.

"Maybe not," said the doctor, "but it will seem like it."

103, 232, 322, 365, 461, 606, 664, 1170, 1201

Aggressiveness

71. The foreman was browbeating one of his men.

"I understand," he said, "that you've been going over my head to ask for more money."

The employee murmured that he hadn't said anything to anyone about more money.

"Oh, yes you have," said the foreman. "Isn't it true that you've been praying for a raise?"

72. Two elderly widows were sitting on the porch of the old ladies' home, talking about their late husbands.

"Life seemed to improve around the house after my husband became too old to chase after other women," the first widow confided.

"Age didn't have anything to do with it at my house," the other woman said. "Why, the only way I used to be able to keep my husband in line was to take the tires off his wheel chair."

340, 520, 639, 1378

Agreement

73.   A state official died and at his funeral an office-seeker got the Governor of the state aside and asked if he could have the dead man's place.

"I have no objection," said the Governor, "if the undertaker will agree."

74.   "We've been married a year and we never quarrel," explained the bride. "If a difference of opinion arises and I'm right, my husband gives in right away."

"But what if he's right?" her friend asked.

"Well," said the bride, "that situation has never come up."

75.   Two truck drivers met on a bridge too narrow for two trucks to pass.

"I never back up for an idiot," shouted the first driver.

"That's okay," yelled the other, as he backed up, "I always do."

76.   A customer in the restaurant asked the manager to lend him a couple of dollars "until payday."

"I'd like to help you out," said the manager, "if only it weren't for my agreement with the bank."

"What do you mean, agreement with the bank?" the man asked.

"They agreed not to sell sandwiches," the manager said, "if I agreed not to lend money."

77.   A group of tourists were fishing off Miami Beach. The mate of the boat had a wooden leg. One of the ladies was talking to him about it. She asked how he had lost it.

"Well, lady," he said. "I fell over the side of the boat and a shark came along and grabbed my leg."

"My," she said. "And what did you do?"

"I let him have it, of course," the man said. "I never argue with sharks."

78.   "Will you marry me, darling?" the young man asked.

"Before I can give you my answer," the young lady said, "I'd like to ask you one question: Do you ever drink anything?"

"Yes," the young man said rather proudly, "anything."

205, 467, 1440

Airplane

79.   The little old lady had watched the tender parting of the young couple at the loading ramp. As the plane taxied down the runway, the young girl burst into tears.

"There, there, my girl, don't cry," said the lady, who was sitting next to her. "Are you crying so because you have to leave your husband?"

"No," said the girl, "because I have to go back to him."

80.   A young man had just passed his examination for his private pilot's license. He wanted to show off and persuaded his grandmother to go up with him.

When they landed, she said, "Thanks for the two rides."

"What do you mean, two rides, Granny?" he asked. "You had only one."

"Oh, no," said his grandmother. "Two. My first and last."

81.   The airline hostess was taking orders for drinks before serving dinner.

"A dry martini, please," said one of her passengers. "And be sure it's dry. You do know how to make them dry, don't you?"

"We try," the pretty hostess said. "We've been serving dry martinis on this same dinner flight for six years and we are still on our first bottle of vermouth."

150, 473, 767, 1804, 1832

Alert

82.   The draftee had an angle figured out that would keep him from being drafted. When he took his physical examination and the doctor asked him to read the letters on the chart, he asked, "What chart?" He was promptly rejected because of poor eyesight.

That night he went to a movie and discovered he had taken a seat next to the same doctor who had examined him that morning. The bad thing was, the doctor recognized him. But, not to be caught off-guard the young fellow said: "Could you tell me, please, what time this bus leaves?"

Alert

83.   It was the middle of a hot afternoon and the laborer decided to sneak up to the corner bar for a glass of beer. Just as he was taking off, he ran into the foreman.

"Hi," said the foreman. "Were you looking for me?"

"I sure was," the man said, "but I didn't want to see you."

89, 201, 404, 549, 620, 950, 1356

Alibi

84.   Coming home late one night from a meeting, a minister saw one of his own parishioners staggering down the street. Always ready to help a friend, the minister took the man home.

At the man's door, the fellow pleaded with the minister to come inside with him. The minister said it was too late.

"Please, Reverend," the man said. "Just for a minute. I want my wife to see who I been out with tonight."

85.   The defendant was telling his side of the story to the judge.

"Your Honor," he said, "I was not going forty miles an hour. No, not twenty. Not even ten. In fact, when the patrolman came up I was almost at a standstill."

"I'd better stop you now," said the judge, "before you back into something. Twenty-five dollars fine."

393, 440, 452, 760, 894, 1547, 1830

Alimony

86.   A hard-pressed victim of a costly divorce asked his lawyer:

"Isn't there some way a man can avoid paying alimony?"

"Yes," the lawyer said. "There are two, in fact. He can either stay single or stay married."

599

Allowance

87.   A father was talking to his son about his plans for the future.

Allowance

"I have about made up my mind," the boy said, "to become an artist."

"That's all right with me," his father said, "so long as you don't draw on me."

88.   "My son is real smart," the father bragged. "He is studying journalism and when he writes home his letters always send me to the dictionary."

"You sure are lucky," his friend said. "My son's letters always send me to the bank."

256, 560, 567, 1952

Ambition

89.   An ambitious young man asked a banker for the secret of success in business.

The banker said: "There is no secret. You must jump when your opportunity comes."

"But how," asked the young man, "can I tell when my opportunity comes?"

"You can't," said the banker. "You've just got to keep jumping."

90.   A high school girl was talking to her vocational counselor: "Would you please suggest a career in life for me? I have been thinking of journalism."

Counselor: "What are your natural inclinations?"

Student: "Oh, my soul yearns, thrills, and pulsates with a desire to give the world a lifework that shall be imaginative in its scope and weirdly entrancing in the vastness of its structural beauty!"

Counselor: "Young lady, you're born to be a designer of ladies' hats."

91.   At a class reunion, the toastmaster asked a man at the head table: "Were any of your childhood ambitions ever realized?"

"Yes," said the man. "When my mother used to cut my hair, I always wished I'd be baldheaded some day."

Ambition

92.   The lady went into the shoe store to buy a pair of loafers. The manager said to her, "Yes, we have quite a selection of loafers. I'll see if I can get one to wait on you."

93.   "There's a fellow who's going places," said a fellow to his friend.

"Why do you say that? Is he ambitious?" asked his friend.

"No," said the man. "His wife is out of town."

94.   Two girls were chatting over lunch. "All I'm looking for," said the first, "is a man who's kind and understanding. Is that too much to expect of a millionaire?"

95.   Keep your eye on the ball
Your shoulder to the wheel
Your ear to the ground
Now, let's see you work in that position.

137, 254, 282, 402, 436, 586, 754, 1270, 1407

Amusement

96.   A traveling salesman was hunting some fun in a country town. No poolroom, no movie, no saloon, no library. "What in the world do you folks do for amusement around here?" he asked. "Oh," said the hotel clerk, "we go down to the store of an evenin'—they got a new bacon slicer."

382, 1008

Ancestors

97.   "Oh, yes," said Mrs. Blue Blood haughtily, "we can trace our ancestors back to—to—well, I don't know exactly who, but I'll have you know we've been descending for centuries."

98.   It was a society function and the turnout was good. The speaker was an expert on ancient history. He spoke on the culture of the Medes and the Persians. After the speech was over, he was approached by an elegant lady who said:

"Your speech was most delightful. I found it especially interesting because, you see, my mother was a Meade."

332, 924, 1046, 1365, 1872

Anger

99. A man had been trying to reach his home by phone for over an hour, but kept getting a busy signal. Finally, he asked the operator if she could cut in on the line. She told him that she could do it only in a case of life or death.

"Well," said the man. "I can tell you this much. If that's my teen-age daughter on the phone, there's going to be a murder."

100. A young man had been arrested for fighting and the judge told him to tell his side of the story.

"Well, your Honor," the young man said. "I was in a telephone booth talking to my girl friend, when this man suddenly opened the door, grabbed me by the neck and threw me out in the street."

"And that is when you struck him?" asked the Judge.

"No, sir, I didn't hit him," the fellow said, "until he grabbed my girl friend and threw her out, too."

474, 525

Anniversary

101. A farmer's wife woke her husband one morning and said, "Today's our 40th wedding anniversary. I think we ought to celebrate. What do you say we kill a chicken?"

"Why in the world," her husband asked, "do you want to punish a poor chicken for something that happened 40 years ago?"

102. A fellow had finished his breakfast and had put on his hat and coat and was leaving the house to go to work, when his wife kissed him good-bye and said, "Honey, don't you know what day this is?"

He didn't remember, so he didn't say anything. He just hurried off to work. But, he thought about it all day long and that night on the way home, he stopped in the store and spent about $20.00 on a gift.

As he walked in the front door he said, "Honey, look what I bought you in honor of this great day."

"My goodness," his wife said, "this is wonderful. This is the happiest Groundhog Day I can ever remember."

62, 117, 231, 357, 909, 1381

Antiques

103. A man was browsing through an antique shop near Mt. Vernon and ran across a rather ancient-looking axe.

"That's a mighty old axe you have there," he said to the shop owner.

"Yes," said the man, "it once belonged to George Washington."

"Really?" said the customer. "It certainly stood up well."

"Of course," said the antique dealer, "it has had three new handles and two new heads."

104. "I thought that joke of mine was rather funny," said the comedian, "but the director of the show said it was far-fetched. I wonder what he meant?"

"Farfetched?" said his friend. "Maybe he meant Noah brought it over with him in the ark."

306, 414

Anxiety

105. A businessman was talking to the banker and asked: "Are you worried about whether I'll be able to meet my note that's due next month?"

"Yes," said the banker. "I must admit that I am a little anxious about it. Are you worried about meeting the payment?"

"Oh, no, not me," said the businessman. "That's why I am paying you six percent."

106. The elderly couple met at a social club in St. Petersburg. He found her attractive and invited her to dinner. After dinner he took her to a movie. During the middle of the movie he started looking for something on the floor.

"What have you lost?" she whispered.

"A caramel," he answered.

"Why go to all that trouble for one cheap caramel?" she asked.

"Because," he said, "my teeth are in it."

107. The bus was crowded and the driver was in a bad mood.

"Where is the money for the boy?" he asked, as the father put the money for himself in the box.

Anxiety

"I don't have to pay for him," the man said. "He is only three years old."

"Three years old?" said the driver. "Look at him. He looks at least eight."

The father did look at the boy and then said, "Can I help it if he worries?"

108.   The haywagon had upset in the road and the young driver was terribly worried about it. A kindhearted farmer told the young fellow to forget his troubles and come in and have some supper with his family. "Then we'll straighten up the wagon," the farmer said.

The boy said he didn't think his father would like it.

"Oh, don't worry about that," said the farmer. "Everything will be all right."

So the young man stayed for supper. Afterwards he said he felt better and thanked the farmer. "But," he said, "I still don't think my father will like it."

"Forget it," said the farmer. "By the way," he added, "where is your father?"

"He's under the hay!" said the young man.

151, 238, 349, 362, 661, 914, 1397

Apology

109.   A rather uncouth and uneducated type had been elected mayor. His new position went to his head and he became overbearing and rude and was inclined to throw his weight around.

At a big public political gathering he was pushing himself ahead of the other guests and stepped on a rather dignified gentleman's toes.

"Well," said the man to the mayor, "the least you could do is to apologize."

"Me, apologize?" said the mayor. "Do you know who I am? I'm the mayor of this city."

"Thank you," said the gentleman, "that may not be an apology, but it certainly is an understandable explanation."

Apology

110.   The newly successful actor was noted for being stuck up and rude to everyone around him. One night after the show, he was having a late dinner at a swanky New York night spot. As the waitress served his table she accidentally spilled a bit of water on him.

"I never saw such sloppy service," he screamed. "You aren't fit to serve a pig."

"I'm sorry, sir," the waitress said, "but I'm trying to do my best."

114, 502, 649, 719, 1323, 1367

Appearance

111.   The doctor had just examined the patient and said to the man's wife: "I don't like the looks of your husband."

"I don't either, Doctor," said the man's wife, "but he is kind to the children."

112.   The man said to the bum on the street who had asked him for a handout, "You would stand more chance of getting a job if you would shave and clean yourself up."

"Yes, sir," the panhandler said. "I found that out years ago."

135, 188, 355, 368, 371, 384, 422, 475, 502, 1698, 2102

Appetite

113.   A sick man got well. "It would do your heart good," his wife said, "just to hear him eat again."

114.   A hostess was insisting that her guest eat more—to the point of annoying him. He said, "Allow me to assure you that though I sometimes eat more than at other times, I never eat less."

115.   The naturalist was imparting some gems of information at a social gathering. "The caterpillar," he explained, "is the most voracious of all creatures. Why, in a month it will eat about 600 times its own weight." A somewhat deaf old lady had been following the discourse as best she could and at this point said, "Whose boy did you say that was?"

Appetite

116.   Several hunters stopped in at a backwoods farmhouse to see if they could buy lunch.

"I guess so," said the farmer's wife, "if you like pork chops—that's all I got."

The hungry men ate as hungry hunters can, enjoying every mouthful. Afterwards they complimented the farmer's wife on the delicious pork chops.

"Well, I should hope so," she said. "That's none of your butchered meat, you know. That hog died a natural death."

156, 300, 364, 418

Appreciation

117.   On her 10th wedding anniversary a lady was in the hospital recovering from an operation. Her husband was at home looking after the five children.

That day she received two dozen roses with this message: "Ten years with you is like ten minutes, but ten minutes without you is like ten years."

118.   The visiting preacher had been invited to the big noon "dinner-on-the-ground" before he was to preach the afternoon service at an all-day meeting at the rural church.

One of the ladies of the church offered to fill his plate for him but he stopped her. "I never eat," he said, "before I preach. I find that it keeps me from preaching a good sermon."

After the service was over, a friend asked that same lady what she thought of the sermon. "As far as I was concerned," she said, "he might as well of et."

119.   "Thanks for the mouth organ you gave me for Christmas," the little boy said to his uncle the first time he saw him after the holidays. "It's the best Christmas present I ever got."

"That's great," said his uncle. "Do you know how to play it?"

"Oh, I don't play it," the little fellow said. "My mother gives me a dime a day not to play it during the day and my father gives me fifty cents a week not to play it at night."

237, 421, 464, 551, 929, 1520, 1676, 1758, 2037, 2115

Appropriate

120. The lady was waiting to see the manager of a loan company in West Palm Beach. Mounted on the wall of his waiting room was a beautiful swordfish.

"All my life," she said to her friend with her, "I've read about loan sharks, but this is the first time I've ever seen one."

121. The monastery was a popular tourist attraction with thousands of visitors a year coming to see the extensive vineyards. Always with an eye out for making money, the brothers opened a small fish and chip shop for the tourists.

One day a tourist came into the shop and said to the brother behind the counter, "Excuse me, but are you the fish frier?"

"No," said the brother on duty, "I'm the chip monk."

289, 343, 372, 401, 755, 1780, 1980

Architecture

122. A man and wife went to see an architect about building a new home.

"All right," he said to them, "suppose you tell me in a general way the style of home you want."

"Well, I think . . . ," the husband said, but was stopped by his wife.

"We're not particular," she said to the architect, "just so it will go good with an antique door knocker I picked up last summer in Virginia."

301

Argument

123. The scene was Hong Kong. Two Chinese were screaming insults at each other with their faces only inches apart. A small crowd had gathered around them.

"What's going on?" asked an American tourist of his guide.

"That's a Chinese fight," the man said.

"A fight?" said the tourist. "I've been watching for ten minutes and nobody has struck a blow."

"You don't understand," said the guide. "In a Chinese fight, the man who strikes first shows he has run out of ideas."

Argument

124. The argument between the husband and wife was at its height. "The next thing you'll say," yelled the man at his wife, "is that your judgment is as good as mine."

"You've got me there," his wife screamed at him. "The way we chose spouses proves that you have better judgment than I do."

361, 416, 512, 587, 710, 800, 1342, 1444, 1766

Arithmetic

125. The first-grade arithmetic teacher asked her star pupil: "If you had four oranges and I asked you for two, how many would you have left?"

The little boy's answer was quick and definite: "Four," he said.

126. The teacher was trying to teach arithmetic by giving a concrete example to the pupils.

"Now, Willy," she said, "if you had 50 cents in one pocket and seventy-six cents in the other, what would you have?"

"I'd have on somebody else's pants," he said.

127. It was time for the arithmetic lesson. "If I gave you four chickens and Miss Smith gave you one chicken," the teacher asked the farmer's little boy, "how many chickens would you have?"

"Seven chickens," he said.

"No, no," the teacher said, "You'd have five."

"No, teacher," said the little boy, "I'd have seven. I already have two."

128. The golfer was choosing a caddy. "Can you count, young man?" he asked.

"Yes, sir," said the boy.

"Let's see how you do," the man said. "How many are two, six, three, and seven?"

"Eleven, sir," the boy said.

"Excellent," the man said. "You're hired."

Arithmetic

129. The teacher gave the little boy a tough problem. "Now, she said, "if your father gave you ten cents and your mother gave you twelve and your uncle gave you six more, what would you have?"

The little boy immediately slipped into deep thought.

"Come on," said the teacher, "certainly you can figure out a simple little problem like that."

"It isn't a simple problem," the boy said. "I can't decide whether I'd have an ice-cream cone or a hamburger."

206, 228, 580, 671, 1562, 2008

Army

130. A hard-boiled drill sergeant stood in front of his platoon after a fouled-up drill session. "When I was a little boy," he said softly, "Santa Claus brought me a set of wooden soldiers. It wasn't long before they were scattered and lost which just about broke my heart. My mother tried to comfort me. Don't cry, son, she said, you'll get them back some day."

The sergeant paused and stared at his men. Then he let them have it. "Mother was right! I got them back—today."

82, 748, 776, 834, 1219, 1643, 1973, 2040

Arrangement

131. Two girls were chatting during the coffee break.

"No girl should be discouraged," said the first. "In this world there's a man for every girl and a girl for every man. You can't improve on an arrangement like that."

"I don't want to improve on it," her friend said. "I just want to get in on it."

132. Two citizens of Skid Row were discussing life.

"Was you ever in love?" asked the first.

"Yep," said his friend. "Once when I was a youngster."

"How come you never got married?" said the first.

"Well, it was this way," said his friend. "The gal wouldn't marry me when I was drunk, and I wouldn't marry her when I was sober."

Arrangement

133. There had been a big scandal in the local church and one of the deacons was telling his friend about it.

"The preacher ran off with the choir leader," he said. "And besides he took all of the money in the treasury—$800. But, they caught them. Three weeks later they found them at a hideout up in the hills. They had spent all of the money on high living."

"Well," said his friend, "what did the people do about it?"

"Oh, they brought them back to town," he said. "Of course, the choir leader was disgraced for life."

"What about the preacher?" asked the man. "Did they put him in jail?"

"Put him in jail?" the fellow said. "Why, certainly not. That preacher had $800 of our money, and we made him preach out every dime of it."

377, 399, 577, 740, 946

Art

134. In an art gallery, one child saw "Winged Victory." "Look at that," she said, "that one ain't got no head." "Sh," said her little friend, "that's art. She don't need no head."

135. A little city girl was busy one evening with her pencil and paper. "Daddy," she said, "how many kinds of milk are there?"

"Well," he said, "There's evaporated milk and buttermilk and malted milk and skimmed milk. But why do you want to know?"

"Oh," she said, "I'm drawing a cow and I want to know how many spigots to put on her."

136. Two teen-agers were visiting an art show. They stopped before a modern abstract painting. The price tag was $200.

"Two hundred dollars!" said one. "For that crazy-looking thing? That's highway robbery."

"Oh," the other said, "that's not much for one of the screwy kind."

Art

137. The art class of six-year-olds had been told to draw a picture of what they wished to be when they grew up. The children went to work with paper and pencil and crayon. Some drew pictures of soldiers, policemen, actresses and all sorts of people. They all worked hard, except one little girl, who didn't draw a line.

The teacher said to her, "Don't you know what you want to be when you grow up?"

"Yes, I know," said the little girl, "but I don't know how to draw it. I want to be married."

138. The society matron from the small town had just returned from her first visit to New York. Her friend said to her, "Did you visit the art gallery when you were in New York?"

"Oh," said the society matron, "we didn't need to. Our daughter has just taken up painting at college."

139. Jones, at his wife's insistence, consulted a prominent artist.

Jones: "Do you think you can make a good portrait of my wife?"

Artist: "My friend, I can make it so lifelike you'll jump every time you see it."

140. The critic said to the sculptor, "It's a fine statue, all right, but isn't that a rather odd position for a general to assume?"

"Maybe so," said the sculptor, "but I was halfway finished when the committee ran out of money and decided that they couldn't afford a horse for him."

141. The young artist gave his model a big hug and kiss.

"I'll bet you do that to all your models," she said when she had caught her breath.

"No," he said, "you are absolutely the first."

"How many models have you had?" she asked.

"Four," he said. "A peach, a pear, an apple, and you."

Art

142.   A friend was chatting with his buddy who had taken up art.

"When I look at one of your paintings," he said, "all I can do is stand and wonder."

"Wonder how I do it?" asked his buddy.

"No," said his friend, "why you do it."

143.   A modern artist was showing off his work. He pointed to a blank canvas and said, "That is a cow grazing."

"Where is the grass?" the visitor asked.

"The cow has eaten it," the artist said.

"Well, then, where is the cow?" the visitor wanted to know.

"You don't suppose," said the artist, "that she'd stay there after she'd eaten all the grass, do you?"

144.   A lady had hired an artist to paint her portrait.

"Will it be pretty?" she asked.

"Of course," said the artist. "You won't know yourself."

145.   Two artists from the Village were chatting.

"How's business?" asked the first.

"Excellent," said the second. "I got a commission yesterday from a millionaire. Wants his three children painted very badly."

"Well, friend," said the first artist, "you are the very man to do it."

146.   The artist stopped beside a country lane and said to the farmer, "My, what a beautiful view that is!"

"Well, maybe," said the farmer. "But if you had to plow it, harrow it, cultivate it, hoe it, mow it, fence it, and pay taxes on it, it wouldn't be such a pretty view."

1, 87, 167, 192, 268, 397, 426, 562, 644, 1042, 1216, 1565, 2033

Assist

147.   A woman driver stalled her car at a traffic light. She tried desperately to start the engine, while behind her an impatient man rudely honked his horn. Finally, she got out and walked back.

Assist

"I'm sorry," she said to the man, "but I can't start my car. If you'll go there and start it for me, I'll stay here and honk your horn."

148. Three boy scouts had been sent out from the meeting to do their good turn for the day.

"I did my good turn, sir," the first said as he reported to the Scoutmaster. "I helped a little old lady across the street."

"I helped her across, too," said the second Scout.

"Me, too," said the third.

"Do you mean," the Scoutmaster said, "that it took three of you to help one little old lady across the street?"

"Oh, yes, sir," the Scouts said. "You see, sir, the little old lady didn't want to cross the street."

435, 460, 765, 949, 1119, 1334, 1639

Asylum

149. The local newspaper editor was invited to speak to a group at the Mental Hospital who were trying to start a hospital newspaper. The superintendent thought the editor might give them some pointers and get them started.

The editor had begun his talk and had been going for about ten minutes, when a fellow in the back stood up and yelled, "Aw, you ain't no newspaper man. You don't know what you are talking about. Besides, you're talking too much. Why don't you shut up and sit down."

"I'll wait a minute until you put that man out," the editor said to the superintendent.

"Put him out?" the superintendent asked. "Certainly not. That poor man has been here for eight years and that's the first time he's ever said anything that made any sense."

150. The plane was cruising at 20,000 feet, when the pilot began to laugh hysterically over the intercom.

"I wonder what's so funny," one passenger said to the other.

Just then the voice on the intercom giggled, "Boy, what they'll say at the asylum when they find out I escaped."

47

Asylum

151. A man reported to the superintendent of the mental hospital and asked, "Have any of your male patients escaped lately?"

"Why do you ask?" said the superintendent.

"Because," said the man, "someone has run off with my wife."

164, 454, 497, 615, 761, 1320, 1339, 1548

Atheist

152. Daughter: "I can't marry him, Mother. He's an atheist and he doesn't believe there is a hell."

Mother: "That's all right, dear, marry him and between the two of us I am sure we can convince him."

540, 1406

Attendance

153. A civic club attendance chairman was out to set a record. One week he stood up to announce the attendance at the weekly meeting. "Out of our entire membership, only Joe Ferguson is absent today. Let us hope it is because he is sick in bed."

154. The attendance chairman of the civic club was reporting: "I'm sure we all regret not having Elmer with us tonight," he said. "It's not so much that we miss his vacant chair, but we certainly do miss his vacant face."

229, 379, 551, 1257, 1384

Attention

155. The girl at the Junior-Senior prom seemed unhappy as the short, homely boy cut in.

"Why did you have to cut in when I was dancing with the captain of the football team?" she asked.

"I'm sorry," the boy said, a bit embarrassed. "But I'm working my way through college, and he was waving a $5 bill at me."

156. Company was coming for dinner and the little girl had been given special permission to eat with the grown-ups if she behaved and watched her manners.

Attention

"You just sit quiet," her mother said, "and let the other people do the talking."

Everything went along all right until dessert time. Through a slipup, the little girl was completely overlooked. Finally, as the older folks began to enjoy their ice cream, she said, "Would anybody like to have a clean plate?"

274, 423, 461, 511, 624, 973, 1845, 1888, 2102

Audacity

157. A woman in the third row at the theatre couldn't hear a word from the stage because of the continued conversation going on behind her.

"I beg your pardon," she finally said, "but I can't hear a word."

"Is that so?" said the talkative man. "And what business is it of yours what I tell my wife!"

158. The couple had been engaged for months, but for some reason or other the young man had never said anything about a definite date for the wedding.

One evening they were sitting together in her living room chatting and reading the newspaper together.

"My," said the young man, looking at an advertisement, "isn't that a beautiful suit for only $65.00?"

"Is it a wedding suit?" asked the girl.

"No," said the young man, "it's a business suit."

"Well, I mean business," said the girl.

361, 419, 597, 1138, 1529, 1716

Audience

159. The fellows were sitting around the country store killing time.

"Did you ever do any public speaking?" asked one of the men.

"The nearest I ever came to it," his friend said, "was to propose to my wife over the party line."

49

Audience

160.   An experienced after-dinner speaker was asked what he considered to be a perfect audience.

"Oh, to me," he said, "the perfect audience is one that is well educated, highly intelligent—and just a little bit drunk."

149, 242, 515, 698, 1544, 1778

Authority

161.   A man said to his friend: "Who is the boss in your house?"

"Well," his friend said, "my wife assumes command of the children, the servants, the dog, and the parakeet. But I say pretty much what I please to the goldfish."

162.   The young man finally spoke to his girl friend's father about marrying his daughter.

"It's a mere formality, I know," he said, "but we thought you would be pleased if I asked."

"And where did you get the idea," her father asked, "that asking my consent to the marriage was a mere formality?"

"From your wife," the young man said.

163.   A newly graduated journalism student said to a seasoned editor, "I'd like some advice on how to run a newspaper."

"You've come to the wrong man," the editor said. "You should ask one of our subscribers."

164.   The governor was visiting the mental hospital, and the superintendent was showing him around.

"My," he said, "what a vicious-looking woman we just passed in the corridor. Is she dangerous?"

"Well, sometimes," said the superintendent.

"Then, why do you allow her such freedom?" asked the governor. "She's under your control."

"No, she's not under my control," said the superintendent. "She's my wife."

249, 434, 494, 756, 773, 1047, 1434, 2051

Automobile

165. A man who was reeling drunk was getting into his automobile when a policeman came up and asked: "You're not going to drive that car, are you?"

"Certainly I'm going to drive," the man said. "Anybody can see I'm in no condition to walk."

166. A man bought a foreign car and, after careful record-keeping, came to the conclusion that he was not getting the high mileage so often claimed for these cars. He took it to the service station and said, "I love that car, but isn't there something I can do to increase its mileage?"

"Well, yes," the mechanic said. "You can do the same as most foreign-car owners do."

"Okay," the man said. "What is that?"

"Lie about it," the mechanic said.

234, 239, 373, 526, 633, 659, 1385, 1648, 1877, 1942

Aviation

167. The professor approached the information desk of the public library.

"Where," he asked, "will I find a book with something on Correggio and his 'Flight into Egypt'?"

"Everything on aviation is in the third stack over," the librarian said.

168. The pilot at the air show was taking passengers up for a spin around town for five dollars a ride. As he circled the city with a rather elderly customer aboard, he cut his engine and began to glide toward the airport.

"I'll bet those people down there think my engine has conked out," he laughed. "I'll bet half of them are scared to death."

"That's nothing," said his passenger, "half of us up here are too."

238, 1489

Baby

169. "This is some town," said the stranger, "any big men ever born here?"

"No, suh!" answered the native. "Just babies!"

51

Baby

170.   The next-door neighbor was asking the little boy about the new baby at his house.

"How do you like your new baby sister?" she asked.

"Oh, she's all right," the little boy said, "but just as Dad says, there are a lot of things we need worse."

171.   "Where's the baby?" a papa kangaroo said to his wife.

She looked in her pouch and shouted, "Help, help, somebody's picked my pocket."

172.   Two men who had not seen each other for many months, met on the street.

"How's the wife?" asked the first.

"Not so well," said the second. "She's just had quinsy."

"Good heavens!" said the first. "How many have you now?"

173.   The expectant mother who was being rushed to the hospital didn't quite make it. Instead, she gave birth to her baby on the hospital lawn. Later, the father received a bill listing delivery room fee $50. Put out about it, he wrote the hospital and reminded them that the baby was born on the front lawn.

A week later he received a corrected bill reading: Greens fee, $25.

174.   A speaker at a civic luncheon had given a tremendous talk and received a standing ovation. The president of the club was so impressed that he said to the speaker, "Everyone here is so enthused about what you said, I wonder if you won't please say a few more words to us since we have about ten minutes left of our regular meeting time."

The speaker stood up and said, "Once there was a little baby cabbage who said to his mother, 'Mommy, I'm worried about something. As I sit in this row of cabbages and grow and grow and grow day after day, how will I know when to stop growing?' 'The rule to follow,' the mamma cabbage said, 'is to quit when you are a head.' " And he sat down.

59, 209, 338, 406, 580, 619, 681, 1641

Bad check

175.   "Did you get my check?" asked the man who owed everybody.

"Yes, twice" said his creditor. "Once when you sent it to me and once when the bank sent it back."

180, 1516

Bald

176.   The rapidly-becoming-bald man said to his barber, "My hair is falling out pretty fast these days. Do you have something to keep it in?"

"How would a cigar box do?" asked the barber.

177.   The man's wife had spread her day's purchases on the dining room table for her husband to see.

"Stupid, that's all I can say, just plain stupid," her husband said. "The way women spend money. I never saw such silly spending."

"Okay, okay," shouted his wife, "maybe so. But, one thing you never saw. You never saw a woman buy a bottle of hair-restorer from a bald-headed barber."

91, 354, 1102

Banker

178.   "Thankful! What do I have to be thankful for? I can't pay my bills."

"Well, then," said the banker, "be thankful you aren't one of your creditors."

179.   A woman said to the bank teller: "All right, if you insist I'm overdrawn, I'll just have to cash this check somewhere else."

180.   A man opened an account for his wife at the bank. A few weeks later the cashier asked the man to inform his wife that she had overdrawn.

The man told his wife and at the same time gave her a good scolding for doing it. The following morning she gave her husband a note to deliver to the cashier.

Banker

The cashier opened the note, which contained only one word—"Tattletale!"

181.　Two lawyers and a banker went fishing in a small rowboat. Suddenly, they found themselves in a heavy squall. The boat sprang a leak and sank, and they all found themselves in the water. The two lawyers began to swim, but the banker floundered helplessly. He was drowning.

"Say," one of the lawyers yelled at him, "Do you think you can float alone?"

"Look," said the banker. "I'm drowning and you want to talk business!"

182.　A poet was complaining about the state of the world.

"This is a very unfair world," he said.

"How so?" asked his friend.

"Well, for one thing," the poet said, "a banker can write a bad poem and people think nothing of it. But just let a poet write a bad check and see what happens!"

183.　The minister was telling the banker about the new choir director.

"He has a marvelous voice," he said. "He can hold one of his notes for half a minute."

"That's nothing!" said the banker. "I have held one of his notes for two years."

33, 76, 105, 195, 413, 436, 573

Bank robber

184.　The bank robber walked up to the cashier, took a quick look around and snarled: "This is a stickup! One false move and I'll fill you full of lead. Now hand over all the money."

The bank clerk swallowed hard, but managed to regain his poise. "Could you k-kindly go to the n-next window?" he whispered. "I'm on my l-lunch hour."

185.　A man accused of bank robbery was given a brilliant defense by an eloquent young lawyer. The jury acquitted him.

Bank robber

Later in his office, the lawyer said to the man, "Tell me the truth, now that the trial is over. Did you rob that bank or not?"

"Well," said the man, "I thought I had until after I heard you make that speech to the jury, but now I am beginning to have my doubts."

305, 577, 663, 1948

Barber

186. A barber was surprised to get a tip from a customer before he even climbed into the chair.

"You're the first customer," he said, "ever to give me a tip before I cut his hair."

"That's not a a tip," said the customer. "That's hush money."

187. The whiskey-smelling barber was shaving the minister and not doing a very good job. Suddenly, the razor slipped and and the minister was bleeding from a bad cut.

"Now you see," said the minister, "what comes from drinking too much."

"Yes, sir," said the barber sympathetically, "drinking sure does make the skin tender, don't it?"

188. A barber was chatting to his customer about hair styles.

"Don't you think," he asked, "that long hair makes a man look intellectual?"

"Not when his wife finds it on his coat," the customer said. "Then it makes him look foolish."

189. "Your hair needs cutting badly," remarked the barber.

"It does not," exclaimed the customer, sitting down in the chair. "It needs cutting nicely. You cut it badly last time."

190. A man said to his barber, "Have you a good tonic for my hair? It's beginning to worry me."

"Oh, don't let it worry you," said the barber. "It will all come out all right in the end."

15, 21, 176, 624, 1591, 1661, 1839, 2111

Bargain

191.　A political office in a small New England town was vacant. The job paid $250 a year and there were several candidates for it. One of the candidates was a genuine Yankee type, and a generous campaign fund was turned over to him by his friends. But, in spite of that, he was defeated.

"I can't figure it out," one of them said to the defeated candidate. "With all that money we should have won. What do you think went wrong?"

"Well," the fellow said, "that job only pays $250 a year, and I didn't see any sense in paying over $1500 to get it, so I bought a small farm instead."

192.　A newly rich oil man engaged a famous artist to paint a portrait of his wife. When it was finished, he refused to pay the price that the painter asked.

"What!" he said, "that's too much to pay for a square yard of canvas and a little paint!"

"Oh," said the artist, "if it's just paint and canvas that you want, here's a half-used tube of paint, and over in the corner you will find some canvas. You can have them with my compliments."

193.　A young fellow who had just been ditched by his girl friend said: "A bargain is a good buy. A good-by is farewell. A farewell is to part. To part is to leave. My girl left me without a good-by. She was no bargain anyway."

194.　The little boy had shopped for an hour in the toy shop, with only a penny to spend. He just couldn't make up his mind.

"Look here," cried the toy shopkeeper, "what do you expect to buy for a penny, the world with a fence around it?"

The boy thought for a moment, and then said, "Maybe, let's have a look at it."

195.　A stranger in town asked a shoe-shine boy, "Son, can you direct me to the bank?"

"Yes, sir, for a quarter," he said.

"Isn't that mighty high?" the man asked.

"No, sir," the boy said, "not for a bank director."

Bargain

196.   One woman has been going to a psychiatrist twice a week, regularly for years. She says it's done her no good, but the doctor gives her green trading stamps. Fourteen more visits and she is through. She says, "By then I'll have enough stamps to buy a couch of my own."

197.   The owner of the country store was enraged at his young son who was learning the business. "You sold the wrong eggs to that last woman," he said.

"Why were they wrong?" the boy asked.

"You sold her some of those that we dated September 10, and it's only September 4."

198.   A farmer had been trying desperately to marry off his daughters. One day when he was visiting the county seat, he met a new young unmarried lawyer who had just moved to town.

"I have several daughters," the farmer told the young man. "I would like to see them comfortably fixed. And I'll say this, they won't go to their husbands without a little bit in the bank, either. The youngest one is twenty-three and she'll take $2,500 with her. The next one is thirty-two and she'll take $5,000 with her. Another is forty-three and she'll take $10,000 with her."

"That's interesting," the young lawyer said. "I was just wondering if you have one about fifty years old."

38, 122, 136, 177, 285, 308, 533, 766, 1370, 1502

Bartender

199.   "Dad," said the little boy, "what do they call the person who brings you in contact with the spirit world?"

"A bartender," his father said.

200.   The man at the counter said, "I'll have a scotch and soda."

"Straight or with ginger ale?" the bartender asked.

201.   A drunk said to the bartender, "Have you seen Walter Miller around here in the last hour and a half?"

"Yes, he was here," said the bartender.

"Good," said the drunk. "Did you notice whether I was with him?"

202.   A rough-looking character rushed into a bar and called for a double bourbon. He drank it down in one gulp and threw a five dollar bill on the bar and rushed out the door.

The bartender folded the five-spot carefully, and slipped it in his watch pocket. Just then he looked up to see that his boss had been standing in the doorway all of the time. He looked at his boss and said, "Did you ever see such a phony in your life? Ordered a double bourbon, gulps it down, leaves a five-dollar tip, then runs out without paying."

203.   Two men walked up to a bar and ordered beers. Immediately after they were served, one of the men threw down two caps off soft-drink bottles in payment.

"What goes on here," the bartender said. "Who is trying to be funny?"

At that, the second man winked at the bartender and motioned him to step down to the end of the bar. As the two walked away, out of earshot of the first, the man said to the bartender, "That is my uncle. He is a little lost up here in his head. Go ahead and humor him. Let him pay you in bottle caps and then after we have finished drinking, I'll settle up with you. Okay?"

"Okay," said the bartender. "I'll do it if you say so."

After the two men had been drinking for about an hour, the bartender said to the second man, "Well, it's closing time now, how about doing like you asked and settle up, okay?"

"Okay," said the man, "how many bottle caps do you have?"

"Twenty-six," the bartender said.

"That's right," the man said. "Now, do you have change for a manhole cover?"

204.   A man walked into a bar and asked for a beer. He had obviously been in some terrible sort of accident because his left arm was jutting out almost straight from his shoulder and his elbow was bent and his hand was twisted back toward his body.

Bartender

The bartender looked at him with great sympathy and said, "This one is on the house. My father was in an accident and ended up being crippled for the rest of his life like you."

The man looked surprised at those words, then glanced at his left arm where the bartender was looking and shouted, "My gosh, I've lost my watermelon."

408, 468, 542, 590, 1145, 1436

Baseball

205. "Now about the salary?" said the newly signed big league player.

"Well," said the team manager, "suppose we call it $5,000 a week?"

"That's okay with me," said the rooky.

"Of course," said the manager, "you understand that the $5,000 is merely what we will call it—you will get $500."

206. A little boy was struggling over his homework and complained: "I don't want to study arithmetic."

"You have to," said his father. "I don't want a son of mine unable to figure out baseball scores and batting averages."

207. The baseball team had hit a terrible batting slump. The coach called a special batting-practice session one morning. Disgusted by the poor showing of his men, he finally grabbed a bat and rushed up to the plate. "Here, you rookies!" he said, "I'll show you something!" He ordered the pitcher to throw a few fast ones.

But the coach was out of pratice. After a dozen wild swings, he threw the bat down. "Now," he said, "that's the sort of thing you guys have been doing for weeks. I want you to get in there and start hitting the ball."

208. A little boy came in the house and told his mother about the ball game. "I was a pitcher," he said, "but they won't let me pitch any more because I am too good."

"What do you mean," his mother asked, "when you say you are too good?"

"Because," he said, "I pitched three home runs in the first inning."

209.   A bachelor uncle said he would be glad to baby-sit with his sister's infant son. About two hours later he was faced with a crisis. Frantically he called a young acquaintance, a recent father, who gave him these directions:

"First, place the diaper in position of a baseball diamond with you standing at bat. Next, fold second base to touch home plate. Then, place baby on pitcher's mound with his head pointing toward center field. Then fold third base, first base and home plate so they meet. Fasten in that position with safety pin."

210.   For years the devil had been challenging St. Peter to a baseball game. St. Peter always said "no." Finally, the Cardinals, White Sox, and Yankees all went to heaven. Now, St. Peter figured he couldn't lose, so he called up the devil.

"I'll play the game of baseball now," he said.

"You'll lose," said the devil.

"Oh, no," said St. Peter. "I've got the greatest collection of ballplayers up here you ever saw."

"You'll lose," said the devil, "because we got all the umpires down here."

211.   A man dropped by the sand lot where a bunch of young boys were playing baseball.

"What's the score?" he asked a little boy sitting on the sidelines.

"Twenty to nothing right now," the little fellow said.

"My," said the man, "it's pretty one-sided, isn't it?"

"Oh, I don't know about that," the boy said. "We haven't had our inning yet."

212.   It was just a week before the World Series and the teacher thought she would be clever and give her pupils a timely subject to write about.

"Your composition today will be about a baseball game," she said. "Write anything you want to about baseball."

Baseball

Most of the students went to work eagerly, but one little boy in the far corner seemed to be having all sorts of trouble. Most of his time was spent gazing out of the window. When the papers were turned in, his read: "No game today—called on account of rain."

775, 1460, 1650, 1910

Bashful

213. The high school class was having an old-fashioned sleigh ride. Everybody except one girl seemed to be having a wonderful time.

"What's the matter?" asked her bashful boy friend.

"Nobody loves me," she said, "and my hands are cold."

"Oh, that's all right," he whispered, "your mother loves you, and you can sit on your hands."

214. John was sitting on the porch with his girl friend, Priscilla. "I've heard it said that kisses are the language of love," he said.

"Speak for yourself, John," said Priscilla.

433

Battle

215. "Haven't I shaved you before, sir?" the barber asked.

"No," the customer said, "I got that scar during the war."

123, 507, 1456, 2085

Beach resort

216. Two fathers were discussing their daughters at lunch.

"What do you think?" said the first. "Should I send my daughter to college or not?"

"Well, I'll tell you my experience," said the second. "It cost me two thousand dollars a year to send my eldest girl to college, and it took her four years to get a husband. I spent three hundred to send the young one to the beach for three weeks, and she came home married. I recommend the beach."

Beach resort

217.　The man had just checked into the hotel at Atlantic City.

"Welcome," said the clerk at the desk. "We want you to know you are welcome. We are going to do everything we can to make you comfortable and to help you feel at home."

"Please don't," the guest said. "I left home so I could find a change. For the next few days I want to feel as if I am at a beach resort."

29, 623, 781, 1010, 1218

Beggar

218.　The lady said to the tramp at the door, "Have you ever been offered work?"

"Only once, lady," the man said. "Aside from that, I've met with nothing but kindness."

219.　A tramp stopped a man and said, "Could you give a poor fellow a bite?"

"I don't bite, myself," the man said, "but I'll call my dog."

220.　The housewife gave the man a sandwich, but asked him, "Haven't you been able to find work?"

"Yes, lady, there's plenty of work," the man said, "but everybody wants a reference from my last employer."

"Can't you get one?" she asked.

"No," the tramp said. "He's been dead twenty years."

246, 572

Behavior

221.　"When I got home last night," the young husband said, "my wife greeted me with a hug and a kiss. She had a delicious dinner ready. Afterward, she wouldn't let me help her with the dishes, but made me sit in the living room and read the paper."

"And how did you like her new outfit?" his friend asked.

222.　A soldier asked the girl he had just met, "What kind of sports do you like best, honey?"

Behavior

"Those who are free with their money and know when to say good night and go home," she said.

223. A mother had just paddled her little boy and sent him into the house from the back yard for getting in a mud puddle and ruining his clean clothes.

A few minutes later, as she came into the house, she saw his pants in the middle of the kitchen floor, just where he had removed them. It was obvious to her where he was, because the door to the utility room was open.

"I know where you are," she yelled into the room, "what are you doing in there anyway, running around without any pants on?"

The answer was a deep, male voice which said, "No, lady, I'm just reading your gas meter."

224. The little boy was a natural-born mimic, much to the annoyance of the fat neighbor next door. She finally complained to the little boy's mother about it.

The next day, seeing his mother in the supermarket she said, "I trust you spoke to your little boy about imitating me up and down the street."

"Oh, yes," said the little boy's mother, "I sure did. I told him to stop acting like a fool where everybody could see him."

123, 259, 459, 531, 740, 825, 942, 1186, 1228

Beneficiary

225. A man was talking to his lawyer about having his will drawn up. The lawyer asked him: "What's to be different about this will?"

"Oh," the man said, "I'm leaving everything to my wife on the condition that she marries again. I want somebody to be sorry I died."

607, 2110

Bequest

226.   The town's richest man had died. At breakfast the next morning, another rich, and particularly miserly, old man said to his sons, "I wonder how much he left."

The elder son said scornfully, "Every cent of it."

404, 1217

Bewildered

227.   A man with a terrible breaking-out on his hands went to the doctor for an examination. The doctor checked his hands carefully, then had him undress completely. The man was covered with the rash.

After studying the man for a long time, the doctor consulted several medical books on his shelf. Finally he said to the patient, "Have you ever had this before?"

"Yes," said the patient, "I've had it three times."

"Well," said the doctor, "all I can say is, you've got it again."

228.   The teacher was teaching a class in arithmetic.

"In order to subtract," she said, "things must be in the same denomination. For example, we can't take three pears from four peaches, nor eight horses from ten cats. Do you understand?"

One little boy in the rear raised his hand.

"Well," said the teacher, "do you have a question?"

"Please," he said, "couldn't you take three quarts of milk from two cows?"

229.   A couple of American sailors, on leave for a few days in Norway, decided to go to church. Not knowing Norwegian, they decided to play safe by picking out a dignified-looking old gentleman sitting in front of them and doing whatever he did.

During the service the minister made a special announcement of some kind. The man in front of them stood up. The sailors got to their feet also. Instantly there was a roar of laughter from the whole congregation.

When the service was over and they were greeted by the minister at the door, they discovered he spoke English. They naturally asked what the laughter was about.

Bewildered

"Oh," said the minister. "I was announcing a baptism, and asked the father of the child to rise."

230. A summer guest was furious with the farmer and said, "This is the end. A filthy pig has been trying to force his way into our room."

"Don't blame him," said the farmer, "because when you city folks ain't here, that's his room!"

21, 480, 540, 947, 1015, 1552

Birthday

231. Married man: "We're celebrating the anniversary of my wife's birthday."

His friend: "That's not right. You celebrate an anniversary or a birthday. They're different ideas entirely."

Married man: "That's what you think. We're celebrating the third anniversary of my wife's fortieth birthday."

232. A newspaper reporter was interviewing a man on his 99th birthday. As he was shaking hands to leave, he said, "I hope I can come back next year and see you on your 100th birthday."

"I don't see why you can't," the old man said, "you look healthy enough."

233. Two chorus girls were shopping together one day.

"I just don't know what to get Jean for her birthday," said the first one.

"Why don't you get her a book?" suggested the other.

"No," said the first, "she's got a book."

234. Two teen-agers were talking about their father's upcoming birthday.

"Tomorrow is the day," the boy said. "What shall we do for him?"

"We might let him use his car for a change," said his sister.

235. "Today is my birthday," said the Broadway actress.

"Wonderful," said her friend. "Congratulations. How old aren't you?"

Birthday

236.   The man was buying a washing machine. "I'm buying this for my wife for her birthday," he said to the clerk.

"Oh, a surprise?" said the clerk.

"I'll say it is," said the man. "She's expecting a diamond watch."

237.   Two women were chatting about their husbands.

"What are you going to give your husband for his birthday?" asked the first.

"Fifty cigars," said the other.

"How much do they cost?" asked the first.

"Oh, nothing at all," said the second. "I just take one out of his box every day for 50 days. He never notices it and he always compliments me for getting his favorite brand."

66, 895, 1301

Bishop

238.   A group of religious leaders were on a return flight from a convocation in Honolulu when one of the plane's engines quit. The pretty hostess hustled about, reassuring the passengers, but a Bishop, observing her, felt she needed a little reassurance herself.

"Nothing can happen to this plane," he told her. "There are eight bishops aboard."

The hostess forced a smile and said she would relay the comforting information to the pilot. After a few minutes she came back, still with a worried look on her face.

"I told the pilot," she said, "but he said he would rather have four engines."

692, 994, 1467

Blame

239.   A woman drove in a garage and asked the mechanic: "Can you fix the dent in my fender so my husband won't know I bumped it?"

66

Blame

"No, lady," said the mechanic, "but I can fix it so that next week you can ask him how he dented it."

240. A man's wife said to him at a buffet supper: "That's the fifth time you've gone back for more fried chicken. Doesn't it embarrass you?"

"Not at all," he said. "I keep telling them I'm getting it for you."

241. Every man should have a wife, because there are some things that just can't be blamed on the government.

242. The mediocre golfer had been invited to play with the club pro and a couple of visiting movie stars. Nearly a hundred people had gathered near the first tee to see them get started. The green golfer was so befuddled over being invited to play in such illustrious company that he completely missed his first swing. On his second swing he was very careful to keep his head down, but he still missed. Then he went to pieces and missed his third swing.

He was terribly embarrassed as he looked up at the sea of faces watching him. He felt he had to say something and the best he could come up with was, "Tough course, isn't it?"

84, 519, 2058

Blessing

243. One evening when a banquet was all set to begin, the chairman realized that no minister was present to return thanks. He turned to the main speaker and said, "Sir, since there is no minister here, will you ask the blessing, please?"

The speaker stood up, bowed his head, and with deep feeling said, "There being no minister present, let us thank God!"

244. The little girl was eating dinner at a friend's house for the first time. As the family sat at the table, they all bowed their heads for the blessing.

"What did you do that for?" she asked in surprise.

Blessing

"We are giving thanks for our food," said her friend's father. "Don't you do that at your house?"

"Oh, no," the little girl said. "We don't have to. We pay for our food."

117, 1222

Blind

245.   A husband and wife were arguing.

"I was a fool when I married you," the wife said.

"I guess you were," her husband said, "but I was so infatuated at the time, I didn't notice it."

246.   The lady contributed to the beggar on crutches, but couldn't resist the temptation to preach to him.

"It must be terrible to be lame," she said, "but think how much worse it is to be blind."

"That's right, lady," he said. "When I was blind, people kept passing counterfeit money off on me."

247.   A man visited his optometrist to have his glasses checked. "They just aren't strong enough," he told the doctor. "Don't you have something that is stronger?"

"Yes," said the optometrist, "there is one lens that is stronger."

"Just one?" asked the man. "What comes after that?"

"After that," the doctor said, "you buy a dog."

23, 358

Boast

248.   "Harry says he was born with a silver spoon in his mouth."

"If he was, I'll bet it had somebody else's initials on it."

249.   "Old George has it made," one married man said to another. "Whenever he opens his mouth around the house, his wife jumps."

"That's right, she does," said his friend, "all over old George."

36, 166, 293, 384, 460, 633, 743, 782, 1939

Boat

250. A couple of country boys rented a boat and went fishing. In a remote part of the lake they found a spot where the fish were really biting.

"We'd better mark this spot so we can come back tomorrow," one of them said.

"O.K., I'll do it," the second one said.

When they got back to the dock, the first one asked, "Did you mark that spot?"

"Sure," said the second, "I put a chalk mark on the side of the boat."

"You nitwit," said the first. "How do you know we'll get the same boat tomorrow?"

32, 509, 773

Bobby sockser

251. Bobby sockser: "Mother, may I hit the flick?"

Mother: "What did you say?"

Bobby sockser: "Oh, Mother, hit the flick means go to a movie."

Mother: "If that's what it means, ask me again after you swish the dish, look the book, rub the tub, scour the shower, and spread the bed."

252. The bobby sockser's grandmother said to her, "I wonder if you would do me one little favor. There are two words that I cannot bear to hear and I wonder if you would promise me not to use them. One is swell and the other is lousy."

"Sure, Grandmother," said the girl, "what are the words?"

538

Books

253. A rather nice little old lady said to the clerk at the library, "I'd like a nice book to read over the weekend."

"Here's one about a cardinal," the clerk said.

69

Books

"I'm not interested in religion," the lady said.

"Oh, but this cardinal is a bird," said the clerk.

"I'm not interested in his private life, either," the little lady said.

254.   A little boy told his little girl friend about his new ambition. He said he wanted to be a railroad conductor.

"But," said his little friend, "wouldn't you rather be an engineer and run the train?"

"Not me," he said. "The conductor gets all the comic books that kids leave on the trains."

233, 601, 685, 704, 795

Borrow

255.   "I have a friend who has an umbrella that has been in his possession for eighteen years."

"That's long enough," his neighbor said. "He ought to return it."

256.   Two men were talking about their money problems.

"Do you give your wife a personal allowance?" asked the first.

"I tried that, but it didn't work," said his friend.

"Why didn't it work out?" asked the first.

"She wouldn't cooperate," said his friend. "She always spent it before I could borrow it back."

573, 742, 807, 1403, 1958

Boss

257.   A henpecked husband was advised by a psychiatrist to assert himself. "You don't have to let your wife bully you," he said. "Go home and show her you are the boss."

The husband decided to take the doctor's advice. He went home, slammed the door, shook his fist in his wife's face, and growled, "From now on, you're taking orders from me. I want my supper right now. And when you get it on the table, go upstairs and lay out my clothes. Tonight, I'm going out on the town with the boys and you're going to stay home. Another thing, do you know who's going to dress me in my tuxedo and tie my black tie?"

"I certainly do," screamed his wife. "The undertaker!"

49, 83, 161, 202, 249, 417, 550, 636, 1505, 1569, 1956, 2004

Boy

258.   It was the little boy's first Sunday school picnic. And, as often happens, he became lost in the crowd. His mother had begun searching for him, when suddenly she heard his plaintive cry, "Wilma, Wilma."

When his mother finally reached him, she asked why he had called her by her name, Wilma, which he had never done before.

"Well," answered the little boy, "it wasn't any good calling 'Mother'—the place is crowded with them."

259.   A mother told her little boy that if he stayed home and behaved himself, she would bring him something from the store.

When she returned home, she asked him, "Well, were you a good little boy?"

"Oh," he said, "I was gooder than good. Why I was so good I could hardly stand myself."

107, 115, 319, 441, 531, 1064, 1301, 2055

Boy friend

260.   "How wonderful," gushed a young lady's friend. "So you and Joe are married. I thought all along it was just going to be another flirtation."

"So did Joe," the young bride said.

261.   One girl said to her friend: "If I could only combine the best qualities of my two boy friends, I'd be the happiest girl in

Boy friend

the world. One is gay, debonair, and rich. He's also handsome and witty. But it's the other one who wants to marry me."

262. Two girls were chatting about their various boy friends. "He seems rather dull and uninteresting until you get to know him," said the first. "After that he's downright boring."

263. One girl said to another, "He is a perfect gentleman at all times, but I guess that's better than not having any boy friend at all!"

368, 584, 768, 1329

Bragging

264. The first little boy was bragging and said, "My dad draws some lines on paper, puts little dots on them, calls it music and gets $50 for it."
"That's nothing," said the second. "My dad's a tax expert. He figures for half an hour with a pencil and calls it a tax return and charges $100 for his work."
"Huh," said the preacher's son. "My dad scratches some notes on a sheet of paper, gets up and reads it off, and it takes six men to collect the money for him."

265. A Texan was bragging about the merits of his watch to some friends in New York City. Finally, one of his friends couldn't stand it any longer.
"That's nothing," he said. "I dropped my watch in the Hudson River six months ago, and it's been running ever since."
The Texan couldn't believe it. "What!" he said, "your watch is still running?"
"No," he said, "the Hudson River."

266. At a cocktail party, a self-made man kept bragging that he had never come in contact with the influence of any schools, colleges, or universities. He admittedly had no education and was proud of it.

Bragging

Another guest asked him: "Do I understand you to say that you are thankful for your ignorance?"

"You might put it that way if you like," he said.

"Well," said the other guest, "you certainly do have a lot to be thankful for."

267. A drunk at a football game was making such a nuisance of himself that the people around him threatened to call the police if he didn't sit down and shut up. At that he shouted, "Show me a policeman, and I'll show you a dope."

The words were no sooner spoken when a big six-foot policeman arrived on the scene and said, "I'm a policeman."

"Wonderful!" said the drunk. "I'm a dope!"

268. A father was bragging about his daughter who had studied painting in Paris.

"This is the sunset my daughter painted," he said. "She studied painting abroad, you know."

"That accounts for it," said his friend. "I never saw a sunset like that in this country."

269. A man was bragging to his wife about his personality.

"One thing you have to say about me. I am a modest man."

"What," snorted his wife, "modest? Why you have never done anything to be modest about."

270. The biggest bragger in the neighborhood was talking. "I can truthfully say I never brag," he said.

"Never brag?" said his friend. "That's wonderful. No wonder you boast about it."

271. Two marines were bragging about their outfits. "Why, our company is so well drilled," said the first, "that when we present arms, all you can hear is slap, slap, click."

"Pretty good," said the other, "but when our company presents arms you can hear only slap, slap, jingle."

"Jingle?" asked the first. "What is that?"

"Our medals," said the other.

Bragging

272.   The outdoor man was showing his girl friend his trophies. "This polar bear I shot in the Arctic," he said pointing to a rug before the fire. "It was a close call. It was a case of me or the bear that day."

"I think you decided wisely," said his girl friend. "The bear definitely makes the better rug."

273.   The Englishman had found the young American woman most charming. "I can't understand your being from Baltimore," he said. "I naturally assumed you were from New York."

"Why New York?" she asked.

"Oh," he said, "I thought all charming Americans were from New York."

"What made you think that?" she asked.

"Oh, I don't know," he said. "I think a lady from New York told me."

274.   A man was bragging to his friend about his family.

"When I go home at night," he said, "everything is ready for me, my slippers, my pipe, the easy chair in the corner with the light turned on, my book open at the same place I left it the night before—and always plenty of hot water."

"I get all that stuff about the slippers and easy chair and book and the pipe," his friend said, "but what about the hot water. Why the hot water?"

"Well," the man said, "my family loves me. You don't think they're going to make me wash dishes in cold water, do you?"

275.   Up to this moment, the record for bragging goes to a Texan who graduated from Yale and who had served two years in the Marine Corps.

97, 302, 314, 429, 526, 912, 1622, 1935

Bravery

276.   The audience was questioning the lecturer who had just spoken on big game hunting in Africa.

"Is it true," asked one, "that wild beasts in the jungle won't harm you if you carry a torch?"

Bravery

"That all depends," the lecturer said, "on how fast you carry it."

277. Two women were gossiping about the recent wedding scandal.

"Just think," the first one said, "it was just as the bride was coming down the aisle that the groom suddenly turned and ran from the church and skipped town. I guess he lost his nerve."

"Oh, I don't think so," said the other, "I figure he found it."

278. The young lady was sinking for the third time when the brave young man dived into the water and rescued her. The girl's father was most grateful.

"How can I ever thank you, young man?" he asked. "How brave you were to face such danger to save my daughter."

"Why, there really wasn't any danger," said the young man. "You see, I'm already married."

279. "Did you know I'm a hero?" said a college boy to his roommate.

"How come you're a hero?" asked his roommate.

"Well, it was my girl friend's birthday," said the first, "and she said if I ever brought her a gift she would drop dead. So, I didn't buy her any and saved her life."

280. The little girl's father was talking to her about being brave.

"But ain't you afraid of cows and horses?" she asked.

"Of course not," said her father.

"And ain't you afraid of bees and thunder and lightning?" asked the child.

"Certainly not," he said.

"Gee, Daddy," she said, "guess you ain't afraid of nothing in the world but Mamma."

281. "With the divorce rate going up all the time," a man said to his friend, "I'd say the United States is really becoming the land of the free."

"Maybe so," his friend said, "but the high marriage rate shows that it is still the home of the brave."

Bravery

282.   There were two skeletons hanging in a closet. One of them said to the other, "If we had any guts, we'd get out of here."

283.   "What in the world happened at the picnic yesterday?" a fellow asked his friend. "They are saying around the office that you acted like a coward."

"Well, I'm no fool," the fellow said. "Some of the girls found a big hornet's nest in the top of a tree and dared me to climb up and get it. And I just didn't do it, that's all."

"Whether you were smart or not," the first fellow said, "that sort of makes you unhonored and unsung around here."

"That's right," the coward said, "but I'm also unharmed and unstung."

18, 489, 721, 741

Bribery

284.   "Come along and vote, dear," the Congressman told his wife. "I need every vote I can get. Besides, it's your duty to vote."

But his wife shook her head. "You can call it bribery or not," she said, "but I will not vote unless you buy me a new hat to vote in."

285.   "My," said a little fellow to his buddy, "how in the world did you ever get your little sister to dig up so many nice fat fishing worms for you?"

"Oh," said his buddy, "I had to bribe her a little. For every ten worms she dug up for me, I let her have one to eat."

186

Bride

286.   A young lady, recently returned from her honeymoon, was complaining to her friend about her husband's drinking habits.

"If you knew he drank, why did you marry him?" her friend asked.

Bride

"I didn't know he drank," the bride said, "until one night he came home sober."

287. A friend asked her newly married friend what she thought of married life.

"Oh, one thing is the same," she said. "I used to wait up half the night for Harry to go home. Now I wait up half the night for him to come home."

28, 277, 374, 414, 439, 478, 630, 1964

Bridegroom

288. A friend came up and shook hands with the future bridegroom.

"Congratulations, friend," he said, "on this, one of the happiest days of your life."

"But I'm not getting married until tomorrow," said the future bridegroom.

"I know," said his friend. "That's what makes this one of your happiest days."

289. The minister was preaching on the sanctity of marriage and all of its joys and blessings.

"Just think," he said, "why the bride always wears white. White—the symbol of happiness, of purity, for the most joyous day of her life."

"Then why does the groom always wear black?" a man asked.

585, 1106

Bridge

290. A man's wife, who had just played a bad hand at bridge, said to her husband, "How should I have played that hand?"

"Under an assumed name," he said.

291. Four men were playing bridge. One of them made a stupid play, realizing it after it was too late. After the hand had been played, his partner asked:

Bridge

"Did you lead that card from strength or from weakness?"
"From ignorance," the other man said.

292.   The bridge tournament was in high gear when suddenly one player tossed his cards down and said: "This game is crooked."

"That is a terrible accusation to make," said his partner, "that someone is cheating. What makes you think so?"

"That man," he said, pointing to the player on his left, "is not playing the hand I dealt him."

293.   The husband played wisely and according to the rules. His wife boasted of knowing no rules. However, one evening, she bid and made a grand slam, doubled and redoubled. Excitedly, she said to her husband, "See, you thought I couldn't do it!"

"Well, darling," he said, "you couldn't have, if you'd played it correctly."

294.   A young doctor received a hurried telephone call from a doctor friend who invited him to make a fourth at bridge.

"Do you have to go, dear?" asked his wife.

"I'm afraid so," he said. "It's an important case. In fact, there are three doctors there already."

295.   The couple were driving home after the bridge party.

"You certainly were a nuisance tonight," the man's wife said to him. "All evening long you kept asking me what was trump. Can't you remember anything at all?"

"Oh, honey," her husband said, "I knew all along what was trump. I just kept asking you so you would know I was taking an interest in the game."

1227

Budget

296.   The doctor had examined his patient and then said to him, "You're working too hard."

Budget

"I know it," said the man, "but that's the only way I can keep up all the easy payments I'm trying to make."

297. The boss said to his recently married employee, "I suppose you find that your wife can live on your income all right?"

"Oh, yes, sir," the young man said. "But now it's up to me to make another one for myself."

298. A housewife was working on the budget for the new year.

"Well," she said, "I worked out the budget all right. But one of us will have to go."

299. Two friends were having a drink in a bar and talking about their wives.

"Did you ever give your wife a budget and lay down the law about economizing as you said you were going to?" asked the first.

"Yes, I did it last week," he said.

"Well," asked the first, "how is it working?"

"How is it working?" said his friend. "I've already given up smoking and playing poker."

140, 506, 605, 744, 933, 1951, 1989

Bugs

300. "Are caterpillars good to eat, Dad?" asked the little boy at the dinner table.

"Of course not," said his father. "Why did you ask such a question?"

"Oh, I was just wondering," said the boy. "There was one on your salad a minute ago, but he's gone now."

520, 2067

Building program

301. The minister was proudly showing a visitor and his family the newly dedicated church and adjoining educational

building. As they stood in front of the building saying goodbye, the seven-year-old daughter said: "It certainly is a beautiful building. What is the name of the artichoke who designed it?"

302.   The local Catholic Church had just finished their $200,000 expansion program. It included an educational building and also a beautiful new parsonage for the priest. One afternoon the neighborhood Baptist minister called on the priest and was being shown the new additions. The priest showed his visitor all of the refinements of his new home: wall-to-wall carpet, the built-in hi-fi set, the indirect lighting, the soundproof study. As the Baptist minister was leaving, the priest asked him: "Well, what do you think of my new quarters?"

The Baptist minister smiled and said: "It's finer than any place I ever lived. It certainly is true that you Catholic priests have finer quarters but remember, we Baptist ministers have better halves."

604, 1968

Burglar

303.   The burglar was not only carrying a mean-looking gun, he also appeared to be drunk. "Get ready to die," he said. "I'm going to shoot you."

"Why shoot me?" asked his victim.

"I've always said I'd shoot anyone who looked like me," the burglar said.

"And do I look like you?" the victim asked.

"Yes, you do," said the burglar.

"Then go ahead and shoot," his victim said.

304.   The visitor at the jail asked the man in the cell, "And why are you locked up?"

"I suppose they think I'd go home if I wasn't," he said.

305.   The social worker was trying to help on a rehabilitation program at the prison. "Do you have any plans for the future, when you are released?" he asked a prisoner.

Burglar

"Yes," the prisoner said. "I've got the plans of two jewelry stores and a bank to start with."

306. The victim of the hold-up was pleading with the gunman.

"I don't have anything," he said. "My watch is old and has only sentimental value."

"Give it to me," said the gunman. "I feel like a good cry."

307. The men who robbed the bank had driven six hundred miles to their hideaway.

"Come on," said the first. "Let's count up how much we made on this job."

"I'm tired," said his buddy. "Let's go to bed and find out on television in the morning."

577, 784, 854, 1144, 1487, 1694, 1922

Bus

308. It was the little lady's first ride on the new deluxe overnight express bus. Before they left the bus station, a porter came through with pillows.

"How much are they?" the lady asked.

"Twenty-five cents, ma'am," the porter said.

"I'll take six," she said as she took the money from her purse.

"You want six pillows, ma'am?" the porter asked.

"Why yes," she said. "I never have seen them that cheap in a department store."

309. A man was telling his friend about his new house in the suburbs.

"We like it," he said, "but it does have its inconveniences."

"I imagine it does," said his friend. "What do you miss most?"

"The last bus home at night," the man said.

310. The lady said to the ticket agent in the country bus station, "I want to return to town on a late bus."

"Well," said the agent, "I'd recommend Number 321. She's usually as late as any of them."

Bus

311. The traveler was complaining about the slowness of the bus to the driver.

After he couldn't stand the complaining any longer, the driver said, "If you don't like it, why don't you get out and walk?"

"I would," said the passenger, "but my daughter is going to meet me and she doesn't expect me until this bus gets there."

312. The bus was late, and the lady was taking her anger out on the ticket agent.

"What good," she asked, "are the times that are printed in the timetables?"

"Why," said the agent, "if it weren't for them, we wouldn't have any way of finding out how late the buses are."

313. A drunk was sitting on the curb in a busy part of the city.

"Look, fellow," a passerby said, "why don't you take the bus home?"

"No use," the drunk said. "My wife wouldn't let me keep it in the house."

39, 82, 107, 454, 493, 583, 592, 629, 657, 660, 1328

Business

314. The high-pressure salesman was trying to get a job as a sales manager for a small firm.

"I'm the best man in the business," he said. "Put me to work for you and your business will really prosper."

"Maybe so," said the hard-pushed owner, "but anybody I hire has to start at the bottom. First you have to be a partner."

315. The farmer was sick in bed and his son was running the farm.

"How are the cows doing?' he asked the boy.

"Not so bad," said his son. "We got twelve gallons yesterday."

"How much skimmed milk did you sell?" asked the old man.

"Ten gallons," his son said.

Business

"And how much cream and whole milk?" the farmer asked.

"Three gallons each," the boy said.

The farmer looked worried and said, "Well, what did you do with the rest of it?"

316. The owner of a shoe store was asked: "How's business?"

"Pretty good," he said. "I haven't had a customer all day."

"What's so good about that?" his friend asked.

"See that fellow over there?" the man said, pointing to the shoe store across the street. "Well, he hasn't had a customer in two days."

317. In spite of a slight depression, the men were holding their convention in Atlantic City as scheduled. Several of the men were complaining and asked the delegate from San Francisco how hard the depression had hit his town.

"Depression?" he asked. "Why, we don't have a depression in San Francisco. Of course, I must admit we're having the poorest boom we've had in a long time."

318. A man was applying for a job. "Does the company pay for my hospitalization?" he asked.

"No. You pay for it," the personnel director said. "We take it out of your salary each month."

"The last place I worked, they paid for it," the man said.

"That's unusual," the personnel man said. "How much vacation did you get?"

"Six weeks," the man said.

"Did you get a bonus?" the personnel man asked.

"Yes," said the man. "Not only that, they gave us an annual bonus, sent us a turkey on Thanksgiving, gave us the use of a company car and threw a big barbecue for us each year."

"Why did you leave?" asked the personnel director.

"They went busted," the man said.

319. A widow in a small southern town decided to go into business for herself and set up a bootleg operation in her home. It was down a dirt street and the kids who used to play out

Business

front would watch the men come up on the porch and knock
on the door. The password went something like this: "What do
you want?"

"You know what us want," the men would say, "us want
some of that stuff."

"You all got any money," the woman would ask.

"Yes," they would say, "us got two dollars."

For two dollars, she would take them into the living room
and sell them a jug of moonshine whiskey. They would then
go down the street whistling and singing and looking real in-
nocent.

One day, a couple of the kids out front decided to see what
it was all about. So, they knocked on the door and it went like
this:

"What do you want?" the woman demanded.

"You all know what us want," the little fellow said, "us want
some of that stuff."

"You all got any money?" she asked.

"Yes'um," the little boy said, "us got ten cents."

She figured to teach them a lesson, so she took them into the
living room, took their dime away from them, then banged
their heads together and pitched them out into the street.

The first little boy got up, dusted himself off, and cried, "Dog-
gone it, I don't think I could of stood two dollars worth of that
stuff."

335, 436, 500, 536, 725, 782, 1492, 1738

Butler

320.   Perkins, the butler of an aristocratic Boston dowager,
had recommended his own mother for the cook's position. When
she arrived, the lady of the house was surprised to discover the
woman was 30 years older than herself. A thin, weak-looking
little old woman.

"Aren't you a little frail for such heavy work?" the lady asked
her new cook.

"Oh, no," she said, "why, ma'am, I've never been sick a day
in my life! I've never had anything but whooping cough and
Perkins."

Butler

321.   The grand old lady had hired a new butler. On his first day on the job, he answered the doorbell to find a middle-aged man standing there.

"Does the lady of the house expect you?" the butler asked.

"Expect me?" the man demanded. "Why she expected me before I was born. The lady of the house happens to be my mother."

Cafe

322.   An irate customer waved down a passing waitress: "Pardon me, are you the girl who took my order?"

"Yes, sir," she said, politely.

"Well, I'll be darned," he said. "You don't look a day older."

323.   A man went into a cafe and sat at the counter.

"What will you have?" the waitress said.

"Anything," said the customer, "that will give me a heartburn immediately, instead of at three o'clock in the morning."

623, 1817

Calm

324.   "Mommy, mommy," the girl cried. "Daddy's just fallen off the roof!"

"I know, dear," her mother said. "I saw him pass the window."

584, 602, 606

Candidate

325.   The election was being challenged by the defeated candidate. "I know it was crooked," he said. "A friend of mine voted for me fifteen times in the third precinct and I didn't get but four votes there."

326.   Two rival political candidates were scheduled to speak at the county fair on the same program. The mayor was chosen to introduce them. He arose and said, "I want to present to you

a man who, above anyone, has the welfare of each and every one of you at heart. More than anyone I know, he is devoted to our great and glorious state."

Then he turned to the candidates and asked, "Which of you fellows wants to talk first?"

327.   The candidate was covering a lot of territory in a hurry, as the campaign was nearing the end. His speech writer was hard pressed to keep up with him. In one town, the writer was still typing the speech when the candidate was introduced. He grabbed the speech out of the typewriter without looking at it, and rushed to the platform.

"Fellow citizens," he said, as he read the speech, "I cannot tell you how happy it makes me to be once more in this, my favorite town, so filled with American tradition and the people who make tradition, and I slip in some soft soap about how pretty this lousy, flea-bitten dump is. . . ."

328.   The man running for office asked an old friend to vote for him.

"I'm sorry I can't vote for you," he said, "but, you are a Republican and I'm a Democrat—a born Democrat. And I always vote the straight Democratic ticket."

"A born Democrat," the candidate said, "what is a born Democrat?"

"Well," said the voter, "my dad was a Democrat, and my grandfather was a Democrat, and I'm a Democrat."

"That's no reason to vote for the party," the candidate said. "Do you mean to tell me that if your dad was an idiot and your grandfather was an idiot, that you'd be an idiot?"

"No," said the voter. "In that case, I'd be a Republican."

329.   The candidate had finished the formal part of his address and was in the midst of the question-and-answer period. The exchange was spirited and the politician was clever not to give an answer that would offend either side.

"How do you stand on foreign aid," shouted a man far out in the audience.

Candidate

"I'm right on that issue, too," the politician yelled back at him without batting an eye.

330. The candidate was getting ready to make his speech and the local newspaper reporter said, "Sir, do you have a copy of your speech for the record?"

"I never speak for the record," the candidate said. "I only speak for publicity."

579, 852, 980, 1579, 1802, 2038

Cannibals

331. Two cannibals were sitting by their campfire chatting after dinner.

"That sure was delicious," said the guest cannibal.

"Yes, my wife does make a good soup," replied the host cannibal, "but I'm afraid I'm going to miss her."

427, 1230, 1442, 1506

Capacity

332. A farmer had a cow for sale. A prospective buyer asked about the cow's pedigree. The farmer didn't know even what pedigree meant. The prospect then asked him about the cow's butterfat production. The farmer said he hadn't any idea what it was. Finally, the prospect asked him if he knew how many pounds of milk the cow gave each year. This time the old farmer said proudly, "I don't know exactly. But she's an honest old cow and she'll give you all the milk she's got."

333. A man at a bar said to the man sitting next to him, "One drink always makes me drunk."

"Really?" asked the stranger, "only one?"

"Yes," the man said. "And it's usually the sixth."

334. The summer visitor asked the farmer, "What happened to the other windmill that was here last year?"

"There was only enough wind for one," said the farmer, "so we took it down."

78, 114, 656, 1180, 1462, 1844, 1897

Carefree

335.   A man was in a bar weeping and complaining.

"I don't have anything to worry about," he said. "My wife takes care of my money. My mother-in-law tends to my business. All I have to do is work."

336.   The PTA meeting was becoming rather spirited as the question of male versus female teachers was being discussed.

"I say that women make the best teachers," said one large and noisy woman. "Where would man be today if it weren't for women?"

"In the Garden of Eden eating watermelon and taking it easy," a man in the back shouted.

93, 943

Careful

337.   One Saturday afternoon, the locker-room boy at the country club, answered the telephone. A female voice said, "Is my husband there?"

The boy answered quickly, "No, ma'am."

"How can you say he isn't there," the voice asked, "before I even tell you who I am?"

"It don't make no difference, lady," the boy said. "They ain't never nobody's husband here."

338.   The young mother was giving her baby a bath, and the four-year-old girl from next door was watching her. The little girl had her own baby with her—a doll that had lost an arm and leg and was badly beaten up.

"How long have you had your baby?" the little girl asked.

"Three months," the young mother said.

"My, but you've kept her nice!" said the little girl.

21, 461, 513, 568, 646, 843, 1492, 1647, 1714

Cat

339.   A lady was visiting the aquarium.

"Can you tell me where I can buy a live shark?" she asked the attendant.

Cat

"A live shark?" he asked. "What do you want with a live shark?"

"Our cat has been eating the goldfish," she said, "and I want to teach him a lesson."

340. The clerk was waiting on a customer at the meat counter in the supermarket, when a woman pushed herself ahead of the customer and said, "Give me a pound of cat food, quick, I'm in a hurry."

Then she turned to the other customer and said, "I hope you don't mind my being waited on ahead of you."

"Not if you're that hungry," said the other woman sweetly.

696

Catholics

341. Three young men were graduated from the seminary and were ordained in the Catholic church. They were Father O'Flaherty, Father Ryan, and Father Secola.

They worked hard at their work and some years later the promotions came through. Now it was Monsignor O'Flaherty, Monsignor Ryan, but still Father Secola. Father Secola didn't like it very much, but being a conscientious man, he didn't say anything. He just worked that much harder.

After another ten years, some more promotions came along. This time it was Bishop O'Flaherty and Bishop Ryan, but still Father Secola. He didn't say anything, but the indignity was almost all he could bear.

After another fifteen years, the big promotion came through. Now, it was Cardinal O'Flaherty and Cardinal Ryan, but always Father Secola.

This time Father Secola couldn't stand it any longer and he went to the head Cardinal and complained. He said, "I graduated with those two men, worked hard all my life, and I never got the first promotion. I think I have a right to know why."

"I think you do," said the Cardinal, "and I'll tell you. Remember in the Catholic church, after you get to be a Cardinal and the top job opens up in Rome, anything could happen, lightning could strike anywhere. And we don't think it would be right for Catholics all over the world to have to refer to you as Pope Secola."

342.   A Protestant was getting ready to apply to a local department store for a job. A friend told him that it was the policy of the store to hire nobody but Catholics and that if he wanted a job there, he would have to lie about being a Catholic.

He applied for the job and the personnel man asked him the usual questions. Then he said to the applicant, "And what church do you belong to?"

"I'm a Catholic," the man said. "And all my family are Catholics. In fact, my father is a priest and my mother is a nun."

32, 302, 386, 986, 1248

Caution

343.   A cute young thing, reading names like "Surrender" and "My Sin" on the perfume counter, timidly asked the saleslady:
    "Don't you have anything for a beginner?"

344.   A woman who had been seriously ill was well again and was shopping in the supermarket when she ran into a friend of her husband.

"How are you these days?" he asked.

"Oh, I'm fine, now," she said, "but I was so deathly sick I almost died. I had ptomaine poisoning from some chicken salad."

"That's terrible," the man said. "What with that and the delirium tremors, you just don't know what is safe to eat or drink these days."

345.   A woman was driving along a country road, when she noticed a couple of linemen start up some telephone poles.

"They certainly are stupid," she said to her friend, "they must think I never drove before."

346.   A little boy's sister came to the principal's office and handed him the following note:

Caution

"Dear Teacher, please excuse Harry today—he caught a skunk."

347.   The man stopped the doctor on the street one summer day. "You remember when you cured my rheumatism last winter, doctor," asked the man, "and told me not to get myself wet?"

"Yes, I remember," said the doctor.

"Well, I just wondered if you think it's safe for me to take a bath yet," said the man.

348.   A man and wife checked in at a swank resort hotel. After cleaning up, the lady forgot to turn off the faucets in the bathroom. Half an hour later, the guest in the room directly under them opened his window, stuck out his head and called upstairs to attract their attention.

"Hey, you up there!" he shouted.

The man upstairs opened his window and stuck out his head. "What's the matter?" he asked.

"Turn off those faucets in your bathroom!" he demanded. "It's pouring down here. What's the matter with you? You must be a dope." He ended his tirade with a wild outburst of profanity.

"Wait a minute," said the man upstairs. "Stop your cursing, I've got a lady up here."

"What do you think I've got down here," yelled the first man, "a duck?"

349.   It was the day of the hanging, and as the convicted man was led to the foot of the steps of the scaffold, he suddenly stopped and refused to walk another step.

"Let's go," the guard said impatiently. "What's the matter?"

"Somehow," the man said, "those steps look mighty rickety—they just don't seem safe enough to walk up."

568, 706, 838, 1402, 1493, 1993, 2087, 2093

Certainty

350.   A funeral director telegraphed a man that his mother-in-law had just died, and asked whether he should bury or cremate her.

The man wired back and said: "Both. Don't take any chances."

351.   "At last," said the writer, "I have written something that will be accepted by any magazine."

"What could that be?" his friend asked.

"A check for a year's subscription," the writer said.

237, 257, 325, 536, 1030, 1452, 1556, 2061, 2094

Chance

352.   A man eating in a dining car gave the waiter two one-dollar bills to pay his check of $1.45. The waiter brought his change, a fifty-cent piece and a nickel. The man looked up at the waiter, then at the change tray. He finally picked up the half-dollar and left the nickel.

The waiter smiled and picked up the nickel and said: "That's all right, sir, thank you. I just gambled and lost."

353.   As usual, the little boy showed up for supper with dirty hands and a dirty face.

"Go wash up," his mother screamed at him. "Night after night I tell you. And night after night you always come to the table without washing. Why don't you ever do it without me shouting at you?"

"Well," he said, "it's always worth a try. Who knows? You might forget once."

498, 877, 2049

Change

354.   The little boy and his mother were looking through the family album. They came to a picture of a handsome young man with a full head of hair and a mustache.

"Who's that?" asked the little boy.

Change

"Why, that's your father," said his mother.

"What?" said the little boy. "Then who's that bald-headed man that's living with us?"

355.   A man sitting at a bar said to the wife of a friend sitting next to him, "Whatever happened to that dopey blonde your husband used to run around with?"

"I dyed my hair," the woman said.

356.   The farmer was back home after visiting his son and his wife in New York.

"How was the city?" asked a friend. "Much different?"

"This different," said the farmer. "In the country we go to bed feeling all in and get up feeling fine. In the city, you go to bed feeling fine and get up feeling all in."

357.   The minister was congratulating the lady on her 40th wedding anniversary. "It requires a lot of patience, tolerance, and understanding to live with the same man for 40 years," he said.

"Thank you," said the lady, "but he's not the same man he was when we were first married."

56, 179, 217, 234, 352, 544, 724, 1050, 1203, 1896

Charity

358.   A commuter who always stopped in the same barroom on his way home from work, noticed one day that the bartender had placed a small slotted box on the bar. Over the box was a neatly lettered sign, "For the Blind."

The commuter, a charitable man, dutifully deposited his contribution. This went on every day for several weeks. Then one evening the commuter noticed the box was gone.

"Where's the box for the blind?" he asked the bartender.

"Oh, I put it away," the bartender said. "I collected enough money for the new blind. There it is behind you. What do you think of it?"

Charity

359.   A woman had called a venetian-blind repairman to come pick up a broken blind. That evening, while the family was having dinner, the doorbell rang. The husband of the woman went to the door, and the man on the step said, "I'm here for the blind."

The husband fished a dollar out of his pocket, gave it to the repairman, shut the door and returned to the table.

"Just somebody collecting," he said.

360.   A drunk knocked on the door and asked the housewife for a handout.

"Certainly not," said the woman. "Look at the condition you are in. Don't you know all that liquor will make a mess of your stomach?"

"Oh, that's all right," the man said. "Go ahead and give it to me. I'll keep my coat buttoned."

361.   A rather well-dressed man called on the minister and told him a distressing story of poverty and misery in the neighborhood.

"This poor widow," he said, "with four starving children to feed, is sick in bed with no money for the doctor, and besides that she owes $100 rent for three months and is about to be evicted. I'm out trying to help raise the rent money. I wondered if you can help?"

"I certainly can," said the minister. "If you can give your time to this cause, so can I. By the way, who are you?"

"I'm the landlord," the man said.

43, 204, 377, 889, 1117, 1296, 1420, 1717

Cheerful

362.   I was at the end of my rope. Broke, lonesome, downhearted, and discouraged.

"Cheer up," a friend said to me. "Things could be worse."

So I cheered up. And sure enough, things got worse.

634, 1597, 1907

Cheese

363.   A customer asked the manager of the delicatessen, "Do you remember that cheese you sold me yesterday?"

"Yes," said the manager of the store.

"Please tell me again," the customer said. "Did you say it was imported or deported from Switzerland?"

1039, 1911

Chicken

364.   An irate customer in a restaurant, after battling a tough piece of chicken, said to the waitress, "This must have been an incubator chicken."

"Why?" asked the waitress.

"Because," said the customer, "no chicken with a mother could be this tough."

365.   A little boy asked the farmhand, "Is a chicken big enough to eat when it's two weeks old?"

"Of course not," said the farmhand.

"Then how does it keep alive?" the little boy wanted to know.

366.   A little girl from the city was visiting her grandmother in the country. She went to help her grandmother feed the chickens. There in the barnyard was a peacock strutting around with its tail fanned.

The little girl shouted, "Grandma! Grandma! Look, one of your chickens is in full bloom!"

367.   The science teacher was trying to get over some of the basic facts of the laws of nature and how they cannot vary.

"For example," he said. "We all know that you can't get eggs without hens."

"My grandmother can," said a bright little girl down front.

"That's silly," the teacher said. "How can your grandmother get eggs without a hen?"

"She has ducks," the little girl said.

101, 127, 344, 372, 533, 718, 1482, 1614, 1762, 1831

Choice

368.   The ardent young lover said to his girl friend, "Darling, will you marry me?"

"But have you seen Father and Mother?" asked the girl.

"Yes," said the boy. "But that makes no difference. I still love you and I want to marry you."

369.   The professor of law was lecturing on courtroom procedure. "When you're fighting a case," he said, "if you have the facts on your side, hammer on the facts. If you have the law on your side, hammer on the law."

"But if you don't have the facts or the law," asked a student, "what do you do?"

"In that case," the professor said, "then hammer on the table."

370.   A young man had been calling on his girl friend for over a year. One evening the girl's father stopped him as he was leaving and asked, "Look here, young man, you have been seeing my daughter for a year now, and I would like to know whether your intentions are honorable or dishonorable."

The young man's face lit up. "Do you mean to say," he said, "that I have a choice?"

371.   A woman went into a man's department store and said, "I want to buy a tie."

The salesman showed her his assortment. "I'll take this green one," she said.

"Excuse me for saying this, lady," said the salesman, "but I don't believe that your husband would wear that kind of tie because it's an off-shade green."

"Listen," she said, "he'll wear anything I buy him. He's dead!"

372.   A young man stood in the department store with a puzzled look on his face.

"May I help you, sir?" a clerk asked.

"Yes, thank you," the young man said. "I was supposed to buy either a camisole or a casserole, but I can't remember which."

Choice

"Maybe I can help you," said the clerk, "if you tell me what sort of chicken you want to put in it."

373. The young high school boy's parents were objecting to the girl their son was dating.

"Gee," he said to them, "what do you all expect? She's the best girl I can get with the car we've got."

45, 124, 198, 283, 581, 629, 1232, 1330, 1805, 1975, 2006

Choir director

374. The minister had just married his beautiful choir director. On their honeymoon he said to her: "My big problem now, dear, is to find somebody to take your place. We will have to hire a new choir director."

"That will be easy," his bride said. "I know just the person. My cousin graduates next week from the conservatory of music."

"Wonderful," said her husband, "what is her name?"

"HIS name is Harold Morgan," she said.

133, 183

Christmas

375. It was Christmas Eve and a couple were coming home from the midnight service.

"Look, dear, what a beautiful scene. The Millers are carrying in a Yule log."

"That's no Yule log," her husband said. "That's Miller."

376. Late one Christmas eve in the lower dock area of town, where it wasn't safe to be out at night, four little boys were dragging a big bag through the alley.

A minister, coming home from a midnight service which he had held in the dock-side mission, spotted them and said, "Well, what have we here? This late at night, dragging that bag down the alley. I'll bet you are up to no good. Don't you children know that if you do that, old Santa Claus won't come to see you?"

The smallest of the little fellows looked up at the minister and said, "Who do you think we've got in the bag?"

377.   Every year the folks over at Boulevard Church picked up all the mail at the post office that had been addressed to Santa Claus. A committee opened the letters and made sure that each child who had written to Santa Claus received a gift. One year, when the committee was opening the letters, they came across one that read:

"Dear Santa Claus: I hate to bother you with my problems, but my wife is in the hospital and I have just lost my job. We have eight children and unless you help us, we won't have a very good Christmas. I wonder if you would be a good Santa Claus and send me a check for $600. Signed, Joe Henderson."

"Why, we know him," one of the committee members said. "He is a member of Central Church just down the street. Anyway, throw it away because we are supposed to send our help to children."

"That's right," said another member, "but here is a man who needs help. He must be pretty desperate or he wouldn't have written to Santa Claus for help. We ought to do something for him."

After much discussion, the committee members decided to send him a gift out of their own pockets. Among themselves they made up a purse of $300 and sent it to him.

They never received a reply from the man. Not a word of thank you. Not even an acknowledgment that he had received the money.

A year went by. Then, when the committee was once again opening Christmas mail, they ran across this letter:

"Dear Santa Claus: I hate to bother you again with my problems. But my wife is back in the hospital again. I still don't have a job and all the kids are hungry. If you won't help us, we won't have a very good Christmas. I wonder if you would be a good Santa Claus and send me a check for $600. Signed, Joe Henderson. P.S. Santa Claus, this year when you send me the money, please send it through Central Church. Last year you sent it through Boulevard Church and the dirty crooks over there kept half of it."

Christmas

378. The little girl's aunt was visiting for the holidays and was talking about Christmas. "What are you going to give your little brother for Christmas?" she asked.

"I don't know," the little girl said.

"Well," asked her aunt, "what did you give him for Christmas last year?"

"The whooping cough," said the little girl.

119, 830, 893, 987, 1243, 1336, 2070, 2074

Church attendance

379. A little boy asked his father: "Did you go to Sunday school when you were little?"

"Certainly," said his father. "I never missed a Sunday."

"See, Mother?" said the little boy. "It won't do me any good either."

41, 229, 665, 730, 814

Cigarettes

380. Customer: "A pack of cigarettes, please."

Clerk: "Yes, sir, regular or king size?"

Customer: "King size."

Clerk: "Filter or plain?"

Customer: "Filter."

Clerk: "Menthol or nonmenthol?"

Customer: "Nonmenthol."

Clerk: "Pack or box?"

Customer: "Box."

Clerk: "Turkish blend or—"

Customer: "Forget it! I just gave up the habit!"

381. A man limped into a doctor's office with a badly swollen ankle.

"Goodness, man," said the doctor, after looking at the man's ankle, "how long has it been in this condition?"

"About three weeks," said the man.

"Why, this ankle is broken," said the doctor. "Why didn't you come to me right away?"

Cigarettes

"Well, I sort of hesitated," said the man, "because every time I say anything is wrong with me, my wife insists that I stop smoking."

70, 655, 1671, 1967

Circus

382.   Two old circus buddies who hadn't seen each other in a long time met on the street.

"How is it going?" asked the first.

"It couldn't be any better," said his friend. "I have a new act. With the world so interested in peace, I figured out an act where I have a lion and a lamb performing together in the same cage."

"That sounds like a good act," his friend said, "but you would think that they wouldn't get along very well together. Don't they ever fight?"

"Well," said the first man, "they do have a bit of trouble now and then—but all we have to do is buy a new lamb."

383.   The little girl had been to see her first circus and her aunt was talking to her about it.

"I'll bet," said her aunt, "that the circus was a lot bigger than you expected it to be."

"Oh, no, auntie," the little girl said. "I went there expecting it to be bigger than I expected."

490, 1871

Civilization

384.   "It's women who have made the world beautiful," a mother told her daughter. "If it wasn't for women, men would always look the way they do on a fishing trip."

385.   A shipwrecked sailor finally was washed ashore on a strange island. He was glad to be on land, but afraid he might be among wild and unfriendly natives, so he explored cautiously, and at last saw smoke from a fire rising from the jungle. As he

made his way slowly through the woods, scared half to death, he heard a voice say, "Pass that bottle and deal those cards."

"Thank God!" the sailor cried. "I'm among Christians!"

356

Clergyman

386. "Rabbi Rabinovitz," said Father Kelly. "When are you going to become liberal enough to eat ham?"

"At your wedding, Father Kelly," said the Rabbi.

387. Instead of going to Sunday school one Sunday morning, a little boy sneaked off to the creek and went fishing. He had wonderful luck, and as he was on his way home with his string of fish, he met the minister.

"Look," the little fellow said, holding up the string of fish, "see what happened to these sinful fish for biting at worms on Sunday."

32, 84, 187, 238, 253, 341, 660, 1469

Clothes

388. Friend to Actress: "Your husband certainly looks handsome in his new suit!"

Actress: "Oh, that's not a new suit—it's a new husband."

389. A man was telling his friend about making a lot of money in a real estate deal.

"Did you give your wife any of the money?" his friend asked.

"Yes, sir," the man said. "I told her that at last we had enough money and she should buy some decent clothes—but she said she had worn decent clothes all her life, and that now she was going to dress like other women."

390. The minister had been substituting for the regular teacher in Sunday school. At the end of the lesson, he said, "And now, children, would you like to ask any questions?"

"Yes, sir," said a little boy. "How do you get into your collar?"

23, 221, 397, 422, 498, 676, 1317

Clumsy

391.   At the breakfast table one morning, the daughter of an old Kentucky colonel noticed that in addition to looking red-eyed and tired, her father's head was rather thoroughly bandaged.

"What happened?" she asked. "Did you have some sort of accident last night?"

"It was nothing," he said. "Just some of the younger brothers at the lodge meeting who can't handle their liquor got a little too much under their belts, and one of them stepped on my hand."

392.   The young boy and his sister were in the kitchen cleaning out and washing the fish bowl. Suddenly, there was an ear-splitting crash.

"What are you all doing in the kitchen?" their mother screamed.

"Nothing," the young fellow said. "It's already done."

21, 634, 1451

Coat

393.   The judge was examining a man accused of theft.

"Did you steal this man's overcoat?" he demanded.

"No, sir," said the accused. "I was just playing a joke on him."

"Where did you take this coat?" asked the judge.

"I took it off the coat rack in the restaurant," he said, "and carried it home with me."

"Fifty dollars fine and ten days in jail," the judge said, "for carrying a joke too far."

1035

Coffee

394.   The amateur gourmet was telling a friend about his love for good coffee. "The fresher it is the better," he said. "In order to have it good and fresh every morning, I get up early and build a fire in my pajamas."

Coffee

"That must be a hot business in the summertime," said his friend. "What are your pajamas made of, asbestos?"

395.   A man sat at the table after breakfast one morning, reading his newspaper for over an hour. Finally he asked his wife for another cup of coffee.

"Another cup of coffee?" asked his wife. "But look at the time. Aren't you going to the office today?"

"Office?" said the man with a start. "I thought I was at the office."

396.   Two cleaning women were chatting during their midnight coffee break.

"Is your husband a good provider?" asked the first.

"Yes, he's real good," said the other. "The only trouble is, I'm always worried about him getting caught at it."

131, 637, 1107, 1129, 1168, 1763, 1979

Cold

397.   A man was chatting with an artist friend.

"Do you ever draw pictures in the nude?" he asked.

"No," said the artist. "I always wear a smoking jacket."

398.   The old man was complaining to his landlady about the lack of heat in his room.

"Sometimes it gets so cold at night," he said, "that I wake up and hear my teeth chattering on the night table."

213, 695, 753, 780, 1095, 1564, 1584, 1868, 2080

Collateral

399.   "I'm sorry," said the customer to the restaurant manager, "but I haven't any money to pay for that meal."

"Oh, that's all right," said the manager. "We'll just write your name and the amount on the wall and you can pay the next time you come in."

"Don't do that," the man said. "Everybody who comes in will see it."

Collateral

"Oh, no, they won't," the manager said. "Your overcoat will be hanging over it."

400.   "How much are your rooms?" a man asked the landlady of a boardinghouse.
"Ten dollars up," she said.
"But, isn't that a little high?" he asked. "I'm a book salesman."
"In that case," the landlady said, "it will be ten dollars down."

College boy

401.   A college boy was having his picture made with his father. The photographer suggested that the boy should stand with his hand on his father's shoulder.
"It would be more appropriate," said his father, "if he stood with his hand in my pocket."

402.   Two fathers were talking about the problems of raising their boys. "Is your son very ambitious?" asked the first.
"Yes," said his friend, "he has such big ideas about being rich and successful, that already he's beginning to look on me as a sort of poor relation."

279, 507, 517, 619, 638, 1571, 1996

Color

403.   It was near Washington at an Air Force party at Andrews Air Force Base. Some of the guests were from nearby Bowling Field. Trying to be sociable, one man introduced himself to another, "I'm Brown from Bowling," he said.
"I'm glad to meet you," the other man said, "I'm green from drinking martinis."

Communication

404.   An old fellow bought one of those new hearing aids that are practically invisible. He was told that he could return it if it didn't prove twice as good as the cumbersome device he had been using.

Communication

He stopped by a few days later to express his satisfaction with the new device.

"I'll bet your family likes it, too," said the clerk.

"Oh, they don't even know I've got it," said the old man. "And do you know what, I'm having more fun with it! In the past two days, I've changed my will three times."

405.   When you tell a man something, it goes in one ear and out the other. When you tell a woman anything, it goes in both ears and out her mouth.

406.   The young minister, wishing to announce the new baby's arrival in a novel manner, sent his parents this wire: "Isaiah 9:6" which is the well-known passage that begins, "For unto us a child is born, unto us a son is given."

His father, far from being a Bible scholar, said to his wife, "It seems John's wife had a boy weighing 9 pounds and 6 ounces, but why in the world did they want to name him Isaiah?"

445, 1247, 1315, 1777

Communism

407.   A traveler was trying to win a convert. "In communism everybody divides—everyone shares and shares alike."

His friend: "Do you mean that if you had $2,000 you'd give me $1,000?"

Communist: "That's right."

His friend: "And if you had two Cadillac cars, you'd give me one?"

Communist: "That's the idea."

His friend: "And if you had two shirts, you'd give me one?"

Communist: "No, not at all."

His friend: "What's the difference?"

Communist: "I've got two shirts."

Commuter

408.   A man rushed into a bar and said breathlessly, "The usual, please, and hurry, I gotta catch my train."

The bartender set up five martinis in a row and the customer gulped the second, third, and fourth, leaving the first and last drinks on the bar. Then he rushed out as rapidly as he had entered.

A bystander asked the bartender why the customer left the two drinks.

"Oh, he does that all the time," said the bartender. "He says the first one always tastes terrible and the last one gets him in trouble at home."

409.   The snowstorm was the worst of the year. The train into the suburbs had been moving forward slowly but steadily for hours. Finally, it came to a full stop and the commuters were stuck for the night. Toward dawn one of the businessmen left the train and fought his way through the snowdrifts to the nearest village. He went straight to the telegraph office and sent a wire back to the city to his boss: "Will not be at work today," he wired, "not yet home from work yesterday."

583

Compatible

410.   "How are things going at home?" one fellow asked another over a bottle of beer.

"Well, the old woman ain't talking to me," said his friend, "and frankly, I'm in no mood to interrupt her."

411.   The confirmed bachelor had been calling on the widow every evening for four years.

"Since you two seem to get along so well together," said a friend, "why don't you get married?"

"If I did that," said the bachelor, "where would I spend my evenings?"

595, 1277, 1359, 1461, 1995

Competition

412. The personnel manager said to the job applicant: "Well, what sort of work can you do?"

"Nothing," said the applicant.

"I'm sorry," said the personnel man. "All those kinds of positions are taken by the boss's kinfolks."

413. The new man in town told the banker, "I've come out here to make an honest living."

"Well," said the banker, "there's not much competition."

211, 1600

Complaint

414. Two bridesmaids were chatting about the bride-to-be.

"My, she's angry," said the first, "and I just can't imagine why. The newspapers carried a full account of her wedding plans."

"That's true," said the second, "they even included the fact that the groom is a famous collector of antiques."

415. A man was complaining about his wife to a friend.

"I don't know what I'm going to do about her," he said. "She has the worst memory in the world."

"You mean she forgets everything?" asked his friend.

"Heck, no," he said. "She remembers everything."

416. The man had been trying to get the attention of the waitress for ten minutes. Finally, he got up from his chair and told the cashier he wanted to see the manager.

"What for?" asked the cashier.

"I've got a complaint," he said.

"Complaint?" said the cashier. "This is a restaurant, not a hospital."

417. The secretary, who was a ravishing beauty, resigned. The men in the small plant immediately went on strike. The boss wanted to know what the trouble could be.

Complaint

"Well," said the spokesman for the workers, "we've always considered her beauty and personality around the place one of our fringe benefits."

418. A man was asked how the banquet was the night before. He said, "If the fruit cup had been as cold as the soup, the soup as hot as the wine, and the wine as old as the turkey, the turkey as young as the girl who waited on us, and the girl as interested and willing to pay as much attention to us as the overweight society matron sitting next to us—the dinner would have been a huge success."

419. The criminal had been tried, found guilty, and sentenced to be hanged. On the morning of the fateful day it was raining and sleeting and the prison yard was an absolute quagmire. As the condemned man was marched through all of the miserable mud and slush toward the gallows, he said to his guard, "You people are the most miserable and inconsiderate skunks who ever lived. It's bad enough to hang me, but you ought to be ashamed to make me walk to the gallows in all this mess."

"What are you complaining about?" the guard said. "Think about me. I've got to walk back through it."

79, 100, 182, 286, 311, 316, 335, 398, 512, 598, 1121, 1712, 2047

Compliment

420. A small boy taking dancing lessons was told by his mother to say something nice to each little girl as he escorted her back to her seat. Trying hard to follow his mother's admonition, all he could think to say to one of his dancing partners was: "Mary, you sweat less than any little fat girl I ever danced with."

421. When her husband returned home in the evening after making a speech at a civic club, his wife said: "Well, how did it go? Did they like your speech?"

"They certainly did," said her husband. "When I finished and sat down, everybody said it was the best thing I'd ever done."

Compliment

422. "Your stockings look rather wrinkled," whispered a young fellow to his girl friend.

"You're horrible," said the girl. "I don't have any stockings on."

423. A hotel guest handed the manager a bouquet of roses and said, "These are for the telephone operator."

"Thank you, sir," the manager said, "I know that she will appreciate the compliment."

"Compliment?" said the guest. "I thought she had died."

424. On their way home following the big banquet where her husband was the principal speaker, a woman said to her husband, "Darling, did anyone ever tell you that you were the greatest speaker in the world?"

"No," he said, "they never did."

"Well," she said, "where did you get the idea?"

25, 116, 224, 954, 1090

Compromise

425. A woman visiting New York applied to an agency which provided male escorts. She was told she could engage either a Northerner or a Southerner. She asked the difference, and was told the Southerners were gallant and debonair, while the Northerners were smooth talkers and romantic.

"Well," she said, "I'd like to take a Southerner from as far North as possible."

426. The strip-tease artist went to the doctor to be vaccinated. "Doctor," she said, "I want to be vaccinated where it won't show."

"All right," said the doctor. "Stick out your tongue."

587, 709, 976, 1448, 1640, 1748

Conceit

427. There was a cannibal tribe that was slowly starving to death. One day, an actor on a safari got lost and wandered into

their village. Immediately, the cannibal chef rushed in to fix him all up, but the Chief stopped him.

"I know you are a big actor," said the Chief to the man. "When I was with the World's Fair, I saw you. You are a great comedian, a great tragedian, a great performer."

"Why we not cook him?" interrupted the chef.

"You don't know actors," said the Chief. "When you praise actors, they get big heads, swell up. First we puff him up, then we eat him."

428.　A friend was talking about an acquaintance: "Joe certainly is conceited. On his last birthday, he sent a telegram of congratulation to his mother!"

429.　"There are two men I really admire," said a young fellow to his date.

"Oh?" said the girl. "And who's the other one?"

430.　A man looked up from his newspaper one evening and asked his wife, "Do you know how many really great men there are in this country?"

"I don't know," said his wife, "but I do know there is one less than you think."

97, 109, 424, 739, 1443

Concern

431.　A man and his wife arrived late at the country club dance. He had slipped on the ice outside and had torn a hole in his trousers.

"Come into the ladies' dressing room," his wife said. "There's no one there and I'll sew it up for you."

His wife borrowed a needle and thread. He removed his trousers and she went to work. A few minutes later, several women were heard rushing toward the room. The man's wife tried to stop them, but they said they had to come in—that Mrs. Williams was sick.

The man's wife, thinking quickly, pushed her husband into a closet and slammed the door.

Concern

But instantly, from the opposite side of the door, came loud thumps and the agonized voice of her husband, demanding that his wife open the door at once.

"But the women are here," his wife said.

"I don't care about the women," the man shouted. "I'm standing on the ballroom floor."

432.   A husband said to his wife, "My dear, this article says women need more sleep than men."

"Is that right?" she said.

"Yes, dear," he said, "so maybe you'd better not wait up for me tonight."

294, 879, 2071

Confession

433.   Bashful Boy: "Do you shrink from kissing?"

His Date: "If I did, I'd only be two feet tall."

434.   The young couple had been doing a little necking in their parked car when the young man said to his girl friend, "I suppose I should confess the truth. You are not the first girl I have ever kissed."

"Since you have been so frank with me," she said, "I might as well be frank with you, too, and say that you have a lot to learn."

168, 386, 458, 712, 986, 2114

Confidence

435.   A doctor came home completely exhausted and hoped to get a good night's sleep. No sooner had he gone to bed than the phone rang. He said to his wife: "Listen, honey, see who it is; say I won't be home until later or anything you think of."

His wife answered the phone. "The doctor is not at home," she said.

"Well," the voice said, "I'm one of his patients. I've got a sudden pain in my chest and I want to see him as soon as he comes in."

Confidence

The doctor overheard the lady and whispered some instructions to his wife. She relayed the advice to the patient: "Do that," she said, "and I'm sure you'll soon feel all right."

"Thanks very much," the lady said, "but tell me, is that gentleman with you qualified to advise me?"

436.   The banker was telling a friend how he got started in the business.

"I was out of work," he said, "so to keep busy, I rented an empty store, painted the word 'Bank' on the window. The same day, a man came in and deposited $300. Next day, another fellow came in and put in $250. Well, sir, by the third day I'd got so much confidence in the venture that I put in $50 of my own money."

3, 165, 208, 214, 641, 1700

Confidential

437.   "You will now repeat to the court the words the defendant used," said the prosecuting attorney to the witness.

"I'd rather not," the witness said. "They were not fit words to tell a gentleman."

"In that case," the attorney said, "you will whisper them to the judge."

438.   "She told me," a woman whispered to her friend, "that you told her the secret I told you not to tell her."

"I guess maybe I did," her friend said, "but I told her not to tell you I told her."

"Oh," said the first woman, "Please don't tell her I told you that she told me."

439.   The young bride's grandmother was giving her a few interesting facts about married life. "I hope," she told the young girl, "that your lot in life is going to be easier than mine was. For the fifty-five years I have been married, I've carried two heavy burdens, Pa and the fire. Every time I've turned around to look after one of them, the other has gone out."

588, 727, 844, 1176, 1683

Confused

440. After a hunter had his cap blown off his head during the deer-hunting season in Kentucky, he made himself a suit of awning cloth with black and white stripes. The first time he wore it, he was shot and killed.

At the inquest, the coroner said, "You're not accused of killing this man intentionally, but it does seem funny to me that he was dressed in striped clothes which could be seen a mile away, while you were standing not a hundred yards from him. How could you mistake him for a deer?"

"I didn't," said the man. "I thought he was a zebra."

441. A young fellow answered a "Boy Wanted" advertisement.

"What kind of boy do you want?" he asked.

"We want a clean, decent, and neat boy," said the manager. "One who is quiet, quick, and obedient, one who doesn't smoke, swear, whistle around the office, shoot craps, lie, or steal."

"Shucks," said the boy, walking out, "you don't want a boy, you want a girl."

442. Hopelessly confused and snarled in a traffic jam, a man's wife cried, "Oh, honey, what can I do?"

"I don't know," he said, "but I'll bet if you climb in the back seat, you'll be able to figure it out."

443. A little lady asked the conductor, "At which end of the train do I get off?"

"Either one, lady," he said. "Both ends stop at the same time."

444. "I'm sure in a bad fix," a fellow told his friend.

"What's the trouble?" his friend asked.

"My wife just found out that I have been dating my secretary. And that isn't the worst of it," the fellow said, "she told our maid about it, too."

445. A clever farmer whose voice had become tired and worn out from calling his hogs day after day, trained them to come when he beat on a hollow log with a hoe handle.

Confused

This worked all right until one summer when all of his hogs went crazy. It seems a flock of woodpeckers had moved into the trees in back of the barn.

123, 372, 480, 693, 758, 789, 2005

Congressman

446.   "I just got out of the penitentiary this morning," a man on the plane told his seat companion. "It's going to be tough facing old friends."

"I can sympathize with you," said his neighbor, "I'm on my way home from Congress."

447.   Weary after a hard trip, a Congressman in Washington handed the menu back to the waiter and said: "Just bring me a good dinner."   A delicious meal was served and the Congressman gave the waiter a generous tip.

"Thank you, sir," the waiter said, "and if you have any friends what can't read either, you just send them to me."

448.   The Congressman had lost out in the last election and was feeling sorry for himself.

"I was a victim," he said, "nothing but a victim."

"A victim?" asked a friend. "A victim of what?"

"A victim of accurate counting," the congressman said.

449.   The Congressman climbed out of the taxi on Capitol Hill, and began thumbing through his wallet for a new dollar bill. "I suppose," he said, "that you are like a lot of other folks these days and would like clean money?"

"Oh, it's all right with me," said the driver. "Any old money will do. I don't care how you made it."

450.   The newly elected Congressman took his little daughter on a tour of the Capitol. After she had seen the splendors of the chambers, committee rooms, the rotunda, and the statuary halls, she grew quiet and thoughtful.

"What's the matter?" asked her father.

"Well, Daddy," she said, "I was just thinking that you're such a big man in our house, but you're not very much around here."

451.   A famous surgeon had developed the technique of removing the brain from a person, examining it, and putting it back. One day, some friends brought him a patient. The surgeon operated on him and took his brain out. When the surgeon went to the laboratory to examine the brain, he discovered the patient had mysteriously disappeared. Six years later, he returned to the hospital.

"Where have you been for six years?" asked the amazed surgeon.

"Oh, after I left here," the man said, "I got elected to Congress and I've been in Washington ever since."

452.   A defeated Congressman was running to get back his seat in Congress. He was traveling through his district, talking to the voters.

"I'll be sure to vote for you this election," a lady told him. "I would have voted for you last time, but I was sick on election day."

"Oh, that's what happened," said the ex-Congressman. "I wondered."

453.   A Congressman arrived in a part of his district where he was rather unpopular. Although he was an hour late for his meeting in the town hall, a rowdy crowd still was hanging around outside to heckle him as he entered.

His local committee wanted to save him this embarrassment and tried to sneak him into the hall through the back door.

"Oh, no," said the Congressman. "Just because I am an hour late is no need to sneak me in the back way. If this crowd waited this long to boo me, it wouldn't be fair to deprive them of that pleasure."

454.   A proud young man had just been elected to Congress. Immediately, he was in great demand as a speaker. Among other places, he was invited to speak in Petersburg. Thinking he could study his speech en route, he decided to take the bus.

But at the bus station he entered the wrong bus. Without knowing it, he entered a bus that was going to Williamsburg to the state mental hospital.

After he had seated himself in the last empty seat, a man came in and began to check up on his load. Pointing to each in turn, he began to count, "one, two, three, four, five, sss . . . who are you?" he demanded of the Congressman, "and where do you think you are going?"

"I'm on my way to Petersburg," the young man said. "I'm going down there to make a speech and tell the folks what is wrong with our foreign policy, how to balance the national budget, what to do about the tax problem, the farm problem, and aid to education. I'm the new Congessman."

The man looked at him for a moment and continued to count, pointing first to the Congressman himself, "six, seven, eight, nine. . . ."

455.   The newly elected Congressman had been settled in his home in Georgetown for only about two weeks when, in the wee hours of the morning, he was awakened by his wife.

"Wake up," she whispered. "I hear a noise downstairs. There's a burglar in the house."

"What did you say?" asked the Congressman, as he gradually began to wake up.

"I said there's a thief in the house," his wife said.

"Oh, no, honey," the Congressman said. "Maybe in the Senate, but never in the House."

456.   A Congressman was speaking on the floor of the House, when one of his colleagues shouted, "You are out of order."

The Congressman stopped his speech and said, "Just how am I out of order?"

"How should I know?" shouted the other Congressman. "Why don't you go see a veterinarian?"

457.   It was the day of the dedication of the new post office in the county seat. The Congressman had flown in from Washington for the big occasion. At a luncheon with his local committee following the ceremonies, he said to them, "Well, as I

said when you worked so hard to elect me, I don't forget my friends. Up to now, I have really delivered for you fellows. And today, you got your new post office."

"Yes, Mr. Congressman," said his local chairman, "but it wasn't a new post office we asked for—it was a new postmaster."

458. A Congressman had been working day and night throughout his district in a life or death struggle for reelection. He was relaxing one evening, following a speech, in the home of a friend.

"I've heard your speeches," his friend said, "but I think the real question is what will you do if you are reelected."

"No," said the Congressman, "the real question is what will I do if I'm not."

284, 579, 1553, 1557, 1601, 1697, 1945

Conscience

459. A man called on a psychiatrist and told him that he had problems and needed help.

"I want to talk to you," the man said, "because my ethics have not been what they should be and my conscience is bothering me."

"I understand," the psychiatrist said, "and you want me to help you build up a stronger will power, is that it?"

"No," said the patient, "that's not it. I want you to try to weaken my conscience."

108, 724, 1408

Conservation

460. The speaker was from the Department of the Interior. He was lecturing on conservation.

"Have any of you here," he asked, "ever done anything to conserve our timber resources?"

After a few moments of silence a voice from the rear spoke up:

"I shot a woodpecker one time."

Consideration

461.   A museum curator said to the moving man: "Be very careful when you carry this vase, it is 2,000 years old."

"You can count on me," the moving man said. "I'll carry it just as I would if it were brand new."

462.   A little girl had been sent to her room as punishment. After a while she reappeared in a gay mood.

"Well, Mamma," she said, "I've thought things over and I prayed."

"That's fine," said her mother. "Now that should help you be a good little girl."

"Oh, I didn't pray to be good," she said. "I asked God to help you put up with me."

463.   As the newly convicted man entered his cell in prison, the oldtimer who already occupied the cell said to him, "How long are you in for?"

"Seventy-five years," he answered. "How long are you here for?"

"Forty years," the old-timer said.

"Then you take the bed near the door," the new man said. "You get out first."

464.   It was almost one o'clock in the morning, and the man was trying to find the home of a friend. He finally located what he thought was the right house. Seeing that there was a light on, he rang the doorbell. The friend's wife came to the door, but since the man had never met her, he said, "Is this where Bill McDonald lives?"

"Yes," said the woman rather tearfully, "you've got the right house all right. Bring him on in and put him on the couch—I'll put him to bed."

465.   A man was showing his friend a new set of matched golf clubs he had just bought.

"Doctor's orders," the man told his friend. "My wife and I have been gaining too much weight and we went to see the doctor about it. He said we needed more exercise, so I joined the country club and bought myself a new set of golf clubs."

118

Consideration

"What about your wife?" the man asked. "What did you buy her?"

"A new lawn mower," the golfer said.

453, 705

Consistent

466.   An extravagant fellow who lived far beyond his means was constantly hounded by his creditors. He was so used to them that their presence caused him no distress. In fact, he treated them with the utmost courtesy. Once he even served a bill collector champagne.

"If you cannot afford to pay your debts," the bill collector demanded, "how can you afford to serve champagne?"

"Don't get sore," the man said. "I assure you, this hasn't been paid for either."

612, 839, 1986, 2119

Contract

467.   A man made a deal with his lawyer. "I'll give you a hundred dollars a month to do my worrying for me," he said.

"That's a deal," said his lawyer. "Where's the hundred?"

"That's your first worry," said his client.

205, 500, 726

Contribution

468.   "Well," said the bartender to an old customer, "I see you've been to the revival meeting and given the evangelist your last dollar. Now you'll have to walk home."

"Yes," said the other, full of pride, "and many a time I've given you my last dollar and couldn't walk home."

469.   The businessman had just given his young visitor a dollar, and was given an "associate membership" card in the local boys' club, that said he had "full rights and privileges."

"Now that I am a member," the businessman said, "just what are my rights and privileges?"

119

Contribution

After a thoughtful silence, the boy said, "Well, mainly it gives you the right to contribute again next year."

470.   A member of the finance committee called on the stingiest man in town.

"I'm calling about the yearly contribution to the fund for converting the heathen," he said. "Last year you gave a dollar."

"What!" the man said in surprise, "Haven't you converted them yet?"

471.   The head of the local Community Fund drive had bad luck getting money out of the richest man in town. Each of his team captains had been turned down. Finally, in desperation, he said to them, "I'll tell you what we should do. We'll all go to see him at one time. We are prominent people in this town and he won't be able to withstand the pressure."

So they all called on the man together.

The man met them at the door of his store and invited them into his private office. "Sit down," he said. "I know why you are here. You want to know why I am not giving to the Community Fund. I suppose you have a right to know, although I don't like to spread my private troubles in front of all my friends. What you don't know is that my brother is an alcoholic. He is married and has seven children. He and his family live out West. It's a terrible case. He hasn't earned a dollar in over five years. Then there's my wife's brother. He was shot up in the war to the point where he draws 100% disability. But, with eleven children, that isn't enough money to keep them in food. And on account of so many children, his wife can't work. And besides all that misfortune, there is my mother-in-law. She is an invalid. She has been bedridden for years. Has to have a trained nurse around the clock. And you know good and well that if I'm not helping them, I am not going to give anything to the Community Fund."

204, 359, 804, 1341, 1957

Convention

472.   It was during the Republican convention in Chicago, and there had been a lively banquet at one of the hotels. The

Convention

next morning, a prominent Democrat met one of the Republican delegates and said:

"I understand there were some Democrats at the dinner last night."

"That's right," said the Republican, "one waited on me."

317

Conversation

473. Two women were boarding the new jet airplane. One of them said to the stewardess, "Please ask the pilot not to travel faster than sound. We want to talk."

474. A little old lady had just returned from a walk to the corner market. She said to her daughter, "I think you had better call the police, there is a crazy man lying on the sidewalk in front of the corner market."

"We shouldn't call the police unless we are sure," her daughter said. "What makes you think he is crazy?"

"Because," said her mother, "he is lying there on the sidewalk cursing at a banana peel."

273, 519, 682, 1054, 1299, 2000

Convincing

475. The man's secretary said to him: "There's a man outside who wants to see you about a bill you owe him. He didn't give his name."

"What does he look like?" asked the boss.

"He looks like you had better pay him," she said.

476. The young man asked his father, "Hey, Dad, what's a sweater girl?"

"A sweater girl," said his fast-thinking father, "is a girl who works in a sweater factory. Where did you get that question?"

"Never mind the question, Dad," asked his son. "Where did you get that answer?"

4, 127, 185, 489, 535, 658, 728, 1147, 1455, 2002

Cook

477.   A man came home from the office and was told by his wife that the cook had quit.

"Again?" moaned the husband. "What was the matter this time?"

"You were!" his wife said. "She said you used insulting language to her over the phone this morning."

"Good grief!" said the husband. "I'm sorry, I thought I was talking to you."

478.   After the bride's first dinner, she asked her husband, "Now, dear, what will I get if I cook a dinner like that for you every day?"

"My life insurance," said her husband.

479.   The young man was eating one of the first meals his bride had ever cooked. "This meat tastes odd," he said. "What is the matter with it?"

"I can't imagine," she said. "I saw it was beginning to burn, so I put sunburn oil on it right away."

480.   The young bride was looking through the cookbook. She was puzzled by a cake recipe.

"It says to add sugar, eggs, and mix," she said, "but it doesn't say what kind of mix!"

481.   Bride: "How did you like that cake I baked for you?"
Hubby: "It was terrible."
Bride: "That's funny, the cook book said it was delicious."

482.   Bride: "The two best things I cook are meat loaf and apple dumplings."
Hubby: "Well, which is this?"

483.   A woman from Boston was visiting her sister in Memphis, Tennessee. Her sister was busy one afternoon and asked her to do the shopping. In the supermarket she stood in front of the dairy counter and finally said to the clerk, "Excuse me, please, but could you tell me which kind of buttermilk I should buy to make cornbread?"

Cook

The clerk shook her head and said, "It wouldn't make no difference, honey, you ain't gonna make no cornbread fit to eat anyway, with that accent."

116, 320, 331, 357, 1076

Cooperation

484.   The tenderfoot from the East had spent all his time since his arrival on the ranch asking all sorts of questions.

"Why is it," he asked the local cowboy, "that you always slap your horse on one side when you get in the saddle?"

"Well," said the cowpuncher, "I figure that if I can get one side started, the other is pretty sure to follow."

485.   A husband came home in a bad mood only to find his wife had not even started dinner.

"What, supper not ready?" he shouted. "This is it. I'm going to a restaurant."

"Please wait five minutes," his wife said.

"You mean it will be ready by then?" he asked.

"No, but in five minutes I can be ready to go with you," she said.

486.   A farmer, plowing with one mule, kept crying out, "Giddap, Joe. Giddap, Alexander. Giddap, Henry. Giddap, Whitey."

A man passing by asked him, "How many names does that mule have, anyway?"

"Only one," the farmer said. "His name's Pete, but he don't know his own strength. So, I put blinders on him, yell a lot of names, and he thinks a half a dozen other mules are helping him."

23, 738, 1012, 1297, 1484, 1733, 1990

Correct

487.   "How do you spell extravagance?" the teacher asked the little boy.

"E-x-t-r-a-v-u-g-u-n-c-e," spelled the boy.

Correct

"No," she said. "The dictionary spells it E-x-t-r-a-v-a-g-a-n-c-e."

"You asked me how I spell it," said the boy.

488.   The tourist was on the outskirts of Boston and was looking for a motel. He drove into a filling station and said to the attendant, "Could you tell me where I could stop at?"

"You could stop just before the word 'at,' " the Bostonian said.

173, 293, 601, 746, 1807

Courage

489.   Wife: "Last week when that bear got out you ran away and left me. Once you told me you would face death for me."

Husband: "Yes, I would—but that bear wasn't dead."

490.   A circus train, traveling through the West, was derailed. Several of the animal cars were wrecked and broken open, including one that held seven lions. Almost immediately, the sheriff began organizing a posse to try to round up the lions.

As he got his men together he said, "Fellows, we might be out most of the night. So, before we go, let's step in the bar here and I'll buy everybody a couple of drinks—then we'll be on our way."

"No, thank you," one of the men said, "I don't care for anything."

"Why not?" asked the sheriff.

"Not when I'm starting on a lion hunt," the man said. "A shot of whiskey is liable to give me too much courage."

507, 1908

Courtesy

491.   A young girl came home from college to visit her folks on the farm. She had new ideas and an entirely different viewpoint about everything. She complained about how old-fashioned things were at home.

"Look at that picture on the wall," she said to her father, "with you sitting and Mother standing. That isn't even the courteous thing to do."

Courtesy

"With all of your education, Daughter, you've got plenty to learn," said her father. "That picture was taken in the country, just after I got through with a ten-mile hike and Mamma got through a day of horseback riding!"

492.   A group gathered quickly around a man lying in the street. A policeman arrived in a patrol car.

"How did you knock him down?" he asked the driver of the nearby car.

"I didn't," said the driver. "I stopped to let him go across the street and he fainted."

493.   The bus was crowded when the little old lady got on, and a soldier stood up. She pushed him back gently and said, "No, thanks."

He tried to rise once again and she pushed him back a second time. Finally, he said to her, "Please let me get up, lady, I'm two blocks past my stop now."

494.   Two soldiers were walking down a country road as a truck passed them. The first soldier saluted it.

"Why did you salute that truck?" the other soldier asked.

"Oh," said the first, "it said on the side, 'General Hauling.' "

6, 29, 876, 1634, 2046, 2096

Cow

495.   "Oh, what a funny-looking cow," the young city girl said to the farmer. "But why doesn't it have any horns?"

"There are many reasons," the farmer said, "why a cow does not have horns. Some do not grow them until late in life. Others are dehorned. Some breeds are not supposed to have horns. This particular cow does not have horns because it is a horse."

496.   The farm boy was taking a walk with a city girl who was visiting in the neighborhood. They came to a pasture where a cow and a calf were rubbing noses together.

"Ah," said the boy, "seeing that makes me want to do the same thing."

"Well, go right ahead," said the girl, "it's your cow."

135, 143, 315, 332, 776, 1185, 1284, 1923

Crazy

497.   A farmer was passing the mental hospital with a load of fertilizer. An inmate called through the fence, "What have you got there?"

"A load of fertilizer," said the farmer.

"What are you going to do with it?" the inmate asked.

"I'm going to put it on my strawberries," the farmer said.

"We put cream on ours," the inmate said, "and people say we're crazy."

498.   A social worker visited a mental hospital. In one of the cells was a man whose only garment was a hat.

"Sir," said the social worker, "that's no way to be sitting around. Why don't you put some clothes on?"

"Because," said the man, "nobody ever comes to see me."

"If that's the reason," said the social worker, "why do you wear a hat?"

"Oh," he said, "you never know. Somebody might come."

499.   Two fellows were chatting. "Are you nuts if you talk to yourself?" asked the first one.

"No, you ain't nuts if you talk to yourself," said the other, "but you are if you talk back."

500.   Two men were sitting and talking in the garden of a mental hospital.

"I've just decided to buy all the oil wells in Texas," said one.

The other thought about that for a few moments, and then said, "I don't know that I care to sell."

501.   A nearby farmer was delivering produce to a mental hospital. A fellow sitting in the yard said, "You're a farmer, aren't you?"

"Yes," said the farmer. "I live just down the road."

"I used to be a farmer once," said the man, "but now I'm crazy. Have you ever been crazy?"

"No," said the farmer, as he started to drive away.

"Well, you oughta try it," the man said. "It beats farming any day."

Crazy

502.   A visitor to a mental hospital stood chatting at great length to one man in particular. She asked all sorts of questions about how he was treated, and how long he'd been there and what hobbies he was interested in.

As she left him and walked on with the attendant, she noticed he was grinning broadly. She asked what was amusing and the attendant told the visitor that she had been talking to the medical superintendent. Embarrassed, she rushed back to make apologies. "I am sorry, doctor," she said. "I will never go by appearances again."

503.   A coal miner had been placed in a mental hospital for treatment. After a few weeks, a friend visited him. "How are you getting on?" he asked.

"Oh, just fine," said the inmate.

"That's good," his friend said. "Guess you'll be coming back to the mine soon?"

"What!" said the inmate. "I should leave a fine comfortable house like this with a swimming pool and free meals to come work in a dirty coal mine? You must think I'm crazy!"

203, 445, 454, 474, 553, 615, 962, 1290, 1707

Credit

504.   A man, watching a sign painter at work, said to a friend:

"I'd be much better off if they'd put that sign on the mail box in the post office."

"What sign?"

"Post no bills."

505.   "You look a bit sick," a fellow said to his friend. "Anything wrong?"

"I'm afraid there is," said his friend. "I've had to give up drinking, smoking, and gambling."

"Well, I must say that's all to your credit," said the first man.

"Oh, no, it isn't!" his friend said. "It's due entirely to my lack of credit."

Credit

506.   A prospective employer asked an applicant for a job, "Do you live within your income?"

"Heck, no," the man said. "It's all I can do to live within my credit."

33, 178, 244, 524, 1036, 1280, 1978

Critic

507.   The college debater was telling his friend about the upcoming debate in which he was to take part.

"It's going to be something," he said. "It will be a real battle of wits."

"How brave of you," said his friend, "to go into battle half prepared."

508.   A composer said to the critic, "Well, how did you like my new waltz?"

"Very much," said the critic. "One of the finest waltzes Strauss ever composed."

509.   A farmer and his friend were watching Robert Fulton getting ready to make his trial run with his steamboat "Clermont."

"They'll never start that contraption," he said gloomily to his friend.

Later, as the Clermont moved away and picked up speed, the farmer said, in the same gloomy voice, "They'll never stop that contraption."

510.   A young playwright gave a special invitation to a highly regarded critic to watch his new play. The critic came to the play, but slept through the entire performance.

The young playwright was indignant and said, "How could you sleep when you knew how much I wanted your opinion?"

"Young man," the critic said, "sleep is an opinion."

145, 481, 552, 802, 1204, 1285, 1287, 1742, 1786

Criticism

511.   The young mother was at the front door ready to go to Sunday school. She had her arms full of coats and hats and three kiddies at her side.

Her husband said, hurriedly, "Okay, let's get going. Don't just stand there."

She handed him the coats and hats. "All right," she said, "This time you put the kids' coats and hats on and I'll go out and honk the horn."

512.   The supermarket was crowded. People were shoving and pushing each other all around, especially at the meat counter. Finally, the boss noticed one of the clerks arguing with a woman customer. Suddenly, she left in a huff.

"What was the matter?" the boss asked.

"Oh, she was complaining about the long wait," he said. "You just can't please that woman. Yesterday, she was complaining about the short weight."

356, 377, 422, 515, 881, 1279, 1340, 1691, 1775

Cure

513.   Laboratory Technician: "Here's a tricky cure for colds. You sit in a bathtub filled with gasoline and light two matches."

Friend: "What's so tricky about that?"

Technician: "Lighting the second match."

514.   A man thought he was going to die with a toothache. He asked his friend, "What can I do to relieve the pain?"

"I'll tell you what I do," his friend said. "When I have a toothache, or a pain, I go over to my wife, and she puts her arms around me, and caresses me, and soothes me until finally I forget all about the pain."

His friend brightened up and said: "Gee, that's wonderful! Is she home now?"

515.   A woman went to a Broadway musical and sat in the front row. Whenever the star appeared, she said, "Ah, good! Ah, good!" which the star could not help hearing. After the show, the star made a point of meeting the lady.

Cure

"I want to thank you," he said, "for being such an appreciative audience."

"What?" asked the woman in surprise.

"All through the show you were saying 'Ah, good! Ah, good!' and I heard you," the star said.

"Oh, that," the woman said. "I've got arthritis, and when they put that very strong light on you, it hit my back, and oh, my, was that good!"

516. The young doctor seemed pleased after looking over his patient.

"You are getting along just fine," he said. "Of course, your shoulder is still badly swollen, but that doesn't bother me in the least."

"I don't guess it does," said the patient. "If your shoulder were swollen, it wouldn't bother me either."

517. A fellow who had been away to school returned to his home town. He met an old friend who said to him, "Where have you been for the last four years?"

"At college," he said, "taking medicine."

"Gee," said his friend, "and did you finally get well?"

518. "Hi, Bill," a fellow said to his friend, "how's it with you? And how's your wife? I haven't seen her lately."

"Oh," said his friend, "she went to Florida for her health."

"For her health?" the man asked. "What did she have?"

"Nine hundred dollars," his friend said, "that was left to her by an aunt."

46, 347, 603, 635, 900, 1582, 1725, 1754, 1903, 1947, 2068

Curiosity

519. The schoolgirl's grandfather was telling her about the way things used to be. "The girls of today are different," he said.

"How different?" she asked.

Curiosity

"Well," said her grandfather, "you never see a girl of today blush. It was different when I was a young fellow, they blushed in those days."

"Why, Grandfather," she said, "what in the world did you say to them?"

520.   The potato bugs were on a rampage in Idaho and a group of farmers were sitting around the country store, complaining about their losses.

"The rascals cleaned up my whole crop in two weeks," said the first.

"That's nothing," said another. "They ate mine up in three days and then sat on the fence to see if I was going to plant any more."

"Gentlemen," said a third farmer, "a person who doesn't know anything about potato bugs might find this hard to believe, but ten days before planting time I was over at the seed store, and I'll swear if two of them weren't in there looking over the books to see who had bought seed."

81, 709, 1015, 1037, 1172, 1509, 1861, 1936

Dance

521.   A visitor to a deaf and dumb school was invited to stay for the weekly dance on Saturday night. He told the president of the school, his host, that he would be embarrassed because he couldn't talk to the people at the dance.

"Oh," said the president of the school, "you don't have to know how to talk to them. All you need to know is how to ask a girl to dance with you. I can show you that in one minute." He then proceeded to show the visitor the sign language. "All you do is make a circle motion with your hand and the young lady will understand."

The visitor stayed for the dance and finally got up enough nerve to ask a young lady just as she walked into the room. The sign language worked, and they danced another dance. After that, they ended up down by the orchestra.

When the music stopped, the saxophone player said, "Say, Edith, how about having the next dance with you?"

Dance

The young lady turned to him and said, "I'd like to, but I can't, Harry, I'm stuck with this dummy."

155, 420, 431, 538, 644, 714, 995, 1736

Dating

522.   The star quarterback took back his fraternity pin from the college queen. He found out she was faithful to the end.

523.   A young man at a community dance said to an atractive girl he had just met, "Let me take you home. I won't try to kiss you, hug you, or make a pass at you. I'll be a perfect gentleman."

"Buddy," she said. "You just talked yourself out of a date."

48, 106, 213, 373, 444, 1422, 1855

Deadbeat

524.   A well-known deadbeat caught a friend on the street one day before the friend could duck.

"I'm really in a jam and need money," he said to his friend, "and I haven't any idea where I'm going to get some."

"I'm sure glad to hear that," said his friend. "I was afraid you might have the mistaken idea you could borrow some from me."

525.   The dentist returned empty-handed and angry after trying to collect a long overdue bill.

"What's the matter," asked his wife, "didn't you get your money?"

"No, I didn't' " he said. "And not only that, he had the nerve to gnash my own teeth at me."

526.   A man was bragging about his car. "I've had it a whole year and I haven't paid a cent for repairs or upkeep."

"Yes," said his friend. "That's what the man at the service station told me."

Deadbeat

527.   A homeowner went to the office of the Electric Light and Power Company. "Why did you cut off my current?" he asked.

"You didn't pay your bill," said the clerk. "No currency—no current!"

175, 203, 466, 470, 532, 1734

Deaf

528.   An insurance adjuster was investigating a fire, and was interviewing people in the neighborhood. He was talking to a hard-of-hearing man.

"How does the consensus of the folks run, concerning the fire?" he asked. "Do they think it resulted from some natural cause or had an incendiary origin?"

"Hey?" said the deaf man.

"He jest wants to know," shouted the man's wife, "was the fire ketched or sot."

529.   A highway patrolman pulled alongside a motorist and waved him to the side of the road. "Sir, your wife fell out of the car three miles back," he said.

"So that's it," said the driver. "I thought I had gone stone deaf."

530.   Two deaf farmers met one day as they drove their wagons down a country road. Each had his fishing pole in plain sight on the wagon.

"Hey, John," said the first fellow, "where you going, fishing?"

"No, Henry," said his friend, "I'm going fishing."

"Oh," said the first, "I thought maybe you were going fishing."

115, 521, 635

Debate

531.   A boy in a small-town high school won first prize for giving the best speech before the class. He was an easy winner because he had memorized Patrick Henry's famous "Give me liberty or give me death" speech.

Debate

Winning first prize went to his head, and he developed the habit of ending everything he said with the dramatic words, "Give me liberty or give me death."

This annoyed his friends so much that they went to the teacher and complained about it. She said she had noticed the habit herself, but that she thought she could cure him.

"What I'll do," she told the boys, "is to get him in front of the class and ask him a question he can't answer—much less answer with his pet phrase."

That afternoon after recess, she called him before the class and said, "I have a question for you. What is the colic? I want a short, concise definition of the colic."

Everybody could tell from the way he stood, first on one foot and then the other, that the teacher had caught him up. But finally, he looked up at her and said, "Well, ma'am, I'm not a doctor or a scientist, but according to my understanding, the colic is an overaccumulation of atmosphere, confined within the framework of the human anatomy crying 'give me liberty or give me death.' "

507

Debt

532.   A man asked his lawyer about collecting an old debt.
"Did you give this man a bill?" asked the lawyer.
"I sure did," the man said.
"What did he say to that?" the lawyer asked.
"He told me to go to the devil," said the man.
"Then what did you do?" asked the lawyer.
"Why, I came to you, of course," the man said.

33, 896

Deceive

533.   The man at the poultry counter had sold everything except one fryer. A customer said she was entertaining at dinner and wanted a nice-sized fryer. The clerk threw the fryer on the scales and said, "This one will be $1.35."

Deceive

"Well," the lady said, "I really wanted a larger one."

The clerk, thinking fast, put the fryer back in the box and stirred it around a bit. Then, he brought it out again and put it on the scales. "This one," he said, "will be $1.95."

The woman said, "Wonderful. I'll take both of them."

534.   "It certainly was terrible about Mary Sue, wasn't it?" said one secretary to another when they were at lunch together. "You know—her marrying that old man who deceived her so."

"Deceived her?" asked her friend. "How did he deceive her? Wasn't he as rich as he told her he was?"

"Oh, he was rich all right," the first secretary said, "but the dirty liar was ten years younger than he said he was."

6, 286, 540, 746, 1981

Definite

535.   A lady was getting on a train and said to the agent, "Is this the train to Chicago?"

"Yes, ma'am," he said.

"Are you absolutely sure it goes to Chicago?" she asked again.

"Well, lady, I'm not really sure," he said, "but the station agent, the engineer, the fireman, the conductor, and the waiters in the dining car all think it does."

536.   Did you ever notice that a girl will wear shorts when she isn't going to play tennis and a bathing suit when she isn't going swimming? But, when she puts on a wedding gown, she means business.

537.   The man's wife was sick in bed and he was trying to fix breakfast. "I can't find the tea bags, dear," he called to her from the kitchen.

"You must be blind," she said. "They are right in front, on the top shelf, in a coffee can marked 'rice.'"

538.   It was the weekly teen-agers' meeting at the church and the minister had been talking against dancing. As a windup to his talk, he said, "Now tell me honestly, do you really think the girls who participate in these dances are right?"

Definite

"Well, they must be," said one of the girls, "because the ones that don't are always left."

539.   Three doctors who had been called into consultation had examined the sick man and then gone into another room to discuss the case. The patient was worried and asked his wife to listen at the door.

"Can you hear what they are saying?" he asked his wife.

"I'm trying," she said, "but it's hard to hear through the door. All I can hear is something about being sure after the autopsy."

86, 500, 731, 978, 1630, 2048

Definition

540.   The Sunday school teacher asked her pupils if they understood the meaning of "False doctrine."

"Yes," said a little boy. " 'False doctrine' is when the doctor gives you the wrong kind of medicine."

541.   "How are the roads in this section?" a visitor asked a local politician.

"Fine," said the politician. "We've abolished bad roads."

"That must have been an expensive job, wasn't it?" asked the visitor.

"Not at all," said the politician. "Wherever the going got too bad, we quit calling it a road. We called it a detour."

542.   A high school boy was doing his homework in social science. He said to his father, "What is it they call a person who brings you into contact with the world and things?"

"A bartender, son," his father said.

88, 160, 251, 531, 692, 727, 966, 1332, 1449, 1913

Delay

543.   A professor at pharmacy school asked one of the students how much of a certain drug should be administered to a patient. The student said, "Eight grains."

Delay

A few minutes later, the same student raised his hand.

"Professor," he said, "I'd like to correct my answer to that question. It should have been two grains."

The professor looked at his watch and said, "I'm sorry, but it's too late. The patient has been dead for two minutes."

544.   A soldier asked for a leave, so he could get married.

"How long have you known the girl?" the Captain asked.

"A week," the young soldier said.

"That's not really long enough," the Captain said. "You should not rush into marriage. I think you should wait six months. Then, if you still want to get married, I'll give you two weeks' leave."

Six months later, the soldier was back. He reminded the Captain of his promise.

"So you still want to get married," he said. "I didn't think you would stay interested in the same girl for that long."

"You're right, sir," he said, "it isn't the same girl."

184, 409, 1089, 1522

Democracy

545.   A Russian was shown a copy of a Sears Roebuck catalogue.

"Do you mean to tell me," he said, "that in America all of these things are available to the masses?"

"Available?" said the American. "In America we have to beg people to buy them."

579

Democrats

546.   The father was telling the candidate about his family.

"Nine boys," he said, "and all Democrats, except John. He learned to read."

328, 472, 1083, 1450

Demonstration

547.   A salesman was explaining to a friend the reason for his sudden prosperity.

"I sell ladies' hosiery," he said. "Sometimes if the woman of the house wants me to, I put them on for her."

"You sure must sell a lot of hose that way," his friend said.

"No," the salesman said, "my legs look lousy in women's hose."

207, 702, 733, 899, 979, 1512

Dentist

548.   The young lady hated to go to the dentist's office. Finally, with a tooth causing much pain, she made an appointment. As soon as the dentist asked her to open her mouth, she started to moan and groan and cry.

"What in the world is the matter?" he said. "Don't you know I'm a painless dentist?"

"Well, you may be painless," she said, "but I'm not!"

525, 905, 1949

Dependability

549.   A lady had just bought a dog and was bragging about his good points to a friend.

"He's not what you would call a pedigree dog," she said, "but no prowler could come near the house without him letting us know about it."

"What does he do?" asked her friend. "Bark and arouse the neighborhood?"

"No," said the proud owner, "he crawls under the bed."

550.   The boss was mad at the young man for not doing a job properly. "Why didn't you deliver the message the way I told you?" he asked.

"I did the best I could, sir," the young man said.

"The best you could!" the boss screamed. "If I had expected to send a dumbbell, I would have gone myself."

Dependability

551.   The conductor of the community orchestra was almost out of his mind because at every rehearsal at least one member would be missing. At the last rehearsal, he called for attention and said, "I wish to thank publicly the first violinist for being the only member of the orchestra to attend every rehearsal."

"It seemed the least I could do," the violinist said humbly, "since I won't be at the concert tonight."

103, 835, 1237, 1798

Description

552.   "What do you think of our little town?" asked the native of his visiting cousin.

"It certainly is unique," said his cousin.

"What do you mean by 'unique'?" asked the native.

"It's from the Latin 'unus' meaning one," his cousin said, "and 'equus' meaning horse."

553.   The murder trial was over and the jury had been locked up for three days. Finally, they filed into the courtroom to render their verdict.

The foreman rose in all of his dignity and said, "The jury is all of one mind, temporarily insane."

94, 209, 826, 1816

Determination

554.   "Sarah sure has a lot of self-control," a lady said to a friend. "I wish I could be like her."

"Why, what makes you say that?" asked her friend.

"Well," the first one said, "she can listen to the commercials on television without discovering that she has even one of the symptoms of a single disease that they are talking about."

555.   The big businessman was giving some advice to a group of new salesmen that had just been hired by his company.

"It takes hard work to succeed," he told them. "You've got to have pluck. I owe everything I have to pluck, pluck, pluck."

Determination

"That's just what I wanted to hear," one of the young men said to him. "Now could you tell us where to find the people to pluck and how to do it after we find them?"

95, 148, 1545, 1860

Devotion

556.   A New York lawyer went to California to try to locate a young woman who had fallen heir to a fortune. A detective agency was called in to help in the search. The case was placed in the hands of a young, clever, and attractive investigator. Several weeks passed without any word, and the lawyer was beginning to feel concerned over the matter. Then, one day the young detective showed up and informed him he had located the heiress.

"Wonderful," said the lawyer, "Where is she?"

"Over at my place," the young detective said. "We were married yesterday."

557.   A little boy said to the pharmacist: "Please give me a small bottle of castor oil."

"The tasteless kind?" asked the druggist.

"No," said the little boy. "It's for my father."

558.   A salesman was trying to sell a woman an insurance policy on her husband. He was having trouble making his point.

"What is the maximum value of your husband's present policy?" he asked her.

She acted as though she didn't understand the question, so he tried again, "If you should lose your husband, for example, what would you get?"

She thought for a moment and then said, "A parakeet!"

559.   A man's wife was feeling a bit sorry for herself. "You don't seem as devoted to me as you used to," she complained. "Do you still love me?"

Her husband looked up from his newspaper and shouted, "Yes, I still love you. Now shut your big mouth and let me read my paper."

Devotion

560.   A lady who was vacationing at Miami Beach opened her mail, glanced at a small piece of paper, stuck it back in the envelope and said to her friend who was with her, "Well, my husband is feeling good, things are going well at the office, there isn't any trouble with the cat or dog at home, and he still loves me."

"My," said her friend, "do you mean to say he told you all that on that tiny piece of paper and you read it in less than two seconds?"

"Yes," said the lady. "It's a check for $300."

60, 274, 959, 1163, 1234, 1302

Diagnosis

561.   A man went to the doctor for a checkup. "If there's anything wrong with me," he said, "don't give it a fancy scientific name, just tell me in plain English."

"Well, to be quite frank," said the doctor, "you're just plain lazy."

"Gee, thanks, doctor," said the patient. "Now give me a fancy, scientific name for it so that I can tell my wife."

562.   An art student had just finished a painting of a friend, and was rather proud of it. He was showing it to a doctor friend of his. The doctor looked at it for several minutes, and then shook his head and said, "It looks to me like it's either a gallbladder attack or a case of acute appendicitis."

227, 458, 604, 700, 1625, 1887

Diamond

563.   Everybody with any experience knows that a gold digger is the hardest known female. It takes a diamond to make an impression on her.

564.   The experienced lady of the world was giving some advice to her younger friends. "Remember," she said, "always wear enormous jewelry. There is nothing like a large diamond to make a girl look petite."

Diamond

565.   The country hick went to the county fair for the day. When he returned, he was wearing a ring set with a three- or four-carat shiner. The jewelry excited all of the local girls and was the cause of much talk. A close friend asked him if it was a real diamond.

"Well, if it ain't, said the man, "I've been skinned out of two dollars."

713, 1677, 1826

Diet

566.   "You look a lot thinner than the last time I saw you," a minister said to a member of his congregation. "Are you taking treatments or dieting to lose weight?"

"Oh, no," she said, "I'm losing weight because of all the trouble I'm having with my new maid."

"Why don't you get rid of her?" asked the minister.

"Oh, I'm going to," said the lady, "just as soon as she worries me down another ten pounds."

567.   Husband: "What happens to all the grocery money that I give you?"

Wife: "Stand sideways and look in the mirror."

116, 300, 774, 1363

Dignity

568.   The big, black limousine drove up to the front of the night club and the doorman ran down the steps of the club to open the door. Halfway, he slipped, and fell down the rest of the way.

"Be more careful," yelled the manager from the top of the steps, "or people will think you are a customer."

123, 455, 1409

Diplomacy

569.   "You heard the last witness' testimony and how it contradicts yours," said the lawyer. "Are you trying to cast doubt upon his veracity?"

Diplomacy

"No, not at all," the witness said. "I merely wish to make it plain what a liar I am if he's telling the truth."

570.　A little boy had just come from a birthday party. His mother worried about his manners, said, "Are you sure you didn't ask Joe's mother for a second piece of cake?"

"Oh, no, Mother," he said. "I only asked her for the recipe so you could bake a cake like it. And she gave me two more pieces."

571.　The wealthy social leader was looking at her new photograph that she had just had made. "That picture is terrible," she said. "Now, I ask you, does that photograph look like me?"

The photographer, who had dealt with her kind many times, said without batting an eye, "Madam, the answer to that question is in the negative."

572.　"Why should a big, strong man like you be out begging?" the housewife asked.

"Well, to tell the truth, lady," said the tramp, "it's the only profession I know in which a gentleman can address a beautiful lady like you without a formal introduction."

162

Disappearance

573.　The police sergeant was questioning the banker about his missing cashier. "Is your cashier tall or short?"

"Both," said the banker. "Six feet tall and $10,000 short."

574　A distraught husband visited the police station and said to the sergeant in charge, "I'd like to report that my wife is missing. Here is her picture. I'd like for you to locate her for me."

After looking at the picture for a moment, the sergeant said, "Why?"

133, 190, 1208

Disappointment

575. "Have you ever been disappointed in love?" said a man to his friend.

"Twice," his friend said. "The first time, the girl ditched me. The second time she didn't."

576. Two men were fishing near each other. After a while one said to the other, "Had any luck?"

"Not yet," the fellow said. "I haven't been able to get the cork out."

83, 175, 841, 1254, 1394, 1874

Disbelief

577. The bank had just installed a new burglar alarm. In case of a holdup, all the teller had to do was to step on a pedal on the floor. This rang a bell at police headquarters.

The first day it was in use, the bank was held up. The teller, before handing over the money, pressed his foot on the pedal. Immediately, the phone in the bank began to ring. As the teller reached to answer it, the holdup man grabbed it himself and lifted the receiver.

"This is the Police Department," a voice said. "Did you know that somebody over there has stepped on the pedal that rings the burglar alarm over here?"

578. An insurance salesman had been talking for hours trying to sell a farmer on the idea of insuring his barn. At last he seemed to have the prospect interested because he had begun to ask questions.

"Do you mean to tell me," asked the farmer, "that if I give you a check for $75 and if my barn burns down, you will pay me $50,000?"

"That's exactly right," said the salesman. "Now, you are beginning to get the idea."

"Does it matter how the fire starts?" asked the farmer.

"Oh, yes," said the salesman. "After each fire we make a careful investigation to make sure the fire was started accidentally. Otherwise, we don't pay the claim."

Disbelief

"Huh," grunted the farmer, "I knew it was too good to be true."

21, 273, 383, 455, 632, 1224, 1959

Discernment

579. A Congressman was being interviewed by the press. One reporter asked: "Do you feel that you have influenced public opinion, sir?"

"No," answered the Congressman. "Public opinion is something like a mule I once owned. In order to keep up the appearance of being the driver, I had to watch the way he was going and then followed as closely as I could."

580. The new young minister was somewhat nervous while calling on members of the church.

"What a fine baby!" he said to a young mother. "How old is he?"

"Just six weeks old today," said the proud mother.

"My, my," the young minister said. "And I suppose this is your youngest?"

581. The ambitious young man had just asked the banker's daughter to marry him.

"Before I say yes," she said, "can you tell me what's the difference between me and a baby elephant?"

The young man thought a moment and then said, "I give up. I'm afraid I don't know."

"In that case," said the banker's daughter, "you can marry the baby elephant."

75, 198, 367, 749, 1114, 1223, 1533, 2064

Discipline

582. A schoolteacher wrote a note home to Jimmy's mother: "Dear Mrs. Jones, your son, Jimmy, is a smart boy, but he spends all of his time with the girls. I am trying to break him of this habit."

Discipline

The teacher received this reply: "I wish you success. Please let me know how you do it. I have been trying for years to break his father of the same habit."

583.   "You certainly are the Southern gentleman," a man said to his friend. "I noticed you got up and gave that lady your seat in the bus."

"It's like this," said the man. "Ever since childhood, I have respected a woman with a strap in her hand."

584.   "Why do you have married men working in your office?" a man asked his friend. "Do you find they're better workers than bachelors?"

"No, it's not that," said the man. "It's just that they're used to taking orders and don't get upset when I yell at them."

1, 223, 746, 940, 1812

Discouraged

585.   A minister put an advertisement in the paper for a handyman. The next morning a well-dressed young man came to the door.

"Can you start the fire and have breakfast ready by 7:00?" asked the minister.

The young man said he thought he could.

"Can you polish the silver, wash the dishes, and keep the house picked up and the lawn mowed?" was the next question.

"Look," said the young man. "I came here to see about getting married, but if it's going to be anything like that, you can count me out."

586.   A woman was fussing at her husband. "All you do," she said, "is sit around with your feet propped up. Don't you ever feel any ambition?"

"Sure, I do," the man said. "I feel lots of ambition when I sit around. That's why I sit. But as soon as I start to work, I get discouraged."

131, 362, 901, 1664, 1838, 1867, 2021

Discretion

587. A fellow in the shop said to the man at the next bench: "You look all worn out, what's the trouble? You're not sick?"

"No, I'm not sick. I just didn't get home until morning, and as I was undressing, my wife woke up and said, 'Aren't you getting up mighty early this morning?' So to keep from having an argument I put on my clothes again and came to work."

588. The hostess was instructing the maid: "When you wait on the table tonight, please don't spill anything."

"Don't you worry, ma'am," said the maid, "I never talk much."

589. "Why are you advertising your saxophone for sale?" a fellow asked his friend. "I thought that you enjoyed playing it."

"Yes, I do," said his friend. "But I figured I had better give it up when I saw my next door neighbor in the hardware store yesterday buying a shotgun."

6, 276, 721, 1077

Dishonest

590. A man came home in a bad mood and said to his wife, "The world's full of dishonest people these days. Today a guy passed off a phoney quarter on me, and if that bartender around the corner wasn't nearsighted, I never would have gotten rid of it!"

591. "Excuse me, sir," the stranger said to the hotel clerk in the small town. "I'm new here and I'm looking for a criminal lawyer. I wonder if you know of one in town?"

"Well," said the hotel man, "there are four in town that most of us are pretty sure about, but nobody has ever been able to prove anything on them."

292, 533, 1880

Distance

592. The smart young man in a car saw a pretty girl on the corner waiting for a bus. He pulled over to the curb and said, "Hello, honey, do you want a ride?"

Distance

"Which way are you going?" she asked.

"North," he said.

"Fine," she said. "Give my regards to the Eskimos!"

593. A draftee had served his time in the Navy and was being discharged. A friend asked him what he thought of the sea.

"Just this," he said. "I'm going to put an oar over my shoulder and start walking. I'm going to keep on walking and walking and walking until someone stops me and asks what I've got over my shoulder. Then I'm going to settle down right there until I die."

594. A man walking down a country road, asked a local farmer boy, "How far is it to the next town?"

"About five miles as the crow flies," the farmer said.

"Well, how far is it if the crow has to walk and carry an empty gasoline can?" the man asked.

104, 393, 1364

Divorce

595. Attorney in a divorce case: "Isn't it true, madam, that your husband led a dog's life?"

"Yes, he did," replied the wife. "He came in with muddy shoes and left his footprints all over the house. He took the best spot near the fireplace. He waited to be fed. He growled at the least provocation and snapped at me a dozen times a day. Are there any other questions?"

596. "You say you want to get a divorce," the judge asked, "on the grounds that your husband is careless about his appearance?"

"Yes," the woman said. "He hasn't shown up in ten years."

597. The judge was trying a divorce case, and asked the husband what the trouble was.

"Well, Judge," the husband said, "I came home and there was my wife in the arms of another man."

"And what did she say when you discovered her?" asked the judge.

Divorce

"Well, Judge, that was what hurt me," said the husband. "She turned around and saw me and then said, 'Well, look who just walked in, old blabbermouth! Now everybody in town will know.'"

598.   A lawyer's wife was complaining to him about their house.

"We need furniture, draperies, carpets, and a new furnace," she said.

"Just be patient, honey, and I'll take care of it," he said. "I'm working on a divorce case for a woman now whose husband has lots of money. Just as soon as I finish breaking up their home, we can fix up ours."

599.   A divorcee was telling her widowed friend about all the trouble she was having with the lawyers over the alimony payments that were due her.

"Oh, you don't have to tell me anything about those lawyers," said her friend. "I've had the same trouble. In fact, I've had so much trouble over my husband's estate that I sometimes wish he hadn't died."

600.   The former henpecked husband was known among his friends for the promptness with which he paid his alimony each month. When asked the reason, he explained, "I'm afraid that if I ever fall behind in my payments, she might try to repossess me."

601.   A woman went to see her lawyer about a divorce.

"What grounds do you think you have for a divorce?" the lawyer asked.

"It's my husband's manners," she said. "He has such bad table manners that he is disgracing the whole family."

"That's bad," the lawyer said. "How long have you been married?"

"Nine years," the woman said.

"If you have been able to put up with his table manners for nine years, I can't understand why you want a divorce now," the lawyer said.

Divorce

"Well," said the woman, "we didn't know it before. We just bought a book of etiquette this morning."

34, 86, 281, 732, 1093, 1142, 1616

Doctor

602.   Nervous patient: "Quick, doctor, do something. I was playing a mouth organ and swallowed it."

Doctor: "Keep calm, sir, be thankful you weren't playing a piano."

603.   "My uncle had an accident with his car," a man said to his friend. "It was a terrible accident but he had a good doctor. The doctor told him he would have him walking in a month."

"And did he?" his friend asked.

"Sure," said the man. "When the doctor sent his bill, my uncle had to sell his car."

604.   Patient: "What's my trouble, Doc?"

Doctor: "I'm not exactly sure what's wrong with you, but if you were a building, you'd be condemned."

605.   A woman's husband had been to see the doctor. When he came home, she said: "Well, did the doctor find out what you had?"

"Almost," her husband said. "I had $40, and he charged me $38."

606.   "Your wife used to be extremely nervous," a man told his friend. "Now I notice she is calm and composed and never ruffled. What cured her?"

"The doctor did," his friend said. "He told her that particular kind of nervousness was the usual sign of advancing age."

607.   A stranger called by the doctor's office and said: "I just dropped in to tell you how much I benefited from your treatment."

Doctor

"But you're not one of my patients," said the doctor.

"I know," said the stranger. "But my uncle was and I'm his heir."

608. "Doctor," asked a banker friend, "did you ever make a serious mistake in a diagnosis?"

"Yes," said the doctor. "I once treated a patient for indigestion, when she could have afforded an appendectomy."

609. A sick business tycoon called on the doctor.

"What is your trouble?" the doctor asked.

"That's what you are supposed to find out," the man said.

"If you'll be kind enough to wait in the reception room, please, I'll call in a specialist. He's a veterinarian, and is the only person I know who can make a medical diagnosis without asking questions."

610. "That's that," said the young doctor as he fell in step with a colleague in the hospital corridor. "I certainly performed that operation in the nick of time. Another few hours and the patient might have recovered without it."

611. A doctor told his patient: "The best thing you can do is to give up drinking and smoking, get up early every morning, take lots of exercise, and go to bed early every night."

"What's the second best?" the patient asked.

612. The patient seemed worried and wanted to question the diagnosis of the doctor.

"Are you sure it's pneumonia, doctor?" he asked. "I've heard of cases where a doctor treated a patient for pneumonia, and he ended up dying of typhoid fever."

"Don't worry," said the doctor. "When I treat a patient for pneumonia, he dies of pneumonia."

613. "You were a very sick man," the doctor said to his patient. "In fact, it was only your iron constitution that pulled you through."

"That's wonderful," said the patient. "I just hope you don't forget that when you send me your bill."

Doctor

614.　A man with a bad case of asthma went to the doctor.

"I've tried a lot of doctors and none of them could help me," he said. "So my friend insisted I see you. They said you have had a great deal of experience with this ailment. Is that right?"

"Yes, I have," said the doctor. "In fact, I've suffered from it myself for the past twenty years."

615.　A doctor examined a man who was mentally ill.

"Your husband is in a serious condition," the doctor said to the man's wife. "You should have brought him to me sooner."

"I wanted to," the man's wife said, "but as long as he was in his right mind, he wouldn't go near a doctor."

616.　Every chair in the doctor's waiting room was taken. Several people were standing. There was no word from the doctor. Finally, one old man stood up wearily and said, "Well, I guess I'll just go home and die a natural death."

617.　The drunk went to get a physical examination. He was so full of alcohol that the doctor said to him, "You'll have to come back day after tomorrow. Any examination we might make today wouldn't mean anything—that's what whiskey drinking does, you know."

"Yes, I know," the patient said. "I sometimes have that trouble myself. I'll do as you say and come back day after tomorrow—when you're sober."

618.　The mountaineer had been shot up pretty badly and was carried into the doctor's office by some friends.

"How bad hurt is he, doc?" his friends asked.

"Well," said the doctor after a quick look at the man's wounds, "I would say that the first two wounds are fatal, but this third one here really isn't serious."

11, 22, 46, 111, 227, 294, 347, 381, 426, 435, 451, 465, 629, 756, 1259, 1678, 1842

Doctor bill

619.　The doctor had told the lady she could pay his fee for delivering the baby whenever she was able to do so. Now she was in his office, making the final payment.

Doctor bill

"And how is the baby?" asked the doctor.

"Oh, he's fine," she said. "He's graduating from college next spring."

603, 613, 662, 1159, 1207, 1719

Dog

620.　Jones has a good watch dog. If you hear a suspicious noise at night, just wake him up and he begins to bark.

621.　An excited woman called the police station.

"Will you please send a patrol car immediately?" she said. "There's a big, bad, vacuum cleaner salesman sitting in the tree in our front yard teasing my dog!"

622.　"What is it," a friend asked, "that you don't like about a dachshund?"

"For one thing," he said, "they make too much draft when they come into a room. They always keep the door open so long."

623.　The customer said to the dining room manager in the small resort hotel, "Why does your dog sit there and watch me so attentively while I eat?"

"I can't imagine," said the manager, "unless it's because you are eating from his favorite plate."

624.　A man in the barber chair said to the barber, "Your dog seems very interested in watching you cut hair."

"He doesn't care about the hair-cutting," the barber said. "He's really only interested when I snip off a bit of a customer's ear."

625.　The doorbell rang and the man answered it, to find a friend whom he hadn't seen for some time. His friend was standing there with a large shaggy and rather muddy dog. The man invited them in, and they sat in the living room and talked about old times. The dog, after sniffing around, finally hopped on the beautiful and expensive couch and settled down for a nap, much to the host's displeasure.

Dog

Finally, the guest rose to leave. "Aren't you forgetting your dog?" asked the host.

"That's not my dog," said the guest. "I thought he was yours."

626.   A farmer came to town on Court Day and saw a man entertaining a crowd with the tricks of his trained dog. The farmer said, "How did you train your dog that way? I can't teach mine a single trick."

The dog's owner said, "It's not easy. To begin with, you have to know more than the dog or you can't teach him anything."

627.   The man had entered his plain cur dog in the dog show and, of course, the dog did not win any of the many prizes. Later, his friend said to him, "You knew your dog wasn't going to win a prize. Why did you go to the expense and bother to enter him in the show?"

"Yes," said the man, "I knew he wasn't going to win a prize, but look at all the high-class dogs he met."

161, 219, 247, 549, 595, 678, 734, 798, 1019, 1123, 1322, 1665, 1985, 2034, 2072

Doubt

628.   It had been a real big night at the tavern. Old George had to be carried back to his shack by his friends. When he woke up the next day, he was startled to see a huge ape sitting on the foot of his bunk. He carefully reached for his 45. He took careful aim and said, "If yore a real monkey, yore in a bad fix. But if you ain't, then I am."

629.   "What in the world happened to you?" a fellow asked a friend who was walking on crutches.

"Got hit by a bus a couple of months ago," the man said.

"Two months ago?" his friend asked. "And you still aren't able to walk without crutches?"

"Well," said the man, "it's this way. My doctor says I can walk without them, but my lawyer thinks I had better keep using them for a while."

319, 480, 1005, 1441, 1457, 1485, 1974

154

Doughnut

630. "Honey," said the bride, "I've just made my first doughnuts. I want you to try them and see what you think. Be perfectly frank in telling me if you can think of anything to improve them."

"Well," said her husband, as he lifted one in his hand, "don't you think it might be better if you made the hole bigger?"

1912

Dream

631. A little girl in Sunday school was telling her friend about a dream she had experienced the night before. "It was terrible," she said. "I was at a birthday party at Joe's house. His mother had baked a chocolate cake three feet high and when she cut it everybody was given a piece that was so large that it hung over the sides of the plate. Then she dipped up some homemade ice cream. She had so much of it that she had to give each one of us our share in a soup bowl."

"What was so terrible about that dream?" her friend asked.

"Oh," said the little girl, "I woke up before I could get the first taste."

632. The little four-year-old came down to breakfast one morning and said to her mother, "My, Mamma, that was a wonderful dream I had last night, wasn't it?"

"I don't know," her mother said. "I haven't any way of knowing what your dream was all about."

"You ought to," said the little girl. "You were in it."

91, 628, 816, 1041, 1357, 1528, 1809

Drinking

633. The man was showing off his new car.

"How far do you get on a gallon?" his friend asked.

"That all depends on what's in the gallon," the man said.

634. A tipsy husband came home about midnight and threw himself on the couch in the living room. He woke his wife up

with his clumsiness and she stuck her head out of the bedroom door and said, "Well, you finally came home. I guess you found that your home is the best place to be this time of night."

"Not exactly," he said, "but it's the only place that's open after midnight."

635.   Barfly: "George, aren't you getting hard of hearing lately?"

George: "Yes. And I went to see the doctor about it."

Barfly: "What did he say?"

George: "He said if I didn't quit drinking so much I'd get as deaf as a post."

Barfly: "Are you going to quit?"

George: "No. I tried it. I went back to drinking because I liked the stuff I was drinking a lot more than I did the stuff I was hearing."

636.   The owner of a sheet metal shop, who was a teetotaler, returned from a trip and found the assistant foreman in charge. "Where's the foreman?" he asked the assistant.

"He's on one of those binges of his," said the assistant.

"Where's the welder, then?" the boss asked.

"He's over at Bill's Tavern drunk," he said.

"I didn't see the stock clerk when I came through the stockroom. Where's he?"

"Oh, he's at the gym getting a steam bath to cure a hangover."

The boss dropped to a chair, shaking his head sadly. "Well," he said, "for a man who never touches a drop, I seem to suffer more from the effects of alcohol than any man in this town."

637.   A woman was telling her friend all of her troubles.

"My husband has been drinking too much lately," she said, "and I went to see the doctor about it."

"What did the doctor say?" her friend asked.

"Oh, he gave me some powders to put in his coffee to cure him," said the first woman.

Drinking

"Did it work?" her friend asked.

"Yes, it worked," the woman said. "It cured him of drinking coffee."

29, 70, 78, 200, 203, 286, 333, 344, 391, 403, 408, 464, 490, 505, 576, 611, 716, 1198, 1265, 1745, 2010, 2035

Drought

638.   A college boy said to his roommate, "The drought back home is really bad this time."

"How can you tell?" asked his roommate.

"I got a letter from Dad," he said, "and the stamp was fastened on with a paper clip."

639.   "No, we haven't had any in a long time, now," the clerk at the supermarket said to the customer.

The manager who was passing by heard the clerk and stepped into the conversation and said, "Oh, yes, we have, lady. This is a new clerk and doesn't know about these things. We have plenty in the warehouse and will get some over this afternoon. If you come back then, we'll have it. Now, just tell me what it was he said we haven't had in a long time."

"Rain," said the lady as she walked away.

576, 1558

Druggist

640.   Now we know what the doctor's scribbling means on a prescription blank: It is a secret message to the druggist saying, "I got my $10, now it's your turn."

641.   A little old lady looked at the drug clerk doubtfully. "I take it for granted," she said, "that you are a qualified druggist."

Druggist

"Oh, yes, ma'am," he said.

"You have passed all the required examinations?" she asked.

"Yes, ma'am," he said again.

"You've never poisoned anybody by mistake, have you?" the lady asked.

"Why, no!" he said.

"In that case," she said, "please give me ten cents' worth of epsom salts."

642. The farmer's boy said to the druggist, "Got any medicine?"

"Yes, we have lots of it. What do you want?" asked the druggist.

"Oh, it doesn't matter much," he said, "just so that it's something peppy. Dad is pretty sick."

Drunk

643. "So," said his wife as he staggered in at 3:00 A.M., "drunk again."

"Yeah," he said, "and thish time I had a speshial reason for gettin' drunk."

"Yeah? And what was the special reason?"

"Whash the difference—so long as it sherved the purpose?"

644. Young girl: "I am the most graceful dancer in this state."

Her friend: "You may be in this state, but you're not when you're sober."

645. "That was some party at the hotel last night," said the man at a convention. "We got George so drunk that it took his wife, three bellhops, and the house detective to put me to bed."

646. Old Joe and a friend went into a bar and Joe ordered four straight shots in about four minutes. Each time he would gulp it down. After the fourth, and before he could order a fifth, Joe passed out—plunk, right on the floor. "Well," said his friend, "one thing about old Joe—he knows when he's had enough."

Drunk

647. The drunk was making a lot of noise as he tried to fit his key into the front door lock. At last a man stuck his head out of an upstairs window and shouted, "Go away, you drunk. You've got the wrong house."

"Drunk yourself," the drunk yelled back. "You're lookin' outta the wrong window!"

648. The drunk was in a gay and hilarious mood as he was brought before the desk sergeant at police headquarters in the early hours of the morning.

"What I want to know," he demanded, "is why I was brought here?"

"You were brought here for drinking," said the sergeant.

"Wonderful. Just wonderful," the drunk said. "I can hardly wait to get started."

649. A drunk, feeling friendly at three o'clock in the morning, telephoned a friend. When a sleepy voice finally answered the phone, the drunk said brightly, "Hope I haven't disturbed you."

"Oh, that's all right," his friend said, "I had to get up anyway to answer the phone."

650. The drunk was back after taking the cure.

"Was the treatment bad?" an acquaintance asked.

"Oh, it was horrible!" said the drunk. "Why for sixty days, I had to live on nothing but food and water."

651. It was the annual office party. This year, one of the staff who was known to be a heavy drinker, began rather early to shake hands with his friends and say good-bye.

"You're not going yet?" asked a friend. "The party's just begun."

"Heck, no," the fellow said. "I'm just telling everybody good-bye while I still recognize them."

652. A drunk came home to his Miami apartment at three o'clock in the morning. His wife met him at the door and screamed, "What do you mean coming home in this state!"

Drunk

"Wha' shtate ja wan' me come home in, m'love?" asked the drunk. "Ohio?"

653.   A drunk was sitting on the bench in the village park, when the minister walked up to him. The minister shook the man's hand and said, "I am so happy that you have reformed and repented. All of your friends were pleased to see you at prayer meeting last night."

"Prayer meeting?" muttered the drunk. "So that's where I was."

654.   A drunk stopped a man on the street and said, "Excuse me, which is the other side of this street?"

"Why, over there," the man said, pointing.

"That's funny," the drunk said. "I was just over there and a gentleman said it was over here."

655.   Two men were fumbling around, trying to get into their apartment. "Say," said one, "you don't open the door with that. That's a cigarette butt."

"Heck," said the other, "I've smoked my key."

656.   A man who was pretty far gone down the road to alcoholism, went to see a doctor.

"How long have your hands been shaking like this?" the doctor asked.

"Oh, it started about five years ago," the man said. "But now it's getting worse."

"It's pretty evident that you are drinking too much," said the doctor.

"How much is too much?" the man asked.

"Oh, I'd say a quart a day," the doctor said.

"A quart a day!" the man said in some surprise. "Why, I spill more than that."

657.   A drunk got on a double-decker bus and climbed to the upper deck. A few minutes later, he staggered down the steps, muttering to himself.

Drunk

"Is anything the matter?" asked the driver.

"It ain't safe up there," the drunk said, "No driver."

658. "How is the man who was brought in last night for being drunk?" the doctor asked the nurse.

"I think he's snapping out of it," she said. "He just tried to blow the foam off his medicine."

659. A man telephoned the police station one night, reporting that the steering wheel, brake pedal, accelerator, and radio had been stolen from his car. The officer on the desk said he would send a patrol car to investigate.

A moment later, the phone rang again. "Don't bother," said the same voice. "I just got into the back seat by mistake."

660. A drunk entered a bus and immediately got into a violent argument with the driver. Instead of putting him off, the driver gave him a good talking to and sent him to the back of the bus.

As the drunk was riding the bus, he happened to notice a Dunkard preacher sitting in one of the seats.

"Hello," the drunk said. "Who are you all dressed up in that funny-looking uniform and wearing that funny hat and with that beard on? Are you with a circus or something?"

The little minister took immediate offense at the drunk's tone, and said, "I'll have you know, I'm a Dunkard pastor."

"Well," said the drunk, "shake hands. That's what the bus driver just called me."

13, 132, 160, 165, 267, 303, 360, 375, 758, 1773, 1879

Duplicate

661. A worried-looking man visited a florist shop and asked for a pot of geraniums. The florist was out of geraniums, and so he suggested chrysanthemums instead.

"No," said the customer. "I have to get geraniums. I promised my wife I'd water her geraniums while she was out of town."

67, 1419

662.   A politician died after a long illness. His savings hardly covered hospital and doctor bills. A friend, after quietly soliciting funds for his funeral, lacked only $1 of having enough. Worn out and exhausted, he said to a stranger, "Could you give me a dollar to bury a politician?" The stranger gave him a $5 bill and said, "Here, bury five of them."

663.   "Why were you discharged by your last employer?" asked the personnel director.

"I was overly ambitious," the man said.

"What do you mean, overly ambitious?"

"I wanted to take work home with me," the man said.

"Who was your last employer?" he was asked.

"The First National Trust and Savings Bank," he said.

664.   Plant Manager: "How long did you work in the other place?"

Welder: "Fifty-five years."

Plant Manager: "How old are you?"

Welder: "Forty-five years."

Plant Manager: "How could you work 55 years when you are only 45 years old?"

Welder: "Overtime."

665.   A minister was traveling through the backwoods. He met an old man and started talking to him.

"Brother, are you lost?" the minister asked.

"Oh, no," said the old man. "Been here 70 years and know every cow path in these hills."

"You don't understand," said the minister. "I mean are you ready for Judgment Day?"

"When's it coming?" asked the old man.

"Well, it might be today or it might be tomorrow," said the minister.

The old man thought a moment and said, "Well, don't tell my old lady or she'd want to go both days."

148, 821, 1164, 1233, 1510, 1593

Early

666.   The tourist said to the motel owner that he had read somewhere that this was the town that had a curfew.

"We did have," said the motel owner, "but we had to give it up."

"What was the trouble?" asked the tourist.

"Well, they never rang the bell until 9 o'clock," said the motel man, "and everybody complained because it woke them up."

587, 611, 747, 861, 1423, 1794

Easy

667.   A woman went to see a plastic surgeon about changing the shape of her nose.

"How much will it cost for you to change the shape of my nose?" she asked.

"One hundred dollars, lady," said the doctor.

"One hundred dollars?" she said. "Isn't there something less expensive?"

"Well," said the surgeon, "you might try walking into a telephone pole."

209, 296, 780, 1154, 1174

Economy

668.   A wife, complaining to her husband, said: "Darling, the lady next door has a hat just like my new one."

"Now I suppose you expect me to buy you another one," he said.

"Well," she answered, "it would be cheaper than moving."

669.   A man was bragging about his rich friends. "I have one friend who saves five hundred dollars a day," he said.

"What does he do?" his friend asked. "How does he save five hundred dollars a day?"

"Every morning, when he goes to work, he goes in the subway," he said. "You know in the subway, there is a five-hundred-dollar fine if you spit, so, he doesn't spit!"

Economy

670.   The tightwad asked the bank for a loan of $10 and was told that he would have to pay four percent interest.

"That's 40 cents, isn't it?" the man asked.

"That's right," said the banker. "And what can you give us for security?"

"Twenty-five thousand dollars in savings bonds," said the man.

The bank accepted the bonds as security and gave the man $10. At the end of the year, the man was back with $10 and 40 cents and asked for the return of his bonds.

As the banker gave them to him, he asked, "With all these bonds, why did you want to borrow $10?"

"Well," said the man, "do you know any other way I could keep my bonds in a safety deposit vault for 40 cents a year?"

671.   The chemistry teacher asked his class, "What can you tell me about nitrates?"

"All I know is that night rates are cheaper than day rates," said a bright young fellow.

86, 299, 506, 759, 968, 1592, 1673, 2027

Editor

672.   The editor had run a story saying that "Half the legislature are crooks." It caused such a storm that he was forced to run a retraction. His apology said, "Half the legislature are not crooks."

673.   A writer went to see the editor of a magazine and said, "Here is the short story I offered you last year."

"What's the idea of bringing it back when I rejected it last year?" the editor asked.

"Well," said the writer, "you've had a year's experience since then."

674.   A man had been arrested for being drunk and was being questioned at the police station.

"So you say you're an editor," demanded the desk sergeant.

Editor

"Yes, sir," said the accused.

"That's not so, Sergeant," said the arresting officer. "I searched him and found $200 in his pocket."

675. "Daddy," said the editor's little daughter, "I know why editors call themselves 'we.'"

"Why?" asked her father with great interest.

"So the man who doesn't like what's printed," she said, "will think there are too many of you for him to lick."

676. "Now," said the art editor, "what we need for our next magazine cover is a girl wearing one of those religious gowns."

"What do you mean, a religious gown?" asked the artist.

"Oh, you know," said the editor, "one of those lo and behold outfits."

677. An editor of a small town weekly received this letter in the mail:

"Dear Sir: Last week I lost my watch which I valued highly. The next day I ran an ad in your paper. Yesterday, I went home and found the watch in the pocket of my brown suit. Your paper is wonderful!"

678. A lady came into the office of the small-town weekly newspaper and said to the young man at the desk, "I put an advertisement in your paper for my lost dog. Has anything been heard of it? I offered a fifty-dollar reward."

"Not yet," the boy said, "but the editor is out looking for him."

679. The editor received a manuscript with a letter which said, "The characters in this story are purely fictional and bear no resemblance to any person, living or dead."

When the editor returned it to the writer, he scribbled across the bottom, "That's what's wrong with it."

41, 149, 163, 1387

Education

680. On opening day a Kentucky mountaineer took his boy to school to enroll him.

Mountaineer: "My boy's after learning. What d'ya have?"

Principal: "We offer English, trigonometry, algebra, spelling, history, and reading."

Mountaineer: "Well, load him up with some of that there trigonometry; he's the only poor shot in the family."

681. "How come," a man said to his wife, "the Greens are taking French lessons?"

"Oh," she said, "they have adopted a French baby, and they want to be able to understand him when he begins to talk."

682. The man who stuttered had been taking lessons in remedial speech. His friend asked how he was doing.

"Fine," the man said. "Listen to what I've learned to say: Peter Piper picked a peck of pickled peppers. If Peter Piper picked a peck of pickled peppers, where is the peck of pickled peppers that Peter Piper picked?"

"Say, that's wonderful!" said his friend.

"It sure is," said the stutterer, "b-but it's s-sure h-hard to w-work it into a c-conversation."

683. The man's friend laughed when he spoke to the waiter in French, but the laugh was on him. The man told the waiter to give the check to his friend.

684. The man and his wife were having a knock-down, drag-out fight over money matters. "You brute," she screamed. "Before we were married, you told me you were well off!"

"I was," he said, "but I didn't know it."

685. The salesman was peddling a ten-volume set on scientific agriculture. He tried to sell one to an old farmer.

The farmer said, "No, I don't want 'em."

"But you ought to have them," said the salesman. "They'll teach you to farm twice as well as you do now."

"Shucks, son," said the farmer, "I don't farm half as good now as I know how."

Education

686. Two graduate students were trying to impress each other.

"Don't you find Gibbon's *Rise and Fall of the Roman Empire* a mighty and noble work?" asked the first.

"Indeed I do," said the other. "When did you last read it?"

"Well," said the first, "I haven't got around to it yet. When did you read it?"

"Oh, I've never read it either," said the other.

687. Although the little boy was only three, he already knew the alphabet. His proud parents were showing off his accomplishment to a friend.

"My, you're a smart young man," said the visitor. "And what is the first letter?"

"A," said the little boy.

"That's right," said the visitor, "and what comes after A?"

"All the rest of them," said the little boy.

688. A boy asked his father, "What is college-bred, dad?"

His father, with another son at the University, said, "College bread is made from the flour of youth and the dough of old age."

689. A truck driver had delivered a load of cement and stopped in the office of the warehouse and asked the secretary if she happened to have a Bible in the office. She located a copy on the desk of the president of the company and borrowed it for the man.

He was standing there looking through it carefully and in apparent deep thought, when the president came out of his office and said to him, "I was interested when my secretary said you wanted to borrow a copy of the Bible. I see you are hunting something. Can I help you?"

"Yes," the truck driver said. "I'm trying to find out how to spell Ezekiel. That's the name of my bootlegger and I want to write him a note."

88, 233, 266, 434, 546, 626, 736, 1137, 1740, 1894, 2089

Efficiency

690.   The man was making his first ocean voyage. He was in his cabin, suffering with seasickness.

"Shall I send some dinner to your stateroom, sir?" asked the steward.

"No," he moaned. "Just throw it through the porthole and save me the trouble."

691.   A man, traveling down a country road in the Tennessee mountains, saw a woman pouring water over two ragged and bearded men lying under a tree. The man stopped to see if something was wrong and if he could help.

"Oh, no," the woman said, "It just keeps the flies off of them."

692.   A young lady who had formerly worked for the Department of Defense, took a job as secretary to a bishop. She at once set about revamping the filing system. She labeled one drawer "Sacred" and another "Top Sacred."

693.   The high school principal had recommended one of his students for a job at the local bank. Several weeks later he saw the banker on the street.

"How is that new boy coming along?" he asked.

"Fine," said the banker. "You sure sent me a smart one. He has everything so mixed up and confused that we can't run the place without him."

577, 1369, 1689

Effort

694.   A man said to his friend, "You shouldn't let your wife go around telling people that she made a man of you. You don't hear my wife saying that."

"That's right," said his friend. "But I heard her tell my wife that she had tried her best."

695.   Back in the old days before central heating and electric blankets, a young city girl visited her aunt on the farm. It was

Effort

a cold night and her aunt told her she should take a flatiron to bed with her.

Next morning, her aunt asked, "Well, how did you make out with the flatiron last night?"

"All right, I guess," said her little niece. "I got it pretty near warm before morning."

332, 730, 848, 1134, 1153, 1335

Elegance

696.   A man was visiting his niece and noticed that after many years, she now kept a cat. "I see you finally got a cat," he said to his niece.

"Yes," she said. "One day he wandered in, discovered we had mice and air-conditioning and decided to stay."

302, 993, 1225, 1718

Elevator

697.   An attractive girl elevator operator, listening for the thousandth time to the corny remark, "I suppose you have your ups and downs," gave this snappy reply, "Oh, it's not the ups and downs that bother me. It's the jerks that make my life miserable."

1136, 1675

Eloquence

698.   A Yale man was called on for an impromptu speech at a dinner one night. Thinking quickly, he spoke of his Alma Mater and praised her by saying that the "Y" stood for youth. He then spoke for 20 minutes on youth. Then he said the "A" stood for appreciation and spoke a quarter of an hour on that subject. He then went to "L" for loyalty and "E" for efficiency —each taking another quarter hour or so.

As he came to a close, somebody in the rear was heard to remark: "Thank goodness he didn't graduate from the Massachusetts Institute of Technology."

Eloquence

699.   A man tiptoed out of the banquet room during the middle of the main speech. As he stepped onto the front steps of the hotel to get a breath of fresh air, he met another man who had left the banquet before him.

"Has the speaker finished what he had to say yet?" the first man asked.

"Oh, he finished that five minutes after he started," the second man said, "but he's still talking."

329, 523, 531, 1699, 1900, 1954

Emergency

700.   The doctor was taken up to the patient's room. A few minutes later he came down and asked to borrow a screwdriver. Five minutes later he was back and asked for a can opener. After another five minutes he returned and asked for a cold chisel and hammer. The worried husband couldn't stand it any longer.

"Please, doctor," he said, "what's wrong with my wife?"

"I don't know yet," the doctor said. "I can't get my bag open."

701.   An aspiring vocalist asked her teacher, "Do you think I will ever be able to do anything with my voice?"

"Well," said her teacher, "it might come in handy in case of fire."

702.   The driving instructor said to his pupil, "This is the emergency brake, lady. You can put it on in a hurry, in case of an emergency."

"Oh," said the pupil, "I see, the same as a dressing gown."

703.   The doctor's phone rang, and a man's voice said, "Please hurry, doctor, my little boy just swallowed my fountain pen."

"I'll be right there," said the doctor.

"What do you think I should do while you are on your way?" asked the man.

"Why don't you use a pencil?" said the doctor.

Emergency

704. "Quick," shouted the doctor to his nurse, "get my hat and coat, I've got a rush call."

"Is it a terrible accident or something?" cried his nurse.

"No," said the doctor, "it's worse than that. Mrs. Sims just called. Her little boy's sick. I don't know what is wrong with him, but she has one of those books that tells what to do until the doctor arrives, and I want to get there before she does it."

705. "Hello," said the doctor as he picked up the phone.

"Hello, doctor," the voice on the line said. "This is Harry Smith. My wife just fell down the basement stairs and hit her chin on the concrete floor. She has a badly dislocated jaw."

"That's terrible," said the doctor, "I'll jump in my car and run right over."

"Oh, no hurry, doctor," said the man. "Any time you happen to be passing this way in the next two or three weeks."

18, 392, 409, 431, 577, 719, 755, 1598

Emotion

706. When the seedy-looking man checked into the hotel, the manager said, "I'll have to ask you to pay in advance. Your luggage is too emotional."

"What do you mean," asked the guest, "that my luggage is too emotional?"

"I mean," said the manager, "it is too easily moved."

707. The funeral was over and the husband was standing alone near the grave looking sad and downcast. Thinking he would comfort the man, the minister came over and said to him, "Thirty-six years is a long time for two people to live together."

"Yes, it is," the man said, "and I suppose that she made me a good wife. But, you know, thinking back on all those years—I never did learn to like that woman."

1626, 1709

Employment

708.   A sympathetic neighbor, talking over the back fence, said, "I understand your husband has got a job at last."

"Yes," said her friend. "It is hard work and he says it is killing him. But, thank goodness, it's permanent."

709.   The neighborhood grocer was interviewing a boy to work in and around his store as a handyman.

"You'll do all right," the man said. "You'll be working half inside and half outside."

"I suppose that will be all right," the boy said, "but what happens to me if the wind should blow the door shut?"

195, 220, 342, 412, 506, 584, 754, 1580

Enemy

710.   "My father and old man Wilson have been fighting and arguing for thirty years, but now they've finally stopped."

"Why? Did they bury the hatchet?"

"No, they buried old man Wilson."

741, 1497

Engagement

711.   "Well, young man, I understand you want to become my son-in-law," said father to daughter's boy friend.

"No, sir, not exactly," he said. "But if I marry your daughter, I don't see how I can get out of it."

712.   A young lady said to an acquaintance: "I hear you are going to marry Harry. Did he tell you that he had proposed to me first?"

The acquaintance said: "Not specifically. But he did say that he had done a lot of foolish things before he met me."

713.   The little girl asked her father: "What makes a man give a woman a diamond engagement ring?"

"The woman," was the quick reply.

Engagement

714.　"So you are going to a dance with a young man, are you?" fumed a critical grandmother. "When I was a girl, no young lady would think of going to a dance with a man unless he was her fiancé."

"Oh, don't worry about that, Grandmother," said the girl. "This is one of my fiancés."

78, 260, 522, 1319, 1684, 1828, 2015, 2030

Enough

715.　A lady answered the doorbell and a man standing there said, "I'm the piano tuner."

"I didn't send for a piano tuner," said the lady.

"I know it, lady," the man said. "Your neighbors did."

716.　Sitting quietly in his office one afternoon, a man began to think about his wife and how wonderful she was. He began to feel that maybe he had been neglecting her lately. He decided to make it up to her. On the way home from work he bought her some candy, two dozen roses, and a bottle of imported perfume.

"Honey," he cried as he came in the front door. "I brought you a few little tokens of my love. Now, how about getting all dressed up in your best dress—we're going to a nightclub for dinner and dancing."

"Oh," she screamed. "I thought I had had enough when the baby upset the fish bowl and the kitchen sink stopped up and the furnace blew a fuse. But, to top it off, here you come home drunk."

114, 646, 1193

Entertainment

717.　"Well," said the old regular at the country store, "I hear Hank Barrow has gone to Las Vegas. Do you reckon there'll be enough going on to suit him?"

"Well," said his friend, "you know Hank. He don't take no chances. He took his checkerboard with him."

Entertainment

718.   Two dirty little boys approached a lady who was wheeling her baby in the park.

"Lady, my brother can do some fine imitations," said the larger boy. "Give us a dime and he'll imitate a chicken for you."

The lady was curious and said jokingly, "What will he do? Crow or lay an egg?"

"Nothing like that, lady," the little boy said. "For ten cents, right before your very eyes, he'll eat a worm!"

96, 383, 701, 723, 1292, 1792, 1850

Escape

719.   A woman, who traveled around the country lecturing on safety, always practiced what she preached. She once arrived at a strange hotel and thought she had better check the location of the fire escape. She started looking for it. She came to an unmarked door and opened it, to find that it was a bathroom. The tub was occupied by a rather heavy-set old fellow.

"Oh, excuse me," she said, "I was just looking for the fire escape."

As she turned and walked down the hall, she heard the patter of bare feet. She turned around to see the refugee from the bathroom, draped in a towel and running after her and shouting, "Wait for me. Wait for me. Where's the fire?"

720.   Two South American wives were talking about their husbands. "No matter what you say about your Juan," said one, "you must admit he is the most handsome man in South America. Everyone agrees on that."

"Oh, I'm not so sure about that," said the other. "It's true he is very, very handsome, but you should have seen the Juan that got away."

721.   The examining board was giving the new policeman his oral examination.

"Suppose you were being chased by a car full of bandits," they asked him, "going seventy-five miles an hour. What would you do?"

"I'd do eighty," the young recruit said.

150, 585

Estimate

722.   "How did you come out selling your cattle this year?"
a neighbor asked a farmer. "Did you get what they were worth?"

"Well, I don't rightly know," the farmer said. "I didn't git as
much as I figgered I might, but then I never thought I would
anyway."

507, 746, 818, 1338, 1573, 1672, 1891

Ethics

723.   Two boxing managers were making plans for the forth-
coming fight.

"Let's get it straight," said one. "At the end of the second
round your man will hit mine and he will go down for the
count."

"No, no," said the other. "Not in the second round; make it
the seventh or eighth. We mustn't cheat the public."

724.   Two women were riding together on a bus. One of them
realized she hadn't paid her fare.

"I'll go give it to the driver now," she said.

"Why bother?" her friend asked. "You got away with it, so
what?"

"I have always found that honesty pays," the first woman said.
And she went up to pay the driver.

"See, I told you honesty pays!" she said when she came back.
"I gave the driver a quarter and he gave me change for 50
cents."

725.   The young stockroom clerk had been stealing from the
petty cash box, when the two owners of the firm caught him.
The first was sore and wanted to turn him over to the police.

The other, giving it more thought, said, "No, let's not forget
that we began in a small way ourselves. I think we should begin
training him to be a junior partner."

726.   It is because of ethics that civilized man developed the
attitude that it is fairer to rob a man with a contract than with
a gun.

Ethics

727.   The owner of a men's furnishing store was teaching his son the business. One day, right after a man had bought a hat, the boy's father called him over and said to him, "Here is something you should learn. It is a lesson in business ethics. You see that man who is just going out the door? He came in and bought a hat. He asked how much it was and I told him ten dollars. He said he would take the hat and gave me a twenty-dollar bill. He thought it was a ten-dollar bill and turned and walked out of the store without getting any change. This, of course, raises a question of business ethics. The question is: Should I tell my partner?"

455, 533, 1156, 1563, 1997

Evaluation

728.   A young lady in Boston volunteered as a blood donor. She was asked by the nurse, "Do you know your type?"

"Oh, yes," she said, "I'm the intellectual type."

729.   The farmer surveyed the damage the flood had done to his place.

"Say," called a neighbor from the road, "I hear your pigs was all washed down the river."

"That's right," said the farmer. "How about Jones's pigs?"

"They're all gone, too," said the man from the road.

"And what about Wilson's pigs?" the farmer asked.

"All gone, too," the man said.

"Well," said the farmer more cheerfully, "things ain't as bad as I thought they were."

730.   The little old lady had been a faithful member of the Baptist church for more than ten years, when one day she showed up at the Methodist church and said she wanted to join.

"But why are you changing?" asked the minister. "Do you find greater truth and comfort in my sermons?"

"No, nothing like that," she said. "It's just that they've cindered the path at the Baptist church and it's too hard to walk on."

Evaluation

731.   A man gave a bottle of cheap liquor to the janitor for Christmas. Later, he asked the janitor how it was.

"It was just exactly right," the janitor said.

"What do you mean just right?" the man asked.

"Well," said the janitor, "if it'd been any better, you wouldn't have give it to me, an' if it'd been any worse, I couldn't have drunk it."

92, 118, 129, 192, 193, 369, 421, 635, 1199, 1337, 1352, 1603

Evidence

732.   The judge had asked the woman why she wanted a divorce from her husband.

"Well, your honor," she said, "for ten years I've had to wash his back every Saturday night."

"You surely don't consider that sufficient reason for divorce," said the judge.

"No," the wife said, "but last Saturday night, his back was already clean."

733.   A man called his wife from the office and said he would like to bring a friend home for dinner that night.

"What?" screamed his wife. "You know better than that. You know the cook quit yesterday, the baby's got the measles, the hot water heater is broken, the painters are redecorating the living room and I don't even have any way to get to the supermarket to get our groceries."

"I know all that," her husband said. "That's why I want to bring him home for dinner. He is a nice young man and I like him. But he's thinking of getting married."

188, 337, 367, 601, 1165, 1173, 1513, 1846

Exaggerate

734.   The little boy rushed into the house. "Mommy," he yelled, "There's a dog in the back yard as big as a horse."

"There you go again," said his mother. "I've told you a hundred billion times not to exaggerate, but it just doesn't seem to do any good."

103, 1507

Examination

735.   The beautiful model who had just been fitted for contact lenses went to see her optometrist. She was terribly upset as she said to him, "It's awful. I've lost my new contact lenses. They were so tiny and hard to see. I think maybe they fell on the floor and were swept out. I'll have to buy another pair. Will you have to examine me all over?"

"Unfortunately, no," said the optometrist, "just your eyes."

82, 194, 227, 581, 617, 1308, 2069, 2092

Example

736.   The boy from the Tennessee mountains wanted to go to Nashville to work. His father was against it.

"But what chance do I have here, paw?" said the boy. "Nothing for me here but being poor and dirty all my life."

"What chance?" said the old man. "Why, look at me, son. When I come here from Kentucky twenty years ago I didn't have a dime to my name. Now I got thirteen kids and eleven dogs."

737.   "And now," said the Sunday school teacher, "I want each of you to recite a Bible verse."

The first little boy got up and said, "And Judas went out and hanged himself."

Immediately, another little fellow in the class said, "Go thou and do likewise."

738.   The little boy had been so much of a problem, that he had been taken to the psychiatrist. The doctor said he must be humored more at home.

His father, trying hard, said to him, "I'll get you anything you want to eat."

"I want a fried worm," the little boy said.

His father fried the worm, and then the little boy said, "Now you eat half."

The father managed to force down half the worm, when, suddenly, the little boy started to scream, "You ate my half!"

115, 134, 207, 656, 864, 1065, 1466, 1858

Exclusive

739.   A man at a cocktail party said to his new girl friend, "I keep hearing you use the word 'idiot.' I hope you are not referring to me."

"Don't be so conceited," she said. "As if there were no other idiots in the world!"

740.   A famous French movie star had just arrived at the New York airport. He was mobbed for over an hour by a crowd of 500 women who wouldn't disperse until each had kissed him. After the experience was over, he said to a friend, "I would have much rather had my choice of one out of that 500 and kissed her exclusively for the entire hour."

31, 141, 668, 1452, 1670, 1704, 1955

Excuse

741.   The lion in the zoo was feeling mean and was looking for a fight. He saw a little field mouse in his cage and roared at him.

"You're the weakest, puniest, most helpless little thing I've ever seen. I can whip you with one swipe of my paw."

"Maybe so," said the mouse, "but don't forget, I've been sick lately."

742.   A man went next door and asked his neighbor if he could borrow his power lawn mower.

"I'm sorry," his neighbor said, "I can't let you have it. My daughter is getting married down in Montgomery, Alabama."

"What's that got to do with you lending me your lawn mower?" the man asked. "That's the silliest excuse in the world. That's no reason for not letting me borrow your lawn mower."

"Listen," the neighbor said. "If I don't want to lend you my lawn mower, any excuse is good enough."

743.   "Insurance is the greatest thing in the world," the eager insurance salesman said to his prospect. "Why, I carry a $75,000 policy on my own life, payable to my wife."

Excuse

"In that case," said the unconvinced prospect, "what excuse do you have for living?"

142, 371, 465, 601, 797, 1054, 2103

Expense

744. Overheard: "I hope they don't raise the standard of living any higher. I can't afford it now."

745. A man and his wife were just checking out of the high-class resort hotel when he noticed a sign over the cashier's desk that read: "Have you left anything?"

As he went out the front door, he whispered to his wife, "That sign should have been, 'Have you anything left?' "

746. The sales manager was talking to the new salesman about his expense account. "I notice," he said, "that a large portion of your expense account is for meals and nightclubs."

"Yes, sir," the salesman said, "I've done a lot of entertaining of buyers and prospective customers."

"That's necessary, and all right," said the sales manager, "but I want to point out that we sell bulldozers, and chorus girls have rarely been known to buy a bulldozer."

87, 518, 541, 1325, 1414, 1479, 2025

Experience

747. A newspaper reporter was interviewing the famous octogenarian.

"If you had your life to live over," he asked, "do you think you'd make the same mistakes again?"

"Certainly," said the old man, "but I'd start a lot sooner."

748. "Have you had any previous military experience?" asked the recruiting sergeant.

"Yes, sir," said the boy from Tennessee. "I was shot at three times before there ever was a war."

Experience

749. The local YWCA displayed a poster offering "A Short Course in Accounting for Women."

The next day, somebody had written, "There is no accounting for women."

750. "You don't love me any more," the man's wife said through her tears. "When you see me crying, you never ask why."

"I'm sorry, darling," he said, "but that sort of question has already cost me an awful lot of money."

751. A personnel director, interviewing an applicant for a job, said, "You ask pretty high wages for a man with no experience."

"Well," the man said, "it's harder work when you don't know anything about it."

4, 483, 614, 664, 673, 768, 1327, 1541, 1797, 2009, 2077

Expert

752. "What does your husband do?" a woman asked her friend.

"He's an efficiency expert," said the other.

"Efficiency expert? What are his duties?" said the first.

"I don't know exactly," said the second woman, "but if women did it, they'd call it nagging."

753. Two men who worked in a service station were chatting. "Do you know how to make antifreeze?" one asked.

"Sure," said the other, "hide her woolen nightgown."

754. The young man had just graduated from college with an engineering degree. He figured he was fixed for life, as he applied for a job with a large corporation.

The personnel director asked him, "What sort of position did you have in mind?"

"A sitting position," the young man said.

755. A man called the hospital in great excitement. "Hurry, get me a doctor!" he shouted. "My wife has appendicitis!"

Expert

"Just a minute and I'll give you the chief operator," said the girl on the switchboard.

756.   The woman was a hypochondriac. She had been pestering the doctors of her small town to death for years. Then one day, a young doctor just out of medical school moved to town. She was one of his first patients.

"I have heart trouble," she told him. She then proceeded to describe in detail a hundred and one symptoms of all sorts of varied ailments. When she was through she said, "It is heart trouble, isn't it?"

"Not necessarily," the young doctor said. "You have described so many symptoms that you might well have something else wrong with you."

"Huh," the woman snorted, "you have your nerve. A young doctor, just out of school, disagreeing with an experienced invalid like me."

3, 53, 57, 264, 484, 685, 773, 910, 1139, 1417, 1920, 1926, 2052

Explanation

757.   Professor: "Of course, you all know what the inside of a corpuscle is like."

Student: "Most of us do, but maybe you'd better explain it for the benefit of those of us who have never been inside one."

758.   A drunk was bouncing up and down as he walked along the street, one foot on the curb and the other in the gutter. A policeman stopped him. "Why are you walking that way?" he asked. "You must be drunk!"

"Drunk? So that's it!" said the man. "For a moment I thought I was lame."

759.   An economist spoke on the "why" and "wherefores" of our economic system. He spoke for an hour and covered the subject well. Following him, the chairman said:

"Ladies and gentlemen, what our speaker has been telling you is that, if your outgo exceeds your income, then your upkeep will be your downfall."

Explanation

760.　A man's wife visited her husband's office unannounced and found his secretary sitting on his lap. "Don't get excited," he cried. "I just didn't have the heart to tell you that business is so bad, I'm studying how to become a ventriloquist."

761.　The bus was crowded, so the gentleman stood up and offered his seat to a young lady.

"Oh, thank you very much," she said. "You're extremely kind."

"Don't pay no mind to what she says, mister," said the woman with her. "I'm taking her to a mental hospital."

762.　A woman was reading the newspaper. "What part of the body is the fracas?" she asked her husband.

"The what?" he asked.

"The fracas," she said, "F-r-a-c-a-s."

"Never heard of it," he said. "What about it?"

"Well, it says here in the paper," his wife said, "that a man was shot last night in the fracas down at the tavern."

763.　A noted minister-humorist was booked to give an evening address in the town hall. Since he was going to be in town, he had consented to speak that same day at a civic luncheon. Because many of the stories he told were the same that he would tell that night, and because he didn't want them to be printed ahead of time, he asked the local newspaper reporter not to put them in his report. The reporter promised not to. Instead, he finished his account of the luncheon meeting with this sentence: "He also told a number of stories that cannot be published."

7, 17, 109, 121, 208, 240, 499, 531, 654, 779, 957, 1258, 1749, 1924

Explosive

764.　Two men were talking about their wives.

"My wife is very touchy," the first one said. "The least little thing sets her off."

"You're lucky," the second man said. "Mine's a self-starter."

Explosive

765.   "Would you please help me," a woman called to her husband from the kitchen. "I can't open this bottle of olives."

The husband tried turning the top but didn't make any progress. He then stepped into the basement workshop. A few minutes later, he returned with the bottle open.

"Thank you, honey," his wife said, "but what did you use to open it?"

"I used a pair of pliers," he said.

"Oh," she said, "from the sound of things down there, I thought you had opened it with a word of prayer."

885, 1096, 1316

Extravagant

766.   Husband: "How much did you pay for that weird-looking hat?"

Wife: "It was on sale, and I got it for a song."

Husband: "Well, if I hadn't heard you sing, I'd swear you had been cheated."

48, 667, 745, 888, 1213, 1309, 1365, 1752, 1849, 2101

Facts of life

767.   A couple of college girls were talking about their future plans. One said she planned to get a job as an airline hostess. "That way," she said, "I'll meet lots of men."

"That might be a good idea," agreed her friend, "but wouldn't you meet just as many men working at some other job?"

"Maybe," she said, "but not strapped down."

768.   Two men, fathers of teen-age daughters, were chatting.

"My daughter doesn't want to get married," said the first.

"That's what you think," the other said. "You just wait until the wrong boy comes along."

86, 367, 439, 1275, 1960

Fame

769. Two overdressed matrons stopped the famous lecturer and author in a theatre lobby one afternoon and said: "Don't you lecture?"

"Yes," said the famous man.

"Oh," said the first lady, "did you lecture yesterday morning at town hall?"

"Yes," he said.

"Oh, we thought we recognized you," said the lady. "We were there. Oh, you were simply won-der-ful, simply won-der-ful! What's your name?"

770. A man took a taxi from the airport to downtown Springfield, Illinois. On the way he asked the taxi driver his name.

"My name is Abraham Lincoln," the driver said.

"That's a mighty famous name around here," the passenger said.

"Well, it ought to be," said the taxi driver. "I've lived here all my life."

771. A famous writer went back to his home town for a visit. While there, he was invited to speak to an audience of his former friends and neighbors. He wanted to show that success had not turned his head and that he was still one of them. So he began, "My dear friends—I won't call you ladies and gentleman, as I know you too well for that."

5, 430, 891, 975, 1459, 1835, 2116

Familiar

772. Two young men met on the street for the first time in over a year.

"I haven't seen you in ages," said the first one. "Did you and Martha ever get married?"

"No," said his friend. "I was out of town for ten months. I wrote her every day. She saw so much of the mailman that she married him."

Familiar

773.   The captain of the river steamer said to the passenger, "I've been traveling this river all my life and I know where every snag and stump and sandbar is."

Just then the boat shook as though it were going to fall apart.

"See," said the captain, "there was one of them."

141, 472, 1187, 1238, 1575, 1834

Famine

774.   Two old buddies met at a class reunion. One was now fat, the other skinny.

"From the looks of you," said the fat man, "there might have been a famine."

"Yes," said his buddy, "and from the looks of you, you might have caused it."

483, 1382

Fan

775.   A baseball fan was making his first visit to the races. He had cautiously put a $2 bet on a 50-to-1 shot. As his horse came down the stretch neck-and-neck with the favorite, he yelled at the top of his voice:

"Slide, yuh bum! Slide!"

Farmer

776.   During the war a farmer stayed home and worked on the farm instead of joining the army. One day while he was milking a cow, a soldier came along and said, "You slacker! Why aren't you at the front?" The farmer said, "Because there ain't any milk at that end."

777.   A man bought a 40-acre place in the country and settled down to farm it. A year later he sold it and moved back to town. One day, he met a friend on the street.

"Back to town again?" asked his friend. "I thought you were a farmer."

"You made the same mistake I did," the man said.

Farmer

778.   A farmer was complaining about hard times.

"But," said the county agent, "you could make a lot of money this year by raising and shipping onions."

"Mebbe so," said the farmer.

"Well, you've got the land and could get the seed onions, couldn't you?" asked the county agent.

"I guess so," the farmer said. "But even if I did, the old woman's too lazy to do the plowing and planting."

26, 27, 42, 53, 57, 58, 101, 315, 332, 495, 497, 501, 578, 1221, 1443, 2088

Fast

779.   A country boy took his city cousin hunting for the first time. As they walked through the woods, a rabbit jumped out of the grass at their feet, ran through the bushes, and disappeared. The city boy never raised his gun.

"Why didn't you shoot?" yelled the country boy.

"Gosh," said his cousin. "He was so fast that I didn't see him until he was out of sight."

780.   "Which travels faster, heat or cold?" asked the science teacher.

"Heat," said the young man.

"What makes you think so?" asked the teacher.

"Well, anybody can catch cold," said the young man.

208, 256, 869, 997, 1267, 1985

Father

781.   A little girl at the beach said to her mother, "Mummy, may I go for a swim?"

"Certainly not, dear, the surf is much too treacherous," her mother said.

"But Daddy is swimming," the little girl protested.

"Yes," said her mother, "but he's insured."

782.   A young lady was bragging to her boy friend about her father. "He always had a natural instinct for business," she said. "By the time he was thirty years old, he had made half a million dollars. Would you like to know how he did it?"

187

Father

"I'd be more interested," he said, "in knowing if he still has it."

59, 216, 234, 264, 280, 324, 368, 379, 400, 450, 476, 557, 582, 642, 1110, 1306, 1577, 1821

Fat man

783.   A 300-pound man was walking past a drugstore when he noticed a penny scale with this notice: "I speak your weight."

He had never seen a scale like that and wanted to try it out. He put a penny in the slot and stepped onto the platform. A voice spoke up:

"One at a time, please, one at a time."

567, 774, 913

Fault

784.   The minister, visiting the prison, said to a man doing six years for burglary, "I hope that since you have come here, you have had time for meditation and have decided to correct your faults."

"I certainly have," said the prisoner. "From now on, when I pull a job, I'll be wearing gloves."

785.   "I'm sure homesick," said one married man as he strolled down the street with his friend.

"Homesick?" asked his friend. "Wasn't that your home that we just passed in the last block?"

"Yes," said the first man, "and am I sick of it!"

82, 261, 1424

Favor

786.   A young lady who knew nothing about flowers was being shown through a friend's new home. On the sun porch she saw a beautiful plant in a pot and asked what it was.

"It belongs to the begonia family," her friend said.

"Oh," the young lady said, "it certainly is nice of you to look after it while they're away."

Favor

787.   The little boy had delivered the bag of apples to the minister's home for the all-day summer festival.

"Thank you, son," the minister said. "It was nice of you to bring the apples by the house. And when I see your mother, I am going to thank her for donating fifteen such beautiful apples."

"Please, sir," the boy said, "when you thank her, how about thanking her for eighteen beautiful apples?"

204, 252, 447, 457, 1127

Fear

788.   When a schoolteacher quit her job, she said to the school board: "In our schools today the teacher is afraid of the principal; the principal is afraid of the superintendent; the superintendent is afraid of the school board; the school board is afraid of the parents; the parents are afraid of the children. And today's children are afraid of nobody."

789.   A man who was really unaccustomed to public speaking, arose in confusion after dinner and muttered hesitatingly:

"M-m-my f-f-friends, when I came here tonight only God and myself knew what I was about to say to you—and now only God knows!"

790.   Two farm boys were talking at recess.

"My dad made a scarecrow last summer," said the first, "that was so real-looking that it frightened every crow off the farm."

"That's nothing," said his friend. "My uncle made one that scared them so much they brought back the corn they stole the year before."

49, 139, 168, 276, 349, 548, 600, 1061, 1756

Fellowship

791.   A bum asked a man for 20 cents for a cup of coffee. The man said, "How come you want 20 cents? Coffee is only a dime."

"Yes, I know," said the bum, "but I've invited a friend to meet me."

Fellowship

792.   A mental patient was chatting with the new superintendent at the state hospital. "We like you a lot better than we did
the last doctor," he said.

The new superintendent was obviously pleased. "And would
you mind telling me why?" he asked.

"Oh, somehow you just seem so much more like one of us,"
the inmate said.

793.   The committee chairman was lining up cars for the fraternity picnic.

"How many will your car hold, Joe?" he asked.

"Well," Joe said, "it'll generally hold four, but you can get six
in if they're well acquainted."

27, 625, 820

Fertilizer

794.   The Sunday school teacher was using an Easter lily to
illustrate the miracle of life. "Now," she said, "who can tell me
what makes this beautiful lily blossom forth from this drab-look-
ing little bulb?"

"God does it," said a little girl promptly.

The small son of a farmer spoke up and said, "Fertilizer
helps."

497

Fiction

795.   A customer asked the manager of the bookstore: "Do
you have a book called *Man, the Master of Women?*"

"The fiction counter is to the left," he said.

796.   Two friends were chatting about a friend who was a
writer.

"Which of his works of fiction do you consider the best?" the
first asked.

"You should have read his last income-tax return," the second
said.

Fiction

797.   A little girl said to her mother, "Mama, do all fairy tales begin with 'once upon a time'?"

"No," said her mother, "Sometimes they begin with 'Honey, I had to work late at the office.' "

798.   "That's a mighty fine dog you have there," a fellow told his friend.

"He ought to be," his friend said. "I paid a hundred dollars for him. He's part beagle and part bull."

"Is that so?" asked the first, "which part is bull?"

"That part about paying a hundred dollars for him," a by-stander said.

679

Fight

799.   A witness had told about seeing a fight where two men had beat each other up with chairs.

"Why didn't you try to establish peace?" the judge asked. "Didn't you think about that?"

"Yes, I did, Judge," the man said, "but I couldn't find another chair."

800.   One night in a resort hotel there was a loud argument in one of the rooms that could be heard all over the place.

"What's all the noise about?" asked a guest.

"They're having a battle of wits," said the desk clerk.

"A battle of wits?" asked the guest. "Who's in the room?"

"Shimkowitz, Lefkowitz and Horowitz," said the desk clerk.

801.   A man was arrested and hailed into police court for creating a disturbance at his girl friend's house.

"Liquor again?" asked the judge.

"No, your honor," said the man. "This time she licked me."

802.   The fight had been a slow one, and as two fans were leaving Madison Square Garden, one said, "What did you think of it?"

Fight

"Awful," said the other. "If me and the wife would put on a bout like that, the kids would boo us."

61, 100, 123, 382, 684, 723, 1396

Filling station

803.   A mother drove into a service station with her young son and asked the man to check her tires. Before the attendant could get to the tires, the boy jumped out of the car and started to check the tires.

"You get back in the car and let the man do it," his mother yelled at him. "What do you think we pay gasoline taxes for?"

594, 753, 1511

Finance

804.   When the fund-raising drive for the new church building was being organized at a church supper, the minister opened the meeting by saying: "I want to begin by asking the $64,000 question. Is there anyone in the congregation who will start this drive by giving $64,000?"

805.   A minister who was putting on a fund-raising drive for a new church school addition reminded his congregation of the late W. C. Fields and his famous remark when a friend tried to borrow some money. "I find myself in a most embarrassing situation," Fields said. "All of my available assets at the moment are tied up in ready cash."

806.   Scientists have come up with a new theory that we are taller in the morning than in the evening. That theory may be new, but we have always known that we're shorter around the end of the month.

807.   A man put a second mortgage on his house to buy a new car. Then he borrowed on the car so he could buy a boat and trailer. Then he went to another loan office to borrow enough to buy an outboard motor.

Finance

"If I make the loan," asked the broker, "how will you manage to buy gas for the car and the boat?"

"Well, it seems to me," the man said, "that anybody who owns his own house, car, boat, motor, and trailer should be able to get credit for gas."

808. A young man was reading the evening newspaper and said to his father: "Dad, it says here that a certain man was a financial genius. What does that mean?"

"That means," said his father, "that he could earn money faster than his family could spend it."

809. Several men were in a bar arguing about who was the greatest inventor. One said Fulton, who invented the steamboat; another said Edison; another said Marconi; and still another said the Wright brothers.

Finally, one of them turned to a quiet man who had not given his opinion. "What do you think?" he was asked.

"Well," he said, "the man who invented 6% interest was nobody's fool."

810. The owner of the supermarket said to the new check-out clerk, "Our daily audit shows that you are $20 short in your accounts."

"Oh, but you're wrong," said the new check-out girl. "The store may be $20 short, but I'm $20 ahead."

87, 119, 120, 126, 179, 470, 506, 1906

Fishing

811. An inmate in a mental hospital sat fishing in a bucket of water. A visitor, wishing to be friendly, asked, "How many have you caught?"

"You're the ninth," the fellow said.

812. An irritated mother said to her young son: "Why didn't you tell me you wanted to go fishing?"

"I guess it was because I wanted to go fishing," he said.

Fishing

813.   Isn't it great to get in the boat and go fishing again and lie in the sun?

814.   Two friends, fishing on a Sunday morning, were feeling rather guilty.

"I suppose," said one, "we should have stayed home and gone to church."

"I couldn't have gone to church anyway," said the other. "My wife's sick in bed."

815.   The man had been fishing all day and hadn't caught a single fish. On his way home he stopped at the local fish market. When the clerk asked what he wanted, he said, "Just stand over there and throw me five of the biggest trout you have."

"Throw 'em? What for?" asked the clerk.

"So I can tell the wife I caught them," he said. "I may be a lousy fisherman, but I'm no liar."

816.   A real dedicated fisherman was telling another real fisherman about a wonderful dream he'd had. "I dreamed I was out on Buckeye Lake, alone in a canoe with the queen of the striptease artists."

"Boy, what a dream," said his friend. "How did it turn out?"

"Perfect," said the first fisherman. "I caught an eight-pound bass."

817.   A man had been fishing all day with no luck.

"Let's see your bait," said the old-timer.

The fisherman showed him his minnows. The old-timer tied a minnow to the hook by its tail, pulled a bottle of corn liquor from his pocket and poured some of it over the minnow. He gave it back to the man and said, "Now try it."

Immediately, there was a strike, and after a battle, the man landed a four-pound bass. He wasn't hooked. Instead, the minnow had it by the throat.

818.   The little boy had been fishing all afternoon. A man, who had just walked up, asked him, "How many have you caught today?"

Fishing

"Well," said the boy, "if I catch this one that's nibbling, and then two more, I'll have three."

819.   A man had a reputation for lying about his fishing exploits. To prove his stories, he bought a meat market scale and installed it on his back porch. After that he could always back up his fish stories.

One day a friend rushed in excitedly to borrow the scales. He was back in 10 minutes, full of excitement. "Congratulate me," he cried. "I'm the father of a 24-pound baby boy!"

820.   The little girl watched her father and his friends put off in their boat.

"But, Mommy," she asked, "why do fish like so much beer?"

821.   The fisherman was arrested for catching 12 more black bass than was permitted by law.

"Guilty or not guilty?" asked the judge.

"Guilty," said the fisherman. "They were biting so well, I just couldn't bring myself to stop catching them."

"Twenty-five dollars and costs," said the judge.

After he had paid the fine, the fisherman asked, "And now, your honor, may I have several copies of the court record to show my friends?"

822.   Two friends met on the street and decided to go fishing the following morning. "You bring your boat and trailer," the first one said, "and I'll bring the lunch."

The next morning about six o'clock the man with the boat and trailer pulled up in front of his friend's house and honked his horn. Right away his friend came out of the house with a big shopping bag full of lunch—four bottles of whiskey and a loaf of bread.

The man with the boat and trailer looked so surprised, that his friend said, "Anything wrong?"

"Oh, no," the man said, "there's nothing wrong. But what in the world are you going to do with all of that bread?"

77, 250, 285, 384, 387, 576, 963, 1181, 1599, 2001

Flattery

823.   "This crime," the state's attorney said, "was the work of a master criminal. It was carried out in a skillful and extremely clever manner."

Embarrassed, the defendant rose to his feet and said, "Sir, flattery will get you nowhere. I ain't gonna confess."

824.   "It's queer," said a man one night at dinner, "but the biggest idiots always seem to marry the prettiest women."

"Oh, now," said his wife, "you're just trying to flatter me."

326, 427, 739, 1399

Flirt

825.   A woman stopped to talk to a little boy she saw smoking. "Aren't you ashamed of yourself," she said. "Does your mother know you smoke?"

He looked up at her and said, "Lady, does your husband know you stop and talk to strange men on the street?"

14, 260, 1630

Florida

826.   A New Englander was listening to the Florida cracker bragging about the weather.

"Do you mean to say," he asked, "that in Florida you have 365 days of sunshine every year?"

"That's right," said the Florida cracker. "And that's a mighty conservative estimate, too."

827.   A man went to the funeral of a friend to pay his respects. In the funeral home, the widow was standing at the end of the casket. The man looked down at his former friend and said, "Doesn't he look wonderful!"

"Why not?" asked the widow. "He was in Miami all winter!"

828.   A Florida cracker died and knocked on the pearly gates.

"Where are you from?" asked St. Peter.

"From Fort Myers," the man said.

Florida

"Well, you can come in if you want to," St. Peter said, "but you won't like it."

829. "The weather here in Florida is so wonderful," said the tourist to the native. "How do you tell summer from winter?"

"In winter we get Cadillacs, Lincolns, and stuffed shirts," the native said. "In summer we get Chevrolets, Fords, and stuffed shorts."

830. "Not for me," said a woman to her friend. "You'd never get me to live in Florida. They never have Christmas down there."

"What do you mean, they don't have Christmas in Florida?" asked her friend. "Certainly they do."

"No they don't," said the first woman. "The sign in the airline office said it's always June in St. Petersburg."

70, 77, 652, 1585

Flowers

831. "What kind of flower is that in your buttonhole?" asked a fellow.

"Why, that's a chrysanthemum," said his friend.

"It looks like a rose to me," the fellow said.

"No, you're wrong, it's a chrysanthemum," said his friend.

"Spell it," the fellow said.

"K-r-i-s . . . by golly, it is a rose!" said his friend.

832. A fellow stopped by the florist's to buy some flowers for his girl friend.

"You want to say it with flowers, sir?" asked the florist. "What about three dozen American Beauty roses?"

"Make it one dozen," the fellow said. "I'm a man of few words."

833. "My, what pretty roses," the lady said as the man stopped his push cart in front of her house. "I don't want any today, but if you will come by next Thursday morning, I would like to buy

six or seven dozen to decorate the living room. My daughter is coming out that day, you know."

"Thanks, lady," the man said. "I'll be here. And I'll bring the prettiest roses I can find. I know how you feel about your daughter coming out. What was she in for?"

423, 661, 786, 794, 846

Food

834.   A recruit asked the mess sergeant what they were going to have for supper.

"Oh," said the mess sergeant, "we have thousands of things to eat tonight."

"What are they?" asked the recruit.

"Beans," said the sergeant.

835.   "Are these good eggs?" the customer asked.

"Yes," the waitress said, "these are the best eggs we have had for years."

"Well," said the customer, "bring me some you haven't had so long."

836.   "It looks like rain," said the waitress as she placed a bowl of soup in front of a customer.

"It sure does," he said, "but it smells a little like soup."

837.   A shoemaker proudly presented his handiwork to the great explorer. "Here are the boots for your next arctic expedition. Did you like the boots I made for the last trip?"

"They were excellent," the explorer said. "In fact, they were the best boots I ever ate on any of my trips."

838.   The man selling hot dogs on the boardwalk was shouting, "I don't care where you go or what you pay, you can't get better."

"That's right, you can't," said a young fellow passing by. "I ate one last week and I'm not better yet."

839.   The lady of the house answered the doorbell. There stood the same tramp back for the tenth time.

Food

"Look here," she said, "why do you always come to my house to beg?"

"Doctor's orders, lady," the tramp said.

"What do you mean, doctor's orders?" she asked.

"He told me," the tramp said, "that when I found food that agreed with me, I should stick to it."

113, 116, 221, 240, 300, 331, 340, 386, 478, 1472

Foolish

840.   A woman who was reading a magazine said to her husband, "Here is an interesting story. It's about a man who reached the age of 50 without learning how to read or write. He met a woman, and because of her, he made a real scholar of himself in two years."

"That's nothing!" said her husband. "I know a man who was highly educated and brilliant at 50. He met a woman, and because of her, he made a fool of himself in two days."

841.   "A man is a fool to get married," shouted a man at his wife during a family fight. "Why, he leads a dog's life."

"That's right," screamed his wife. "He growls all day, lies around underfoot all evening, and snores all night."

188, 245, 283, 712, 1801, 1810

Football

842.   While watching a football game that was being played on a muddy field, one coed said to the other, "My, I don't see how the players ever get clean!"

"Oh, don't be naïve," said her friend. "That's what the scrub team is for."

155, 267, 522

Foresight

843.   A young man bought an engagement ring and said to the jeweler, "I'd like some names engraved on it."

"What names?" asked the jeweler.

Foresight

"From Joe to Hazel," said the young man.

"Take my advice," the jeweler said, "and have it engraved simply, 'From Joe.' "

844.   The father thought he would prepare his little three-year-old daughter for the impending arrival of the stork.

"The stork has been flying over our house," he told her one evening when they were alone in the living room.

"I hope he doesn't frighten Mommy," the little girl whispered. "She's pregnant, you know."

845.   A fellow was whistling at his work one morning and seemed much gayer and happier than usual.

"You seem to be unusually cheerful this morning," his friend said. "What's going on?"

"It looks like I am finally making headway with my new girl friend," the fellow said. "I think we'll be getting married before long."

"Congratulations," his friend said. "Did she accept your proposal?"

"Not exactly," said the fellow, "but last night when I asked her again to marry me, she said she was saying no for the last time."

190, 750, 964, 1411, 1463, 1504, 1885

Forgive

846.   "Jack and I have parted forever," a girl said to her friend.

"Good gracious," her friend said. "What does that mean?"

"A dozen roses in about an hour," said the girl.

649, 1395

Fortunate

847.   A bachelor was complaining about being single. "A bachelor has no one to share his troubles," he said.

"Huh," said his married friend. "A bachelor doesn't have any troubles."

Fortunate

848.　The crowded cocktail party was at its height. In an effort to keep things moving, the hostess was introducing everybody to everybody else as she moved through the room.

"I'd like you to meet Mr. Simmons," she said to a pretty young girl who just happened to be a former girl friend of the young man.

Figuring she would put him in his place a bit, the young lady held out her hand and said, "I'm sorry, but I didn't get your name."

"I know you didn't," the young man said, "but it wasn't because you didn't try."

263, 1400, 1909

Fortune

849.　A little boy lost a baby tooth and tucked it under his pillow. The next morning he collected a dime from the fairies. That night he snitched grandma's upper plate and tucked it under his pillow, hoping to get enough money to buy a bicycle.

850.　A rich old fellow was chatting with a pretty girl he had just met at a cocktail party. "I don't want to sound fresh," he said, "but you are one of the prettiest young ladies I have ever met. I'd give fifty dollars just for one of your kisses."

"How terrible," she said.

"Please," he said, "I didn't mean to offend you."

"Oh," she said, "I wasn't offended. I was just thinking what a fortune I have been throwing away."

858, 1977

Fortune-telling

851.　"What does this mean?" cried a customer at the drive-in. "There's a roach in the bottom of my teacup."

"Don't ask me, lady," said the waiter. "If you want your fortune told, go to a gypsy teahouse."

783, 1048

Frankly speaking

852.   One man who told the truth was the candidate who was defeated in the election and who said he was glad he was defeated because he wouldn't have to keep all the promises he had made during his campaign.

853.   A local Republican candidate said he would give the Negro who showed the best reason for being a Republican the generous reward of a fine, live turkey.

The first said he was a Republican because the Republicans had set the slaves free. The second said he was a Republican because it stood for economy in government.

The third man won when he said, "I'm a Republican because I want that turkey."

854.   The holdup man was ready for trial and he asked his lawyer:

"How long do you think this business is going to last?"

"For me, two hours," the lawyer said. "For you, two years."

855.   A girl said to her date: "You remind me of the sea."

"You mean," he said, "because I am so wild, magnificent, and romantic?"

"No," she said, "because you make me sick."

856.   "Doctor," a woman said as she rushed into the office, "I want you to tell me frankly exactly what's wrong with me."

He looked her over from head to foot, then said, "Madam, I have three things to tell you. First, you are about fifty pounds overweight. Second, your looks would be improved if you took off several layers of rouge and lipstick. And third, I'm an artist. The doctor's office is across the hall."

857.   A wife said to her husband at breakfast, "You swore at me in your sleep last night."

"Who was asleep?" he asked indignantly.

858.   Three ministers were having lunch together and wandered onto the question of what they would do if they were given a check for a million dollars. The first said he would build a

new addition to the church. The second said he would start an orphanage. They turned to the third and asked him what he would do.

"The first thing I'd do," the minister said, "would be to tell the church board to go jump in the river."

176, 261, 434, 721, 1530

Freedom

859. The man had just been freed after a long prison term. It was a happy day in his life. He stood in front of the prison gates and cried, "I'm free, I'm free."

A little girl who was playing across the street, looked at him for a few moments and said, "That's nothing to holler about. I'm four."

860. "You are guilty of assault and battery," the judge said. "But before I sentence you, do you have anything you would like to say?"

"Yes, your honor," the man said, "I would like to explain that all I was doing was waving my arms around taking exercises and all that happened was my hand hit his nose. A man has a right to swing his arms around, doesn't he?"

"Yes, he has," the judge said, "but a man's freedom to swing his arms around ends where the other man's nose begins."

596, 974, 2091

Friendship

861. Two men were talking about a friend.

"Since he lost his money," the first man said, "half his friends don't know him."

"And what about the other half?" the other man said.

"Oh," said the first man, "they haven't found out he lost it."

862. "When I was broke," a man told his neighbor, "Harry volunteered to lend me $100."

"Did you take it?" his neighbor asked.

"No," the man said. "That kind of friendship is too valuable to lose."

Friendship

863.   Two long-time friends of the neighborhood were greeting each other. "Good morning," said the first. "You're looking fine this morning."

"I'm sorry I can't say the same for you," said the second.

"You could," said the first, "if you were as big a liar as I am."

864.   Two men were chatting, when the name of a mutual friend was mentioned. "Are you a friend of Harry's?" the first asked.

"Are we friends?" the man said. "Twenty years we're friends. There's nothing I wouldn't do for Harry and there's nothing he wouldn't do for me. In fact, for twenty years, as I said, we've gone through life together, doing absolutely nothing for each other."

865.   The home-town boy had become a successful television star. One day, on a visit back home, he bumped into an old friend.

"How are things with you?" the television star asked.

"Well, since you asked," said the friend, "my wife's in the hospital. I just lost my job. My mother's sick, and I'm behind in the rent. I sure could use a small loan."

The television star stalled around for a few minutes, explaining his own situation. In the end, his answer was "no."

"There's one thing I have to say about you," said his old friend. "Success hasn't changed you a bit."

866.   "I'm sick of marriage," said the new bride. "Bill hasn't kissed me once since I came back from my honeymoon."

"Why, that's been three months," her friend said. "Why don't you divorce him?"

"Divorce him?" said the bride. "Oh, you misunderstand. I'm not married to Bill!"

867.   The little girl came home rather upset, after playing all afternoon with her next-door neighbor. "I just don't know what was wrong with Jean, Mother," the little girl said. "She was rude and mean all afternoon and she kept fussing and fighting."

Friendship

"I should think that you'd have come right home in that case," said her mother.

"Well, I didn't," said the little girl. "I just slapped her face and stayed."

868.   A man was in an accident and sued the insurance company for $1,000 and won his case. When he received his check, he called on his lawyer to settle up.

"How much do I owe you?" he asked the lawyer.

"Well," said the lawyer, "I'll tell you how it is. Since I am an old friend of yours and your father before you, my fee will be only $900."

"I'm sure glad," the man said as he made out his check for $900, "that you weren't a friend of my grandfather's too."

869.   A doctor who had developed his work to a streamlined, fast routine was consulted by a young man. After a ten-minute examination, he gave the young man a prescription, shook his hand, and pushed him toward the door.

The young man thanked the doctor and said, "I came to see you because my father, Bill Miller, spoke of you so often."

"What?" said the doctor. "You are old Bill's son? For goodness' sake, young man, tear up that prescription and come in my office and tell me what's wrong with you."

13, 31, 204, 260, 407, 464, 627, 1524

Fun

870.   The four-year-old's birthday party was well organized by the neighborhood ladies, with games, races, and treasure hunts. In the midst of the confusion, one little boy asked, "When this is all over, can we play?"

645, 898, 1177, 1333, 1405, 1883

Funeral

871.   At a funeral when no one had gotten up to say a good word about the deceased and all was quiet, one man stood and said, "If nobody has anything else to say, I'd like to say a few words about Texas."

Funeral

872.   As the speaker was standing at the head table chatting with people following his address, the local minister shook his hand and said, "That certainly was an interesting and inspiring talk. It gave me some good ideas for a funeral."

34, 73, 350, 371, 423, 707, 1062, 1160, 1970, 1991, 2013

Furniture

873.   A furniture salesman won a free trip to France as first prize in a sales contest. He didn't speak a word of French, but that didn't seem to bother him. The first night he was there, he decided to go out on the town. In the lobby of his hotel, he saw a rather charming young lady.

He asked her if she spoke English. But, instead of speaking to him, she drew pictures for him on her notebook.

She drew a picture of a wine glass. All the salesman had to do was nod his head, and they ended up in a cafe drinking champagne. Later, she drew a picture of a stage and after nodding his head, they went to the theatre. After the show was over, she got out her pencil and notebook and this time she drew a picture of a four-poster bed.

Later, when he told his friends back home about his trip, he said, "How in the world she knew I was in the furniture business, I'll never know."

625

Futility

874.   "Did he leave much money when he died?"

"No, not a cent. It was this way, he lost his health getting wealthy, then he lost his wealth trying to get healthy."

130, 392, 637, 1188, 1471

Gallantry

875.   One day a man visited a large department store to buy his wife some nylon hose. Inadvertently, he got caught in a mad rush at a counter where a bargain sale was going on. He soon

Gallantry

found himself being pushed and stepped on by frantic women. He stood it as long as he could. Then with head lowered and elbows out, he plowed through the crowd.

"You, there!" said a woman. "Can't you act like a gentleman?"

"Not any more," he said. "I've been acting like a gentleman for an hour. From now on, I'm acting like a lady."

876.　Two women were chatting about a neighbor.

"Is he ever gallant," said the first. "A perfect gentleman."

"What do you mean he's gallant?" asked her friend.

"Well, yesterday, coming home on the bus, he saw that I was tired, bushed from the whole day's work," she said. "So what did he do? He made his wife get up and give me her seat."

283, 420, 425, 761, 1437, 1994

Gambling

877.　A businessman was stopped in front of the post office one day by a stranger. "I'm sure you don't remember me," said the stranger, "but five years ago I came to this town broke. I asked you for ten dollars and you gave it to me. You said you never turned down an opportunity to start a man on the road to success."

"I remember that day," said the businessman.

"Well," said the stranger, "are you still game?"

878.　"Are you sure about what you have just said?" the lawyer shouted at the witness.

"Yes," he said, "I'm sure."

"You'll swear it is true?" the lawyer said.

"Yes," said the witness, "I swear it is true."

"Would you bet a thousand dollars on the truth of that statement?" the lawyer cried.

"Yes, I would," the witness said. "That is, if I could get the right odds."

879.　A man rushed into the police station at three o'clock in the morning.

Gambling

"Sergeant, you've got to help me," he said. "My wife stays out every night gambling. She's a fiend for it. She neglects the children and her home. It's terrible! Now, at three o'clock in the morning, she's in a dive—gambling."

"Do you know where?" asked the police sergeant.

"Yes, she's playing in a clubroom up over a cafe on Decatur Street," said the man.

"I'll tell you what I'll do," said the obliging sergeant. "I'll throw the fear of God into her. I'll send a police car and raid the place."

"That's fine," said the man. Then after a brief moment he asked, "Do you think you can arrange it without arresting my mother?"

880. A man was stopped on the street and asked for a handout by a tramp. The man said, "I never give to tramps. But, here's a cigar, that will cheer you up anyway."

"I don't smoke, thank you," said the tramp.

"Well," said the man, "I just happen to have a bottle in the glove compartment of my car, how about a drink to warm you up a bit?"

"No, thank you," the tramp said. "I don't drink."

"Well, as I said, I don't give money to bums, but I'll make you a sporting proposition. I have two dollars running on a horse at the track tomorrow. I'll put a couple of bucks on him for you and tomorrow after the race, I'll give you half of the winnings—how's that?"

"No, sir," said the tramp. "I don't gamble. Look, mister, all I want is something to eat. How about buying my dinner?"

"All right," said the man. "I'll do it, on one condition. Get in the car and go home with me. I want to introduce you to my wife. I want her to take one look to see what happens to a fellow who doesn't smoke or drink or gamble."

881. Two farmhands had been shooting crap one Saturday night and had lost all of their money. They got in their pickup truck and headed for home. They soon came to a country lane where an old sow was sound asleep just over the fence.

Gambling

"Hey," said one of the boys. "I know a man in town who would give me five dollars on that old sow and we could get back in that game and clean it out."

They agreed that would be a good idea and set about to get the sow into the back of their truck. The hard part was getting her over the fence. Just as they were ready to put her in the truck, they looked up to see a car coming. The little red light, flashing on the top, told them it was the sheriff. They didn't know what to do. They didn't have time to put the sow back over the fence. Instead they had the bright idea of putting the sow in the cab of the truck between them. They were just driving off, when the sheriff pulled alongside and threw his spotlight on them.

"Who are you and what are you doing down this country road this time of night?" he shouted.

"Oh, our car just stalled. We're on our way home. We're the McGee boys. We live just down the road," one of them said.

"The McGee boys?" demanded the sheriff. Then, pointing his light, he said, "What's your name?"

"I'm John," the boy in the driver's seat said.

"And what's your name?" the sheriff said, shining his light in the face of the boy on the far side of the cab.

"Oh, I'm Henry," the boy said.

"And you in the middle, there," the sheriff said, shining his light on the sow, "what's your name?"

Just then the driver gave the sow a mighty poke in the ribs to which she responded with a loud "Oink."

"O.K., you boys," the sheriff said. "I guess you are all right. Get going. And don't stop on the road late at night like this, if you don't want to get into trouble."

The boys took off in the truck as fast as they could go. The sheriff turned around and headed back to town. As he drove down the road, he said to his deputy, "You know, I've been around here all my life, but that Oink McGee is the ugliest man I ever saw."

882. The horse player's wife was having a hard time getting her husband to visit the doctor's office for a checkup. Finally,

she talked him into going if she would go with him. So, on the day of the appointment, they went together to the doctor's office.

As they walked down the hall toward the office, the husband came to a full stop and said, "It's all off. I'm not going through with it. Especially not to that doctor."

"What do you mean," cried his wife, "especially not to that doctor? What's wrong with that doctor?"

"Look at the odds against me," the horse player said as he pointed to the sign on the doctor's door. "Nine to four."

883.   A man had listened to the encouragement of a friend who had touted a certain horse pretty highly. The next day, after the horse had come in last, he saw the tipster and screamed, "Brother, have I got it in for you. That horse you told me to bet on came in last."

"Last?" the fellow said. "I can't understand it. He should have been able to win that race in a walk."

"That's the way he tried it," said the man, "but he still came in last."

352, 505, 717, 775, 1063, 1218, 1392

Gardener

884.   A rather snobbish type woman was visiting the rich writer and was being shown through his formal garden.

"What is that?" the lady asked as she passed a sundial.

The writer told her it was a sundial and explained how the sun moving through the heavens cast a shadow, which is recorded on the dial, thereby telling the time of day.

"My goodness," said the lady, "these modern inventions! What will they think of next?"

Gas

885.   The inspector from the fire department was interviewing the badly burned man in the hospital. "Tell me if you can," he said, "exactly what happened."

Gas

"Well, I went home with my friend and as he opened the front door, I thought I smelled gas. I mentioned it to him and he said he thought he smelled it too. He lit a match to see. . . ."

"A match?" cried the inspector. "Why, that was the last thing to do."

"Yes," said the man. "That was the very last thing he did."

166, 223, 513, 594, 1393

Generosity

886.   A man came home drunk without his pay check and his wife asked him what he had spent it for and he said, "I bought something for the house."

"What," she asked sarcastically, "did you buy for the house?"

"Ten rounds of drinks," he said proudly.

887.   The country boy was visiting the county fair with his girl friend. As they passed a popcorn stand, the girl said, with a hint in her voice, "That's sure nice, ain't it?"

"What's nice?" asked the boy.

"That popcorn. Doesn't it smell grand?" asked the girl.

The boy sniffed for a moment, and said, "It sure does. Here, let's walk a little closer so you can get a better smell."

888.   Two college boys were chatting. "Yesterday, I took a girl to the coke bar in the afternoon," one said, "and I paid for that. Then I took her to the drive-in for a hot dog and I paid for that. After that, I took her to a movie, and I paid for that. Then I took her to a nightclub and I paid for that. Do you think I should have kissed her good-night?"

"No," said the other. "I think you did enough for her for one day."

889.   "I feel real generous today," a woman told a friend. "I started the day out by giving a dollar to a bum."

"You gave a bum a whole dollar?" her friend asked. "What did your husband say?"

"He said, 'Thanks,'" the first woman said.

133, 222, 377, 407, 466, 746, 791, 1371, 1715

Genius

890.   A man and wife were at the theatre and the husband was admiring the leading man. "He's good," whispered the man to his wife. "Isn't it wonderful how convincingly he displays affection for the leading lady?"

"Yes, he's pretty good," said his wife, "but after all, he's been married to her for fifteen years."

"What!" said her husband. "Really married? Gosh, what an actor! Pure genius."

891.   During homecoming day at the college, visitors and students lined up in the cafeteria and ate together in the crowded dining room.

One pretty young co-ed sat at the same table with the world-famous astronomer who had returned for a day at his alma mater.

"And what do you do?" the co-ed asked.

"I study astronomy," the man said.

"What, at your age?" she said. "Why, I finished astronomy in my freshman year."

687, 808, 1856

Gentleman

892.   A rather battered-up and crestfallen-looking fellow ran into a friend.

"What's the matter?" he asked. "You really look sad."

"I am sad," said the man, "because last week I saw a man hit a girl."

"You didn't let him get away with it?" asked his friend.

"I did not," said the man. "I walked right up and told him that only a coward would strike a lady. I asked him why he didn't hit a man. I just came out of the hospital this morning."

263, 425, 523, 572, 583, 1078, 1637, 1965

Genuine

893.   A rich playboy was telling a friend about giving his girl friend a string of pearls for Christmas.

Genuine

"Why," said his friend, "didn't you give her something more practical—like an automobile?"

The playboy smiled and said, "Did you ever hear of an imitation automobile?"

894. "Why, that's a counterfeit five-dollar bill," a man screamed at his wife. "How in the world were you stupid enough to let somebody slip a counterfeit five-dollar bill in your change?"

"How could I tell?" she asked. "You never let me have enough real money for me to learn to tell the difference."

483, 739, 1261

Gift

895. Niece: "Thanks very much, Uncle Wilbur, for the birthday gift."

Uncle Wilbur: "Oh, that's nothing to thank me for!"

Niece: "That's what I thought, but Mother told me to thank you, anyway."

896. "What is the difference between electricity and lightning?" the teacher asked her class.

"The main difference," said a little boy, "is you don't have to pay for lightning."

102, 192, 233, 279, 284, 378, 731, 1283, 1893

Girls

897. "See that girl over there?" the smart young man said. "She's fresh from the country and it's up to us to show her the difference between right and wrong."

"Okay, pal," his friend said. "You teach her what's right."

898. There are more important things in life than money—but they won't have anything to do with you if you're broke.

131, 370, 441, 476, 519, 538, 582, 1184

Golf

899. The self-confident golfer teed up, looked toward the green, and said to his friends: "This is good for one long drive and a putt." He took a powerful swing and topped his ball. It rolled about 35 feet.

He walked over to his ball, took his stance, and snapped, "Now for one record-breaking putt."

900. A nerve specialist was explaining his technique to a colleague.

"I always ask the patient," he said, "if he plays golf. If he says yes, I tell him to stop, and if he says no, I tell him to start playing."

901. At a local country club golf tournament, the club secretary caught one of the members driving off about two feet in front of the teeing mark.

"Here," he cried. "You can't do that. You're disqualified!"

"What for?" demanded the golfer.

"Why, you just drove off in front of the mark," the secretary said.

The player looked at the secretary angrily. "Go back to the clubhouse where you belong," he said, "I'm playing my third stroke."

902. "What do you think of my game?" said the duffer to his friend.

"Oh, it's all right, I guess," said his friend, "but I still prefer golf."

903. A golf pro was trying to teach a new pupil how to swing his club.

"Now just go through the motions," he said, "without hitting the ball."

"I can already do that," the pupil said, "I want you to teach me to hit it."

Golf

904. "If you don't keep your big mouth shut," the golfer cried to the caddy, "you'll drive me out of my mind!"

"That ain't no drive, mister," said the caddy. "That's a putt."

905. A dentist was leaving his office to play golf, when the phone rang.

"Oh, doctor, I'm in great pain," said a voice. "I must see you at once."

"I'm sorry," the dentist said, "but I already have an appointment to fill eighteen cavities this afternoon."

906. The man was so proud of his skill at golf that he had brought his mother-in-law along to watch him play. He sent her on ahead of him so she would get a good view of his first tee shot.

As he teed off, he said to his friend, "I really want to make a terrific drive today. That's my mother-in-law standing down there."

The other man looked and shook his head in doubt. "I don't think you can make it. You can't expect to hit her at two hundred and fifty yards."

907. The duffer was slicing and hooking his way around the course. He felt the look of scorn from his caddy, and he said to him, "I'm not playing my usual game today."

"No, sir," said the caddy, "and what game is that?"

908. A pretty girl was seated next to a golfer at dinner, and all he talked about was golf. Toward the end of the banquet, he said apologetically, "Goodness! I'm afraid I've ruined the evening by talking about nothing but golf."

"That's all right," said the girl, "but would you mind telling me, what is golf?"

909. The golf widow was complaining to her husband about the time he spent playing golf. "You don't love me anymore," she said. "All you do is think about golf. Why, you don't even remember the date of our anniversary."

"I certainly do," he said. "It was the day after I shot one over par at Greenwood Country Club."

910.　　Two female members of the country club approached the new golf pro the first day he was on the job.

"Do you want to learn to play golf, lady?" he asked the first lady.

"Oh, no, it's my friend here who wants to learn," she said. "I learned last week."

911.　　Four men were putting out on the 18th hole when a ball landed at their feet and rolled within six inches of the hole.

"Who would do a silly thing like that?" one of the men cried. "He didn't even holler at us. It might have hit somebody."

"I don't know about that," one of the others said, "but he sure made a good shot. He almost got a hole in one."

"Hey," said the third, "let's give him a big thrill. Let's kick it in the hole and when he comes up in a few minutes, he'll think he got a hole in one and it will tickle him to death."

That's what they did. In a few minutes, a man walked up with his putter in his hand. "Did anybody see a ball come this way?" he asked.

"Yes," said one of the foursome, "there it is—in the hole."

"In the hole?" the man screamed. "Wonderful, I made a nine."

912.　　The minister had given up golf during Lent. But his golf clubs were still in the trunk of his car.

One day as he passed the golf course, he decided he'd just drive a few. "That's not the same as playing," he said to himself. But, after driving a few, the minister found himself playing down the fairway in absolute disregard to his lenten pledge.

Looking down on this was a little angel, who ran to his boss and said, "Lord, look what is happening. The minister broke his pledge. What should we do about it? What sort of punishment should we give him? How about letting me hit him with a bolt of lightning?"

Golf

"How terrible!" said the Lord. "We've got to punish him properly. Lightning isn't bad enough. But first, let's see how he does on this next hole."

As the Lord and the angel watched, the minister teed up his ball and made a mighty swing. It soared for three hundred yards, hit a tree and bounced off to the right, up a dogleg for a hundred yards, hit a rock and bounced another hundred yards to the green, where it rolled gently into the cup.

"Did you see that?" cried the angel. "A hole in one on a four-hundred-and-twenty-yard dogleg. Why, Lord that's the greatest golf shot in the history of the game. What sort of punishment is that?"

"That is his punishment," the Lord said. "The greatest golf shot in history—and whom can he tell?"

913. The fat, overdressed golfer joined a foursome on the first tee. Seeing that he had two caddies, one of the players asked, "Why do you have two caddies?"

"It's this way," said the duffer, "I always have to send one back for laughing."

914. Golfer (to foursome ahead): "Excuse me, but would you mind if I played through? I've just heard that my wife has had a bad accident."

128, 173, 242, 465, 1182, 1490, 1847

Good-bye

915. "My husband has lost all his money on the stock exchange," the woman told her neighbor.

"How terrible," said her friend. "I do feel sorry for him."

"Yes, so do I," said the man's wife. "I'm afraid he'll miss me so."

916. The foreman had been at the plant about eight months. He still had the feeling that he wasn't popular with his men. One day, he asked an old-timer, "What's wrong here that the men don't seem to like me? Why, when I left my last job, the men presented me with a 17-jewel wristwatch."

Good-bye

"Only 17-jewels!" cried the worker. "Gee, if you'd leave here, we'd make it a 21-jewel watch."

917.   After about an hour of listening to one of the guests at a cocktail party do bird imitations, his listeners were fit to scream.

"And now," he said, "I'll show you a real tough trick. You name a bird—any bird—just name any bird, and I'll imitate it."

"A homing pigeon," shouted half a dozen voices at once.

79, 193, 222, 298, 304, 581, 592, 616, 651, 972, 1122, 1380, 1770, 1992, 2060

Gossip

918.   An understanding wife received a call from a gossipy neighbor. "I feel that I should tell you that I saw your husband at Atlantic City," she reported, "walking along the beach with a pretty blonde on his arm."

"Well, what would you expect him to have on his arm at his age?" the wife said, "a bucket and shovel?"

919.   A lady asked her next-door neighbor, "What did you hear at the Opera yesterday?"

"All sorts of exciting things," said the neighbor. "The Wilsons are going to have a baby, Mrs. Jones has dyed her hair, and the Johnsons are getting a divorce."

920.   Two women were talking over the back fence. "Wasn't that something," the first one said, "the way Lucy's stove exploded last night? The explosion blew her and her husband right out of the front door into the street!"

"Yes," said the other. "That's the first time they've gone out together in thirty years."

72, 277, 405, 588, 596

Government official

921.   A stranger walked up to a farmer and showed him his card:

Government official

"I am a government inspector," he said, "and I am entitled to inspect your farm."

A few minutes later the farmer heard screams from his pasture, where the inspector was being chased by a bull. Leaning over the gate, shouting at the inspector at the top of his voice, the farmer cried: "Show him your card, mister—show him your card!"

73, 164

Grafting

922. A boy who was reading a political editorial looked up and asked his father:

"Dad, are political plums raised from seed?"

"No, my boy," was the answer, "only by expert grafting."

726

Grammar

923. The third-grade teacher was quizzing the class in English grammar.

"Is it correct to say 'You have et'?" she asked.

"No, that's wrong," said the boy in the front seat.

"Why is it wrong to say, 'You have et'?" the teacher asked.

"Because," said the boy, "it's only ten o'clock and I ain't et yet."

252, 488

Grandma

924. A little boy's grandmother came to visit the family. This was the first time he had met her.

"Who are you?" asked the little boy.

"I'm your grandmother," she said, "on your father's side."

"Well, all I can say is, you're on the wrong side around here," said the little boy.

925. Grandmother was trying to get on the good side of her five-year-old grandson. "Will you give me a kiss if I give you a penny?" she asked.

Grandma

"A penny!" he said. "Shucks, I get that much for taking castor oil."

926.   One of the greatest puzzles in the world is how the boy who wasn't good enough to marry the daughter can become the father of the smartest grandchild in the world.

80, 366, 439, 714, 1300, 1521

Grapes

927.   Two drunks were chatting at the bar. "They say that more than 60,000 carloads of grapes were grown in California last year," the first drunk said to his buddy.

"We'd better start drinking," said the second, "they're gaining on us."

Gratitude

928.   A minister married a young couple who came to his house late one night. Following the ceremony, the groom took him aside, and whispered: "I am sorry, sir, I don't have any money to pay your fee, but if you will take me down to your cellar, I'll fix your electric light meter so that it won't register."

929.   A man asked his boss: "Is it all right if I take tomorrow afternoon off to go shopping with my wife?"

Boss: "Absolutely not, we are too busy."

Employee: "Thanks a lot."

930.   The woman had received a beautiful skunk coat for Christmas—a gift from her husband.

"My," she said with excitement, "I just can't understand how a beautiful coat like that could possibly come from such a miserable evil-smelling little beast."

"Well," said her husband, "I didn't exactly expect any gratitude from you, but I do think I deserve a little bit more respect."

202, 278, 607, 916, 1531, 2043

Grief

931. A farmer's mule once kicked his mother-in-law in the head and she died. A huge crowd turned out for the funeral, most of them men. The minister, following the ceremonies, said: "This lady must have been very popular. Look at the large number of people who have left their work to come to her funeral."

"They're not here for the funeral," said one of those who had come. "They're here to bid on the mule."

34, 599, 1702, 1870, 2121

Grocer

932. The farmer's wife sold her butter to the local grocer. One day when she came to deliver some butter to the grocer, he complained.

"The butter you brought in last week was underweight," he said.

"That's odd," the woman said. "Somehow I had misplaced my pound weight, so I just used that pound of sugar you sold me last week."

933. A lady said to the supermarket manager, "It sure is tough when you have to pay ninety cents a pound for meat."

"Yes," said the manager, "but it's tougher when you pay only forty."

96

Growth

934. A little girl was telling her father about the things she had learned that day at school. "The teacher told us about a baby that was fed on elephant's milk and gained over twenty-five pounds in a month," she said.

"Ridiculous!" said her father. "Why, that's impossible. Whose baby was it?"

"The elephant's baby," said the little girl.

1498

Guarantee

935.   "You said when you sold me this car," the customer said, "that you would replace anything that broke or was missing?"

"Yes, sir, we guarantee to do that," the car salesman said. "What is it?"

"Well," said the customer, "I want two front teeth and a collarbone."

936.   "How do I get ahead fast in business?" a young college graduate said to an older friend with lots of experience.

"The first thing to do is to find a girl with a good job and marry her," his friend said.

376

Guest

937.   The weekend guest was being driven to the station by the family chauffeur.

"I hope you won't let me miss my train," he said.

"No, sir," the chauffeur said. "The boss said if I did, I'd lose my job."

938.   There were guests coming and the little boy had been sent to wash his hands. A moment later, from the bathroom, he called, "There's only clean towels in the bathroom, mamma. Shall I start one?"

217, 348, 403, 1747, 1969

Habit

939.   Husband: "My wife has a habit of sitting up every night until two and three o'clock in the morning and I can't break her of it."

Sympathetic friend: "Why does she sit up that late?"

Husband: "Waiting for me to come home."

940.   Lecturer: "What a man becomes in later life depends on the formation of his habits when a child."

Habit

Man in audience: "That's right. When I was a baby my mother paid a nurse to wheel me about, and I have been pushed for money ever since."

380, 582, 732, 960, 1028, 1104, 1240, 1594, 1755

Happiness

941.   If you want to bring happiness to a loved one, repeat one of the six phrases: (1) I love you; (2) dinner is ready; (3) all is forgiven; (4) sleep until noon; (5) keep the change; (6) here is that ten.

942.   The Sunday school teacher said to her class, "It is our duty to make someone happy during the week. Have you done it?" she asked the little boy.

"Yes," he said without a moment's hesitation.

"That's fine. What did you do?" asked the teacher.

"I went to see my Aunt Jane, and she was happy when I came home," he said.

261, 288, 501, 1070, 1273, 1514

Hard work

943.   A man who habitually came home drunk was cornered by his wife in a bar where he was dreamily toying with a shot of whiskey. Being in a gracious mood, he offered her a sip, but when she took it she gagged and sputtered, and said:

"How in the world can you stand to drink that horrible stuff?"

"See, I keep telling you," he said, "and all the time you thought I was out having a good time!"

944.   "How long have you worked in that bank?" a fellow asked his friend.

"Ever since they threatened to fire me," the friend said.

57, 146, 155, 218, 296, 320, 335, 395, 555, 586, 1126, 1151, 2113

Hat

945.   A young man went into a department store to buy a pillowcase.

Hat

"What size?" asked the saleslady.

"I don't know," he said. "But, I wear a size seven hat."

66, 90, 284, 498

Health

946.   A man of 80 got a perfect score on a medical checkup. The doctor asked him how he kept in such good condition.

"When I was married 50 years ago," the man said, "my wife and I agreed that if I lost my temper, she would remain quiet. If she lost her temper, I would take a walk. I attribute my good health to the well-known advantages of a daily hike in the woods."

947.   "You've got to give up smoking," the doctor said.

"I don't smoke," the patient said.

"Well, then, you've got to give up coffee," the doctor insisted.

"Never drink it," the patient told him.

"Whiskey," the doctor said. "You've got to give up whiskey."

"But," said the man, "I don't drink whiskey either."

"What do you do?" the doctor shouted at him. "If you don't have anything to give up, how do you expect me to be able to treat you?"

113, 232, 300, 320, 381, 456, 1612, 1953, 2080

Heaven

948.   "Stand up," shouted the preacher, "if you want to go to heaven."

Everybody stood up but one old man.

"Don't you want to go to heaven, brother?" asked the preacher.

"Yes, sir," the man said, "but I ain't going with no excursion."

828, 1162, 1517, 1539, 2065

Help

949.   A lady who had just passed her test for her first-aid certificate was on her way home. Suddenly, she saw a man lying

224

face down in the street. Without a second thought, she threw herself upon the man and began applying artificial respiration.

After a while, the man raised his head and said, "Lady, I don't know what you're trying to do, but I'm trying to fish a wire down this manhole."

950. A man fainted on the street and a crowd quickly gathered.

"Give him air!" shouted a man. "Clear the way. Hurry up someone, get him a drink!"

The man's eyes fluttered open and he gasped, "Please, make it a double martini."

951. "Did you know," a fellow asked his friend, "that George was held up on the way home last night?"

"Well," said his friend. "How else could he have made it?"

44, 148, 462, 471, 486, 659, 765

Helpful suggestion

952. A lady in a supermarket said to the manager: "Please give me a pound of those turnip greens. My husband is fond of them. Have they been sprayed with any kind of poison?"

"No, lady," said the supermarket man, "you'll have to get that at the drugstore."

953. The businessman had been speaking before the high school assembly. During the question-and-answer period a young man asked, "Sir, in one sentence, what would you give as a rule for success in business?"

"That's easy," said the businessman. "Sell your wrist watch and buy an alarm clock."

23, 58, 705, 1071

Hen

954. The young married woman and her husband had moved to the country to live, and she was on her first visit back home to the city.

Hen

"So you like country life," her father said. "Are your hens good layers?"

"They're experts," the young lady said. "They haven't laid a bad egg yet."

955.   A woman in the supermarket said to the clerk, "How much are your eggs, today?"

"Eighty-four cents a dozen, lady," the clerk said.

"That certainly is high," the woman said. "That's seven cents an egg. That's ridiculous."

"That may be ridiculous to you, lady," the clerk said, "but it's a full day's work for a hen."

54, 365, 1034, 1108, 2105

Henpecked

956.   "You ought to stand on your two feet and show your wife who is running things at your house," a big, bossy fellow said to his henpecked friend.

"There's no need to," his friend said, "she already knows."

957.   Invited to stop for a drink with his friends following the lodge meeting, a henpecked husband said he had to hurry home. "I can't stop," he said, "I've got to go home and explain to my wife."

"Explain what?" one of his friends asked.

"I don't know," he said, "I'm not home yet."

958.   "Dad," said a little boy, "there's a limerick contest in the magazine. I can win a hundred dollars if I guess the last words. Can you help me out?"

"Get your mother to do it," said his father. "She's better at last words than I am."

959.   "Why don't you stop picking on me?" a husband said to his wife. "I'm trying to do everything possible to make you happy."

"There's one thing you haven't done that my first husband did to make me happy," she said.

Henpecked

"What's that?" asked her husband.

"He dropped dead," she said.

960.   The police chief said to the sergeant, "Did you give that hoodlum the third degree?"

"Yes," the sergeant said. "We browbeat him and badgered him with every question we could think of."

"And what did he say?" the chief asked.

"All he did was doze off and whisper now and then, 'Yes, my dear, you are perfectly right,' " the sergeant said.

961.   A jury was being selected in a murder trial. The attorney for the defense was challenging prospective jurors. He questioned one man, "Are you married or single?"

"Married, for ten years," the man said.

"Have you formed or expressed an opinion?" asked the attorney.

"Not for ten years," said the man.

962.   The doctor was giving some bad news to a friend about his wife. "This is a serious case," the doctor said. "I hate to tell you, but your wife's mind is gone, completely gone."

"Well, I'm not surprised," said the man. "She's been giving me a little piece of it every day for fifteen years."

963.   Some of the fellows were going on a fishing trip and thought it would be nice to invite their new neighbor, a young Chinese student. Although the student learned rapidly, he still got a bit mixed up in his English.

The evening before the fishing trip, he called his friends to say he could not go because, as he said, "Something came down."

One of his friends laughed and said, "You mean to say that something came up."

"No," said the Chinese, "down is the right word. My wife's foot."

19, 101, 161, 257, 584, 600, 764, 2024

Heredity

964.   "I hope you understand," said the girl's father, "that when you marry my daughter you will be getting a bighearted and generous girl."

"Oh, I certainly do," the fellow said, "and I hope she inherited those fine qualities from her father."

965.   Two men were talking about a used-car salesman.

"I've never heard a man talk so fast in all my life," said the first.

"That's not surprising," said his friend. "His father was a tobacco auctioneer and his mother was a woman."

966.   Asked to define heredity, a small girl wrote, "Heredity means that if your parents didn't have any children, you won't have any either."

97, 332, 926

High cost of living

967.   "From our scientific studies," the professor said, "we find that other planets may not be able to support life."

The hard-pressed student said: "It isn't exactly easy on this one either."

968.   The man's wife had gone home to spend two weeks with her mother. A friend of his stopped him on the street and said, "How do you manage without your wife these days?"

"A lot cheaper," he said, "a whole lot cheaper."

504, 744, 1480

High pressure

969.   The new real estate salesman asked his boss if he shouldn't refund the money to a customer who was sore because the lot he had bought was under water.

"What kind of a salesman are you?" shouted the boss. "Go out there and sell him a motor boat."

155, 314, 471, 1876

Hillbilly

970.   The hillbilly was on his first visit to town. He couldn't get over the asphalt streets. He stomped his feet on the hard surface and said, "Well, I can't blame 'em for building a town here. The ground's too hard to plow, anyhow."

971.   A hillbilly stopped at a tavern with his wife and six-year-old boy. "We're thirsty, bartender," he said. "How about two shots of straight whiskey?"

"What's the matter, Paw?" the little boy asked, "ain't Maw going to drink with us?"

691, 736, 748, 1389, 1651, 1925

Hint

972.   A bus driver had been looking particularly downcast for several days. Finally, his boss asked: "What in the world is wrong? You look like you had lost your best friend."

"Oh, it's my wife," the bus driver said. "I think she wants to get rid of me."

"What gave you that idea?" asked his boss.

"Oh, for the past week," the bus driver said, "she has been wrapping my lunch in a road map."

973.   Two fathers of teen-age daughters were talking in their car pool. "What is the tactful way for a girl's father to let her boy friend know it's time to leave?" asked one.

"The way I do it," said his friend, "is to casually walk through the room with a box of breakfast food."

102, 589

History

974.   The history teacher asked her class, "What did the Puritans come to this country for?"

"To worship in their own way," said the little girl, "and to make other people do the same."

975.   The professor was lecturing on literature and said, "If Shakespeare were here today, he would be considered the greatest man alive."

History

"That's easy to understand," said a student. "He'd be more than 300 years old."

98, 1032, 1190, 1914

Hobo

976.   Two men of the road were lying on the green grass beside a country road. Above them was the warm sun. Birds were singing in the trees. It was a quiet, restful, peaceful scene.

"Boy," said the first, "right now I wouldn't change places with anybody—not for a million bucks."   .

"How about five million?" asked his friend.

"No, not even for five million," said the first tramp.

"Well," said the other, "how about ten million?"

The first one sat up. "Well," he said, "that's different. Now you're talking real money."

218, 1155

Homesick

977.   The woman with the nasal, raspy voice was singing "My Old Kentucky Home." An old man in the corner bowed his head and wept quietly.

A lady leaned over and whispered, "Excuse me, but are you a Kentuckian?"

"No, lady," said the man. "I'm a musician."

978.   A mother received this letter from her little girl at camp:

"Dear Mommy: I am having a wonderful time. I am not homesick. The food is good. The camp is good. The weather is good. The Counseler is good. Love, Annie. P.S. When you come to visit me, please take me home."

230, 785, 1946

Home town

979.   A freshman reported to the coach for basketball. He said, "I'm a little stiff from bowling."

Home town

The coach said, "I don't care where you're from. Get in there and show me what you can do."

5, 517, 552, 771, 865, 1210

Honesty

980.   In a political debate, one of the candidates said, "There are hundreds of ways to make money, but only one honest way."

"How is that?" demanded his opponent.

"Aha," said the first, "I knew you wouldn't know."

981.   The tailor said to his client: "I'm sorry, but I can't give you any more credit, sir. Your bill is bigger now than it should be."

"I know it is," said the man. "Make it what it should be and I'll send you a check."

982.   As the three ladies picked up the concert program, each put on a pair of glasses.

"Of course, I really need mine only for close reading," said the first.

"I wear mine only when the light is poor," said the second.

The third was honest. "I rarely wear mine," she said, "except when I want to see."

983.   "Why are you washing your spoon in your finger bowl?" asked the waiter.

"So I won't get egg all over my pocket," replied the customer.

984.   A Tennessee mountaineer was sitting under a tree chatting with a neighbor, when his boy came up the road carrying a chicken.

"Where did you get that chicken?" he asked the boy.

"Stole it," the boy said.

The mountaineer turned to his friend and said, "That's my boy. He may steal, but he won't lie."

Honesty

985.   The little boy was standing a little too close to the apple counter. The supermarket manager said to him, "Say, son, are you tryin' to steal those apples?"

"N-no, sir," the boy said, "I'm tryin' not to!"

986.   A man had been working for a lumber yard for twenty-five years. During that time, whenever he wanted any lumber, he had helped himself to it. In fact, he had stolen so much lumber that he became one of the richest men in town. He became so rich and prominent that he was made a deacon in his church.

This worried him because he felt he shouldn't serve as a deacon with this terrible sin on his conscience. One night, as he pitched and tossed in his bed, the thought occurred to him that he could go to the local priest and confess. The next morning he asked the local priest about it and the priest said it was a bit unusual for a Protestant to come to confession, but he would be glad to hear him.

After the man had told the priest about stealing all of the lumber, he said, "You know, Father, this thing they say about confession is good for the soul, that's right. I never felt so relieved in my life, and that's all there is to it, isn't it?"

"Why, no," said the priest. "You can't lie and steal and lead a life of sin for twenty-five years and come down here and talk to me for thirty minutes and wipe the slate clean. You've got to do something to make it right with the Lord. Did you ever make a Novena?"

"No, I never did," said the man, "but if you've got the plans, I can get the lumber."

987.   It was during the Christmas rush and the parcels at the post office had been treated rather roughly. When the package was delivered to the minister's study, it was broken open and very little remained of the wrapping except some loose paper and a bit of string. But the contents were all there—a dozen Bibles.

"Excellent," said the minister. "No harm done at all. The Bibles are undamaged. And all twelve of them are here. We certainly are lucky that none of them is missing."

Honesty

"Oh, I don't know," said the postman. "I just think it's because none of the fellows over at the post office are religious enough to want to steal a Bible."

145, 332, 396, 413, 448, 723, 787, 1837

Honeymoon

988. "Darling," said the bride, "let us try to act like old married folks and make people believe we've been married a long time."

"Okay, honey," he said, "but do you think you are strong enough to carry both suitcases?"

989. The bride and groom from the hills of old Kentucky had just registered in the motel and had been shown to their room. The bride had been thrilled with everything up to that point, but when she saw the twin beds her face fell.

"What's the matter?" asked her husband.

"Oh, nothing, I guess," she said, "but I was hoping we would have a room all to ourselves."

286, 630, 866, 1852

Hookey

990. A boy, who played hookey from school to go fishing, met a friend on his way home. His friend saw that he was carrying a fishing pole, and said, "Did you catch anything?"

"No," said the boy, "I ain't been home yet."

1726

Hope

991. The schoolteacher was trying to persuade her children to buy a copy of the class picture. "Just think," she said, "how nice it will be to look at this picture when you're grown up and say there's Mary, she's married, or that's Harry, he's a lawyer."

A little fellow added innocently, "And there's teacher, she's dead."

Hope

992.   One night while the men at the firehouse were playing checkers a man wandered in rather casually and said to the captain, "I hate to bother you fellows, but my wife has disappeared again and I want to report her as a missing person."

"We are sorry to hear that," the captain said, "but you aren't supposed to make a report like that to the fire station. You should go see the police."

"Oh, no," cried the man, "not the police. I told them the last time and they went out and found her and brought her back."

383, 658, 667, 849, 1294, 1679

Hopeless

993.   A man's wife came home late for dinner. "I've been to the beauty parlor," she said.

Her hungry husband looked at her and said: "Oh, you didn't get waited on, did you?"

994.   "Please don't get upset," said the curate to one of his parishioners. "You mustn't cry, really, dear lady. The bishop will assign you a fine pastor to take my place. I'm sure he will be much better than I."

"But," said the little lady, "that's just what they promised us the last time."

995.   Two college boys were chatting. "Did you hear what happened to the girl who wore cotton stockings to the dance?" said the first.

"No, what happened?" asked the second.

"Nothing," said the first.

176, 442, 749, 1263, 1390, 2022

Horse racing

996.   A minister visited a small church in the Kentucky Blue Grass. His sermon was against horse racing. Later he was told that the principal supporter of the church was a wealthy horseman. The next week he said to the man, "It seems that I touched

on one of your weaknesses, sir, but I assure you, it was not personal."

"Oh, that's all right," the horseman said. "It's a mighty poor sermon that doesn't hit me somewhere."

997.   A man from Arizona showed up at Pimlico with an eight-year-old that had never raced before. Since an eight-year-old nonstarter is a pretty poor gamble, he was the long shot of the day. He won and paid $480.

The stewards suspected dirty work and asked the owner, "Why haven't you raced him before?"

"To tell the truth," said the Westerner, "we couldn't catch him till he was seven."

998.   A confirmed horse player was on the way to the track with a friend.

"Gosh," he said, "I hope I break even today. I sure do need the money."

882

Horses

999.   "He's a nice-looking horse," the man told his friend, "and the owner says I can have him for a song. Do you think that's a good deal?"

"It all depends," his friend said, "on your eye for a horse and his ear for music."

1000.   "Son, go fetch the old horse," a farmer told his son.

"Why the old one, Paw?" the boy asked.

"My motto is wear out the old one first," his father said.

"Then you go fetch the horse, Paw," the boy said.

1001.   A young lady had just had her first riding lesson.

"I never thought," she said, "anything filled with hay could be so hard."

1002.   The farmer went up to the barn to see how the new farmhand was doing. "Where's that horse I told you to take out and have shod?" he asked.

"Did you say 'shod'?" asked the new man. "I thought you said 'shot.' I've just buried her."

1003.   The owner of the third-rate race horse had just put his jockey up and was giving him some instructions for the upcoming race.

"Hold him back a little," he told the jockey. "We don't want everybody to know what he can do. Try to bring him in about third or fourth."

When the race was over, the owner said to his jockey, "That was fine. You came in third, just as I wanted. But tell me, do you think you could have passed those other two horses?"

"Oh, sure," said the jockey, "our horse could beat them any day, but I'm not so sure about him beating those four horses behind us."

1004.   It was the man's first day at the dude ranch. The cowboy assigned to him asked, "Do you prefer an English saddle or a Western?"

"What's the difference?" the man asked.

"The Western saddle has a horn," said the cowboy.

"Oh, I don't think I'll need a horn," the man said. "I won't be riding in heavy traffic."

1005.   A crowd had gathered on the courthouse lawn to witness what looked like the makings of a fight.

"What's going on?" a fellow asked.

"Oh," said the other. "Two men arguing. They swapped horses about an hour ago and each one claims the other one cheated him."

"Well, why don't they swap back?" the first asked.

"I don't know," said the other, "unless they are afraid of getting cheated again."

1006.   It was the young man's first visit West and he was staying at a dude ranch. His first day there he sat watching a cowboy do a bit of fancy riding. When the show was over, he said he would like to ride and so a rather gentle horse was picked out for

Horses

him. He had no sooner mounted than he found himself lying in the dust at the horse's feet.

"That horse sure does buck, doesn't he?" the fellow said.

"Buck?" said the cowboy. "Why, that little filly didn't do anything but cough."

140, 484, 491, 495, 734, 1620, 1693, 1918, 1932

Hospital

1007. A man entered a hospital for an examination. Just as soon as he had been assigned to his room, he heard a knock at the door. "Come in," he said.

In came a woman. "I'm your doctor," she said. "Please take off your clothes."

The man asked her if she meant for him to remove all of his clothing. She told him yes, that she wanted to give him his examination. So he took off all his clothes and she examined him, thoroughly. When she finished her examination she said, "Now, you may get into bed. Before I leave, do you have any questions?"

"Just one," said the man. "Why did you knock on the door?"

1008. A young minister was just getting acquainted with his duties. One of his first chores was to visit the hospital where a member of his flock was confined as a result of an automobile accident. The man had been seriously injured: a broken leg, both arms broken, a broken collarbone, terrible cuts over his face and head, and several broken ribs.

He was so thoroughly bandaged and taped and strapped up that only his two eyes and mouth were showing.

The young minister was at a loss for words, but realized that he must say something, so he asked the man: "How do you feel today? I suppose all of those broken bones and cuts cause a great deal of pain. Do you suffer very much?"

"No, not much," the man said, "only when I laugh."

173, 416, 650, 755, 892

Hospitality

1009. A man had been duck shooting in the marshes. When it grew dark, he found that he had wandered miles from the motel where he was staying. Rather lost, he walked until he came to a farmhouse. It was a very cold night and he was tired and hungry. He pounded on the farmhouse door, and at last a window opened and a man's voice yelled, "What do you want?"

"I want to stay here all night," shouted the man.

"That's all right with me," yelled the farmer, slamming the window, "stay there all night."

1010. As the guest was leaving the resort hotel, the room clerk said, "I hope you enjoyed your stay with us, sir."

"The bed was too hard," the guest said, "and the price too high. The food was lousy, the service was slow, and there was too much noise. But, I must say, I certainly enjoyed your ice water."

1011. A man said to his wife one evening, "We ought to have the Wilburs over some evening."

"The Wilburs? I should say not," said his wife.

"Why not, dear?" asked her husband.

"Because we had them over three months ago," she said, "and she never has recuperated."

1012. "Well," said the young man to his bride, "I guess if worst comes to worst, we could go and live with your parents."

"Oh, we couldn't do that," she said. "They're living with their parents."

1013. A man checked into a hotel and when he was getting ready for bed, picked up a little book on the telephone table titled *The Bedside Reader*.

On the inside cover was a suggested list of articles to read for certain occasions. "If you are down in the dumps and discouraged," it read, "read page 42."

The man read that article and looked again in the front of the book. "If you are lonesome and restless," it read, "read page 67." The man turned to page 67 and read it. Then, he noticed that someone had written at the bottom of the page with a ball-point pen, "If you're still lonesome and restless, call AT 8-0479 and ask for Irene."

466, 1130

Hotel

1014. A young man from a small town, who had a good job in the city, invited his old mother to come to town for a visit. He gave the old lady the best room in the hotel, one with a private bath adjoining. The next morning the boy asked, "Did you have a good night's rest?"

"Well, no, I didn't," she replied. "The room was all right, and the bed was comfortable. But I couldn't sleep very much, for I was afraid someone would want to take a bath, and the only way to it was through my room."

1015. The man had just registered at the hotel and the bellhop was walking away with his key and bag when the clerk said, "Excuse me, sir, do you mind telling me your name?"

"My name," cried the man, "can't you see what I have written on the registration card?"

"Yes," said the clerk, "that's why I asked."

217, 348, 423, 591, 623, 645, 706, 745, 1058, 1649, 1941

Humility

1016. A man wrote to a company for some information and said: "I don't want any advertising material—and no salesman." Like most companies, they ignored the warning and sent a salesman.

When the salesman showed up, the man said: "I told them in plain language, no salesman!"

The salesman, a young man making his very first call for the company, said: "Mister, I'm the nearest thing to a no-salesman they've got."

1017. A father asked his son one evening about his schoolwork. "How do you stand in your class?" he asked.

Humility

"I'm second from the top, Dad," said the boy. "There's just one girl ahead of me."

"What!" cried his father. "Surely you're not going to let her get away with that. When I was a boy, I would never let a mere girl get the better of me."

"What you don't realize, Dad," the boy said, "is that girls aren't nearly so 'mere' as they used to be."

911

Hunger

1018.   A tramp knocked on the door of a house. "Lady," he said when the lady of the house opened the door, "I haven't had a bite in days." So, to be kind to him, she bit him.

1019.   The new dog chewed his leash in two in the middle of the night and proceeded to raid the pantry. The incident was announced throughout the house as soon as Mamma entered the kitchen.

Right on her heels was Papa who said, "What all did he eat?"

"Everything in the pantry," Mamma said, "except the dog biscuits."

115, 219, 240, 340, 416, 624, 1100, 1298, 1771, 1976

Hunting

1020.   After all day in the duck blind, one hunter said to his friend, "It's getting late and we haven't shot a thing. Let's go home."

"Okay," said the friend, "but first let's miss two more big Canadian geese and then go home."

1021.   A customer was carefully stirring and searching in his bowl of oyster stew. The waiter watched him for some time and finally said, "You sometimes find a pearl in an oyster stew."

"I'm not looking for pearls," the customer said, "I'm trying to find an oyster."

Hunting

1022. The smart little boy said to his father, "Dad, do you know how to catch a squirrel?"

"No," said his father, "how do you catch a squirrel?"

"Climb up a tree," the little boy said, "and act like a nut."

1023. Two men had been sitting in a duck blind for about ten hours. They had taken more shots from their bottle than they had at any ducks. After the bottle was empty, they decided they would give it up as a bad day. Just one more shot, they said. In a few minutes a solitary duck flew over. The hunter, who was much the worse for his day in the blind, raised his gun and blasted the duck out of the sky.

"Wonderful," said his friend. "A fine shot."

"That's nothing," said his drunk friend. "Usually, when I shoot into a flock like that I get half a dozen."

55, 272, 440, 779, 1051

Husband and wife

1024. Husband: "I passed Harry on the street today and he didn't speak to me. I suppose he thinks I'm not his equal."

Wife: "You sure are his equal! Why, he's nothing but a card-playing, whiskey-drinking bum."

1025. A meek little man appeared before the judge in an accident case.

Judge: "Did you have complete control of yourself at the time?"

Little man: "No, Judge, my wife was with me."

1026. A man was fussing with his wife about her extravagance.

"What do you mean, extravagant?" she screamed. "All the money I spend is for the necessities of running this house. You are the one who spends our money foolishly."

"When have I ever spent any money foolishly?" he asked.

"Well, for one thing," his wife said, "look at that stupid fire extinguisher you bought for the kitchen. That was two years ago and we've never used it yet."

Husband and wife

1027. The badly bruised woman was telling the judge her story: "Your Honor, he gets up every morning and starts knocking me around the bedroom. He hits me in the head with his fist. Sometimes he uses a shoe. If I don't fix his meals just the way he likes them, he throws the pots and pans at me. If I dare to open my mouth, he hits me with a beer bottle. Your Honor, that man ought to be in jail."

Looking at the defendant, the judge asked: "What have you to say about this?"

"You can't believe a word that woman says, your Honor," said the man. "She's punch drunk."

1028. Two women were having lunch together and gossiping about their various friends.

"I hear that Helen has married again," said the first woman. "Isn't that her second husband?"

"Second?" cried her friend. "Goodness, no. It's her fifth husband."

"Her fifth?" said the first. "Why, he's not a husband, he's a habit."

14, 117, 162, 231, 245, 269, 388, 430, 559, 778, 920, 1618

Idea

1029. The young lady was blonde and pretty. She said to the floorwalker in the department store, "Do you have any notions on this floor?"

"We do, lady," said the man, "but we have been told to suppress them during working hours."

402, 424, 491

Identification

1030. The young lady stood at the teller's desk in the bank. The teller looked at the check she wished to cash and asked her if she could identify herself.

Identification

For a moment she seemed bewildered. Then, she pulled a small mirror from her handbag, glanced in it, and said, "Yes. This is me all right."

1031. A man's wife gave him a new electric razor for a birthday present. The razor was made for alternating current, and when the man traveled, he always checked to make sure the hotel had AC current.

Once in Ft. Lauderdale, he phoned the switchboard of his hotel and asked, "Is there AC current or DC current in this hotel?"

The girl at the switchboard said, "Just a moment, please, and I'll let you know."

After a few minutes, the telephone operator came back on the line again and said, "I'm sorry, sir, but neither of the gentlemen is registered."

1032. "I'm Mr. Brown's wife," said a beautiful brunette, introducing herself to a ravishing blonde at the annual office party.

"Oh, I'm so pleased to meet you," said the blonde. "I'm his secretary."

"Oh," said Mrs. Brown, "you were?"

1033. A friend of the judge dropped in for a visit one morning before court opened and looked around. "My, you certainly have a tough-looking bunch of roughnecks and crooks to try this morning, haven't you?" he said.

"Oh, not so bad," said the judge. "You're just looking at the wrong bunch. Those are the lawyers."

1034. A high wind caught the nearsighted farmhand's hat, and took it across the field. He started after it at once.

Suddenly, a woman cried out from a nearby farmhouse, "What are you doing there?"

"I'm after my hat," he said.

"Your hat," said the woman. "That's our little black hen you're chasing."

Identification

1035. A man was getting ready to leave the restaurant, when he was tapped on the shoulder. "Excuse me," he was asked, "but do you happen to be Mr. Wilson of Trenton, New Jersey?"

"No, I'm not," the man said.

"Well," said the first man, "I am Mr. Wilson of Trenton, and that's his overcoat you're putting on."

1036. "Is this Bill?" said the voice on the phone.

"Yes, this is Bill," the fellow said.

"Doesn't sound like Bill," said the first voice.

"It's me all right," said the second voice.

"Can you lend me $10, Bill?" asked the first.

"I'll ask Bill as soon as he comes in," said the second.

1037. "Is there any alcohol in cider?" the man asked.

"Inside whom?" his friend wanted to know.

1038. The new maid was lazy and the lady of the house was trying to tell her so without giving her an actual reprimand.

"Look," she said to the maid as she pointed to the dust on the piano, "the dust is so thick that I was able to write your name in it last night."

"Yes," said the new maid. "I noticed that and I meant to speak to you about it. You should have spelled it with two r's."

97, 223, 258, 328, 337, 359, 440, 477, 486, 1067, 1115, 1391, 1282, 1611, 1631

Ignorance

1039. Two truck drivers had been invited to dinner at the home of their employer. During the meal, the conversation touched subjects out of their range.

"Do you enjoy Omar Khayyam?" asked the boss's wife, trying to make conversation.

"Pretty well," one of the men said, "but, personally, I prefer Chianti."

The subject ended there, but on the way home his buddy said:

Ignorance

"Why don't you say you don't know whenever you're asked something you don't understand? Omar Khayyam ain't a wine, stupid. It's a kind of cheese."

1040. The football coach had just given his men a tough workout. As they were changing their clothes in the locker room he called for their attention and said, "Now, remember, you guys, there's other things you've got to learn here at this college besides football. You're to stay eligible to play. So, right after you get dressed, Professor Wilson is going to give a lecture on Keats and all of you are supposed to be there."

Later, as they filed out of the dressing room into the auditorium for the lecture, the coach said to his assistant, "Look at that bunch of lunkheads going to hear a lecture on Keats. And I bet there isn't a one of them who knows what a keat is."

98, 266, 291, 626, 908, 1026, 1807

Imagination

1041. One little second-grader said to his friend, "Did you see that horror movie on TV last night?"

"No," said the other, "I don't have to watch TV. I just go to bed, shut my eyes, and I can dream scarier things than you can ever see on TV."

90, 128, 479, 486, 722, 1890

Imitation

1042. A young lady was showing her aunt through the art museum. "And this," she said, "is the famous Blue Boy by Gainsborough."

"Well," said her aunt. "It's nothing but a copy of a calendar that has hung in our kitchen for the past three years."

1043. "Let's go to the show tonight to see Jimmy Stewart," said a fellow to his friend.

"I don't care to see Jimmy Stewart," the friend said.

"Did you ever see Jimmy Stewart?" asked the first.

Imitation

"No, and I don't care to," his friend said.

"What kind of an attitude is that?" the first one asked. "You never saw Jimmy Stewart and you don't want to. Just why don't you want to see him?"

"I saw a man on television imitate him once," said the friend, "and he was terrible!"

24, 37, 483, 718, 917, 1255, 1291, 1610

Impatience

1044.   Her grouchy uncle had been left to put the little girl to bed. His patience with children was just about zero.

"Please tell me a bedtime story, Uncle," she begged, "Please, please, please."

"All right," growled her uncle. "Once upon a time there was a little girl named Red Riding Hood and she met a wolf and the wolf ate up her grandmother. Now shut up and go to sleep!"

147, 700

Impressed

1045.   The snobbish lady met a writer at a cocktail party, and said to him, "I'm so thrilled to meet you. It was only last week that I read something of yours, about something or other, in some magazine or newspaper."

1046.   A woman was trying to impress her friend. "My ancestors," she said, "spring from a long line of peers."

"Well, that's nothing, I had an uncle once who jumped off the dock," her friend said.

273, 450, 686, 772, 1001, 1731

Impression

1047.   A teacher asked a pupil: "What is the term 'etc.' used for?"

The pupil said: "I think it's used to make people think we know more about something than we really do."

261, 295, 356, 563, 627

Inaccurate

1048. A man stepped on a scale to weigh himself. His wife grabbed the little card and read it:

"You are dynamic, a leader of men, and admired by women for your good looks and strength of character," she read. Then she added, "It's got your weight wrong, too!"

128, 659

Income tax

1049. A man was complaining to his Congressman about taxes.

"Quit complaining," the Congressman said. "Don't you know that death and taxes are inevitable?"

"That's right,'" the man said, "but there's one thing you've got to say in favor of death—it doesn't get worse every time Congress meets."

796, 1905

Indian

1050. An Indian went before the court in Oklahoma to ask that his name be changed.

"What is your name now?" asked the judge.

"Chief Screeching-Train-Whistle," said the Indian.

"And what do you wish to be called in the future?" asked the judge.

The Indian grinned and said, "Toots."

1051. The little boy's mother pointed to a picture of the Pilgrims going to church, in an effort to interest him in churchgoing.

"They went to church every Sunday," she said.

The little boy looked at the picture which showed the men carrying guns. "Gee," he said, "I'd go every Sunday, too, if I could shoot Indians on the way!"

1052. An Eastern tourist had stopped at an Indian trading post in the West. She looked at rugs and pottery, but the jewelry interested her the most. She picked up a necklace made of odd-

Indian

looking teeth and asked the Indian proprietor, "What kind of teeth are these?"

"Those are grizzly bear teeth, lady," said the Indian.

"Oh, yes," said the lady. "And I suppose they have the same value for you Indians that pearls have for us."

"Not exactly, lady," said the Indian. "Remember, anybody can open an oyster."

1693

Indifference

1053.   The man was getting his car inspected.

"Your horn is broken," the inspector said.

"No, it isn't," said the driver. "It's just indifferent."

"What do you mean, indifferent?" asked the inspector.

"It just doesn't give a hoot," the man said.

307

Indulgent

1054.   "Where have you been for the last two hours?" demanded the man's wife.

"I met Mrs. Wilson in front of the post office and made the mistake of asking her how she was feeling," said the man.

645, 918, 1344, 1776

Inflation

1055.   A mechanic sold a friend a car he had fixed up and repaired. The next day he was sorry he sold it, so he went to see his friend.

"I'll buy the car back from you," he said, "and give you fifty dollars' profit."

So the friend sold him the car. The following day, he looked up the mechanic.

"I'm sorry I sold the car back to you," he said. "I'll give you seventy-five dollars' profit for it."

Inflation

So, he bought the car back. The next day, the mechanic was sorry he sold it and bought it back again, giving his friend one hundred dollars' profit. The following day, his friend came to buy it back, but learned that the mechanic had sold it to a used-car dealer.

"You dope! Why did you sell it to a stranger?" said the mechanic's friend, "especially when we were both making such a wonderful living out of it."

1056. Two men met casually as they were looking over the paperback books at the airport bookstore.

"I wonder where the dime novel went," said the first.

"Oh, it's right in front of you," the other one said, "only now it's gone to a dollar and a half."

1057. A tourist was talking with a young man in the Kentucky mountains.

"I suppose," said the tourist, "that even up here in the mountains the necessities of life have increased in price."

"They sure have," said the young man. "And when you are able to buy it, the stuff ain't worth drinking."

1058. The man had just checked into a swanky resort hotel, and the bellman was carrying his bags to the room. Not being sure about the tipping rates in such a fancy place, the man just asked the bellman, "What's the average tip here?"

"Three dollars," was the fast reply.

Not wishing to appear stingy, the guest gave the bellman three dollars. But he said to him, "Three dollars is a pretty big tip. At that rate, you must be getting rich."

"No, sir," the bellman said. "All the time I've been working here, this is the first average I was ever able to get."

1059. One stormy night in Leopoldville, a big gorilla walked up to the bar in a neighborhood tavern and ordered a double Manhattan.

The bartender served the Manhattan. The gorilla downed it in one gulp, and placed a $5 bill on the bar which the bartender took, rang up $3, and returned the change.

"Strange, you know," said the bartender, "we don't get many

gorillas in here."

"No," said the gorilla, "and you never will at these prices."

195, 400, 925, 1500

Influence

1060. A man had just bought a new baby-blue Cadillac. The salesman was interested in uncovering the effects of their advertising program.

"I wonder if you would tell me what was the one dominating thing that made you buy this car?" asked the salesman.

"My wife," said the customer.

1061. The little boy's mother was enrolling him in school. She was telling the teacher how to treat her little darling.

"I want you to remember," she said, "that my Percy is much too delicate for physical punishment. If he should misbehave, just slap the boy next to him and that will frighten Percy."

768, 840, 1025

Ingenuity

1062. A widow, viewing her husband laid out at the funeral home, said she was sorry she had ordered a gray, rather than a blue suit for her husband.

"We can take care of that," said the funeral director. "We'll have him fixed up properly by about 6 o'clock."

When the widow returned that evening, the change had been made. "It was really no trouble," the funeral director said. "The woman whose husband is in the next room preferred her husband in a gray suit."

"So you traded suits?" the widow asked.

"Oh, no," said the funeral director. "We just changed heads!"

1063. A twelve-dollar-a-week stockroom clerk was living it up. He was driving an auto, running around with girls, spending at night clubs and wearing fancy clothes. His boss became suspicious and asked him:

"Where do you get all of the money to do those things?"

Ingenuity

"Oh, I have a good thing going," the clerk said. "Every Saturday I hold a raffle. I sell a thousand tickets at a quarter each."

"What do you raffle?" asked the boss.

"My pay check," said the clerk.

1064. The little boy came home from school and said to his mother, "Well, I got two free ice cream cones again today."

"How did you do that?" asked his mother. "I certainly hope you didn't steal them."

"Oh, no," said the little boy. "I just took one ice cream cone in my right hand, the other one in my left hand, and said to the lady behind the counter, 'Would you please get the money out of my pocket, but be careful not to hurt my pet garter snake.' "

1065. It was arithmetic time in the third grade. The lesson was on fractions. "If your mother had five children to feed," asked the teacher of a little girl, "and she had only three potatoes for them, and she wanted to divide them so each of the children had an equal amount, how would she do it?"

"She'd give them mashed potatoes," the little girl said.

119, 1305, 2029

In-laws

1066. A lady was visiting a zoo and was being shown around by a guide. They came to a cage occupied by a kangaroo.

"Here, lady," he said, "we have a native of Australia."

"Good gracious," she said, "and to think my sister married one of them."

1067. A henpecked husband took to drink. In fact, he became a real lush. He drank so much that it began to worry his friends. Finally, they figured out a plan to cure him. The plan was for one of them to dress up like a devil, with horns and a pitchfork. They planned to scare their friend into giving up drink.

Late one night, as he headed home drunk, his friend jumped from behind a tree and shouted, "You'll have to stop drinking!"

"Who are you?" asked the man.

In-laws

"I'm the devil," said his friend.

"Oh, you're the devil," the man said. "I'm glad to meet you. I'm the guy who married your sister."

1304, 1586

Innocence

1068. A lady was scolding a little boy who had just beaten up his brother.

"Why did you kick your little brother in the stomach?" she asked.

"Well, it was his fault," said the little boy. "He turned around."

1069. The man had been arrested for stealing a hog. The trial was short and sweet. There was no concrete evidence against the man and the judge dismissed the case against him. For some reason, the man seemed not to understand.

"The case is dismissed," the judge said. "It is over. You are acquitted. You can go."

"Well, thanks, Judge," the man said, "but do I have to give him back his hog?"

382, 860, 897, 1111

Insomnia

1070. "What do you take when you can't sleep?"

"A glass of wine or whiskey at regular intervals."

"Will that make you sleep?"

"No, but it makes me satisfied to stay awake."

1071. The man who couldn't sleep asked the doctor: "Is it true that sleeping outdoors will cure insomnia?"

"That's right," the doctor said. "But sleeping indoors will do the same thing."

56, 1782

Inspiration

1072. The playwright became inspired with a big idea for a story. He immediately phoned a noted producer.

"Not only is it a great comedy and just suited for your star," he said, "it also has a message."

"A message?" asked the producer. "Listen, just write me a good comedy. Messages are for Western Union."

1073. The great man was delivering the graduation speech at the university. It was well written and was being delivered in a most inspiring manner. The theme was one of optimism and hope for the future.

Two foreign students were in the audience. One of them said to the other, "What is he saying?"

"School is out," said the other.

586, 676, 872, 919

Instant love

1074. A sixth grader rushed home after school one afternoon and headed straight for the telephone and dialed a number.

"Hello," he said. "Betty, can you go with me to the movies tonight?"

After a moment's silence, he said, "O.K., I'll call you tomorrow."

"What was that excitement and rush all about?" his mother wanted to know. "Who is Betty? And, another thing, it isn't right to ask a girl out the same day you call. You should ask her some time in advance."

"But, gosh, Mom," the boy said, "I didn't even like her until two hours ago."

1075. A young fellow and his girl friend were paddling a canoe on a moonlit lake. The situation was most romantic. "Please say the words that will make you mine forever," he pleaded.

"One million dollars," she said.

28

Instruction

1076. The bride was trying to cook a pudding according to the directions in the book. She ran into so much trouble, that she called her mother on the phone.

"There's something wrong with this cookbook," she cried. "I'm trying to make a pudding and it says I was supposed to bring it to a boil on a brisk fire, stirring for two minutes. Then I was to beat it for fifteen minutes. And I did, and when I got back it was burnt to a cinder."

1077. The lawyer was giving his son some business instruction. "You must always enter any business transaction with honesty and discretion," he said.

"What do you consider to be the best measure of honesty?" his son asked.

"Honesty," his father said, "is keeping your word. Once you have given your word, never go back on it."

"And what is discretion?" he asked.

"Discretion," his father said, "is never giving your word."

207, 420, 588, 704, 727, 1680, 2106

Insult

1078. A terrible-tempered boss was dictating a letter to a competitor. "Sir," he growled, "my secretary, being a lady, cannot type what I think of you. I, being a gentleman, cannot think it. You, being neither, will understand well exactly what I mean."

477, 1098, 1660

Insurance

1079. The farmer had just taken out a fire-insurance policy on his barn. As he signed the application blank, he said to the insurance agent, "Now, if my barn were to burn down tonight, what would I get?"

"Oh, about two years," the insurance man said.

1080. Life insurance salesman: "At the age of 75, there are 18 per cent more women than men."

Insurance

Insurance prospect: "At the age of 75, who cares?"

1081. "Mother," the new bride asked, "what is the best way to protect a wedding ring?"

"The best way," said her mother wisely, "is to dip it into dishwater three times a day."

1082. "This is the last class before final examinations," the professor told his students. "I want to urge you to study hard for the examination. The questions already have gone to the printer. And before the class ends, I wonder if any of you have a question."

"Yes," said one of the students. "What is the name of the printer?"

54, 330, 478, 528, 558, 578, 743, 781

Integrity

1083. A witness was called in the election bribery case.

"You say," asked the judge, "that you were given $10 to vote for the Democrats, and you got another $10 to vote for the Republicans?"

"Yes, sir, your honor," said the witness.

"And how did you vote?" asked the judge.

"Your honor," he said, "I voted according to my conscience."

1084. The personnel director of a bank was interviewing applicants for the job of cashier. After talking to a fine-looking fellow, he decided to check his references. He called a man who had been listed as a former employer.

"We are thinking of hiring your former employee as a cashier," the personnel director said. "I wonder if you could tell me whether or not he is perfectly honest."

"Honest," said the voice on the phone. "I should say he is. He has been arrested nine times for embezzlement and he was acquitted each time."

26, 449, 724, 985

Interference

1085.   The boss said to his foreman one morning, "Your nose is suspiciously rosy this morning. What makes it so red?"

"Well," said the foreman, "it's just the reflection of my soul, blushing with pride at my ability to mind my own business."

158, 410, 691, 1703

Interpretation

1086.   The woman listened carefully as the doctor prescribed a remedy for her nervous condition. "Lady," he said, "you need frequent baths, plenty of fresh air, and you should dress in warm clothes."

That night after supper she told her husband about it. "The doctor," she said, "told me I am in a highly nervous condition, and that I must go to Atlantic City, then to a dude ranch out west, and buy myself a full-length mink coat."

1087.   A widow with asthma asked a friend about a summer resort. "Would that be a good place for me to go for my asthma?"

"Yes," her friend said. "The men there are so dumb they can't tell it from passion."

1088.   A woman was filling out an application and she came to the blank marked "age." Without hesitation, she wrote, "Atomic."

1089.   Another lady was filling out a credit card form. When she came to the line that said "age," she hesitated a long time.

Finally, the clerk leaned over and whispered, "The longer you wait, the worse it gets."

1090.   "Your eyes," said the young sailor to the girl he had just met at the dance, "they're beautiful. I see dew in them."

"Take it easy," said his girl. "That ain't dew. That's don't."

1091.   The young lady's hopes had been high for two years while her boy friend remained silent on the question of marriage. Then one evening he said to her, "I had a most unusual dream

Interpretation

last night. I dreamed that I asked you to marry me. I wonder what that means."

"It means," said his girl friend, "that you have more sense asleep than you have awake."

229, 432, 489, 541, 1006, 1073, 1772

Introduction

1092. A Baltimore newspaperman was invited to speak at a Chamber of Commerce meeting in a small Texas town. He was almost frightened to death when he noticed that most of the men in his audience were wearing six-shooters. His fears increased after he had finished speaking and sat down, because one of the men drew his guns and rushed toward the head table.

"Don't be afraid of him," the president of the club said. "He's not going to bother you. He's after the man who introduced you."

1093. A judge was trying a divorce case. He had never had a case like this one before, because the woman had been married only one day.

"Why is it," he asked, "that you want a divorce? You married the most eligible man in town. He is the richest man in town, the best looking, the best dressed, doesn't drink, doesn't smoke. He ought to make an ideal husband. That's what all of your friends have been telling you. Now, you want a divorce after being married one day. Why? What's your reason?"

"Well, Judge," she said, "I guess that's the reason. That man was just naturally overintroduced."

1094. A speaker was introduced as the man who had just made $800,000 in an oil deal in Oklahoma.

In response, he said, "It wasn't an oil deal, it was a real estate deal. It wasn't in Oklahoma, but in Virginia. I'm sorry, but the man had his figures mixed up. It wasn't $800,000 but $800. And besides that, it wasn't a profit, but a loss."

1095. A speaker had received a deafening roar of applause following his introduction. Looking out over his audience, he said, "As the cow said to the farmer on a winter day—thanks for the warm hand."

359, 403, 572, 1374, 1787

Inventor

1096. The landlady of a rather rundown rooming house led a prospective tenant to a third-floor room with badly spotted wall-paper.
Landlady: "The last man who lived in this room was an inventor—he invented some sort of explosive."
Prospect: "Oh, these spots on the walls are chemicals?"
Landlady: "No, the inventor."

1097. A woman called the Electric Light and Power Company and asked them to come out to the house and install a meter jumper.
"A meter jumper," the man said, "where in the world did you ever hear about such a thing?"
"Well," said the woman, "a neighbor of mine down the street has one on her meter and she says it cuts her electric bill in half every month."

1098. When Eli Whitney was working on the patents for his cotton gin, a group of businessmen formed a syndicate and tried to swindle him out of his rights. His constant fight kept him in and out of Washington. On one of his trips there, he was walking up the steps to the patent office, when two of the attorneys for the syndicate came out the front door. Angered at the very sight of them, he shook his fist in their faces and screamed, "You keep your cotton-picking hands off my gin."

809, 884

Invitation

1099. A lady opened a letter and said to her husband, "Do you remember that couple we met on the boat and took such a violent fancy to, the couple we invited to visit us?"

Invitation

"Yes," said her husband. "You don't mean to say . . ."

"Yes, that's right," said his wife. "The idiots actually are coming."

1100. She was the most beautiful girl at the cocktail party. The young man was looking for an opportunity to get acquainted and said, "How heavenly you are. You look sweet enough to eat."

"I do eat," she said. "Where shall we go?"

50, 510, 696, 1013, 1927, 2062

Jail

1101. The new boarder was talking. "For fifteen years," he said, "my habits were as regular as clockwork. I rose exactly at six. Half an hour later I was at breakfast. At seven I was at work. I had lunch at one, had supper at six, and was in bed at nine-thirty. I ate only plain food, and didn't have a day of sickness during all those years."

"My," said a stranger who was listening, "and what were you in for?"

12, 44, 304, 446, 463, 1483

Jealous

1102. A jealous wife used to give her husband a regular inspection every night when he came home from the office. Every hair she discovered on his coat would be cause for a terrible scene.

One evening, when she didn't find a single hair, she screamed at him, "Now, you're even running after bald-headed women."

1103. The man's wife was upset and was confiding in her maid. "Do you know," she said, "I suspect my husband is having an affair with his stenographer."

"Oh," cried the maid. "You can't believe that. You're just saying that to make me jealous."

597

Judge

1104.   The judge was questioning the town drunk, who had been in court many times. "This time," the judge said, "you are charged with habitual drunkenness. What explanation can you offer for your offense?"

"Habitual thirst, your honor," said the drunk.

1105.   The judge, a political appointee with no legal training, sat half asleep while the plaintiff's counsel presented his case.

When the lawyer for the defense arose, the judge said, "Now, what're you gonna do?"

"I'm going to present our side of the case," he said.

"I don't want to hear both sides," said the judge. "It has a tendency to confuse the court."

1106.   A former judge, who had taken up the ministry, was conducting his first marriage ceremony.

"Wilt thou take this man to be thy lawfully wedded husband?" he asked the bride.

"I will," she answered.

"And you," he said to the bridegroom, "what have you to say in your defense?"

1107.   It was a hot summer day in Georgia. A couple of the local lawyers had invited the judge to have lunch with them.

When the judge ordered hot coffee with his lunch, one of the lawyers said to him, "Coffee? You shouldn't be drinking hot coffee on a day like this. You should be drinking something cool and stimulating. Did you ever try whiskey and gingerale?"

"No, I haven't," said the judge, "but I've tried a lot of men who have."

26, 52, 85, 393, 437, 597, 1938

Judgment

1108.   A writer and a friend were arguing about a new book. The author finally said to his friend, "There's no use in your talking. You never wrote a book yourself, so you can't appreciate the fine points of one."

Judgment

"Oh, I don't know about that," his friend said. "I never laid an egg either, yet I can spot a bad one quicker than any hen in the country."

1109. "I would like your permission, sir, to ask your daughter to marry me," the young man said.

"All right, you have my permission," the man said. "I have given her a fine education, sent her to the best schools, sent her abroad to meet the best people. If she doesn't have sense enough to say no, I'm afraid there isn't anything else I can do for her."

118, 124, 419, 552, 732, 2081

Junior

1110. When the doorbell rang, the little five-year-old boy opened the door and stared at the visitor outside.

"I'd like to see Mr. Jones," said the man.

"I'm Mr. Jones," said the little boy. Then as an afterthought he added, "But, maybe, you want to see old Mr. Jones. I'll call him."

570, 725

Jury

1111. A country lawyer had made up his mind to save his client from hanging. Just to play safe, he made a deal with one of the jurors. "I'll see that you are well rewarded," the lawyer said, "if you get the jury to bring in a verdict of manslaughter in the second degree."

That was the verdict of the jury, just as the lawyer had arranged, and the prisoner got twenty years. The lawyer paid off the juror and thanked him.

"It was hard to do," said the man. "They were all for turning him loose, but I talked them out of it."

185, 553, 961

Justice

1112. The courtroom in the small county-seat courthouse was packed. The noise of whispering was so great that nothing could be heard.

"We must have less noise in the court," roared the judge. "There's already been a half-dozen men convicted today without the court's being able to hear a word of the testimony."

1113. A father was surprised when his son handed him one of his old report cards and said, "Well, son, you're right. This old report card of mine you found in the attic isn't any better than yours. And I guess the only fair thing to do is give you what my father gave me."

1114. "Do you think I'll get justice in this court?" asked the man accused of murder.

"No, I don't," said his lawyer. "I see three men on the jury who I know are opposed to hanging."

182, 1269, 1540, 1724

Juveniles

1115. Three young boys were brought into court for causing trouble in the neighborhood. "Now," said the kindly judge, "we'll take one at a time. What are you here for, young man?"

"Nothing much, I just threw peanuts in the water," the first boy said.

"Well, that doesn't seem like such a terrible thing," said the judge. He turned to the second boy and asked, "And what did you do?"

"The same thing, sir, I threw peanuts in the water."

"And I suppose," said the judge to the third boy, "you threw peanuts in the water too?"

"No, sir," the boy said, "I'm Peanuts."

793

Kindness

1116. A mother was giving her daughter some advice about a new boy friend.

Kindness

"Before you become serious with that new friend," she said, "be sure that he is kind and considerate."

"Oh, I'm sure he is, Mother," said her daughter. "Why, only the other day he told me that he had put his shirt on a horse that was scratched."

1117. The Sunday school teacher was trying to teach her little pupils the principles of charity and kindness and compassion.

"Suppose I was walking down the street," she said, "and saw a man beating a donkey and I made him stop. What virtue would I be showing?"

"That would be brotherly love," a little boy said.

1118. The lonely vacationer entered a restaurant in Miami Beach.

"May I take your order?" the waitress asked.

"Yes," said the lonely man. "I'd like two eggs and a kind word."

The waitress brought the eggs and was walking away, when the man called to her. "What about the kind word?" he asked.

The waitress came back, leaned over, and whispered, "Don't eat the eggs."

1119. A policeman stopped a drunk and said to him, "Do you know who I am?"

"I can't say that I do," the drunk said, "but if you'll tell me where you live, I'll help you home."

94, 111, 218, 761, 1018

Kiss

1120. New neighbors had moved in and had been under observation for several days.

"They seem like a most devoted couple," a wife said to her husband. "Every time he leaves for work she comes out on the porch and he hugs and kisses her. Why don't you do that?"

"Me?" said her husband, "I should say not. I haven't even been introduced to her yet."

Kiss

1121. "I assure you," a young bride said to her friend, "that my husband is the only man who has ever kissed me."

"Really?" said her friend. "Are you bragging or complaining?"

1122. The young man had kissed his girl friend good-night about a dozen times. They just couldn't seem to say good-night. Finally, he said, "Love is wonderful. Darling, do we really have to say good-night?"

A voice from deep within the house said, "Certainly not. Stick around another half hour and you can say good-morning."

10, 102, 141, 214, 221, 433, 496, 740, 1132, 1525, 1619, 1636, 1687, 1919

Knighthood

1123. It was snowing and sleeting. A terrible night. Sir Lancelot leaped from his horse and ran into the stable. "I am carrying an important message to the king," he cried. "I need a fresh horse. Can you let me have a horse?"

"I am sorry," said the stableman, "all my horses are out. The only animal here is that St. Bernard dog you hear barking."

"Well," said Sir Lancelot, "he'll have to do. I'll take him."

"Oh, no!" begged the stableman, "I wouldn't dare send a knight out on a dog like this!"

Knowledge

1124. A Sunday school teacher was pointing out the difference between right and wrong to her pupils.

"Now, children," she said, "if I put my hand in a man's coat pocket and took all of his money, what would I be?"

"You'd be his wife!" said a little girl.

1125. The phone rang at eight o'clock in the morning in the small electronics plant in Alexandria, Virginia. The only man on duty at that hour was the janitor. He picked up the phone and said, "Hello."

"This is Major Roberts in the Pentagon," the voice on the line said. "I'm calling to find the resistance rating and the total connected load of your model ARC-46283 unit."

264

Knowledge

There was dead silence on the other end of the line.

"Hello, hello," the Major shouted, "don't you know anything about electronics?"

"Listen, Major," the janitor said, "when I picked up this phone and said, 'hello,' I told you everything I know about electronics."

128, 292, 739, 842, 956, 1141, 1178, 2007

Labor

1126. "Why don't you work?" the lady asked the panhandler. "Hard work never killed anyone."

"You're wrong, lady," the man said. "I lost both of my wives that way."

1127. A woman telephoned a restaurant and spoke to the manager. "Would you mind calling my husband to the phone, please?" she asked. "He's Bill Miller, a waiter there."

"Bill Miller, a waiter?" the manager asked. "Does he work for me?"

"Yes," she said, "but right now he's outside picketing the place."

1128. A little boy asked his father, "Dad, what is the difference between Capital and Labor?"

"If you lend money," his father said, "that's Capital. And when you try and get it back, that's Labor!"

184, 318, 417, 708

Landlady

1129. A doctor told his patient, "You are suffering from nervous tension. You should drink a glass of hot water first thing every morning."

"Oh, I do that," said the patient, "only the landlady calls it coffee."

1130. The landlady was complaining to her neighbor. "I'm being bothered with rats," she said. "They're running all over the place."

Landlady

"Why don't you buy some rat biscuits for them?" said her neighbor.

"What kind of place do you think I run, the Statler?" cried the landlady. "It the rats can't eat what the rest of us do, they can go hungry!"

400, 504, 1566

Language

1131. Everybody these days knows how telephone operators use certain codes when they handle long distance calls. These codes speed up the service. For example, "D-A" means "the party doesn't answer" and "B-Y" means "the number is busy."

An operator from New York recently rang an exchange in a small rural community in South Georgia. The operator tried to get the number and reported back that the number was "O-M-C."

"O-M-C," the northern operator said, "What does that mean?"

"Oh," said the Georgia operator, "that means out milking cows."

1132. The teacher wrote on the chalk board LXXX. She then said to a girl in the back row, "Can you tell me what that means?"

"Love and kisses," the girl said.

214, 229, 477, 488, 541, 561, 640, 1268, 1321, 1690, 1819

Late

1133. Suddenly, in the middle of his lunch, a man looked at the clock on the wall and made a rush for his hat and coat.

"It's two o'clock," he said. "I've got to get over to the corner. My wife is supposed to meet me there at one o'clock, and I don't dare be late."

1134. After a hard run toward the departing train, the man gave up and returned panting to the gate.

Late

"Just missed her, huh," said the gateman.

"Oh, I wasn't trying to catch it," the man said. "I was only chasing it out of the station."

1135. The secretary's only trouble seemed to be her inability to get to work on time. Not once had she ever arrived on schedule. Finally, the office manager decided to do something about it.

"I'm sorry," he said, "but I'm going to suspend you for a week without pay. When do you want to take the week, now or later?"

"If it's all the same to you," she said, "I'd rather use up the time being late."

1136. A businessman, with offices on the twentieth floor of a skyscraper, was put out because a farmer friend was half an hour late for an appointment. The door finally opened and his friend came in, all out of breath. "Some walk up those stairs," he said.

"Stairs?" said the businessman. "Why on earth didn't you ride the elevator?"

"I wanted to," said the farmer, "but I missed the thing."

1137. A father was chiding his son gently for coming in so late at night. "You should take a lesson from the busy bee," he said.

"I did, Dad," said the young man. "I was out with a honey last night."

56, 381, 1596

Law

1138. "Look here," said the guest to the hotel manager, "don't you know that roller towels in hotels have been prohibited in this state for three years?"

"Certainly," said the hotel man, "but that towel in your room was put up before the law was passed."

1139. "Hi, there," a fellow said to a friend. "Where have you been lately—haven't seen you around."

Law

"I've been serving on the jury," the man said. "We're in our eighth week already."

"Eight weeks," his friend said. "I'll bet you have heard so much law in that time that you are almost a lawyer yourself."

"That's right," the man said. "I'm so full of it that when I get off the jury and back to my business, I'll never be able to keep from cheating my customers as long as I live."

86, 369

Lawyer

1140. Two young lawyers went into partnership. The name of their firm was Rosenberg and Finkelstein. After being in business together for two or three years, they still weren't doing very well.

One day when Rosenberg came to work, he found a sign painter changing the sign on the front door to read, "Rosenberg and O'Reilly."

"What's going on here," he said to his partner. "Are you moving out on me?"

"Oh, no," his partner said. "Business has been bad lately and I thought maybe it was because of our names. So, I went down to the courthouse yesterday and changed my name.I thought about it a long time and figured that O'Reilly would be about the best name for me."

Two weeks later, the newly named O'Reilly went on a trip to Chicago. Upon his return, he saw that the sign on the front door had been changed to read "O'Reilly and O'Reilly."

"What goes on?" he asked.

"I thought your idea was a good one," his partner told him, "so I decided to do the same thing. I thought about it a long time. I decided that the finest name in the world was O'Reilly, so I changed my name to that."

All went well. The business prospered. They made money. They installed a switchboard and hired a switchboard operator. She had only been on the job a few minutes when the first call came in: "I want to speak to Mr. O'Reilly," the voice said.

"Which one do you want," the girl asked, "Rosenberg or Finkelstein?"

Lawyer

1141. A judge asked the witness if he knew any of the jurors personally. "Yes," he said, "I know eight of them."

"You mean you know more than half of the jurors in the box?" the judge asked.

"Heck," said the witness, "as far as that goes, I know more than all of them put together."

1142. "So you want to know if you have grounds for divorce," said the lawyer. "Are you married?"

"Yes."

"Then you have grounds for divorce."

1143. The lawyer was defending a badly beat up man charged with desertion. To make his point, he told his client to remove his bandages, exposing a black eye and assorted cuts and bruises.

"Your Honor," said the lawyer, "I submit that one look at this man will convince you he is not a deserter, but a refugee."

1144. The two burglars worked as a team. One stayed outside as a lookout, while the other robbed the house. One night, when the inside man returned, his buddy said, "How much did you get?"

"Nothing," the other said. "The fellow who lives there is a lawyer."

"Gee!" said his buddy. "How much did you lose?"

1145. "Have you ever been arrested or in court before?" the lawyer asked the witness.

"No, sir," said the witness.

"Are you sure about that?" asked the lawyer. "Your face certainly looks familiar. I'm sure I've seen it some place before."

"I'm sure you have," said the witness. "I'm the bartender in the bar across the street."

1146. The lawyer was examining a hostile witness. "Just when did this accident take place?" he demanded.

"Well," said the witness meekly, "I think it . . ."

"Stop," shouted the lawyer. "I don't want to know what you think. I want you to tell the court what you know."

Lawyer

"In that case, I may as well go home," the witness said, "because as I'm not a lawyer, I can't talk without thinking."

1147. The lawyer was defending a man who had been arrested for drunkenness. He was cross-examining the arresting officer. "But if a man is on his hands and knees in the middle of the road, officer," said the lawyer, "does that prove he is drunk?"

"No, sir, it does not," said the officer, "but this man was trying to roll up the white line."

1148. It seemed that every time the poor businessman turned around, he had some added legal fees. It worried him to the point of ulcers. Then one day, he met his lawyer in the post office and said, "Nice day, isn't it? And remember, I'm telling you, not asking you."

44, 45, 181, 185, 437, 467, 532, 591, 629, 1167

Lazy

1149. The laziest man in the county finally reached the age of 90. A newspaper reporter from town came out to take his picture and write a story about him. The reporter was talking to a neighbor about the old man and asked him, "How do you figure your friend was able to live so long?"

"I guess," said the neighbor, "it was because he never did anything else."

1150. Two political bosses were discussing the behavior of one of the precinct workers who had been put on the county payroll.

"I thought," said the first boss, "that when we gave him that soft job down at the county jail, he would be satisfied. Why, all that fellow has to do is tear a page off the office calendar each month!"

"That's right," his friend said, "but now he's starting to complain because February is such a short month."

1151. The foreman was angry and demanded, "Why is it that you carry only one plank while all the other men carry two?"

"I guess," said the fellow, "they're just too lazy to make two trips as I do."

270

Lazy

1152. Visitor: "How many people work in your plant?"
Plant Manager: "Oh, about one in every ten."

1153. The worker was being bawled out by the foreman. "I know your kind," said the foreman. "You'd like a job where you could lie in bed all day and get everything done by pushing buttons."

"Not me," said the man. "You wouldn't catch me pushing buttons all day."

1154. "This book," said the salesman, "will do half your work."

"Fine," said the executive. "I'll take two of them."

1155. Two hoboes were sitting under the bridge listening to the holiday traffic passing overhead. "I hate holidays," said the first.

"Yes," said his buddy, "It makes you feel right common when nobody ain't working."

1156. The lazy mountain boy was sleeping in the shade. The flies buzzed around and settled on his face, but he didn't bother to shoo them away. Then, a bee lit on him and stung his nose. He slowly wiped his face and said, "As long as some of you won't behave, you'll all just have to get off."

1157. A family from up north moved into Tennessee. Being used to locking everything, they put a padlock on their toolshed. A neighbor saw what they had done and laughed at them. "Don't you know," he said, "that no one in Tennessee ever stole anything to work with?"

1158. When the town's laziest man died, his wife decided to have him cremated. The attendant at the crematory showed his widow a display of beautifully decorated urns for his ashes.

"No," she said. "I don't want any of those things. I want you to put his ashes in an hour glass. I'm going to put it on the mantelpiece. That lazy rascal never did a day's work in his life, but believe me, he'll be busy all day long from now on."

92, 561, 586, 778, 1567, 2073

Legacy

1159. "Since we have been close friends for so many years, doctor, I do not to intend to insult you by paying my bill. Instead I have left you a generous legacy in my will."

"I certainly appreciate that," the doctor said. "By the way, let me have that prescription I just gave you. I want to make a slight change in it."

1160. At the funeral, a friend asked the nephew of the dead man, "Was your uncle's mind vigorous and sane up to the very last?"

"I don't know," the man said. "The will won't be read until tomorrow."

1161. The boss's son had been working for the company for several months. It was obvious that he was unhappy with the boy. One day he called him into his office.

"Son," he said, "I just don't understand you young people. You have no ambition. You don't know what get-up-and-go means. Now look at you. You're twenty-two years old. You are still not head of your department."

"Yes, sir," said the boy. "But, after all, sir, this is my first job, and I've only been here a few months."

"A few months," said his father. "Son, you're a failure. Why, when I was your age, I had already inherited my third million!"

1162. A little widow was in the hospital and knew that her days were numbered. She sent for her long-time friend, another little widow and said to her, "I know that I'll never get out of this hospital bed. The doctors have told me that. So, I wonder if you would do me a favor?"

"Certainly," said her friend. "I'll do anything I can."

"Well," said the first little lady, "when I pass away, I want you to be sure to have me buried in that new black dress I just bought. You know, the full one hanging in my closet that I have worn only once."

"Yes," said her friend, "I know the dress you mean."

"And when you bury me," the little widow said, "I want you to take the dress, cut out the back, and keep the material for yourself. That is a full dress and there is enough material in the back for you to make a dress."

"I'll do nothing of the kind," her friend said. "I never heard of such a silly thing. Why . . . what . . . what would the angels think? After you have passed away and you join up on the other side with your poor departed husband and the two of you go hand in hand up to the Pearly Gates. What would the angels think when you walked up there in a dress that didn't have any back in it?"

"Well," said the little widow, "the angels wouldn't be paying any attention to me. They'd be looking at Pa. I buried him in his long, red underwear."

1163. A recent widow was being visited by a lady from the church who was trying hard to be sympathetic.

"I suppose your husband left you quite a lot?" she asked.

"Yes, he did," the widow said, "nearly every time he got a chance."

1164. "Do you believe in heredity?" asked one society dame of her friend, as they sipped cocktails at the country club.

"I certainly do," said her friend. "That's how my husband got his money."

225, 478, 518, 607, 1710

Liar

1165. A lawyer was questioning the witness about the truthfulness of a neighbor.

"Well," said the man, "I wouldn't say he was a liar, but I can tell you this, when it comes time to feed his hogs he has to get somebody else to call them for him."

1166. "If a fellow took you out to the show one night and to dinner the next night and to a concert the next night and then to a night club the night after that and never even tried to kiss you goodnight, what would you do?" a young lady asked her girl friend.

"I'd lie about it," her friend said.

Liar

1167. The defendant was trying his own case and was making a complete mess of it. The judge finally said to him, "I gave you the right to defend yourself, but you are lying so obviously that I think you need the help of a more experienced man. I really think you should have a lawyer."

520, 534, 863

Library

1168. "I trust you found that book interesting," the librarian said.

"It really was rather dull," the borrower said, "but the letter someone left in it for a bookmark was certainly something to read."

1169. The young man rushed up to the librarian and said, "Can I draw out that same book I had last week?"

"I suppose so," said the librarian. "Did you find it so interesting?"

"No, the book's terrible," said the fellow, "but it's got my girl's phone number in it."

167, 253

Lie

1170. A father was getting ready to spank his six-year-old son for having told a lie.

"I never told lies when I was your age," he said.

The little boy thought a moment and then asked, "How old were you when you started, Dad?"

1171. "I wish there were some easy way to get rid of that boy friend of mine," a young lady confided to her friend.

"Why don't you just tell him to get going?" her friend asked. "Are you afraid he will go around spreading lies about you?"

"Oh, no," the young lady said. "I'm afraid he'll go around telling the truth."

166, 441, 674, 1833

274

Life

1172. For 20 years of a man's life his mother asks him where he is going. For the next 40 years his wife asks the same question and at his funeral so do his mourners.

99, 743

Light

1173. One night, a farmer noticed a light in his barn. He went to see what it was all about and he found a farmhand with a lantern, all dressed up.

"What are you doing all dressed up and with that lantern?" he asked.

"I'm going to call on my girl friend," the farm hand said. "I've got to go through the woods and it's dark."

"When I was your age calling on my wife for the first time," said the farmer, "I went through the woods without a lantern."

"I know," said the farm hand, "but look what you got!"

1174. The lecturer at the high school was trying to make the point that even though man had made great scientific progress, he did not know the basic truths about the universe.

"Even though I have studied physics for years," he told the students, "I still do not know all of the mysteries of electricity. I still don't know what makes the electric light work."

"Why, that's not hard to understand," said a young girl in the back. "You just snap on the switch—and it works."

515, 527

Limit

1175. A man checked in a hotel and asked the clerk, "Can you give me a room and bath?"

"I can give you a room," the clerk said, "but you will have to take your own bath."

80, 334, 543, 699

Listen

1176. If you want your wife to pay close attention to what you are saying, whisper it to another woman in a low voice.

554, 1148, 1802, 1899

Literary

1177. Serious boy: "Do you enjoy Kipling?"
Young girl: "I don't know—how do you kipple?"

1178. Two students were cramming for a test in English literature.
"Great Scott!" said the first, "who wrote Ivanhoe?"
"I'll help you with that," said the other, "if you will tell me who the dickens wrote David Copperfield."

254, 1039, 1168, 1426, 1783, 1799, 2117

Little boy

1179. A little boy was asked his age by a visitor.
"I'm at the awkward age," he said.
"Is that so," said the visitor. "What do you mean by the awkward age?"
"Too old to cry and too young to swear," the little boy said.

1180. The story that Sunday was about Elisha and the bears. "And when the children mocked him," the teacher said, "they were punished by two she-bears who came out of the woods and ate forty-two of them. Now, what does that story tell us?"
"It tells us," a little boy said, "how many children two she-bears can eat at one time."

1181. A little boy who had been absent from Sunday school for several weeks showed up one Sunday bright and early.
"I'm so glad you came today," the teacher said. "We have been missing you."
"Well," said the little boy, "I almost didn't make it. I started to go fishing but my father wouldn't let me."
"I'm glad he wouldn't let you go fishing on Sunday," the teacher said. "And I hope he told you why. Did he?"

Little boy

"Yes," the little boy said. "He said there wasn't enough bait for both of us."

1182.   "Is your father at home?" the minister asked the little boy as he came to the door one Sunday afternoon.

"No, sir, he's not here," the boy said. "He's over at the country club." Then, realizing what he had said, he hastened to cover up for his father. "But, he isn't going to play golf. He never plays golf on Sunday. He just went over there for a couple of highballs and a few hands of poker with some friends."

64, 119, 125, 170, 194, 211, 224, 285, 346, 353, 703

Little girl

1183.   While guests were present, the four-year-old was a perfect lady. But the moment they left, she became ugly and disobedient.

"Why is it," her mother said, "that you are so naughty now? You were so nice while our guests were here."

"Well, Mother," said the little girl, "you don't use your company silver all the time, do you?"

1184.   A young mother was on a bus with a cute youngster at her side.

"A fine child," said an elderly man sitting next to her. "I hope you will raise him to be an upright and conscientious man."

"Yes," said the mother, "but I'm afraid it's going to be a bit difficult because. . . ."

"Oh, nonsense," said the man, "remember as the twig is bent so is the tree inclined."

"I know," said the young mother, "but this twig is bent on being a girl, and we are inclined to let it go at that."

1185.   The little girl from the city was visiting her grandparents on the farm. When she found half a dozen milk bottles lying in the grass behind the barn, she rushed into the house and said, "Oh, Grandma, I found a cow's nest."

Little girl

1186. The Sunday school teacher was amazed at the sudden improvement in the behavior of a particular little girl. She thought she should praise her a bit. "You've been a real good girl today," she said.

"Yes, ma'am," the girl said, "I couldn't help it. I've got a stiff neck."

1187. The Sunday school teacher was quizzing her little pupils. "What can you tell me about King Solomon?" she asked.

"I know about him," said one little girl. "He liked women and animals."

"Women and animals?" the teacher asked. "Where did you learn that?"

"Well," the little girl said, "the Bible says he had a thousand wives and three hundred porcupines."

137, 156, 244, 280, 301, 378, 462, 2086

Loan

1188. Man to his friend: "I can't imagine what Joe does with his money. He's always broke. Yesterday, the day before, and still broke today."

Friend: "What did he do—try to borrow from you?"

First man: "No, I've been trying to borrow something from him."

1189. "If a farmer had 4,000 bushels of corn," the teacher asked, "and it was bringing 40 cents a bushel, what would the farmer get?"

"He'd get a government loan," said the smart farmer's son.

76, 105, 120, 181, 524, 670, 742, 1128

Location

1190. It was history time and the teacher asked her class, "Where was the Declaration of Independence signed?"

"All over the bottom half of the page," said a little boy who had seen a copy of it.

Location

1191. "What are you doing hiding under the bed?" a mother asked her little girl.

"It's all that lightning and thunder," she said. "I don't want to get struck by lightning."

"Oh, that's silly," said her mother. "If lightning is going to strike you, it will strike you no matter where you are."

"That's all right," the little girl said, "but if it's going to strike me, I just want to be hard to find."

268, 425, 464, 537, 762, 1324, 1574, 1813, 1902, 1928, 1940, 2050

Logic

1192. A teacher was lecturing to her students on the evils of drink. "And in conclusion," she said, "I shall prove my point with a demonstration. I have here two glasses, one filled with water, the other with whiskey. I now place a worm in each glass. Notice how the worm in the water squirms and wiggles with the very spark of life, while the worm in the whiskey twists in agony and dies. Now, what is the moral of this story?"

A voice in the rear said: "If you don't want worms, drink whiskey."

1193. A teacher who was punishing a little boy, said to him: "This is the fifth time I have punished you this week, what have you got to say about it?"

Little boy: "I'm sure glad it's Friday."

1194. A lady at the zoo stood before the penguins and asked the keeper all sorts of questions.

"How can you tell," she asked, "whether these queer birds are male or female?"

"It's easy, lady," said the keeper. "You just tell a joke. If he laughs, it's a male, and if she laughs, it's a female."

1195. The teacher of English literature was preparing her class for a test. "Can you tell me anything about the great poets of the 17th century?" she asked.

"They are all dead," said her star pupil.

Logic

1196. A college freshman was talking about girls with his friend. "Which would you advise me to do? Marry a sensible girl or a beautiful girl?" he asked his friend.

"I don't think you will be able to marry either," his friend said.

"Why not?" the freshman said.

"It's logical," said his friend. "A beautiful girl could do better and a sensible girl would know better."

1197. A college boy, home from school, was talking to his father about the "Law of Compensation" which he had studied. "If a person loses one eye," he explained, "the sight in the other becomes stronger. If he loses the hearing in one ear, the hearing in the other becomes more acute. If he loses one hand, he becomes more agile with the other."

"I guess that is right," the boy's father said. "I have always noticed that when a man has one short leg, the other is longer."

1198. Two Southern gentlemen, who had spent a convivial evening together, met on the street at about 10 o'clock the next morning.

"How do you all feel this morning, Colonel?" asked the first.

"I feel awful, Colonel," roared the other genially, "just as any Southern gentleman should at this unreasonable hour of the morning, sir."

1199. "This is a lesson in logic," the professor said. "If the show starts at nine and dinner is at six and my son has the measles, and my brother drives a Cadillac, how old am I?"

"You're forty-four," said a student promptly.

"Right," said the professor. "Now tell the rest of the class how you arrived at the correct answer."

"It was easy," the fellow said. "I've got an uncle who is twenty-two and he's only half nuts."

7, 279, 312, 1019

Longevity

1200. At the revival meeting, the visiting preacher said, "If there is any man here who has no enemies, let him stand up."

A ninety-six-year-old fellow in the back stood up.

"Do you mean to stand there and say you have never had an enemy," the preacher shouted.

"No," said the man. "I've just outlived all of them."

1201. The tourist was talking to the man who had just celebrated his ninetieth birthday. "And to what do you owe your great age?" he asked.

"Well, I'm not sure yet," the man said. "I'm dickering with a couple of breakfast food companies."

1202. "What do you mean writing a $50,000 insurance policy on that 99-year-old man?" the insurance broker demanded of his new salesman. "Don't you know he is not a good risk?"

"He seemed to be a good risk to me," said the salesman. "I looked it up on the charts and you'd be surprised how few men 99-years old die each year."

65, 72, 232, 382, 1386, 2003, 2118

Looks

1203. The attractive cashier asked for a vacation.

"I must rest up," she said, "my beauty is beginning to fade."

"What makes you think that?" asked her boss.

"I've noticed the men are beginning to count their change," she said.

1204. A lady at a concert leaned over and whispered to her husband, "Doesn't that soprano have a large repertoire?"

"Yes," he said, "and that dress she has on doesn't help it any."

1205. Two old college chums met after many years. "And how is your wife?" asked the first. "Is she as beautiful as ever?"

"Oh, yes," said the other, "only it takes her a lot longer now."

1206. The rather fussy society type was shopping in the fish market. "I want to buy some fish for supper," she said, "but I certainly don't like the looks of your mullet."

Looks

"Well," said the man, "if it's looks you are after, why don't you buy some goldfish?"

1207.   The elderly society dame had just been examined by the famous plastic surgeon regarding a possible face-lifting operation.

"And how much will it cost?" she asked.

"The entire operation and costs will come to $2,500," he said.

"Why," said the woman, "that's outrageous. Isn't there something that I could do that wouldn't be so expensive?"

"Yes," said the doctor, "you might start wearing a veil."

111, 188, 368, 384, 417, 475, 720, 1226, 1362

Lost

1208.   The lesson was on natural history, and the teacher asked, "Where is the elephant found? I want Wibur to tell us."

Wilbur looked puzzled for a moment, then said, "To tell the truth, the elephant is such a big animal that it's hardly ever lost."

1209.   The little girl in the department store was crying, and the floorwalker asked her, "What's the matter, little girl? Are you lost?"

"No," she said between tears. "I'm here, my mother's lost."

1210.   A drunk approached the policeman on the corner and said, "Pardon me, officer, but where am I?"

"You're on the corner of Main and Forsyth," the policeman said.

"Never mind the details," the man said. "What town am I in?"

1211.   The little boy was lost at the fairgrounds. He was weeping his heart out when a policeman found him and asked him what was the matter.

"I'm lost," said the little boy.

"Who were you with?" asked the officer.

"My father," the boy said.

Lost

"Oh, we'll find him," the officer said. "What's your father like?"

"Whiskey and poker," said the little boy.

1212. A tramp stopped a lady and said, "Can you help an unfortunate soul? I've lost my leg."

"Well," said the lady. "I haven't found it. Why don't you put an advertisement in the newspaper?"

1213. The lady was lost. She really didn't know where she wanted to go. She had been pestering the bus driver to death. Finally, she asked him, "Does this bus stop at the Roney-Plaza?"

"No, lady," he said, "it can't afford the Roney-Plaza. It has to stay in the garage overnight."

1214. It was beginning to get dark and the two deer hunters hated to admit it but they were lost. As darkness came on they began to worry about finding their way. Finally, with panic in his voice, one of them said, "We're lost. I say we're lost. Lost, do you hear? Lost."

"Aw, keep quiet," the other man said. "Don't lose your head. We'll keep going the way we're headed and we'll find our way. If we don't, all we'll have to do is to shoot an extra deer and the game warden will show up in about five minutes."

106, 204, 258, 729, 1169, 1761

Love

1215. Girl's father: "What reason do you have, young man, for wanting to marry my daughter?"

Young man: "I haven't any reason. I'm in love."

1216. Salesman to his friend: "Was that a new girl friend I saw you with last night?"

His friend: "No, just the old one painted over."

79, 102, 117, 132, 213, 274, 411, 575

Luck

1217. Friend: "My luck's run out."

Neighbor: "What's the matter?"

Friend: "Three weeks ago my grandfather died and left me $50,000."

Neighbor: "You call that bad luck?"

Friend: "No, but two weeks ago my aunt died and left me $30,000. Last week an uncle left me $40,000."

Neighbor: "So, what do you mean, your luck's run out?"

Friend: "This week—nothing."

1218. A big tipper at a resort found a new waiter serving him breakfast one morning.

"Where is my regular waiter?" he wanted to know. "You know, the one they call Willy?"

"Excuse me, sir, but Willy ain't serving you any more, 'cause I won you in a crap game last night."

1219. The owner of the restaurant was carefully checking the work of his new cook.

"You say you were an army cook during the war?" he asked.

"Yes, sir," the cook said. "I cooked for officer's mess for over two years and was wounded three times."

"Huh," said the boss. "You're lucky they didn't kill you."

1220. A Washington newspaperman was interviewing a noted scientist who had just been assigned to the Atomic Energy Commission. He noticed that the great scientist was wearing a rabbit's foot on his key chain.

"You don't mean to tell me," said the newspaperman, "that you, a man dedicated to science, believes in that old superstition?"

"Certainly not," said the scientist, "but a friend of mine from down in Alabama tells me it's supposed to bring you luck whether you believe in it or not."

1221. An old college chum was visiting his friend in New England for the first time since graduation years before. The New Englander was a not-too-successful farmer.

Luck

"I've never seen such a poor-looking farm," the old chum said to the farmer. "Nothing but rocks and hilly ground. I don't see how you are able to get along."

"The truth is," said his friend, "I'm a lot better off than you think I am. At least I don't own this place."

1222. "Everybody has something to be thankful for," the minister said to the man who was sitting in his office telling a tale of woe. "Look at the man across the street from you who just lost his wife in an automobile accident."

"Yes," the man said, "but everybody can't be that lucky."

126, 178, 387, 576, 602, 999, 1433

Lying

1223. Neighbor: "Can you tell by your husband's face if he's lying?"

Veteran wife: "Yes, if his lips are moving, he is."

1224. A man was telling about being rescued during his recent vacation at a seaside resort. "At 7:15," he said, "I suggested to my wife that we take a sail. At 7:30 we started. As soon as we were beyond the breakers, a high wind capsized the boat. We would have drowned if a passing porpoise hadn't taken us on his back and brought us to land."

His friend appeared to be skeptical, so the man asked, "Don't you believe the story?"

"No, sir," he said, "trying to tell me your wife got ready in 15 minutes!"

569, 813, 984

Maid

1225. A hostess was instructing a new maid about her duties. "When you set the table for dinner tonight, be sure you put the forks on the left side of the plate. And be careful to put the plates so that the designs are straight and even. And above all, make sure that the napkins are folded neatly."

Maid

"Yes, Ma'am," said the new maid, "but why are you so superstitious?"

1226. A vacuum cleaner salesman rang the doorbell and was admitted by a woman, who immediately left the room. After saying hello to the man in the room, the salesman said, "Was that your wife who let me in?"

"Certainly. Do you think I'd hire a maid as homely as that?" asked the man.

31, 444, 566, 588, 1038, 1103, 1943

Mail

1227. The college girl wrote home to her mother: "I realize, Mother, that Father is paying a lot to keep me in college. And to show him that I appreciate all he is doing for me, I am taking up contract bridge."

504, 560, 772, 1768

Manners

1228. The six-year-old went to school, all dressed up in a new blouse and skirt. When she came home, her mother asked if anyone had commented on her new clothes.

"Yes," the little girl said, "the teacher did. She said since I was dressed like a lady, I should act like one."

1229. Two young ladies were chatting.

"What sports do you like best?" asked the first.

"Those who are free with their money," said the second, "and know when to say goodnight and go home."

1230. The cannibal mother scolded her son for his bad manners. "How many times must I tell you," she said, "not to talk with someone in your mouth?"

158, 263, 425, 453, 583, 1183

Marriage

1231. A young lady went to a married friend for advice. She said to her: "Should I marry a fellow who lies to me?"

Her friend said: "Yes, unless you want to be an old maid."

1232. "I'll never forget my wedding day," said Joe. "When the time came, I couldn't find the ring. Boy, did I get an awful fright!"

"Yes," said his friend, "I know, and you've still got her."

1233. A young man was describing the newly finished church to a girl friend.

"You should see the new altar in the sanctuary," he said.

"Boy, lead me to it," she replied instantly.

1234. A bachelor asked a married friend about wives in general.

"Well, I'll tell you about wives in general," his friend said. "A wife is a woman who will stick by you through all the trouble you would never have got into if you hadn't married her in the first place."

1235. As a pretty girl passed by, the husband turned to look. His wife said with a pout, "Every time you see a pretty girl, you forget you're married."

"That's where you're wrong," he said. "Nothing makes me more aware of the fact."

1236. Two friendly taxi drivers stopped at a stop light. "How's your old jalopy?" yelled the first one.

"Oh, my wife's fine," said the other. "How's yours?"

1237. The young man had just proposed, and his future bride was bubbling over with happiness—and plans. "And just think," she said, "I shall always be there to share your troubles."

"But, honey," said the young man, "I don't have any troubles."

"But," she said, "I was talking about after we are married."

25, 47, 241, 261, 281, 289, 368, 411, 534, 544, 733, 1196, 1470, 1692

Matronly

1238. A rich society matron visited the hospital to see her chauffeur, who had been badly injured in an automobile accident.

The head nurse said, "He's a very sick man and is not supposed to see anyone but members of his family. Are you his wife?"

Highly indignant, the society leader said, "I certainly am not, I'm his mistress."

728, 769

Medicine

1239. A medicine-show quack was passing the house of a well-to-do family in a small town and said to the yardman, "Anybody sick in this house?"

"No, not now," said the man. "The lady of the house was sick, but I heard the doctor say this morning she was convalescent."

"Nothin' to it," said the quack. "Why, I can cure convalescence in twenty-four hours!"

1240. A woman had been taking tranquilizers and her friend was asking her about them.

"There are times when I get nervous," the first woman said. "I have thought of taking a tranquilizer now and then, but I am afraid they are habit forming. Are they?"

"Habit forming?" her friend said. "Certainly not. Not if you take them regularly."

8, 435, 517, 540, 557, 604, 641, 1346, 2083

Memory

1241. A woman asked her neighbor, "Does your husband remember your wedding anniversary?"

"No," said her friend. "He completely forgets. So I remind him of it in January and June, and I always get two presents."

8, 12, 415, 487, 687, 1235

Minister

1242. The preacher's car broke down one Sunday morning. On Monday he drove it to the local garage for repairs.

"I hope you'll go a little easy on the price," he told the mechanic. "After all, I'm a poor preacher."

"I know it," the mechanic said, "I heard you yesterday."

1243. A minister, called suddenly away and unable to officiate at the Christmas services in his own church, entrusted his new assistant with the duty. When he returned home, he asked his wife what she thought of the young man's sermon.

"The poorest I ever heard," she said. "Nothing in it at all. It didn't even make sense."

Later that day, the minister, meeting his assistant, asked him how he had managed.

"Fine, sir, absolutely wonderful," he said. "I didn't have time to prepare anything myself, so I preached one of your old sermons."

1244. A minister and a doctor were joking with each other about their respective professions. When the minister inquired about the health of an elderly member of his congregation whom he knew the doctor was attending, the doctor looked real serious about it.

"The poor man," he said. "To tell the truth, he needs your help more than mine."

"Is it that bad?" the minister asked with great concern.

"Yes," said the doctor, shaking his head, "I've been trying to get him to take a nap every afternoon and he just can't seem to get to sleep."

1245. How to get rid of a minister:

1. Look him straight in the eye when he is preaching, and say "Amen" once in a while. He'll preach himself to death in a few weeks.

2. Pat him on the back and brag on his good points. He'll work himself to death.

3. Start paying him a living wage. He's probably been on starvation wages so long, he'll eat himself to death.

4. Rededicate your own life to the church and ask the preacher to give you a job to do. He'll probably die of heart failure.

5. Get the church to unite in prayer for the preacher. He'll become so effective, some larger church will take him off your hands.

1246. A minister was being entertained at dinner and the other guests were praising his sermon. One of them turned to his host's young son, who was at the table, and asked, "Young fellow, what did you think of the sermon?"

"Oh, it was all right," said the boy, "only he passed up three real good places where he could have stopped."

1247. One Sunday, during the church service, the wife of a deacon became worried about the roast at home in the oven. She thought she had left the oven on. Worried, she sent a note to her husband by another usher. This usher thought the note was for the preacher. He tiptoed down and laid it on the pulpit.

The preacher paused in his sermon, opened the note, and read, "Please go home and turn off the gas."

1248. A Protestant minister was walking down the street dressed in ministerial black, when he met two small Catholic boys. One of the boys, recognizing the dress, said, "Good morning, Father."

The other boy nudged him and whispered, "Don't be stupid, he ain't no father, he's got a wife and three kids."

1249. The minister was visiting the man in the hospital, who had been badly injured in a fight. "I'm going to pray so you'll forgive your enemy for hitting you with a brick," the minister said.

"It might be better," the man said, "if you waited until I get out of here and then pray for the other fellow."

1250. A Methodist minister was invited to conduct services at an Episcopal church. Before the service, he and the rector were in the rectory getting prepared.

"I suppose you'll want to wear a surplice," said the rector. "Surplice!" said the other. "I am a Methodist. What do I know about surplices? All we have is deficits!"

1251. "Oh," said the member of the congregation to the minister's wife, "didn't you think your husband's sermon last Sunday, 'One Day's Rest in Seven,' was absolutely inspiring?"

"I can't really say, because I didn't hear it," said the minister's wife. "I had to stay home and get his dinner."

1252. The ship was sinking rapidly. The captain cried out, "Does anybody know how to pray?"

"Yes, captain, I do," said a minister who was a passenger.

"Wonderful," said the captain. "You start praying. The rest of us will put on life belts. We are one short."

1253. The farmer and his wife were talking about their contribution to the annual benefit for their minister.

"What'll we give this year?" the farmer's wife asked.

"Well, it's hard to figure," the farmer said. "Potatoes are up, pork is up, turkey and chicken are way up. You know, we'll save money by giving him money."

1254. The minister had announced that he was going to read that day from The New English Bible. When the service was over, and he was greeting people at the door, a little lady said to him, "I didn't like it. If the King James version of the Bible was good enough for Paul and Silas, then it's good enough for me."

1255. "Nothing," said the preacher, "that is false, ever does anybody any good."

"You are wrong there," said the old man. "I have false teeth and they do me a lot of good."

1256. The minister of the local Christian Church helped organize a community church in a nearby rural area. It was the only church for several miles and since everybody in the neighborhood had contributed to it, it was called the community church. Later, a group wanted a name for it. The Christian minister was in favor of calling it a Christian Church but felt that in fairness, the congregation should vote on it.

On the night of the decision, he was presiding and said to the congregation, "Tonight we are going to vote on whether or not to call this a Christian Church. Before we vote if anyone has anything they would like to say, we would like to hear it now."

A fellow got up in the back and said, "Yes, I've got something to say. I am a Baptist. And I have been a Baptist for 67 years and you're not going to make a Christian out of me."

1257.　One Saturday night, the local poker party continued all night long and did not break up until after 11:00 o'clock Sunday morning. On their way home, several of the players passed a church where the services had just begun.

"I feel terrible," one of them said. "Here it is Sunday morning and we should be in church instead of being on our way home from drinking and playing cards all night long."

"I feel the same way," his friend said. "Here is a church. We could slip in and sit on the back seat, and nobody would pay any attention to us."

And that is what they did.

When the congregation stood up to sing, these fellows, still a bit under the influence, sang louder than anybody else. And when the collection plate was passed, their consciences bothered them so much that each one put in a $20 bill.

The minister had never seen a $20 bill in the collection plate before and when the service was over, he asked the deacon who the visitors were and what church they belonged to.

"I don't know what church they belong to," the deacon said. "They sang like Methodists, they contributed like Catholics, but they sure smelled like Episcopalians."

1258.　A preacher was reading his sermon, but in the last-minute rush to start the service, he had accidentally dropped a page as he entered the pulpit.

As he finished the first page, his sermon went something like this: "And Adam said to Eve . . . . that's funny, there seems to be a leaf missing."

16, 52, 118, 133, 183, 243, 264, 341, 361, 374, 390, 580, 585, 653, 660, 1491, 2108

Miracle

1259. "Well, Doctor," asked the man, following his annual examination, "how do I stand?"

"I don't know," replied the doctor. "But I think it's a miracle."

1915, 2082

Miss

1260. Two old friends were sitting in what had once been their favorite saloon. The old place had been modernized and redecorated. The old boys fell to chatting about the good old days.

"I suppose it's all right," the first one said, "all these new-fashioned trappings and everything, but I miss the old spittoon."

"Yes," said the other, "and you always did."

25, 154, 1020

Missionary

1261. A young medical missionary arrived in Africa to take up his life's work of bringing health and enlightenment to the savages. He was surprised to find that the cities were modern, with paved streets and modern buildings. He told a guide: "I want to see the real Africa. I want to go where few white men have ever been. Where the primitive ways of the ignorant medicine men are still practiced—where I can truly carry the light of modern medicine."

His guide proceeded to take him to the deepest interior of the Black Continent. After a month's safari, the guide announced that when they reached the next village, they would be at a place where only one other white doctor had ever visited —a Doctor Dawson from Johns Hopkins. As they approached the native huts, the entire population of the village came forward to meet them. The chief headed the group. Beside him was an aide who carried a large wooden tray on which stood a tiny man only six inches tall. The man was dressed in American style clothes and was carrying a tiny black bag.

"We're in luck," cried the guide. "Here is the chief and his aide. And there on the tray is Doctor Dawson. Dr. Dawson, it's good to see you again. This is our new medical missionary I am bringing to the village. Please tell him that fascinating story about the time you called the local witch doctor a faker."

1262. The lady from Boston tried not to show her feeling of superiority. But somehow, she never quite succeeded. Once when she was in Salt Lake City, she was talking with a little Mormon girl.

"I'm from Boston," she said. "Do you know where Boston is, young lady?"

"Why, certainly," said the little girl. "Our church has a missionary there."

665

Mistake

1263. A man brought a cheap watch to a jeweler to be repaired.

"The mistake," he said, "was in dropping it down a flight of stairs."

"No" said the jeweler. "Your mistake was picking it up."

1264. A romantically inclined young lady said to her mother, "What made you marry Daddy?"

"So you're beginning to wonder, too," said her mother.

10, 126, 163, 293, 359, 395, 440, 457, 540, 608, 647, 777, 2107

Mistrust

1265. Two inebriated gentlemen were staggering along the road together one dark night. One of them snapped on his flashlight, pointing it skyward.

Mistrust

"I betcha fifty dollars," he said, "you can't climb that beam."

"Oh, no, ya don't, I'm not gonna fall for that old gag," his friend said. "I'd get halfway up and you'd turn it off."

577, 1881

Model

1266. A young lady was talking to a friend: "The man I marry," she said, "must shine in company, be musical, tell jokes, sing, dance, and stay home nights."

"You don't want a husband," her friend said. "You want a television set."

141, 735, 880, 1706

Modern age

1267. Modern lad: "Grandpa, do you think the world is getting faster or slowing down?"

Grandpa: "Definitely slowing down, son. For example, when I was a boy you could hear any record in three minutes and now it takes an hour."

1268. The little fellow was having a hard time keeping his Wild West television program and his space ship program separated in his mind. Dressed in his space helmet, he said to his dad, "Put 'em up, you ornery old horned toad, or I'll plug you with my six-shooter."

"You've got it wrong," said his dad. "You're talking Western, not space."

"I," said the little boy, "am from West Mars."

69, 967, 1017

Modesty

1269. The sheriff's deputy stood on the lake shore and said to the young girl in swimming, "I'm sorry, young lady, but swimming is not allowed in this lake."

Modesty

"Why didn't you tell me before I undressed?" she asked.

"Well," he said, "there ain't no law against undressing."

269, 430, 751, 823, 1007, 1606, 1682, 1848, 1884

Money

1270.   A fellow was explaining his ideas to a friend.

"They say that people with opposite characteristics make the best marriages," he said. "That's why I'm looking for a girl with money."

1271.   Two men were chatting at a bar. "Do you have the same trouble with your wife that I have with mine?"

"What trouble?"

"Why, money trouble. She keeps nagging me for money, money, money, and then more money."

"What does she want with all the money you give her? What does she do with it?"

"I don't know. I never give her any."

1272.   He didn't want to marry her for her money, but he didn't know any other way to get it.

1273.   Man's wife: "Which do you think is more satisfied, honey, a man with a million dollars or a man with six children?"

Husband: "That's easy, a man with six children is the happiest."

Man's wife: "What makes you think so?"

Husband: "Because a man with a million dollars wants that much more."

1274.   A six-year-old was telling his younger brother about the value of money.

"This," he said, "is a dime. It will buy two candy bars. And this is a nickel. It will buy only one candy bar."

Finally he reached in his pocket and brought out a penny.

"And this," he said, "is a penny. It's only good for Sunday school."

Money

1275. A rich American girl was a guest at a party in England, and one of the women there was being just a bit catty. "You American girls are so pale," she said. "Your complexions are not nearly as rosy as ours. I simply can't understand what our men see in your white faces."

"Don't kid yourself," said the American girl. "It's not our white faces they like, it's our greenbacks."

1276. Maybe you can't take money with you, but where can you go today without it?

1277. A woman told her friend, "My husband and I like the same thing. The only difference is he likes to save it, and I like to spend it."

1278. A mother-in-law was being a bit critical of the way her daughter-in-law was raising the children.

"One thing I notice that you do," she said to her daughter-in-law, "is to pay the children for keeping quiet. I saw you give little George a dime to be good. I never had to give his father anything to behave—he was always good for nothing."

1279. It was the evening of the masquerade ball.

"I wonder what our friends will say when they see me dressed in these circus tights," the woman said to her husband.

"They'll probably say I married you for your money," he said.

126, 140, 184, 205, 226, 264, 319, 389, 436, 449, 1253, 2044, 2054

Monkey

1280. "Are you trying to make a monkey out of me?" asked the husband.

"Why should I take the credit?" said his wife.

628, 1326, 1695, 2120

Motel

1281. A couple stopped at a motel and the man's wife asked, "Do you have hot and cold running water in this motel?"

Motel

"Of course, lady," said the clerk. "It's hot in summer and cold in winter."

488, 989

Mother

1282. A rather old-fashioned fellow was watching the youngsters put on their horse show. He said to a bystander, "It's terrible the way they dress today. Just look at that young boy with the cigarette, sloppy haircut, and tight breeches."

"That is not a boy," said the other. "It's a girl and she's my daughter."

"Oh, excuse me, sir," said the man. "I meant no offense. I did not know you were her father."

"I'm not," said the other, "I'm her mother."

130, 258, 280, 320, 338, 354, 364, 428, 511, 580, 632, 1209

Mother-in-law

1283. Lady at the front door: "Will you donate something to the Old Ladies' Home?"

Man answering the door: "With pleasure. Help yourself to my mother-in-law."

1284. The farm girl was milking a cow, when suddenly a bull tore across the meadow toward her. The girl didn't move, but kept on milking. Several men, who were watching from the next field, were surprised when the bull stopped dead within a few yards of the girl. He then turned around and walked away.

"Weren't you afraid?" asked the men.

"Of course not," said the girl. "This cow is his mother-in-law."

335, 350, 906, 1278

Movies

1285. A husband said to his wife as they left the triple-feature movie, "Well, if you must know, it gave me a colossal, sensational, stupendous, terrific, breathtaking headache!"

106, 251

Mule

1286. It was a hot day and the farmer was having a hard time trying to drive his two mules into a field. Just as he was giving them a piece of his mind, the local minister came by.

"Excuse me, parson," said the farmer. "I need your advice. Just how did Noah get these two into the Ark?"

42, 486, 579, 609, 931, 1589

Music

1287. Once, when a young concert pianist's concert was panned by the critics, an old-timer in the business patted him gently on the shoulder.

"Remember, young man," he said, "there is no place anywhere in the world where a statue has been erected to a critic."

1288. The music publisher was talking about a new song to his promotion manager: "I've never heard such corny lyrics, such simpering sentimentality, such repetitious uninspired melody. Man, we've sure got a hit on our hands!"

1289. "You say your son plays the piano like Paderewski?" a man asked a friend.

"Yes," his friend said. "He uses both hands."

1290. A man in the upstairs apartment yelled to the man downstairs, "If you don't stop playing that clarinet, I'll go crazy."

"Too late, now," the man said. "I stopped an hour ago."

1291. A composer was commissioned to write the complete score for a Hollywood musical in ten days.

"That certainly will take a lot out of you, won't it?" commented a friend.

"Not out of me," the composer said, "but out of Brahms, Bach, and Beethoven."

1292. A man took his wife to the Shrine circus. The man on the trapeze, high above the crowd, hung precariously by his toes as he swung through the air.

Music

The man's wife watched incredulously as the trapeze artist, still hanging by his toes and swinging, arched his back and forced his head between his legs. He then caught a violin that was pitched to him, and then the bow.

As he swung 100 feet above the audience, hanging on by his toes, with his head between his legs, he began playing a tune on his violin.

"Oh," said the woman. "Isn't he wonderful?"

Her husband shrugged and grunted, "He ain't no Heifetz."

1293.   The little girl's parents considered themselves to be concert violinists. A visitor asked the little girl, "Who do you think plays better, your mother or your father?"

"Fritz Kreisler," said the little girl.

1294.   A neighbor was talking across the back fence to his friend.

"Your son is making good progress with his saxophone," he said. "He is beginning to play quite nice tunes."

"Do you really think so?" asked his friend. "We were afraid we had just begun to get used to it."

1295.   A hostess kept begging the noted pianist to play.

"Well, all right, since you insist," he said. "What shall I play?"

"Anything you like," his hostess said. "It's only to annoy the neighbors."

1296.   A man was talking to the music teacher about a student.

"What do you think of her playing?" he asked.

"She plays in the true spirit of Christian charity," the teacher said.

"What do you mean by that?" the man asked.

"Her right hand does not know what her left hand is doing," said the teacher.

1297.   The local, small-town, community band was giving their weekly concert and had finished an extremely loud number. The musicians were resting and enjoying the enthusiastic applause.

Music

"What's the next number?" asked the tuba player.

The leader checked his program and said, "The Stars and Stripes Forever."

"Gosh," said the musician. "I just got through playing that!"

38, 47, 264, 374, 508, 589, 602, 715, 977, 998

Nagging

1298.   A henpecked husband was complaining to a friend.

"My wife is a nagger," he said.

"What is she fussing about this time?" his friend asked.

"Now she's begun to nag me about what I eat. This morning she asked me if I knew how many pancakes I had eaten. I told her I don't count pancakes and she had the nerve to tell me I had eaten 19 already."

"And what did you say?" asked his friend.

"I didn't say anything. I was so mad I just got up from the table and went to work without my breakfast."

1299.   A young fellow was studying his homework and said to his father, "Dad, what is a monologue?"

"A monologue," his father said, "is a conversation being carried on by a woman with her husband."

19, 61, 511, 752, 1271

Names

1300.   A young man about to be married said to his friend, "What did you call your mother-in-law after you were married?"

"Well, that sort of took care of itself," his friend said. "For the first year I got by with addressing her as 'Say' and from then on we called her 'Grandma.' "

1301.   A proud father was passing out the traditional cigars at the office. "Boy or girl?" asked his boss.

"It's a boy," the young father said.

"What did you name him?" the boss asked.

"John," said the father.

Names

"Why did you name him John?" asked the boss. "Don't you know that every Tom, Dick, and Harry is named John?"

1302.   "This is the first day of school," the teacher said to her class, "and I want to get acquainted with all of you and to learn about your families."

Then, looking at a little girl in the front row she said, "And what is your father's name?"

"His name is Daddy," the little girl said.

"No," said the teacher. "I mean his name. What does your mother call him?"

"She doesn't call him anything," the little girl said. "She likes him."

337, 406, 486, 496, 770, 1140, 1576, 2042, 2057

Neat

1303.   A lady in the restaurant asked the waiter, "Is there any hollandaise sauce on the bill of fare?"

"No, lady," he said. "There was, but I wiped it off."

189, 360, 388, 983, 1720, 1999

Neglect

1304.   A wife complained bitterly to her husband. "I'm absolutely ashamed of the way we live. Mother pays our rent. My aunt buys our clothes. My sister sends us money for food. I don't like to complain, but I'm ashamed that we can't do better than that."

"You should be ashamed," her husband said. "You've got two uncles that don't send us a dime."

19, 661

Neighborly

1305.   "Why is your next-door neighbor so unpopular?"

"He's rigged up his lawn mower so you have to drop a nickel in it to make it go."

Neighborly

1306. The man and his wife had just moved into the suburbs and wanted to get acquainted. The man's wife asked him to drop in on a neighbor and give her an armful of roses from the garden. He found the neighbor's front door open, stepped inside, and asked if anybody was at home.

"Yes, we are, and we're busy," said the lady's voice from the kitchen. "What are you doing here at this time of day? Sit down and keep quiet."

The man did as he was told. Ten minutes later, the lady and her little girl came out of the kitchen. The lady was speechless, but the little girl said, "She thought you were Daddy."

1307. After several poor years in school, the little boy had begun to bring home all "A's" on his report card. Just about the time his parents had begun to develop a real sense of pride in his work, his grades fell off again. They were right back where they had been for so long.

"What is wrong?" his father asked. "Why aren't you getting good grades any more?"

"It's the teacher's fault," the boy said. "She moved that smart little girl who was sitting in front of me."

1308. Two women were having a neighborly chat over the back fence.

"Our new neighbor down the street sure does love her husband," the first woman said. "You should see her meet him at the door every evening when he comes home from work and give him a big kiss."

"Huh," said the other. "That isn't love. She's just checking up on him to make sure he hasn't been drinking."

710, 715, 742, 862, 1120, 1458, 1806, 1882

New car

1309. A man was showing his friend his new car.

"I sure wish I could afford a car like this," his friend said

"So do I," the owner said.

New car

1310. The man was looking over the new car, and asked the salesman, "What's the main difference between this model and last year's?"

"Well," said the salesman, "the cigarette lighter is about an inch nearer the steering wheel."

659

Newspaper

1311. A small town is a place where everybody knows what everyone else is doing, but he reads the local paper to see if they've been caught at it.

1312. The editor of the country paper seemed unusually happy.

"What are you so happy about?" asked his wife at supper.

"Oh, I had some good luck today," the editor said. "An old farmer who hasn't paid for his paper in over 10 years came in today and canceled his subscription."

163, 330, 395, 414, 559, 677, 747, 1963

Noise

1313. Man from downstairs: "Didn't you folks hear me pounding on the ceiling?"

Host to the party upstairs: "Oh, that's perfectly all right. We've been making quite a lot of noise ourselves for the past hour or so."

1314. "They tell me you love music," the show-off at the piano said.

"Yes," said the kind lady, "but please keep on playing anyway."

1315. "Good morning," said the boss to the proud new father. "I hear you have a new baby at your house."

Noise

"For goodness' sakes," said the man. "you can't hear him all the way up here, can you?"

1316.   A man was awakened suddenly in the middle of the night by what he thought was an explosion next door. He listened for a few moments. Not hearing anything more, he turned over and went back to sleep. Next morning at the bus stop he saw his next-door neighbor and said, "I thought I heard an explosion at your house last night. What was it?"

"It was an explosion," his neighbor said, "caused by a bit of powder on my coat lapel."

2, 147, 158

Nudist

1317.   Two little boys were walking past the high board fence that surrounded a nudist colony. One of the youngsters spotted a knothole and peeked in. "Hey," he shouted to his companion, "there's a lot of people in there."

"Men or women?" the other little boy asked.

"I can't tell," said the first little fellow. "They don't have any clothes on."

9, 397

Numbers

1318.   There are 1,000 evils in the world: two are wine and song and the other 998 are women.

1319.   The young man had mustered up the courage to ask his girl friend's father for her hand in marriage.

"And you want to marry my daughter?" her father said.

"Yes, sir," the young fellow said.

"Do you think you can support a family on your salary?" the man asked.

"That depends," the young man said, "on how many of you there are."

811

Nurse

1320.   A badly injured man came to, to find himself in bed with a nurse watching over him.

"Where am I? Where am I?" he cried.

"This is number 127," the nurse said.

"Room or cell?" the man asked.

59, 658, 704

Obedience

1321.   "Lay down, doggie, down, down," ordered the man. "Good doggie, lay down."

"You'll have to tell him to lie down, Mister," said a bystander. "He's a Boston terrier."

1322.   "Is your dog well behaved?" asked the lady.

"Yes, he is," said the little boy. "When I say to him, come here or don't come here, just as you please, he comes or he doesn't come, as he pleases."

579

Obituary

1323.   The editor was confronted by a hot-tempered man who shouted, "That report of my death in your paper was a lie. I'll horsewhip you publicly if you don't apologize in your next issue." When the next edition appeared, it contained the following item: "We regret very much that the notice of Mr. George Brown's death that appeared in our last issue was not true."

1324.   A banker was sitting down to breakfast one morning when he read an announcement of his own death in the newspaper. He quickly called his cashier at home and said:

"Have you read the morning paper? Did you see the announcement of my death?"

"Yes," said his cashier. "Where are you calling from?"

1325.   A woman went to the office of the local paper and said she would like to put a notice in about her husband's death. "How much will it cost?" she asked.

Obituary

"We charge fifty cents an inch," the editor said.

"Oh, I can't afford that kind of money," said the widow. "My husband was six feet tall!"

Occupation

1326. "What is your occupation?" the lady asked.

"I used to be an organist," the poor man said.

"And why did you give it up?" the lady asked.

"The monkey died," he said.

1327. One evening at supper a woman told her husband that her nephew had just lost his job. "Do you think you could help him find one?" she asked.

"I might," her husband said. "I have a friend who is the manager of the Eagle Laundry. I think I could get him a job there."

"I don't think that would work," said his wife. "I'm sure he has never had any experience washing eagles."

90, 500, 736, 777, 1158, 1853

Offensive

1328. As the bus passed a fertilizer factory, a lady passenger opened her bottle of smelling salts. About that time, the bus slowed down for a traffic light. The odor from the factory was almost unbearable.

A man on board stood it as long as he could, but finally cried out, "Please, lady, would you mind putting the cork back in the bottle? You're smelling up the whole bus."

1329. "I don't like that young man you are going out with," the young girl's father said to her.

"That makes it mutual," she said, "because he can't stand the sight of you."

582, 1595

Old maid

1330. Voice on phone: "Is this the Police Department?"

Police Sergeant: "Yes, what can we do for you?"

Voice on phone: "I just found two strange men hiding in my apartment. I want you to come and arrest one of them."

1331. An old maid rang the fire alarm and 25 firemen responded. When they arrived she said, "The fire's out, so 24 of you can go back."

1332. "Are you unmarried?" asked the census taker.

"Oh, gracious, no," said the old maid. "I've never even been married."

1333. "What kind of time did you have in Miami Beach?" an old maid asked her friend who had just come back from her vacation.

"Eastern standard time," the friend said.

1334. An old maid came home and went upstairs to go to bed. She thought she heard a noise and looked out the window. Sure enough, there was a man trying to get in.

She dialed the phone as quickly as she could and when a voice answered she said, "Hurry, send that wagon out here right away. There's a man trying to get in my second-story bedroom window."

"Lady," said the voice on the phone, "you have the wrong number. You want the police department. This the fire department."

"I know who I'm calling," she said. "Send that wagon out here right away. That poor man needs a longer ladder."

1335. An old maid checked into the Embassy Hotel. She had been in her room only about five minutes when she called the desk and said, "Get up here right away. You've got to arrest a man for indecent exposure."

In less than five minutes the manager of the hotel arrived, along with the house detective and two bellmen. "Where is that man?" the manager asked.

Old maid

"Right out that window in that room over there," the old maid said, pointing to a hotel about a block away.

"Way over there, lady?" the manager asked. "Why, that's a quarter of a mile away. I can't see anything."

"Well," said the old maid, "you use these binoculars and you can see him all right."

1336.   Two old maids were talking about Christmas and what they wanted Santa to bring them.

"Do you think that one long, wide stocking would hold all you want for Christmas?" the first asked.

"No," said the other, "but a pair of short socks would."

1337.   An old maid walked up to the policeman on the corner and said, "Officer, I want you to arrest that man. He's been following me all over town. I think he must be drunk."

The policeman looked long and carefully at the old maid, then said, "Yes, lady, I guess maybe you're right. He must be drunk."

1338.   A little girl was talking to her old maid aunt who was visiting for the summer.

"Auntie," said the little girl, "why don't you get married?"

"I'll tell you why," she said. "I have a fireplace that smokes and spews ashes all over the rug, a dog that growls all day long, a parrot that swears at everything I do, and a cat that stays out all night. Why should I want to get married?"

1231, 1551

Opinion

1339.   A farmer had been to the state legislature. After he'd spent thirty days with his fellow legislators at the state capitol, he came home for a weekend.

In telling his wife about it, he said: "I've discovered one thing—it's the first insane asylum I've ever seen that's run by the inmates."

Opinion

1340. A guest at a concert turned to the man sitting next to him and criticized the voice of the woman who was singing.

"What a terrible voice," he said. "Do you know who she is?"

"Yes," the man said. "She's my wife."

"Oh," said the embarrassed guest, "I beg your pardon. Of course, it isn't her voice that's bad, it's that awful song she has to sing. I wonder who wrote it."

"I did," said the man.

1341. "When I want your opinion," the man's wife told him, "I'll give it to you."

1342. A drunk cowhand rushed into a bar waving and firing his guns at random and shouting, "All you dirty, lousy skunks get outta here."

Within a minute everybody had scattered and disappeared except one mild-looking fellow who sat at the bar finishing his drink.

"Well?" barked the cowhand, waving his smoking gun. "What about it?"

"My," said the man, "there were certainly a lot of them, weren't there?"

1343. "I am so glad you enjoyed my sermon," the minister said to a lady as they shook hands at the church door. "I noticed your husband walked out during the services. I hope he wasn't ill."

"Oh, no," the lady said, "he walks in his sleep."

1344. The man had just put the finishing touches on the concrete driveway, when a little boy chased a playmate right across it. The man got back on his hands and knees and worked for an hour to erase the footprints and smooth out the damage. As he worked, he kept muttering about the kids who had caused all the trouble.

A man passing by heard him and said, "It sounds as though you don't like children. You shouldn't feel that way."

Opinion

"Oh, I don't dislike children," the man said. "I have children of my own. I like children in the abstract—but not in the concrete."

1345.   Two fight managers were talking about some of their boys. "I hate to talk about Jose behind his back," the first one said, "but it's safer that way!"

1346.   The hobo knocked on the back door and said to the woman of the house, "The lady next door gave me a piece of homemade pie. Won't you give me something, too?"

"Yes," said the lady. "I'd better give you some bicarbonate of soda."

1347.   "Tell me, sir, who was braver than Lawrence of Arabia, wiser than Solomon, wittier than Will Rogers?" asked the lecturer.

"My wife's first husband," the man said.

1348.   The tramp went to the back door of the restaurant with the classic name of George and the Dragon. "I haven't had a bite for days," he said to the woman who seemed to be in charge. "Do you think you could spare me something to eat?"

"No," she shouted. "We don't feed tramps here."

"Thank you," he said and went away. A few minutes later he was back.

"What do you want now?" she asked.

"Could I have a few words with George?" asked the tramp.

1349.   One of the local businessmen had been invited to speak to the children in the third grade. He decided to talk about the progress of the world during the past 50 years. He spent half an hour talking about the great inventions that had been developed during his lifetime.

"And now, before I go, I'd like to ask this question," he said. "What is the most important thing in the world today that wasn't here just twenty years ago?"

"Me," said a little boy in the front row.

74, 145, 290, 384, 421, 450, 481, 510, 593, 1242, 1532, 1795, 2032

Opportunity

1350. "Where are you rushing off to in such a hurry?" a wife asked her husband.

"Over to Joe's house," he said. "He has just phoned and asked if I could lend him a corkscrew. I'm taking it to him."

"Couldn't you send Willy with it?"

The man threw out his chest and said in a rather pompous manner: "The question you just asked shows why women are unfit to lead armies and make quick decisions in big business deals. When the psychological moment comes, you don't know how to take advantage of it."

1351. A used-car dealer was demonstrating an old heap. As he started up a hill, he said, "This is the opportunity of a lifetime."

"Yes," said his prospect, "I can hear it knocking."

1352. Two young ladies were talking about a certain rich bachelor.

"I know he's rich," said the first, "but isn't he too old to be considered eligible?"

"Not at all," said her friend. "He's too eligible to be considered old."

1353. After talking steadily all evening, a man's host said, "Speaking of Africa makes me think of the time. . . ."

Instantly his guest said, "My goodness, you're quite right. I had no idea it was so late. I'll be seein' you. Good-night."

1354. "Why do they make such a fuss over Miss Sims's voice? I think Miss Wilson has a much richer voice."

"Yes, but Miss Sims has a much richer father."

1355. The defendant was not doing very well on the witness stand, so the judge advised his lawyer to withdraw with his client and give him the benefit of the best advice he could think of. Twenty minutes later, the lawyer returned to the courtroom alone.

"Where is the prisoner?" asked the judge.

Opportunity

"Oh, he took off," said the lawyer. "After thinking over his chances here in court, that's the best advice I could give him."

1356.   A group of deer hunters, outfitted in their colorful coats and equipped with high-priced firearms, met a small boy walking down a backwoods road. He was armed with nothing more than a slingshot.

"Hi, son," said one of the men. "What are you out hunting for?"

"I don't know," the little boy said. "I ain't seen it yet."

89, 93, 413, 469, 485, 1246, 1638

Optimist

1357.   The confirmed optimist always said: "Oh, well, it might have been worse."

One day an acquaintance stopped him and said, "I dreamed last night that I died, went to hell, and was doomed to everlasting torment."

"Oh, well," said the optimist, "it might have been worse."

"What do you mean!" cried the man. "How could it have been worse?"

"It might have been true," the optimist said.

1358.   A West German was chatting with an American newspaperman, who asked him how to distinguish between an optimist and a pessimist in Germany.

"It's easy," said the German. "All the optimists are learning English and all the pessimists are studying Russian."

1359.   "That young man you are going with seems to be hanging around a lot lately," a man said to his daughter. "Do you think his intentions are serious?"

"I'm beginning to think so, Dad," she said. "He has already asked how much my allowance is, what brand of whiskey you drink, how good a job you have, and whether or not you and Mother are easy to live with."

257, 315, 504, 513, 729

Oversight

1360.　A woman was telling a friend about a wedding she had attended a few days before. "The bride was a veritable dream," she said, "all in white satin, with her long veil, slender slippers, huge bouquet, and everything."

"And what did the bridegroom wear?" asked the friend.

"Oh," said the first woman, "that was the only thing wrong at the wedding. That so-and-so never showed up."

1361.　The customer said to the waiter, "I haven't tasted any ham in this sandwich yet."

"Try another bite," the waiter suggested.

The customer took another bite and said, "Nope, none yet."

"Shucks," said the waiter. "You must have gone right past it."

1362.　A girl was asking her friend about her new boy friend. "What does he look like?" she asked. "Does he have a mustache?"

The girl thought a moment and said, "I can't say for sure, because if he does, he keeps it shaved off."

24, 102, 661, 1473, 1623

Overweight

1363.　A woman put a penny in the scales and weighed herself. As she stepped down, her husband said to her, "Well, how is it? Are you overweight?"

"Oh, no," said his wife, "but, according to that table printed on the front, I am about six inches too short."

465, 566, 856

Own

1364.　The tourist slapped his neck and looked at the owner of the summer cabins. "You told me you didn't have any mosquitoes," he said.

"I haven't," said the man. "Those that are biting you have come over from the cabins across the lake. They ain't mine."

248, 619

Painting

1365.   The owner of a house was showing it to a friend. He pointed to a portrait and said: "This is one of my ancestors."

"Yes," said his friend. "You know, he came very nearly being my ancestor. I bid up to $300 for that picture at an auction, but I decided not to waste any more on it."

1366.   The artist opened his mail and shouted to his friend: "Oh, boy! Do you remember the painting I sent to the Chicago exhibit? Well, here's fifty dollars for it."

"Wonderful," said his friend. "So they decided to keep it?"

"Heck, no," said the artist. "This is from the express company. They lost it."

562

Panhandler

1367.   It was the "better part of town" and the lady who came to the door said to the tramp: "I should think you would be ashamed to beg in this neighborhood."

"Don't apologize for it, lady," the bum said, "I've seen worse."

1368.   The beggar asked a man for a handout. "Can you give me two dollars for coffee?" he asked.

"I thought it was ten cents for a cup of coffee," the man said.

"That's what the others say," the bum replied, "but I'm putting all my begs in one ask-it."

1369.   The tramp had said he would be willing to work for a few days in order to get on his feet.

"But I couldn't give you enough work to keep you occupied," the man told him.

"Sir," said the tramp, "you'd be surprised what a little bit of work can keep me occupied."

1370.   "Friend," said the panhandler, "will you give me a dime for a sandwich?"

"Maybe," said the man. "But first let's see the sandwich."

Panhandler

1371. The lady gave the bum a quarter for a cup of coffee and said "But there must be many generous persons in the world."

"Yes," said the bum, "there are lots of them, but they don't have any money."

1372. The panhandler asked the lady of the house, "Would you help a poor man out of his troubles?"

"I sure would," she said. "Would you rather be shot or hit with an ax?"

112, 358

Pants

1373. Two college boys roomed together. They were close friends and on occasion they even shared their clothes. One night, one of the fellows was pressing his pants for a date. In the process, he burned a hole in the seat.

"Hey," he said to his roommate, "I've got a date with a girl and I ruined my pants. Will you lend me your pants for this evening?"

"Sorry," his friend said. "I can't. I'm going out myself tonight."

"Look," said the first one, "if you don't lend me your pants, you're going to lose my friendship."

"Listen," the other fellow said. "I can go lots of places without your friendship, but I can't go any place without my pants."

1374. It was at a political barbecue. Everybody was there from high society to low society to no society. The music was blaring over the loudspeaker, the air was festive. One prominent businessman was standing and chatting with some of his friends when his tailor wandered over and joined the group.

"Your face seems familiar," the man said to his tailor.

"I made your pants," the tailor whispered to his client.

"Oh, sure, I remember you now," the man said. Then he turned to his friends and said, "I want you to meet an old friend of mine, Major Pants."

126

Parking

1375. Women drivers wouldn't have trouble squeezing into parking places if they would only imagine they were putting on a girdle or a pair of shoes.

1376. A painter parked his truck in a no-parking zone in front of an office building. Figuring he could get away with it, he stuck a note on the windshield that said: "Painter working inside."

Later, when he returned, he found his note had been removed. In its place was a parking ticket with a note attached: "Policeman working outside."

52

Parrot

1377. A little old lady was shopping in a pet shop.

"Are you looking for anything special?" asked the manager.

"Yes," she said, "I want a parrot."

"Well, here's a fine bird," he said. "Speaks three languages, recites poetry, sings The Boola Song and tap dances, and only $200."

"Oh, I'm not interested in his talents," she said, "I just want to know—is he *tender*?"

1378. A man finally bought a parrot at an auction after some rather spirited bidding.

"I assume the bird talks," he said to the auctioneer.

"Talks?" the auctioneer said. "Who do you think has been bidding against you for the past half hour?"

558

Party

1379. A secretary was chatting with a girl from the office across the hall:

"Your bookkeeper was at the masquerade party last night, but I couldn't tell him from Adam."

"My heavens!" the girl across the hall said. "Did they dress like that?"

Party

1380. "This sure is a lousy party," a guest at a cocktail party said to the man next to him. "I'm going to finish this one and then get out of here."

"I would, too," said the other man, "but I've got to stay. I'm the host."

1381. "Today marks my 25th anniversary as warden of this penitentiary," said the warden to a trusty. "Tonight we're going to celebrate. What kind of party do you think the boys would like?"

"Well," said the trusty, "I think they would like to have an open house."

1382. The little boy had been to a birthday party the day before and his grandmother was asking him about it. "How was the party?" she wanted to know.

"How was it?" he said. "My, it was wonderful. Say, I ain't even hungry yet."

1383. "That was a wild party we went to last night," she said. "One couple came dressed as Carmen and a matador. Carmen even had a rose between her teeth. After a few drinks, they got into a fight and Carmen threw her rose at the matador."

"Then what happened?" asked her friend.

"Then the matador picked up the rose," she said, "and threw her teeth back at her!"

1384. The man had been to a party the night before. When he woke up the next morning, he knew he was in no condition for work. He called his boss at his home and said, "I'm sorry, but I'm afraid I won't be able to get to the office today. I've caught a bad cold."

"That's too bad," said his boss, "but you didn't have to bother to call; this is Sunday."

23, 570, 631, 645, 1313, 1549

Patience

1385. He had choked her. He was certain she was dead. There was little doubt about it. He had listened to her dying gasp. Now she was cold—stone cold. In his anger, he gave her one furious kick. To his amazement she gasped. Then she sputtered and began to hum softly.

"All it takes is a little patience, Willie," said his wife from the back seat of the automobile.

1386. A man celebrating his 95th birthday was asked by a friend:

"Don't you hate growing old?"

"Heck, no," he said. "If I wasn't growing old, I'd be dead."

1387. The editor of the newspaper was beside himself. "What are we going to do for our front page tonight? Nothing scandalous has happened in town for almost twenty-four hours!"

"Take it easy," said the police reporter. "Something'll happen. You shouldn't lose faith in human nature."

1388. After waiting for an hour, a waiter finally approached the customer and said, "What is it you wish, sir?"

"Well," said the customer. "What I came in for was breakfast. But if dinner is ready now, I'd like to order supper."

1389. A hillbilly went to see his friend in the hospital and asked the nurse at the desk, "Can I see how my friend, Harry Miller, is getting on?"

"Just fine," said the nurse. "He's convalescing now."

"That's all right," said the hillbilly, "I'll just sit here and wait."

1390. The two young ladies were being followed through the park by a lone soldier. Finally, one of the girls stopped and said to the young man, "Either quit following us or get another soldier."

1391. The young father was pushing the crying baby down the street with what appeared to be absolutely calm and self-assurance. People on the street could hear what he was saying as he passed.

Patience

"Take it easy, Donald," he said. "Don't let it get you down, Donald, you'll soon be safe back home. Things will be all right, Donald, if you just keep calm."

One motherly type woman waiting for a bus, heard and saw the young father and said to him, "I think you are wonderful the way you are taking care of the baby." Then she leaned over to the baby and said, "Now, don't cry, Donald, everything's going to be all right."

"Lady," said the father, "you've got it all wrong. His name is Henry—I'm Donald."

1392. The boss passed through the warehouse during lunch hour and saw a crap game going on down behind a huge pile of shipping crates. He called his foreman into his office and told him in no uncertain terms, "That's a disgrace. I want you to go out in the warehouse and break up that game."

It was two hours before he saw his foreman again. "Did you break up that game like I told you?" he asked.

"Yes, sir, I broke it up," said the foreman.

"Well, what took you so long?" the boss asked.

"Gosh," said the foreman. "I thought I did it pretty fast considering I only had twenty cents to start with."

81, 196, 307, 357, 493, 517, 707

Payment

1393. The boy was doing his homework. "What's a retainer, Dad?" he asked.

"Oh, that's money you pay a lawyer before he does any work for you," explained his father.

The boy thought a moment, then said, "Oh, I see. It's like the quarter you put in the gas meter before you get any gas."

1394. A man was in an automobile accident and sued the driver of the other car for $10,000. He won his case and the insurance company sent the check to the man's lawyer. The next day, the lawyer called up his client and invited him to come by his office and receive the payment.

Payment

"Here is the balance due after deducting my fee and all the costs," the lawyer said, handing the man a one-hundred-dollar bill.

"What's the matter with this hundred-dollar bill?" the man asked. "Is it counterfeit?"

105, 203, 205, 244, 296, 351, 448, 466, 475, 525, 1895, 2026

Peace

1395. A man was in the hospital close to death. His minister came to see him and asked: "Have you made your peace with God?"

"I didn't know," the man said, "that we had ever quarreled."

1396. Two college boys were walking across the campus. "Why are you so down in the mouth?" asked the first.

"Aw," said the second, "I just heard a guy call another fellow a liar. And that fellow said that if he didn't apologize, he'd whip him."

"Well, why should that make you so sad?" asked the first.

"Because," said his friend, "the guy apologized."

799, 1572

Peace of mind

1397. A mother, worrying about her daughter's safety, said to her:

"Didn't I say you shouldn't let that man come over to your apartment last night? You know how things like that worry me."

"But I didn't invite him to my apartment," her daughter said, "I went over to his apartment. Now you can let his mother do the worrying."

1398. "I can't find anything organically wrong with you," the doctor said. "As you know, many illnesses come from worry. You probably have some business or social problem that you should talk over with a good psychiatrist. A case very similar to yours came to me only a few weeks ago. The man had a $5,000 note

Peace of mind

due and couldn't pay it. Because of his money problem, he had worried himself into a state of nervous exhaustion."

"And did you cure him?" asked the patient.

"Yes," said the doctor. "I just told him to stop worrying; that life was too short to make himself sick over a scrap of paper. Now he's back to normal. He has stopped worrying entirely."

"Yes, I know," the patient said sadly. "I'm the one he owes the $5,000 to."

190, 503, 758, 847

Perfect

1399. A young lady became angry with her boy friend and said, "You're a perfect dope!"

"Don't try flattery," he said. "None of us is perfect!"

1400. "I'm going to get a divorce," a man told his friend. "My wife hasn't spoken to me in three months."

"I'd think twice about that if I were you," his friend said. "Wives like that are hard to find."

160, 209, 271, 508, 560

Perfume

1401. A lady was buying some perfume and the salesgirl told her, "I would advise you not to use this if you're bluffing."

1402. The pretty girl was shopping at the perfume counter and said to the clerk, "Do you have something that will bring out the mink in a man without disturbing the wolf?"

343, 716, 887

Permission

1403. The young man was calling on his girl's father to ask permission to marry her. The girl was waiting anxiously in the kitchen.

Permission

"Well," said the young man when the interview was over, "it's all set. He asked me how well off I was and I told him I had $2,000 saved up and in the bank."

"What did he have to say to that?" his girl asked.

"He borrowed it," the young man said.

1404. It was a summertime romance. The young man had been sitting on the girl's front steps talking to her for hours and hours. Finally, she said to him, "It's such a pretty night, would you like to take a walk?"

"Yes," he said, "I'd love to."

"Okay," she said, "don't let me stop you."

50, 251, 438, 544, 938, 1109

Persistence

1405. Gay blade: "Do you ever expect to find the perfect girl?"

His buddy: "No, but it's lots of fun trying."

1406. A young girl's family was upset because the fellow she was planning to marry was an atheist.

"We'll not have you marrying an atheist," her mother said.

"What can I do? I love him," the young girl said.

"Well," said her mother, "if he loves you, he'll do anything you ask. You should talk religion to him. If you are persistent, you can win him over."

Several weeks went by, then one morning at breakfast the young lady seemed absolutely brokenhearted.

"What's the matter?" her mother asked. "I thought you were making such good progress in your talks about religion to your young boy friend."

"That's the trouble," the young girl said. "I overdid it. Last night he told me he was so convinced that he is going to study to be a priest."

1407. A bum was sitting on his cot in a flophouse.

"You know," he said to the fellow on the next cot, "when I was seventeen years old, I made up my mind that nothing was going to stop me from getting rich."

Persistence

"Well, how come you never got rich?" his friend asked.

"Oh," the first bum said, "by the time I was nineteen, I realized it would be easier to change my mind."

65, 353, 493, 752, 867, 1348, 1829

Personal

1408.   A little lady in a country church kept shouting "Amen" as the minister blasted every sin from murder to whiskey drinking. Then he got on the subject of dipping snuff. At this point, the little lady flared up and said to her neighbor, "Now he's done quit preachin' and gone to meddlin'!"

1409.   Business was pretty bad and Old George was looking rather seedy. One day, when he came home from work, he found his wife sporting a new dress.

"What, another new dress?" he cried. "Every day, it's another new dress. I can't afford it. Look at me, working like a slave and you spend all our money on clothes."

"It's your own fault, Old George," she said, "because wherever I go, they say, 'There goes Old George's wife, look how she's dressed.'"

"Good gracious," he said, "look how I'm dressed, and I'm Old George."

31, 471, 487, 623, 992, 1481

Perspective

1410.   A boy was doing his homework and asked his father, "Is a ton of coal very much, dad?"

"That depends," his father said, "on whether you are shoveling or buying it."

370, 634, 1542

Pessimist

1411.   The man's wife woke up one beautiful spring morning, looked out the window, then turned to her husband, still half-asleep in bed and said:

Pessimist

"My, this is a beautiful day! It's too bad you have to get out of bed and louse it up."

1412.   A father took his little boy to the zoo.

"See," he said, "those are wild animals. If they ever got out of those cages, they'd tear a person to pieces!"

"Gee, Dad, if that lion got out and grabbed you and tore you to pieces," said the boy, "what number bus do I take to get home?"

1413.   A poor workingman had been in a serious accident, and said to a friend, "I'd like to hire a lawyer, but I haven't any money."

"Well," said his friend, "why don't you get one to take it on a contingent fee?"

"What's that?" asked the man.

"A contingent fee," said his friend, "means that if you don't win the case, the lawyer doesn't get anything, and if you do win, you don't get anything."

1414.   A pessimist is a fellow who sits and worries when everything is all right because he knows if he worries when things are all right he is bound to worry more when things get worse, and he knows that because things are so good now, they are sure to get worse.

108, 509, 539, 628, 768, 1295, 1358

Pianist

1415.   A seedy-looking entertainer in a bar sat down at the piano, placed his beer glass carefully on top and started banging away tunelessly.

Finally, when he could stand the noise no longer, a patron at the bar went over to the piano player and said: "I suppose you know you are probably the world's worst piano player."

"Yeah," the piano player said, "I know."

Pianist

"Well, for heaven's sake," the man said, "isn't there something *else* you can do?"

"Yes," said the poor fellow, "I suppose I could go back to the violin, but then I wouldn't have any place to put my beer."

1416. "My wife used to play the piano," a man told his friend, "but since the children came, she hasn't had time to touch it."

"Children sometimes are a comfort, aren't they?" his friend said.

1417. The young lady was idly playing on the piano and humming a tune. The young man listened for a while, then asked, "Do you sing and play much?"

"Not much," the girl said. "I just do it to kill time."

"Well, you've certainly chosen the perfect weapon," the fellow said.

47, 602

Picnic

1418. "You've got to have more recreation and relaxation," said the doctor to the overworked businessman.

"But I'm too busy," said the businessman.

"That's silly," said the doctor. "Ants have the greatest reputation for being busy all the time, yet they never miss an opportunity to attend a picnic."

258, 283, 1652

Picture

1419. The customer was raging at the photographer. "I certainly don't like these photographs you took," he said. "I look like an ape."

The photographer gave him a long look. "Yes, I guess you do," he said. "But you should have thought of that before you had them taken."

135, 251, 268, 354, 401, 491, 562, 570, 573, 1645

Pity

1420. The rich business magnate was visited by a boyhood friend whom he had not seen for years. The man told him a long story of misfortune: bankruptcy, death of wife and children, personal illness. He ended by asking for a loan.

The magnate pushed a button, and a big, athletic-type walked in. "Joe," the magnate said, "throw this poor fellow downstairs; he's breaking my heart."

833

Plan

1421. "How did you teach your neighbor to keep his chickens in his own yard?" a fellow asked his friend.

"One night I hid a dozen eggs under a bush in my back yard," he said, "and the next day I let him see me gather them."

1422. The young man kissed his girl friend good-night and started to leave, when she said, "Remember, we are going on a picnic next Sunday."

"I won't forget," he said. "But suppose it rains?"

"Well, in case of rain," his girl friend said, "we'll make it Saturday."

221, 305, 394, 402, 753, 1022

Playing

1423. A mother was telling her small son about the good times she had when she was a little girl; riding a pony, sliding down a haystack, sledding, and wading in a brook at the farm.

"My," he said, "I wish I'd met you sooner."

211, 292, 870, 1314

Poet

1424. The editor had just returned a sheaf of poems to the budding young poet.

"Do you think it would help if I put more fire into my poetry?" the young man asked the editor.

"No," said the editor. "I would recommend the reverse."

Poet

1425.   The editor tried hard to read the poet's handwriting. "This handwriting's so bad I can hardly read it," he said. "Why didn't you type out these poems before you brought them in?"

"Type them!" cried the poet. "Do you think for a minute that if I could type, I'd be wasting my time trying to write poetry?"

1426.   A young lady asked an aspiring poet, "Why do they call it free verse?"

"That's easy," said the poet. "Did you ever try to sell any?"

182, 1040, 2031

Point of view

1427.   A welder was shortchanged two dollars in his pay envelope, and complained to the foreman.

"You were overpaid two dollars last week and didn't object," the foreman said.

"I know," said the welder. "I didn't mind overlooking one mistake, but when it happened the second time, I thought it was time to complain."

1428.   A quiet-looking man, carrying a chair, walked up to the owner of a secondhand store and asked how much it was worth.

"Three dollars," said the secondhand dealer.

The quiet-looking man seemed surprised. "Isn't it worth more than that?" he said.

"Three dollars is the limit," the owner said. "See that? Where the leg is split? And look here where the paint is peeling."

"Okay then," said the customer. "I saw it in front of your store marked $10, but I thought there must be a mistake. For $3 I'll take it."

1429.   A tall girl was shopping for a new outfit.

"Have you a skirt that will make me look shorter?" she asked the saleslady.

"No, I haven't," said the saleslady, "but I have a skirt that will make everyone else look longer."

Point of view

1430. The waitress said to a friend, "Where I work, one man's meat is another man's croquette."

1431. Two refugee women were talking about their children who had gone to the United States to live. "How does your daughter like America?" the first one asked.

"Wonderful," the woman said. "She married an American boy. He helps her with the house, he washes the dishes, he stays with the baby when she wants to go out. He does everything for her. And how is your son doing?"

"Oh, the poor boy. It is terrible," she said. "He married an American girl. He has to help her with the house, and wash the dishes, and stay with the baby when she wants to go out. Everything, he has to do!"

1432. The teacher was giving an arithmetic lesson. "How old," she asked, "is a person who was born in 1910?"

"Man or woman?" asked the little boy.

83, 108, 146, 168, 290, 410, 471, 491, 1410, 1961

Poker

1433. The man was sneaking in at 2:00 A.M. after playing poker with his friends. In spite of all precautions, his wife awoke.

She shouted at him, "I suppose you've been out holding a sick friend's hand all night!"

"If I had been holding his hand," her husband said, "I'd have won enough money to buy you a mink coat."

1434. It was the final hand of the night. The cards were dealt. The pot was opened. Plenty of raising went on. Finally, the hands were called.

"I win," said one fellow. "I have three aces and a pair of queens."

"No, I win," said the second fellow. "I have three aces and a pair of kings."

"None of you-all win," said the third one. "I do. I have two deuces and a thirty-eight special."

Poker

1435. The minister ended his sermon on a soft note. He asked Deacon Brown to offer the benediction. But there was no response. So he repeated more loudly, "Deacon Brown, will you lead us?"

It now was clear that the deacon was asleep, so in a loud voice the minister said, "Deacon Brown, will you please lead?"

The deacon woke up with a start and blurted out, "Lead yourself, I dealt!"

299, 1211, 2017

Policy

1436. A man with a talking mynah bird went into a bar and ordered a straight bourbon. The bird ordered a double martini.

"Sorry," said the bartender, "it's our policy not to serve mynahs."

337, 342

Polite

1437. "I don't guess I have anything to complain about," said the mussed up young man as he listened to another mussed up young man describe his ejection from a dance hall. "They treated me all right."

"What do you mean, treated you all right," said the second young man. "They threw you out, didn't they?"

"Yes," said the first. "They threw me out the back door, but when I told the bouncer that my family was in the social register, he picked me up gently, brushed me off, and escorted me back into the dance hall. Then he threw me out the front door."

1438. As soon as he arrived home from school, the little boy rushed up to his mother and said, "Oh, Mommie, my teacher kissed me today."

"Well," she said, "were you a good boy and did you kiss her back?"

"Oh, no," he said. "I kissed her face."

30, 75, 420, 493, 625, 875, 1011, 1588

Politics

1439. A civics teacher asked one of her pupils to name the three great American parties.

His answer, as quick as a flash, was:

"Democratic, Republican, and cocktail."

1440. The Congressman's local confidential henchman was reporting to him. "Some of your constituents are beginning to disagree rather seriously with you," he said. "Well," said the Congressman, "keep a close record on them and when enough disagree with me to form a dependable majority, let me know, and I'll turn about and agree with them."

1441. Two senators, a Democrat and a Republican, met on the subway car which runs to the Capitol. They began discussing a bill they were about to vote on and found that they were in agreement on it. "Goodness," said the first one, "this is the first time we have ever agreed on a matter of public policy." "I was just thinking about that," the other said, "and it makes me more than half suspect that I may be wrong in how I'm planning to vote."

1442. A cannibal rushed into the village dragging a man on the end of a rope: "I've captured a politician!" he cried. "Now I can have a bologna sandwich."

1443. During a political race in the South, a man who had been elected Senator several times, and who thought that he had a lifelong right to the office, was addressing a meeting:

"My friends," he said, "I stand on my record. If you had a hired man who had worked for you for a long time, and if he had done a good job, would it not be right for you to keep him on the job?"

A voice from the rear cried out: "Not if he got to thinking that he owned the whole darned farm."

1444. Three men were arguing over whose profession was first established on earth.

"Mine was," said the surgeon. "The Bible says that Eve was made by carving a rib out of Adam."

"Not at all," said the engineer. "An engineering job came before that. In six days the Earth was created out of chaos. That was an engineer's job."

"Yes," said the politician, "but who created the chaos?"

1445.   The candidate's name had been kicked around rather roughly and frequently in the press, and he was complaining to a friend about it.

"I don't see anything wrong in that," said his friend. "You're getting a lot of publicity out of it."

The candidate couldn't see it that way at all. "Half those lies they are printing about me aren't true," he said.

1446.   At a first aid course for newly elected Congressmen, a member was asked:

"What would you do if you found a man in a fainting condition?"

"I'd give him a drink of whiskey," was the answer.

"What if there wasn't any whiskey?" the instructor asked.

"Then, I'd promise him some," the Congressman said.

1447.   "That baby's going to be a great politician," said his grandfather.

"How can you possibly tell that?" asked the baby's mother.

"It's quite obvious," explained the grandfather. "That child can say more things that sound good and mean nothing than any kid I've ever seen."

1448.   The election was four days away and the politician was out canvassing for votes. "I hope I'll have your support," he said to a farmer.

"I'm afraid not," the farmer said. "I've already promised my support to your opponent."

The politician smiled and said, "In politics, promising and doing are two different things."

"Well, in that case," said the farmer, "I'll be happy to give you my promise."

Politics

1449. The professor of political science asked his class, "Can any one of you give me a clear, concise, easy to understand definition of a politician?"

"Yes, sir, I can," said a young fellow. "Just tell me whether you mean a Republican or Democrat."

1450. It was election day and a farmer was driving to town. He picked up two farmhands on the road and asked them where they were going.

"We're going to town to vote," the first one said.

"That's fine," said the farmer. "That's where I'm going. How are you going to vote?"

"I'm a Republican," one farmhand said. "I'm going to vote for the party."

The farmer stopped his car and put him out.

As he drove down the road, he said to the other fellow who was still in the car, "How are you going to vote?"

It was 14 miles to town and the fellow didn't want to walk, so he thought about it a moment and then said, "I'm a Democrat."

That must have pleased the farmer because he didn't say anything. But as they passed a watermelon patch the farmer said, "Hey, there isn't anybody looking. How about getting over the fence and picking a couple of melons? We'll cut them on the way to town."

The farmhand did it. Then, as they were resting in the shade of a tree eating the melons, the farmhand started laughing.

"What's so funny?" the farmer asked. "What are you laughing at?"

"It sure is funny," the farmhand said. "Here I've been a Democrat for only 20 minutes, and I'm stealing already."

1451. A politician is a man who constantly looks for trouble, who finds it everywhere, who diagnoses it incorrectly, and who then applies the wrong remedies.

1452. The president of the small town bank had just been elected mayor of the town. Two weeks later, he attended the

State Bankers' Convention where he ran into an old friend who was interested in the election.

"Congratulations on winning the election," he said. "I suppose you won because the people in your town know that you are honest and upright and always deal fairly with your customers."

"Maybe so," the mayor said, "but I really think it was because I was the only one running."

1453. In a town election in the solid Democratic state of Georgia, one Republican vote was discovered before the tabulation had been completed. Election officials stopped to ponder this marvel, then decided to complete the count before deciding what to do about it. Later, another Republican vote showed up.

"That settles it," said one official. "Throw both votes out. Some so-and-so voted twice."

1454. When the Congressman was making his first speech, he was pleased to see a lot of the older heads among his colleagues nodding in approval. But when his proposal came to a vote, only a handful of the members voted with him.

Later, a fellow member said, "That was a good speech and I want you to know that I agreed with much of what you said."

"If you were with me," the new Congressman said, "why didn't you vote with me?"

"I was with you," said the man of experience, "only as long as you were talking."

1455. A young fellow, studying political science, asked his father, "Dad, what is a traitor in politics?"

"Any man who leaves our party," said his father, "and goes over to the other one is a traitor."

"Well, what about a man who leaves his party and comes over to yours?" asked the young man.

"He'd be a convert, son," said his father, "a real convert."

1456. The political rally ended in a blazing gun battle.

"What started the shooting?" asked a visitor in town.

Politics

"A fellow made a motion that was out of order," an old-timer said.

"That question must have been highly controversial," the visitor said. "What was the motion?"

"Toward his hip pocket," the old-timer said.

1457. The candidate was working the rural precincts and getting his fences mended and the votes lined up. On this particular day, he had his young son with him to mark down on index cards whether the voter was for him or against him. In this way, the candidate could get an idea of how things were going.

As they were getting out of the car in front of one farmhouse, the farmer came out the front door with a shotgun in his hand and screamed at the top of his voice, "I know you—you dirty filthy crook of a politician. You're no good. You ought to be put in jail. Don't you dare set foot inside that gate or I'll blow your head off. Now, you get back in your car and get down the road before I lose my temper and do something I'll be sorry for."

The candidate did as he was told. A moment later he and his son were speeding down the road away from that farm.

"Well," said the boy to his father, "I might as well tear that man's card up, hadn't I?"

"Tear it up?" cried his father. "Certainly not. Just mark him down as doubtful."

109, 191, 325, 326, 328, 472, 541, 662, 672, 922, 1150

Popularity

1458. "Why," a man asked the most popular man in the neighborhood, "are you so popular in the neighborhood?"

"I don't know," said the man, "except that I told everybody that I always play the saxophone when I get lonely."

1459. The teacher asked one of his pupils about another member of the class. "She seems to be one of the prettiest, sweetest girls in school," the teacher said. "Yet you all seem to dislike her. Why is she so unpopular?"

"Don't you know?" asked the pupil. "It's because she won the popularity contest last year."

450, 1781

Position

1460. Rookies had come from everywhere for the opening day of spring training. The manager of the ball club was trying to sort them out and assign them their positions.

"Hey, you," he said, stopping an awkward-looking young fellow. "What's your position?"

"I'm a utility man," the fellow said.

"Whom were you with last year?" the manager asked.

"The light and power company and I still am," he said. "I'm here to check the lighting system."

1461. A man and his wife were strolling through a cemetery one Sunday afternoon and came to a gravestone with the following inscription: "Here lies a lawyer and an honest man."

"My," said the man, "isn't it odd that they buried these two fellows so close together?"

73, 501, 621, 754

Poverty

1462. A beggar was obviously envious of the rich man who had just given him a dollar.

"You have no reason to envy me," said the rich man, "even if I do look prosperous. I have my troubles, too, you know."

"You've probably got plenty of troubles," said the beggar, "but the difference is, I ain't got nothing else."

1463. A city man had given up urban life and moved to the country to become a farmer. A year later he was visiting his friend back in town and was complaining how hard it was to get along.

"What are you complaining about?" his friend asked. "You have it made. All the butter and milk and eggs and vegetables and fruit you could want. Plenty to eat and a place to sleep. All you need is another year and you'll have it made."

"Well," said the would-be farmer, "if you come by my place a year from now you will see the sleekest, fattest, and nakedest farmer in America."

361, 1250

Practical

1464.   The man in the restaurant had been waiting an hour. Finally, he ran out of patience.

"Look here," he said to the waiter. "How long do I have to wait for the half-portion of duck I ordered?"

"Till somebody orders the other half," the waiter said. "We can't go out and kill half a duck."

1465.   A little boy went to the do-it-yourself garden department of the garden supply store. "My mother wants a spray," he said, "that will kill crab grass, Japanese beetles, weeds, and spinach."

1466.   The farmer's brother from the city was visiting on the farm.

"Just what's the difference between these theoretical and practical farmers that I'm hearing about?" he asked.

"Well," said the farmer, "a theoretical farmer is a fool what insists on trying to make a living by farming the place, while a practical farmer has sense enough to take in summer boarders and start a hot-dog stand."

236, 308, 399

Prayer

1467.   A bishop and a young minister were driving in the country one winter. It was snowing. Their car broke down. They finally reached a farmhouse and were welcomed for the night. The house was cold, and the attic in which they were invited to spend the night was like an icebox.

Stripping to his underwear, the bishop jumped into a featherbed and pulled the blankets over his head.

The young minister was slightly embarrassed. "Excuse me, sir," he said, "don't you think we ought to say our prayers before going to bed?"

The bishop stuck one eye out from under the covers. "Son," he said, "I keep prayed up ahead for situations just like this one."

1468.   The little boy ended his prayer by saying, "and please, Lord, could you put the vitamins in pie and cake instead of in cod-liver oil and spinach? Amen."

Prayer

1469. A country preacher arrived at prayer meeting a half hour late and absolutely soaking wet. He told a story of meeting a big brown bear on the log across the creek and of how he had jumped in the water to save himself.

"Why didn't you pray?" asked one of the congregation.

"The way I figure it," the preacher said, "prayer is for prayer meeting—not bear meeting."

71, 462, 653, 765, 1252, 1435, 1602, 1642, 2056

Prediction

1470. Two women who hadn't seen each other since school days met accidentally one day.

"It's nice to see you after all these years," said the first. "Are you married?"

"Yes," said the second.

"I remember," laughed the first, "you always said you wouldn't marry the best man in the world."

"Well," said her friend, "I didn't."

1471. A man was told by a fortune-teller, "You'll be poor and unhappy and miserable until you are fifty."

"Then what?" asked the man.

"By that time," the fortune-teller said, "you'll be used to it."

597, 899

Prejudice

1472. "Do you like spinach?" the host asked her young guest.

"No," he said. "And I'm glad I don't like it, because if I liked it, I'd eat it, and I couldn't stand that because I hate it."

615, 1072, 1105

Premature

1473. A fellow was laughing and a friend asked him what was so funny.

Premature

"See that fellow over there?" he said. "He brings a boiled egg in his lunch every day and cracks it over his head, just to show off."

"So what?" his friend said.

"Well," the fellow said, "this morning his mother forgot to boil the egg."

1474. An old-time lawyer had finally retired and turned his practice over to his son who had just passed his bar examination. Two weeks later, his son came home and said, "Well, Dad, you'll be proud of me I know. Today, I settled that old railroad suit that you have been working on for the past fifteen years."

"Settled it," cried his father, "why, son, I left you that lawsuit as an annuity for the rest of your life."

186, 197, 659

Present

1475. The man's wife had given him a box of cigars for his birthday, but they were not to his liking and he was complaining about them.

"Well, I asked for the best," she said.

"The best!" said her husband. "What kind did you ask for?"

"I told the clerk that I wanted them for a distinguished-looking, middle-aged man who always dresses in gray," she said.

236, 259, 378

Price

1476. Two traveling salesmen, working together, arrived at a hotel and were shown a shabby, run-down room.

"What," said the first, "does this pigsty cost?"

"For one pig," the manager said, "four dollars, for two pigs, six dollars."

1477. A man picked up a menu in a restaurant and said to the waiter, "What! You charge two dollars for a veal cutlet here?"

"Yes," he said, "That's the price."

339

Price

"The place down the street charges only ninety cents for a veal cutlet," the man said.

"Then why don't you eat in the restaurant down the street?" asked the waiter.

"Because they're out of veal cutlets," the man said.

"Oh," said the waiter. "We do better than that. When we are out of veal cutlets, we charge only seventy-five cents."

1478.   A man saw a friend standing in the rain in front of a fancy nightclub. "What are you going to do?" he asked. "Stay outside and get wet, or go in and get soaked?"

1479.   The president of the gas company was addressing a Chamber of Commerce meeting. He managed to mention his company in his speech. "The gas company," he said, "has played an integral part in all developments of the community. I might well say, to make a pun, 'Honor the Light Brigade.'"

From the rear came a loud voice, "Oh, what a charge they made!"

1480.   A young fellow was talking to a long-time married friend about getting married.

"How much does the marriage license cost?" the young man asked.

"Four dollars down," the veteran said, "and all of your salary for the rest of your life."

36, 136, 192, 400, 751, 868, 955, 1056, 1428, 2018

Pride

1481.   A rundown-looking rug peddler was hawking his wares in the native quarter of Saigon.

"Will you buy a carpet, sir?" he asked a tourist.

"No," growled the tourist. "They stink!"

The peddler drew himself up in indignation. "How dare you say that!" he cried. "I'll have you know that my carpets do not stink! It's only me."

Pride

1482. A recruit came home to the country on leave. To celebrate the occasion, his mother killed a couple of chickens. She cooked them both and the boy ate every bit, right down to the bones.

The next morning, as the young soldier drove out, the rooster began to crow as loud as he could. One little hen said, "What's he crowing so loud for this time of day?"

The other hen said, "He has a right to. He now has two sons in the Army."

1483. A woman was visiting her friend. "My boy has just written me from jail," she said. "He says they're going to cut six months off his sentence for good behavior."

"My," said her friend. "You must be proud to have a son like that."

1484. The presidents of the town's four service clubs had met to discuss an upcoming interclub project for the city. Present were the president of the Lions, Kiwanis, Rotary, and Civitan.

As they sat chatting over a cup of coffee, the president of the Rotary Club said to the president of the Kiwanis Club, "You know, I have always admired the work you fellows do in this town and if I were not a Rotarian I would be a Kiwanian."

"I feel the same way," said the Kiwanian. "If I were not a Kiwanian, I would be a Rotarian."

At that point, the Civitan president said to the Lion president, "You're a Lion. If you weren't a Lion, what would you be?"

"Well," said the loyal Lion, "if I weren't a Lion, I'd be ashamed of myself."

1485. A local lawyer had been elected judge. His young daughter was so proud of her father being a judge that whenever she introduced herself she said, "I'm Judge Williams' daughter."

After her mother had heard her introduce herself that way several times, she called a halt to it. "It isn't right and you mustn't do it," her mother said.

Pride

The next day while she was helping her mother shop in the supermarket, a lady said to her, "I think I know you. You're Judge Williams' little girl, aren't you?"

"Well," said the little girl, "I always thought so, but Mother says I'm not."

109, 206, 301, 428, 455, 468, 639, 1166, 1474, 1605, 1621

Prison

1486. A social worker, visiting a prison, was much impressed by the melancholy attitude of one man she found.

"My poor man," she sympathized, "what is the length of your term?"

"Depends on politics, lady," replied the melancholy one. "I'm the warden."

305, 833, 1101, 1584, 1620

Prisoner

1487. A rookie patrolman radioed his precinct. "A man has been robbed down here, and I've got one of them."

"Which one have you?" the desk sergeant asked.

"The man that was robbed," the rookie said.

1488. "And what is your name?" the social worker asked the prisoner.

"69994," the prisoner said.

"That's not your real name, is it?" the social worker asked.

"No," the prisoner said. "That's only my pen name."

463, 859, 1069, 1711, 1822

Privilege

1489. A certain airline started a VIP service. To their best customers, they gave a permit to buy tickets without having to stand in line. One day a man with a VIP permit went to the airport to buy a ticket.

Privilege

"Get in that line over there," he was told.

"But," he said, "I'm a VIP and this permit allows me to buy a ticket without standing in line."

"I know that," said the ticket agent, "and that is the line for people that don't have to stand in line to buy tickets."

469, 1550

Profanity

1490. The marble tournament was at its height. One little fellow had missed an easy shot, and let go a man-sized cuss word.

"Hey," called the minister from the spectator's bench, "what do little boys who swear when they are playing marbles turn into when they grow up?"

"Golfers," said the boy without batting an eye.

1491. "Grand Coulee!" screamed the minister as he hit his finger with a hammer.

"Grand Coulee? What do you mean, Grand Coulee?" asked his next door neighbor.

"Grand Coulee—that's the world's largest dam, isn't it?" said the minister.

1492. A self-righteous citizen had heard two telephone linemen having a heated argument. She had them arrested and brought before the judge on a charge of public profanity.

One of them explained, "It was this way, Judge. Joe, here, was working above me on a pole. He accidentally spilled a little hot lead. And I said, "See here, Joe, that hot lead doesn't feel very good dropping down my back. Please be more careful."

348, 474, 2019

Professor

1493. Professor to his students: "This examination will be conducted on the honor system. Please sit in alternate rows—three seats apart."

343

Professor

1494. Someone has said that a professor is a man whose job is to tell students how to solve the problems of life which he himself has tried to avoid by becoming a professor.

1495. "Who was John Donne?" the professor of literature asked of the young man who was standing idly by the window as he walked into his classroom.

"I don't know," the young man said. "I never heard of him."

"Never heard of him?" the professor shouted. "Why, I assigned that question last week. If you haven't learned that, how do you expect to pass the course?"

"I don't expect to pass it," the young man said. "I just came to fix the electric lights."

8, 9, 167, 369, 543, 757

Profit

1496. A man was chatting with a business acquaintance at lunch. "We're a nonprofit organization," he said. "We didn't mean to be, but we are."

119, 318, 810, 1055, 1312, 1764

Progress

1497. A little girl was telling a friend about her stay at summer camp:

"The first day I didn't have hardly any friends. The second day I had a few friends. The third day I had friends and enemies."

1498. The personnel director was interviewing the applicant for a job. "How old are you?" he asked.

"Twenty-four," said the young man.

"And just what do you expect to be five years from now?" asked the personnel director.

"Twenty-nine," said the young fellow.

1499. The town's most eligible bachelor had been going out with the pretty young widow who had just moved into the community.

Progress

"How are you making out with that new widow?" a friend asked him.

"I think maybe she has her eye on me," the bachelor said. "Last night when I took her home after the movie, she asked me if I snored."

1500. The family stopped at the farmer's wayside produce stand while they were out Sunday driving.

"My," said the housewife, "vegetables certainly do cost a lot more than they used to."

"It's like this," the farmer said. "Farming isn't what it used to be. We sent the boy off to agricultural college and he knows the botanical name for everything we raise, the entomological name for the bugs that eat it, and the chemical formula of the stuff that kills the bugs—and somebody's got to pay."

96, 247, 318, 730, 934

Promise

1501. "Darling," the young man said, "I could die for your sake."

"You are always promising that," said his girl friend, "but you never do it."

1502. "Honey," said the young farmer, "if you will only marry me I'll put in electricity, build a modern kitchen, paint the house, buy a clothes dryer and install a milking machine."

"Darling," said his girl friend, "suppose you do all those things first and then ask me."

1503. A couple were getting married in the minister's living room. The minister said to the groom, "Do you take this woman for better or for worse, through sickness and health, in good times or bad, whether she be . . ."

"Oh," said the bride tearfully, "please don't say anything more. If you're not careful, you are going to talk him right out of it."

345

Promise

1504. A man was in the hospital dying. Just before he passed away, he said to his wife who was sitting by the bedside, "Darling, I have only one regret as I pass on. I hate to leave you behind in all of your loneliness. I just want you to know that, if you should ever want to remarry, you have my blessing. Only, if you do, I wonder if you would promise me something?"

"Yes, darling," his wife said. "What is it?"

"Would you promise not to let your new husband wear my old clothes and remind you of me?" he asked.

"Why, certainly I'll promise you that," his wife said. "I wouldn't think of doing such a thing. Besides, all of your suits are too small for Harry anyway."

35, 544, 661, 994, 1446, 1635

Promotion

1505. An employee asked his boss for a raise in pay. "I have been here 10 years," he said, "doing three men's work for one man's pay. I think I deserve more money."

"Well, I can't give you a raise," said the boss, "but if you'll tell me the names of those other two men, I'll fire them."

1506. The newspaperman had been shipwrecked and was found by a tribe of cannibals and taken before their chief. "And what is your business?" he asked.

"I am a newspaperman," the man said.

"An editor?" asked the chief.

"Not really an editor," the man said, "just a reporter."

"Well, I have a surprise for you," the chief said. "You are about to be promoted. After dinner tonight, you will be editor-in-chief."

341, 953, 1666

Promptness

1507. A husband, impatient with his wife, yelled into the bedroom: "For goodness' sakes, honey, aren't you ready yet?"

His wife shouted back and said, "Haven't I been telling you for the last hour that I'll be ready in a minute."

Promptness

1508. The boss told Joe that if he couldn't get to work on time, he would be fired. So Joe went to the doctor, who gave him a pill. Joe took the pill, slept well, and was awake before he heard the alarm clock. He dressed and ate breakfast leisurely. Later he strolled into the office, arriving half an hour before his boss. When the boss came in, Joe said:

"Well, I didn't have any trouble getting up this morning."

"That's good," said his boss, "but where were you yesterday?"

1509. "You should have been here at nine o'clock," the boss said to the late-arriving office boy.

"Gosh," he said, "what happened?"

1510. The newly married young businessman was leaving his wife for his first trip after their marriage. "Goodbye, dear," he said. "Look after the home well, and if you need money while I'm gone, just go to the bank."

"Yes, dear," she said. "What time does the bank open this morning?"

1511. The owner of a service station was complaining to an employee about his constant tardiness. "It's funny," he said. "You are always late in the morning and you live right across the street. Now, Billy Wilson, who lives two miles away, is always on time."

"There's nothing funny about that," said the man. "If Billy is late in the morning, he can hurry, but if I'm late, I'm here."

514, 600, 779, 937

Proof

1512. "Lady," said the pet-shop owner to a customer, "This is the finest dog you can buy—a thoroughbred bloodhound."

"How do I know it's a bloodhound?" she asked doubtfully.

"Towser," the man said, "bleed for the lady."

1513. Two women met for the first time since they were in school together.

"How long have you been married, Jean?" asked one of the girls.

"Twenty-odd years," Jean said.

"What do you mean, odd years? Why do you call them odd?" asked her friend.

"You'll understand what I mean when you come by my house," said Jean. "Wait till you see my husband."

1514. A little fellow was bragging about his status at school. "My second-grade teacher sure does like me," he told his mother.

"What makes you think that?" asked his mother.

"I heard her tell the principal that the happiest day of her life was the day I was promoted into the third grade."

1515. An old maid, the "do-gooder" type, accused a local man of wasting time in taverns because "with her own eyes," she said, she had seen his sports car in the tavern's parking lot. The man didn't say anything, but that night he parked his car in front of her house and left it there all night.

1516. A hotel owner wired an egg broker for a truckload of eggs: Please ship one truckload of eggs; if good, I will send check.

The broker wired back: Send check; if good, I will ship the eggs.

1517. A man who had been in such a coma that he had been taken for dead, suddenly came to as they were about to bury him.

"What did it feel like to be dead?" asked a friend later.

"Shucks," he said, "I wasn't dead and I knew it. I was hungry and my feet were cold."

"But what would that prove?" his friend asked.

"Well," he said, "I knew that if I were in heaven I wouldn't be hungry, and if I were in the other place, my feet wouldn't be cold."

Proof

1518. A wife was complaining to her husband. "Why do you go on the balcony when I sing?" she asked. "Don't you like to hear me?"

"It isn't that. I love to hear you," he said, "but I want the neighbors to see that I'm not beating my wife."

1519. The kindergarten teacher was upset when the little boy told her he had just eaten a worm. She was trying to teach him not to eat worms and was appealing to his reason rather than telling him flatly not to do it.

"You should not have eaten that little worm," she said, "because now his mother will be real unhappy and distressed."

"Oh, no she won't," he said, "because I ate her, too."

84, 124, 208, 398, 460, 591, 674, 1701

Propaganda

1520. "I see by the paper," said a wife to her husband, "that the concert we attended last night was a huge success."

"Yes," he said, "I had no idea we enjoyed it half so much at the time."

1521. A little girl was packing her things for a visit to her grandmother's house. She went into the library and brought back three books, *Peter Rabbit, Little Black Sambo,* and *Child Guidance.*

Her mother saw what she was doing and said, "You won't need that *Child Guidance.*"

"Oh, yes I will," said the little girl. "Grandma still believes in spanking."

266, 330, 819, 1421, 1445

Proposition

1522. "We can pay you seventy dollars a week now," said the personnel manager to the job applicant, "and seventy-five dollars a week in six months."

"Thank you, sir," the man said. "I'll be back in six months."

Proposition

1523. "There you are," said the lady as she handed a bread and butter sandwich to her little boy and his friend from across the street.

"Thank you," the little neighbor boy said.

"You are a nice little boy," the lady said to him. "I like to hear little boys say 'thank you.' "

"Well," he said, "if you want to hear me say it again, how about putting some peanut butter in this sandwich?"

503, 524, 850, 1413

Protection

1524. A man ran for sheriff in a small southern town. He was badly beaten at the polls, receiving only a mere 150 votes out of a total of 27,847 that were cast.

The next day he walked down the main street with two guns hanging from his hips. He was stopped by a group of puzzled and indignant citizens, who said:

"Look, you don't have any right to carry those guns. After all, you weren't elected sheriff."

"Listen," he said, "a man with no more friends than I've got in this community has to carry a couple of guns."

1525. A little boy explained why he didn't mind wearing glasses:

"They keep the boys from fighting me and the girls from kissing me."

1526. A girl was giving her preference in boy friends. "I like men that are tall, dark, and handsome," she said.

"Not me," said her friend. "I like them tall, dark, and handcuffed."

54, 338, 343, 675, 1655, 1823, 1987

Psychiatrist

1527. A burly fellow walked into a psychiatrist's office, opened a tobacco pouch, and stuffed his nose with tobacco.

Psychiatrist

"Man, I can see that you need me," the psychiatrist said. "Come on in and tell me your problem."

"My only problem is," the man said, "I need a light."

1528. "Start by telling me about the dream you had," the psychiatrist said to the young lady who had come to him for treatment.

"It was terrible," she said. "I dreamed I was walking down the street with nothing on but a hat."

"And I suppose you were embarrassed?" the doctor said.

"I certainly was," the young lady said. "It was last year's hat."

1529. A beautiful woman psychiatrist was attending a convention. At one of the seminars the man sitting next to her pinched her. Upset over it, she was about to give him a piece of her mind, but thought better of it.

"Why should I worry?" she said to herself. "After all—it's his problem."

1530. A man was visiting his psychiatrist. Among the many questions the doctor asked was: "Are you bothered by improper thoughts?"

"Not at all," said the patient. "The truth is I rather enjoy them."

1531. Late one night a psychiatrist found himself staring into the muzzle of a large pistol. He was shocked to recognize the gunman who was holding him up.

"See here," he said. "Don't you remember me? I'm your benefactor. Don't you remember the time I saved you from the electric chair by proving you were crazy?"

The holdup man laughed and laughed. "Sure I remember you. Ain't robbing your benefactor a crazy thing to do?"

1532. "Don't worry about your son playing with his blocks all day long," the psychiatrist told the upset mother. "It's quite normal."

"Well!" she said. "I don't think he's normal and neither does his wife."

Psychiatrist

1533. The young girl had been sent to the psychiatrist who was questioning her. "What would you say would be the difference between a little boy and a dwarf?" he asked.

The young girl thought for a moment and said, "Well, there might be a lot of difference."

"What, for instance?" asked the psychiatrist.

"Well," said the young girl. "The dwarf might be a girl."

1534. The kangaroo went to see the psychiatrist.

"And what seems to be your trouble?" the doctor asked.

"I don't know, exactly," said the kangaroo, "I just don't feel jumpy anymore."

1535. The patient told his psychiatrist that he had the same nightmare over and over again night after night.

"And what do you dream about?" asked the doctor.

"I dream that I am married," the man said.

"And to whom are you married in this dream?" the doctor wanted to know.

"To my wife," the patient said. "That is what makes it a nightmare."

196, 257, 459, 738, 1800, 2109

Psychology

1536. You find amateur psychologists everywhere. Even waiters try it.

"There's nothing to it," said a waiter in Miami Beach. "You see, I'm an expert on food and character. Tell me what you eat and I'll tell you what you are."

A little man at the next table said, "Please cancel my order for shrimp salad."

499

Public relations

1537. Owner of restaurant: "Now girls, I want you all to look your best today. Add a little dab of powder to your cheeks and take a bit more care with your hair."

Public relations

Waitress: "What's on—something special?"
Owner: "No, the beef's tough."

1538. A man went into a restaurant for dinner. He sat at a table and waited—and waited—and waited. Four waiters, at a table in the rear, were playing poker. After about half an hour, the manager came in. He saw the situation at a glance.

"What a way to treat the public," he roared. "I got four waiters and they can't even wait on one lousy customer."

1539. The Washington public relations man's little girl came home from Sunday school one Sunday with her little Sunday school paper and a colored picture illustrating a Bible text.

"What did you bring home today?" her father asked.

"Oh," said the little girl, "just some advance publicity about heaven."

330, 453

Punishment

1540. It was the day after the trial of the man's brother for murder. A neighbor stopped to ask, "Well, how did your brother come out?"

"They're gonna put him in jail for a month," the man said.

"A month!" the neighbor said. "That's certainly a light sentence for a cold-blooded murder."

"Oh, I don't know," the man said. "At the end of that month, they're gonna hang him."

1541. "You sure do look downhearted. What's the matter?" a man asked his friend.

"It's my future that worries me," said his friend.

"What makes your future look so black?" the man asked.

"My past," his friend said.

1542. The teacher made two little boys stay after school for misbehaving. She told them that before they could go home, they had to write their names on the blackboard 500 times.

Punishment

After about half an hour, one of the little fellows said to the teacher, "It isn't fair, giving us the same punishment. His name is Joe Ace and my name is Knickerbocker Van Boskirk."

61, 462, 943, 990, 1950

Pure

1543. There was a farmer in Kentucky who always covered his eyes with one hand as he drank his bourbon.

"Why do you do that?" his friend asked.

"Bourbon," the farmer said, "is the noblest of all beverages and every time I see bourbon my mouth begins to water. I don't want to look at it because I don't want to drink my whiskey diluted."

1643, 1739, 2036

Purpose

1544. A famous designer told a class she was teaching, "In designing clothes for women, there's always one thing to keep in mind—men."

1545. The situation was desperate. The woman had been bitten by a rabid dog and the doctors were not certain that she had begun treatment in time to save her.

After a consultation on the matter, they came into the room and told her the plain truth—that she might develop hydrophobia—that her chances were pretty bad.

Instead of seeming to be upset at the news, she asked for a pen and paper and began to write at great length. After an hour of steady writing, her nurse said to her, "What are you writing? Is it your will or a letter to your family?"

"No," said the patient, "it's a list of people I'm going to bite."

142, 339, 372, 574, 643, 952

Questionnaire

1546. The school principal sent a questionnaire home with the students, requesting information about their home environment, number of brothers and sisters, father's occupation, and so on.

Questionnaire

The next day, one little boy returned with a scrap of paper on which was written: "We have 18 children. My husband can also do plumbing and carpentry work."

499

Quick thinking

1547. "Young man," said the angry father, "didn't I hear the clock strike four when you brought my daughter home?"

"Yes, sir," said the boy. "It was going to strike ten, but I grabbed the gong and held it so it wouldn't disturb you."

"I'll be a so-and-so," said the girl's father. "Why didn't I think of that in my younger days?"

1548. The foreman was repairing the roof at the mental hospital. He was working with several of the inmates who had been assigned to him. Everything was all right until quitting time, when one of the inmates grabbed him by the neck and said. It's time to quit. Let's jump down."

The foreman did some fast thinking and then said, "Shucks, anybody could do that. Come on, let's walk down and jump up."

7, 82, 392, 432, 533, 760, 1350

Quiet

1549. A little boy asked the girl next door if his father could borrow her hi-fi.

"Yes," she said. "Do you have a party on?"

"No," said the little boy. "Dad wants to go to bed early."

1550. A drunk sat next to a minister on a bus. Trying to start a conversation, he said, "I ain't going to heaven. There ain't no heaven."

The minister never said a word.

"I say there ain't no heaven," said the drunk in a loud voice.

The minister still didn't answer him.

"I said I ain't going to heaven," shouted the drunk.

The minister quietly turned to the drunk and said, "Well, go to hell, then; but be quiet about it."

156, 186, 441, 904, 1112, 1416, 1865

Quiz

1551. A sports expert was on a quiz show. His question was: "If two old maids, ages 45 and 53, took a bottle of 8-year-old Scotch to a baseball game and sat in row six, section H, what is the situation on the ball diamond?"

Sports expert: "I'm afraid I don't know."

"That's easy," he was told. "It's the last of the fifth and the bags are loaded."

1552. One student looked so bewildered during an examination, that the professor said to him, "You look worried. Does the question bother you?"

"Oh, no sir," said the student. "The question is all right. It's the answer that bothers me."

1553. The newspaperman was interviewing the Congressman on television but he wasn't getting very good answers. In a rather sarcastic manner he said to the Congressman, "I always thought that Members of Congress knew all of the questions of the day."

"Oh," said the Congressman, "I know all of the questions, but that doesn't mean I know the answers."

228, 329, 390, 476, 923

Rabbi

1554. A rabbi from Chicago was visiting New York and went to dinner at a famous Jewish restaurant.

He gave his order in Yiddish, and suddenly realized it was being taken by a Chinese waiter.

"Amazing," he said to the headwaiter as he was leaving. "Where did you find a Chinese waiter who could speak Yiddish?"

"Sh-h-h," said the headwaiter, "he really thinks he's learning to speak English."

386

Race horse

1555. A charitable little lady noticed a seedy-looking man always standing at the corner of the street near the bus stop. One morning, during Lent, she took compassion on him, pressed a dollar into his hand and whispered, "Have hope."

The next day she saw him and he stopped her and slipped six dollars into her hand.

"What does this mean?" she asked in great surprise.

"It means, lady," said the man, "that 'Have Hope' won and paid 6 to 1."

1556.   When the race track opened at the country fair on the day of the big race, the first man at the betting window was a farmer who said, "I want to put five hundred dollars on Blue Belle, to win."

He took his five hundred dollars' worth of tickets and put them in his pocket and went down behind the paddock. After about an hour, he came back. In the meantime, he had been sampling a bit of mountain dew and had gained a lot of enthusiasm about that horse. This time he said, "Buddy, I want to put five hundred more dollars on old Blue Belle, the greatest horse that ever ran on any track. Five hundred dollars to win."

He put those tickets with the others and went back to that bottle.

Later, when the bugle blew for post time, here he came again. He had finished that bottle and was about halfway through another. He could hardly remember what he was trying to do and was talking to himself about it.

"I wanna put five hunner dollars on old Blue Belle," he was muttering as he stood in the line leading to the betting window.

Standing in front of him was a distinguished-looking gentleman, who turned and said to him, "Friend, I'd like to give you some advice. You should get out of line and save yourself five hundred dollars. There are six horses in that race and Blue Belle is not the fastest horse. I ought to know because I own Blue Belle."

The farmer looked at the man for a moment and then said, "Well, friend, all I can say is, it's sure going to be a mighty slow race, because I own the other five."

775, 883, 1116

Rain

1557. The Congressman had just delivered a speech to a group of farmers in the drought area. He had promised all sorts of government help and assistance.

After his speech he asked the chairman of the group what he thought of his speech.

"Well," said the farmer, "it wasn't too bad. But a half-hour of rain would have done a lot more good."

1558. It was a hot dusty summer day in Kansas, when the tourist pulled into the service station.

"Do you think we'll get any rain?" he said to the manager of the gas station.

"I sure hope so," said the man. "Not so much for myself, but for the kids. I've seen rain."

212, 639, 836, 1478, 1746, 1760, 2059

Razor

1559. One morning a fellow started to curse and swear at the top of his voice in the bathroom.

"What's the matter?" called his wife.

"My razor," he said. "It just won't cut."

"Don't be silly," she said. "Do you mean to tell me your beard is tougher than linoleum?"

21, 1031, 1651

Real estate

1560. A man shopping for a house got off the train at a suburban station and asked how far it was to the new subdivision. "About a twenty-minute walk," said a man at the station. "That far?" the first man asked. "The ad in the paper said five minutes." "Well," the local man said, "you can believe me or the ad, but I ain't trying to sell 'em."

1561. A man, driving through the back country, asked a native, "How does the land lie out this way?"

"It ain't the land that lies," the man said. "It's the real estate salesmen."

Real estate

1562. A man up north owned some real estate in Florida. He knew that land prices had soared and he had an overinflated idea of what the property was worth. One day he received a telegram from a real estate broker in Florida offering him a good price for the land.

"Will be happy to sell," he wired back to the broker, "but must have double your price, otherwise count me out."

Two hours later, the owner received another telegram which read: "One, two, three, four, five, six, seven, eight, nine, ten."

1563. The enraged northerner stormed into the Florida real estate broker's office and screamed, "You dirty crook. When you sold me that piece of swamp, you told me that I wouldn't sell it in six months for $50,000 profit."

"That's what I said," replied the real estate man, "and I'm sure you haven't, have you?"

389, 969

Realism

1564. "What," a man asked, "is the difference between a rich man and a poor man?"

"A rich man," his friend said, "has acute laryngitis and a poor man has a head cold."

1565. "I believe in realism," the artist said. "Here is my latest painting. It's called 'Men at Work.' It's modern realism."

"But," said his friend, "the men really aren't at work."

"That's right," said the artist, "that's why it is so real."

1566. The long-time star boarder fell in love with the land-lady. "Will you marry me?" he asked her one evening after supper.

"You've been here four years," she said, "never grumbled about the food, never fussed about the hot water, always paid on time. I'm sorry, but you're too good a boarder to put on the free list."

Realism

1567. The lazy husband put down his newspaper and said to his wife, "If I'd been in Napoleon's place, do you know what I would have done?"

"I sure do," she said. "You'd have settled on a farm in Corsica and let it grow up in weeds."

1568. The man was coming to after a serious operation. He was just conscious enough to feel the softness of the comfortable bed and the warmth of gentle hands on his forehead.

"Where am I?" he asked. "In heaven?"

"No," said his wife, "I'm still right here with you."

127, 144, 458, 731, 790, 1251, 1662

Reason

1569. "Why did you leave your last position?" the personnel director asked.

"Because of illness," the man said. "The boss got sick of me."

1570. The waitress said to the customer, who had been waiting for half an hour, "Excuse me, but was yours ham and beans or ham and eggs?"

"Why ask me after all this time?" the customer wanted to know.

"Because," said the waitress, "we're out of ham."

1571. The boy was doing so poorly in school that he had been called to the office of the Dean. "Why did you come to college, anyway?" asked the Dean. "You aren't even trying."

"Well," said the young man. "I don't really know myelf. My mother says it is to fit me for a great career, Uncle Harry says to sow my wild oats, my sister says to find a friend for her to marry, and Dad, to bankrupt the family."

1572. Two soldiers were talking one day in the PX. "What made you join the army?" asked the first.

"Well, I didn't have a wife and I love war," said the second. "What made you join up?"

"Me?" said the first. "I had a wife and I love peace."

7, 142, 346, 452, 471, 484, 495, 643, 1215

Reasonable

1573. A man was chatting to a friend who was a rabid fisherman.

"I notice," he said, "that when you tell about the fish you caught, you vary the size of it for different listeners."

"Yes," said the veteran fisherman, "I never tell a man more than I think he will believe."

601, 776, 981

Recognition

1574. First stranger: "Where in hell have I seen you before?"
Second stranger: "I don't know. What part of hell are you from?"

1575. Mother to daughter: "Did any of your friends admire your engagement ring?"

Daughter: "They did more than that. Two of them recognized it."

1576. Two prehistoric scientists were out one day, naming the various animals, when they saw a rhinoceros.

"Just look at that one," said the first scientist. "What in the world can we name it?"

"Let's call it a rhinoceros," suggested the second.

"But why that name?" asked the first.

"Because," said the second, "it looks more like a rhinoceros than anything we've come across yet."

1577. A lady was driving her little boy home from school.

"Mother," he asked, "where are all the infernal idiots today?"

"Why," she said, "they only drive on the highway when your father is driving."

1578. The little girl, visiting the zoo for the first time, walked up to the outdoor bird cage with several pieces of bread in her hand. Immediately, a stork rushed over and began to beg for something to eat. As fast as the little girl would give him a bite, he would gobble it down and nod his head for more.

"What kind of bird is that?" she asked her mother.

Recognition

"That's a stork, dear," her mother said.

"Oh," the little girl said, "no wonder he's so friendly. He recognized me."

83, 120, 375, 430, 483, 1825

Recommendation

1579.   Two farmers were attending a political meeting where a candidate was making a speech. He did a good job of praising himself and making a lot of promises.

After the speech, one said to the other, "Who was that man?"

"I don't know who he was," the other farmer said, "but he sure does recommend himself, doesn't he?"

1580.   A prospective employer asked the job applicant, "Do you have any letters of reference?"

"Yes, sir," he said. "Here is one."

The employer read: "To whom it may concern: John Jones worked for us one week, and we were satisfied."

1581.   As proud as she could be, the young bride went to the bank to cash her husband's pay check for the first time.

The teller said, "We can't cash this without an endorsement on the back."

Without a moment's hesitation, the bride turned the check over and wrote on the back, "I hereby endorse my husband. He's the sweetest man in the world."

1582.   A doctor told his patient, "The best thing for you to do is give up drinking and smoking, get up early, and go to bed early."

"I don't deserve the best," said the patient. "What's second best?"

216, 273, 310, 447, 570, 693

Reference

1583.   A young fellow said to a girl, "If you'll give me your telephone number, I'll call you up sometime."

Reference

"It's in the book," she said.

"Fine," he said. "What's your name?"

"Oh, that's in the book, too," she said.

220, 689, 996, 1084

Refuge

1584. Two college presidents were discussing their retirement plans.

"I'd like to be superintendent of an orphan asylum," said the first. "No visits from parents."

"I have a better idea," said the second. "I want to be warden of a penitentiary. No alumni reunions."

1585. A man and his wife were traveling one summer in upper Michigan. While they stopped at a filling station for gas, the man said to the manager, "This is pretty country up here, but doesn't it get mighty cold in the winter?"

"I'll say it does," the filling station man said. "It gets so cold that my wife and I can't stand it any more. We always go south for the winter."

"Florida?" asked the tourist.

"No, Ann Arbor," the man said.

345, 1143

Relatives

1586. "It certainly is hard," said the sad individual, "to lose one's relatives."

"Hard?" said his rich friend. "Hard? It's practically impossible!"

1587. The out-of-state motorist had been arrested in a small town following an accident. "But, officer," he said, "I had the right of way. I wasn't speeding. And this young man deliberately hit me. Yet you say I'm to blame. Why? Why blame me?"

"Why?" said the officer. "Because his dad is the mayor, his brother is my boss, and I'm going steady with his sister."

Relatives

1588. The farm boy had just bought his first pig and was sitting on the edge of the pigpen watching it.

"How are you, young fellow," asked his next door neighbor, "and how is your new pig?"

"Oh, fine, thank you," said the boy. "And how are you and all your folks?"

1589. The farmer awoke one morning to look out his front gate and see a dead mule lying beside the road. Not knowing what to do or whom to notify, he called the sheriff.

"Don't bother me with things like that," the sheriff said. "It's none of my business. Get rid of him yourself. Bury him."

"Oh," said the farmer, "that was what I was going to do. I called you because I wanted to notify his next of kin."

98, 1624

Relaxation

1590. Friend: "Why didn't you take a vacation this year?"
Neighbor: "I thought I needed a rest."

221, 1418, 1534, 1841

Repeat

1591. The customer had settled down in the barber's chair when the barber said to him, "Your hair wants cutting badly, sir."

"Well," said the customer, "go ahead. That's the way you have been cutting it for the past five years."

1592. "What do you want with your old letters?" a girl asked her exboyfriend. I have given you back your ring. Do you think I'm going to use your letters to sue you or something?"

"Oh, no," he said, "it's not that. I paid a fellow twenty-five dollars to write them for me and I may want to use them over again."

Repeat

1593.   An embarrassed young lady gave the clerk a telegraph blank containing only the name, address, and the word "Yes."

"You know, of course, you can send fifteen words for the same price," the clerk said.

"I know," the young lady said, "but wouldn't I look too eager if I repeated the same word fifteen times?"

1594.   One Thursday night, a man came home to supper. His wife served him baked beans. He threw his plate of beans against the wall and shouted, "I hate baked beans."

"I can't figure you out," his wife said. "Monday night you liked baked beans, Tuesday night you liked baked beans, Wednesday night you liked baked beans and now, all of a sudden, on Thursday night, you say you hate baked beans."

1595.   A wife was complaining to her husband, "Our new neighbor must be offended at something I said or did. She hasn't been over for almost a week now."

"Well," said her husband, "when she does come over, be sure to find out what it was you said, so we can try it on her again."

225, 325, 395, 437, 469, 477, 513, 575, 772, 1113, 1427, 1523, 1784, 2039

Reporter

1596.   A reporter rushed to the scene of a murder, but was stopped at the door by the deputy sheriff.

"All right, buddy," he said, "You can't come in here."

"But I've been sent to do the murder," the reporter said.

"Well, buddy, you're too late," the deputy said. "The murder's already been done."

1597.   A newspaper reporter was talking to a seriously injured passenger in an automobile accident.

"I am going to die," the injured man said feebly.

"Cheer up, mister," the reporter said. "How do you spell your last name?"

88, 232, 747, 763, 1658

Reprimand

1598.   An excited visitor rushed up to the beekeeper at the zoo and complained: "A bee just stung me," she said, "and I want you to do something about it."

"Certainly, lady," said the beekeeper, "just show me which bee stung you and I'll give him a reprimand."

1599.   A little boy was sitting on the creek bank fishing. His luck was terrible and he was telling the fish what he thought of them in no uncertain terms. Suddenly, without his knowing it, his minister walked up behind him.

"You shouldn't swear like that, young fellow," the minister said. "The fish won't bite if you swear like that."

"Well," the little fellow said, "I'm doing the best I can with the words I know. Here, you take the fishing pole and see what you can do with them."

71, 180, 1085

Republican

1600.   A young lawyer from up North wanted to set up a practice in the South. He wrote to a friend there and asked him what he thought the chances would be for "an honest young lawyer and Republican."

His friend wrote back: "If you are an honest lawyer, you will have no competition. As for being a Republican, the game laws will protect you."

1601.   A campaigning Congressman said to his audience: "I was born over a drugstore. On account of the lumber shortage the year I was born, only a few wealthy Republicans could afford log cabins."

1602.   It was a big outdoor Republican barbecue and rally. The local minister, himself a staunch member of the GOP, was called on to offer the invocation.

After praying for several minutes, the minister began to put a bit of politics into his invocation. ". . . and too, Lord, we thank

Republican

thee for sending us our great presidents, Lincoln, McKinley, Roosevelt—that's Theodore I'm speaking of, Lord. . . ."

328, 472, 853, 1083, 1450

Reputation

1603.   Once a middle-aged banker fell in love with a lady much younger than he was. He wanted to ask her to marry him but was afraid she was more interested in his income than in him.

So, under an assumed name, he hired a private detective agency to check the girl's background and to give him a detailed report on her activities.

After a careful investigation, the banker was given the report. "Miss Jones," the report read, "is a person of the highest character. But we are sorry to inform you that during the past few weeks she has been seen frequently in the company of an older man of very questionable reputation."

400, 427, 446, 951, 1811

Resemblance

1604.   A man said to his wife, "Did you see how pleased she looked when I told her she didn't look a day older than her daughter?"

"I didn't notice," said his wife. "I was too busy watching the expression on her daughter's face."

1605.   A man and his wife called on a friend in her home for the first time. She took great pride in showing off her house full of antique furniture.

On the way home afterward, the man said to his wife, "I wonder where she got that huge chest?"

"I don't know," said his wife. "But they say her mother was built the same way."

508, 532, 565

Resourceful

1606. The little three-year-old was in her room for the night, when her little brother wanted to come in.

"You tant' tum in," she said, "'cause I'se in my nightie an' Mommie says little boys shouldn't see little dirls in their nighties."

Her brother kept banging on the door. Finally, the little girl said, "It's aw wight, now you tan tum in. I tooked my nightie off."

1607. "I married a brilliant woman," one man bragged to another. "She loves to work in all sorts of civic groups. She can speak on nearly any subject."

"That's nothing," the other fellow said. "My wife can talk without a subject."

209, 570, 639, 675, 1086

Responsibility

1608. "For this job," said the personnel director, "we are looking for a responsible man."

"That's for me," said the applicant. "Everywhere I've worked, whenever anything went wrong, they said I was responsible."

1609. After the accident, the lady driver was apologizing. "I'm afraid it was my fault," she said.

"No," said the man who had been driving the other car. "It was my fault. I could tell your car was being driven by a woman at least 300 feet away, and I could easily have driven over into the field and avoided the accident."

239

Restaurant

1610. A husky fellow mounted a stool in a roadside restaurant and said to the man behind the counter: "I'd wike thum scwambled ekkth with chicken wiverth—and no withe cwackth!"

"Scrambled ekkth with chicken wiverth," the waiter sang out to the cook.

Restaurant

"Thtop twying to mock me!" snarled the customer angrily.

"I wathn't," said the waiter. "Tith ith the way I talk."

The customer quieted down. Just then another man sat down at the counter. "I'll have waffles with syrup and sausages," he said.

"Waffles with syrup and sausages," cried the waiter.

With that the first customer rose up and shouted, "Tho you were mocking me after all."

"I wath not!" said the waiter. "I wath mocking him!"

1611.   An irate customer called the waiter to his table.

"Would you please tell me what this stuff is?" he asked.

"That's bean soup, sir," said the waiter.

"I don't care what it's been," said the customer. "I want to know what it is now."

1612.   A man sat down at a table in a restaurant in a small Georgia town and said to the waitress, "How's the chicken?"

"Oh, I'm all right," she said. "How are you all?"

1613.   A traveling salesman asked a man in a hotel lobby if he knew a good place to eat.

"I'd suggest you try the Deluxe Cafe," the man said.

"Do you always eat there?" the salesman asked.

"No, I've never eaten there," the man said, "but I have eaten at all the other restaurants in this town."

1614.   A man was complaining to the waiter, "What on earth is this broth made from, waiter? It's practically tasteless."

"Well, sir," said the waiter. "It's chicken broth in its infancy. It's made out of the water the eggs were boiled in."

1615.   A man was literally having a tough time with his steak. "Waiter," he said, "this steak is as tough as leather!"

"Why," said the waiter, "that is a veal steak. Less than a month ago it was actually chasing a cow."

"Maybe so," said the customer, "but not for milk."

76, 364, 399, 416, 1538, 1554, 1744

Revenge

1616. "Under the circumstances," said the judge, "I think you might as well give your husband a divorce."

"What!" screamed the man's wife. "I have lived with that bum for thirty years and now I should make him happy!"

1617. A little boy had been telling his Sunday school teacher about the terrible things he was going to do to another little boy next day at school.

His Sunday school teacher was upset and said, "You shouldn't talk like that about your playmate. Have you ever thought about heaping coals of fire upon his head?"

"Gee," said the little boy, "I never thought about that, but it sure sounds like a good idea."

339, 1249

Reverse

1618. The hard-working husband had just settled down with his pipe to read the evening paper.

"I've got a lot of things I want to talk to you about," said his wife.

"That's wonderful news," he said, "usually you want to talk about a lot of things you haven't got."

1619. A fresh young fellow said to his girl friend, "What do you say we do something different tonight, for a change?"

"O.K.," she said. "What do you suggest?"

"You try to kiss me," he said, "and I'll slap your face!"

1620. Two men were talking about their experiences with horses.

"Once a horse ran away with me," said one, "and I wasn't out and around for five weeks."

"That's nothing," said the other. "I once ran away with a horse, and I wasn't out and around for five years."

63, 175, 511, 621, 740, 932, 1068, 1398

Reward

1621. A confirmed drunk decided to quit drinking. To prove to himself that he could do it, he passed by his favorite tavern that evening on his way home from work. Fifty feet past the tavern, he stopped and said to himself: "Boy, I'm proud of you! You're a real hero and have won a great moral victory! I didn't think you could do it, and I'm going to reward you! I'm going to take you right back to that tavern and buy you a double bourbon."

1622. A farmer was bragging at the country store one night. "The man who marries my daughter," he said, "will get a prize."
"That sounds interesting," said one of the local boys. "What's the prize?"

274, 627, 731, 930, 1079, 1486, 1659, 1774

Romance

1623. "Why do you call it love at second sight instead of first glance?"
"That's easy. I didn't know he was rich when I saw him the first time."

1624. A six-year-old boy asked his young girl of the same age if she would marry him when they grew up.
"Oh, I can't," she said. "In our family we always marry relatives. My father married my mother, my grandfather married my grandmother, and even my uncle married my aunt."

1625. A young lady told her friend that she was going to marry a rather eccentric millionaire.
"But," her friend said, "everyone thinks he's a little bit cracked."
"He may be cracked," the young lady said, "but he certainly isn't broke."

1626. Two older than young ladies were chatting about their future.
"I've decided to accept Bill's proposal and marry him," the first one said.

Romance

"He has a reputation for being fast with the ladies," her friend said. "You can bet he'll lead a double life."

"Maybe so," said the first one, "but if I don't marry him, I'll lead a single life, and that would be worse."

1627.   The young lady was really trying to make the most out of a blind date. She and her partner were sitting out a dance in the moonlight.

"And couldn't you be happy with a girl like me?" she asked.

"Maybe," the boy said. "That is if she weren't too much like you."

1628.   "Now that we're engaged, darling," said the young lady eagerly, "you're supposed to give me a ring, aren't you?"

"Sure, honey, what's your telephone number?" said her boy friend.

1629.   "Matrimony is a serious word," said the city editor.

"Word?" said the old-timer. "We thought it was a sentence."

1630.   A gay man-about-town strolled into a hotel lobby one afternoon and sat down beside a pretty girl. After a moment he said, "What's your name, honey?"

"Grape Fruit," she said.

"Grape Fruit?" he asked.

"Yes," she said. "Every time some fresh guy tries to spoon, I hit him in the eye."

1631.   The doctor applied his stethoscope to the young man and listened carefully. "I don't like the sound of your heart," he said. "You've had some trouble with angina pectoris, haven't you?"

"You're right about the trouble," said the young fellow, "only you've got the wrong name."

1632.   An old maid said to her friend, "I'm going out tonight with a used-car salesman."

"What's the difference," said her friend, "as long as he is healthy."

Romance

1633. A man always thinks he is doing the chasing until the girl catches him.

1634. A young man bought a shirt with one of those new style collars. When he was unwrapping it, he found a slip pinned inside with a girl's name and address and this note: "Please write and send a photograph."

Thinking he had a romance going, he sent off a letter and a picture of himself.

A week later this letter arrived: "Thanks, I just wondered what kind of dunce would wear such a dopey shirt."

1635. "Do you take this woman for thy lawful wedded wife?" asked the minister.

The little man, five feet tall and weighing 120 pounds, standing beside the bride who stood six feet and weighed a good 200 pounds, said meekly, "I am not taking anything. I'm the one who's being took."

1636. Her lips quivered as they approached his. Her chin vibrated and his body shuddered as he held her close to him. His whole frame trembled as he looked into her eyes.

The moral of this: Never kiss a girl in a jeep with the engine running.

1637. It was 98° in the shade and the bar was crowded. A hot and weary-looking little man squeezed his way up to the bar and said, "Give me something tall and ice cold and full of gin."

A man who had obviously been at the bar for some time, turned and said to him, "Be careful there, buddy, you are talking about my wife."

1638. A fellow was talking to a friend about his recently broken romance. "Do you mean at her request, you gave up drinking, and smoking, and gambling, and dancing, and playing pool?" he asked.

"Yes, just because she insisted," his friend said.

"Then why didn't you marry her?" the fellow asked.

"Well, after all that reforming," his friend said, "I decided I could do better."

Romance

1639. The young lady heard a tapping on her window in the early hours of the morning. There on a ladder was her boy friend. Their elopement was going according to plan.

"Are you all ready?" her boy friend asked.

"Yes," whispered the girl, "but don't talk so loud, you might wake up my father."

"Wake him up?" her boy friend asked. "Who do you think is holding the ladder?"

28, 117, 260, 534, 720, 1075, 1264, 1404

Rules

1640. First Man: "Dr. Barker says it's his rule never to take a drink when you feel like you need one. And Dr. Webber says never take a drink except when you do need one. How does a man know what to do?"

Second Man: "Follow both rules and you'll be all right."

456, 583, 1029, 1453, 1788

Safety

1641. The little girl said, as she rushed into kindergarten, "We just got a new baby boy at our house. Why don't you come and see it, teacher?"

"Thank you," said teacher, "but I think I'll wait until your mother gets better."

"Oh, you don't have to be afraid," said the little girl, "it's not catching."

1642. A sailor's wife approached the pastor of her church just as he was stepping into the pulpit, and handed him a note. The note said: "Harry Jones, having gone to sea, his wife requests the congregation to pray for his safety."

The minister hastily unfolded the note, and with his mind on the sermon he was about to deliver, read as follows: "Harry Jones, having gone to see his wife, requests the congregation to pray for his safety."

Safety

1643. The new commanding officer, inspecting the camp's water supply, asked what was being done about pollution.

"Well, sir," said the sergeant, "first we boil it."

"Fine," said the general.

"After that we filter it," said the sergeant.

The general nodded approvingly.

"And then," said the sergeant, "just to be on the safe side, we drink beer."

1644. The fellow had taken one too many when he walked up to the police sergeant's desk.

"Offisher, you'd better lock me up," he said. "I jush hit my wife on the head with a beer bottle."

"Did you kill her?" asked the officer.

"Don't think so," the drunk said. "Thash why I want you to lock me up."

1645. A young lady was showing her boy friend the old family album.

"Doesn't dad look funny," she said, "in those old-fashioned suspenders?"

"Yes," her friend said, "but he'd look a lot funnier without them."

1646. A young man six-feet-nine-inches tall applied for a job as a lifeguard. After the usual questions, the manager of the pool said:

"I take it for granted you are an expert swimmer."

"Well, the truth is, I can't swim at all," said the applicant, "but I sure know how to wade in deep water."

1647. A condemned man was scheduled to die in the gas chamber. On the morning of the day of his execution, he was asked by the warden if there was anything special he would like for breakfast.

"Yes," said the man, "mushrooms. I've always been afraid to eat them for fear of being poisoned."

Safety

1648.   Safety Instructor: "What part of an automobile kills the most people?"

Student: "The nut behind the wheel."

1649.   A man checked into a hotel. Along with his baggage was a large coil of rope.

"What's the rope for?" the manager asked.

"That's a fire escape," said the man. "There have been a lot of hotel fires lately. I carry this with me so I can let myself down from the window in case of fire."

"That's a good plan," said the manager, "but all guests with fire escapes like that have to pay in advance at this hotel."

1650.   "I notice you always talk about the weather to your barber," a man said to his friend. "Why?"

"I wouldn't dare talk about anything as exciting as politics or baseball to a man with a razor in his hand, would you?" he said.

1651.   A New Yorker was traveling through the Kentucky mountains and stopped for gas. In back of the station was a real mountaineer boy shaving himself with a bowie knife.

"My," said the New Yorker, "that looks dangerous. Did you ever cut yourself?"

"Well," said the mountain boy, "I have been shaving nigh onto two years now and I haven't cut myself either time."

1652.   The family was on a picnic. The father was standing near the edge of a high cliff, admiring the sea dashing on the rocks below. His young son came up and said, "Mom says it's not safe here. Either you stand back farther or give me the sandwiches."

1653.   The first-grade teacher had been telling the children about the different animals. "Now," she said, "name some things that are very dangerous to get near, and that have horns."

"Cars," said half a dozen kids at once.

1654.   Sign on a truck rolling down a superhighway: "This truck has been in six accidents and ain't lost a one."

Safety

1655. The little boy had been wearing glasses for about a month.

"Do you find that your glasses help your eyes?" asked his teacher.

"Yes, they sure do," he said. "I don't get my eyes blacked any more."

18, 38, 278, 345, 349, 385, 589, 657, 719, 750, 1331, 1345, 1669, 2095

Salesman

1656. A salesman and his boss were traveling together. They checked in a motel and before going to bed they visited a bar where they proceeded to get stinko drunk. Finally they returned to the motel and in their drunken condition, unknowingly crawled into the same bed. After a few minutes the salesman said, "There's someone in my bed."

"That's funny," said his boss, "There's someone in my bed, too."

"Let's kick them out," said the salesman.

"Okay," said his boss.

So they began to kick and scuffle, and the salesman finally kicked his boss out of bed.

"Okay," he cried, "I kicked him out."

His boss, lying on the floor said, "I didn't do so good. The guy in my bed kicked me out."

"That's all right," said the salesman, "you can sleep with me."

1657. A used-car salesman entered a lunchroom, sat at a vacant stool, and ordered bread and milk. The man sitting on the next stool said:

"Are you on a diet?"

"No," the salesman said, "a commission."

1658. A reporter said to the city editor: "Here's the perfect news story."

"Man bites dog?" asked the city editor.

"No," said the reporter, "the bull throws the salesman."

377

Salesman

1659. "Gentlemen," said the sales manager, "I've called you in to announce a big sales contest. It starts today and will run six weeks."

The men were excited, and an eager voice from the rear asked, "What does the winner get?"

"He gets," announced the sales manager, "to keep his job."

1660. A rather shiftless used-car salesman in Pittsburgh was talking to a friend. "What do you think? I have just received the biggest insult of my life. A car dealer in Miami offered me a job."

"Why do you call that an insult?" asked his friend.

"It's not the job, but the salary," the salesman said. "They offered me thirty dollars a week."

"Well," said the friend, "thirty dollars a week is better than nothing."

"Thirty dollars?" said the salesman. "Why, I can borrow more than that right here in Pittsburgh."

1661. A man climbed into a barber's chair and asked, "Where's the barber who used to work on the next chair?"

"Oh, that was a sad case," the barber said. "He became so nervous and despondent over poor business, that one day when a customer said he didn't want a massage, he went out of his mind and cut the customer's throat with a razor. He is now in the State Mental Hospital. By the way, would you like a massage, sir?"

"Absolutely!" said the customer.

1662. The persistent salesman finally managed to get into the manager's office.

"I'm a very busy man," the manager said. "What's your proposition?"

"I'm about to offer you something," said the salesman, "that will make you a million dollars."

"Well, leave me your sales literature," said the manager. "Right now I'm too busy to talk to you. I'm working on a deal that should make me two hundred dollars in real money."

Salesman

1663. "No," said the little boy's mother to the clerk, " I don't want a whistle for my little boy. The other day he nearly swallowed one."

"Well," said the salesman, "we have some nice bass fiddles I could show you."

1664. The new traveling salesman was chatting with an old-timer on the road, who asked him how he was doing.

"Not so good," said the new man. "Every place I go, I get insulted."

"That's funny," said the old-timer. "I've been traveling for more than forty years and I've had my samples pitched out the door, been thrown out myself, kicked down stairs, and was even punched in the nose once—but, I was never insulted."

1665. The owner of a men's store put on a big sale in order to move some suits which had been in stock for several years. One of the suits was particularly loud, with broad yellow and green stripes running through the material.

On the opening day of the sale, he put it on the front of the rack and told his clerk that he wanted that suit sold—or else.

When the owner came back from lunch, the suit was gone. He went to congratulate his clerk and found him standing in the back in absolute tatters. He was all bloody and beat up as though he had been in a car accident.

"I see you sold the suit," the owner said, "but don't tell me that the customer did that to you?"

"Oh, no, sir," the salesman said. "The customer was perfectly satisfied, but his seeing-eye dog nearly tore me to pieces."

1666. The greatest hunting dog in North Carolina was named "Salesman." People from all over would engage him for the hunting season a year in advance. He was made. His fame had spread.

Then one season, the hunters showed up and the dog refused to budge. Instead of the greatest hunting dog in North Carolina, he had turned into nothing.

"What happened?" the hunters asked his owner.

Salesman

"Well, it's a sad story," he said. "He did so well that we changed his name from Salesman to Salesmanager. Now, all he does is sit around and bark at the other dogs."

25, 38, 92, 96, 314, 380, 400, 545, 547, 621, 1310, 1857, 1998

Samson

1667.   Few people know it, but Samson was one of the greatest actors of all time. He never had to say a word. All he did was throw out his chest, reach out with his hands and pull against a couple of the pillars—and he brought down the house.

1668.   One hot day down in Georgia a fellow named John Henry Simpson took a job with a road contractor. The crew was building a new road through the red clay hills of the state. The temperature was better than 100° in the shade and the foreman was working his men relentlessly. After several hours of this sort of grueling labor, John Henry went over to the timekeeper and asked him: "Boss, has you got a fellow on your list named Simpson?"

The timekeeper looked at his time sheet and then said, "Yes, I've got a man on my sheet named Simpson, what did you want to know about him?"

"Oh, nothing, boss. But, from the way they's been working me, I thought maybe they had it down as Sampson."

Sanitary

1669.   The young doctor from the medical center was going from house to house in the farm area trying to check an epidemic.

He asked one farmer, "Are you taking all necessary precautions to prevent the spread of contagion?"

"Yes, sir," said the farmer. "We even bought one of those sanitary paper cups and we all drink out of it."

1670.   A little boy had the sniffles. This annoyed a woman who was standing next to him. "Listen young man," she said, "have you got a handkerchief?"

Sanitary

"Yes," said the little boy, "but my mother won't let me lend it to anybody."

497, 1814

Save

1671. Friend: "How are you getting on in your new six-room house?"

Neighbor: "Oh, we're doing fine. We have already furnished one of the rooms by saving cigarette coupons."

Friend: "Haven't you furnished the other five rooms yet?"

Neighbor: "No, we can't. They're full of cigarettes."

1672. Two farmers met at the annual farm bureau meeting. "What was your peach crop like?" the first asked.

"Well," said his friend, "a heavy storm blew down 50 per cent of it one night and the next night another wind blew down the rest."

"That was bad luck," the first said. "Could you do anything with them?"

"Well," said the man, "my wife ate one and I ate the other."

1673. A wife was proudly reporting to her husband. "Well," she said, "I followed your advice. I saved a hundred dollars this month."

"Great," said her husband. "It isn't so hard after all, is it?"

"No," said his wife. "All I did was tear up most of the bills."

191, 196, 669

School

1674. The teacher asked a little girl, "What is the plural of man?"

"Men," answered the little girl.

"That's right," the teacher said. "And what is the plural of child?"

"Twins," the little girl said.

206, 212, 531, 680

Science

1675. The television network was putting on a live documentary about the Kentucky mountain folks. They had brought to New York, a man who had spent his entire life in the mountains. He was absolutely amazed at all of the things around him. He was almost breathless as he stood in the lobby of the RCA Building. His eyes were popping with interest as he saw a little old lady enter an elevator. The door closed, the little red light went on and she was gone. He almost dropped dead when a few minutes later, the same door opened and out stepped a beautiful young girl.

"Well, I'll be doggoned," he said. "If I'd a known about that contraption, I'd have brung along my old woman."

561, 780, 806, 1220

Scotch

1676. Three blood transfusions were necessary to save a man's life in a hospital. A Scotchman offered his blood. The patient gave him fifty dollars for the first pint; twenty-five dollars for the second pint; but the third time he had so much Scotch blood in him he only thanked the blood donor.

Search

1677. A woman in tears came running into her husband's office one morning. "Oh," she cried, "I've lost my diamond ring. It must have slipped off my finger somewhere and I can't find it any place."

"Don't worry," he said. "I found it a few minutes ago right here in my pants pocket."

1678. "Have you ever been operated on for appendicitis?" the nurse asked the patient as she was filling his medical record for the doctor.

"I don't know for sure," the man said. "I was operated on once but I never knew whether it was appendicitis or professional curiosity."

385, 464, 520, 556, 678, 1021, 1191, 1723, 2045, 2076

Seasick

1679. A lady was on her first ocean voyage and was deathly ill. Trying to comfort her, the steward said, "Don't be so downhearted, ma'am, I have never heard of anyone dying of seasickness."

"Oh, don't tell me that," she moaned. "It has only been the hope of dying that has kept me alive."

1680. It was her first trip aboard ship and she was afraid of getting seasick.

"Could you tell me what to do in case of an attack?" she asked the captain.

"I don't need to tell you, lady," the captain said. "You'll do it."

593, 690, 855, 1983

Secret

1681. A holdup man ordered a man to give him his money. Instead, the victim put up a terrific battle. Finally, the holdup man tripped him, and his victim fell to the street. He quickly searched his pockets and found seventy-five cents.

"Why did you put up a battle like that for a lousy seventy-five cents?" he asked the man.

"Because I was afraid you might find the thousand-dollar bill I've got hidden in my shoe," said the man.

1682. A young man met a bikini-clad girl on the beach. They were sitting in the sand chatting. "I've had a miserable week," she said. "I was vaccinated last Monday and it has become so sore and painful that I couldn't work."

The young man looked her over and saw no mark. "Where were you vaccinated?" he asked.

She smiled and said, "In Baltimore."

1683. A fellow was talking to the thinly clad girl at the ice-skating rink. "I can't see what keeps you girls from freezing," he said.

"You're not supposed to," she said.

Secret

1684. A young man asked his father, "Dad, is it possible for a woman to keep a secret?"

"Oh, yes," his father said. "Your mother and I were engaged for six weeks before she said anything to me about it."

89, 438, 539, 640, 727

Secretary

1685. A little boy asked his aunt about her job. "I am a secretary," she said. "All I do is look like a doll, think like a man, act like a lady, and work like a dog."

1686. Man, hiring a secretary: "Can you write on the typewriter?"

"Yes, sir," she said, "I use the biblical system."

"I never heard of it," the boss said. "How does it work?"

"Seek and ye shall find," the secretary said.

1687. Secretary to her boss: "This is your wife on the line. She wants to kiss you over the telephone."

The boss: "Take the message and give it to me later."

1688. The man was giving a test to a prospective secretary. "Suppose I dictate a sample letter," he said. "Kowenski and Khroensteiner, 840 Rhumic Avenue, Okahumka, Florida, Gentlemen,"

"Excuse me, sir," the prospective secretary said, "how do you spell 'gentlemen'?"

1689. The president of the company called in his personnel director. "That new secretary you hired for me is quite capable and efficient," he said, "but she's so pretty and glamorous that everyone stops to talk to her and wastes too much time. I want you to get me a plain secretary."

The next morning, when the president buzzed for his secretary, a thin, sour-looking, wrinkled old lady came in. Later, the president called for his personnel man.

"I know," he said, "that I asked for a plain secretary, but there was no need for you to get sarcastic about it."

Secretary

1690. The man had just hired a new secretary and was telling her about the job. "I hope you understand the importance of punctuation," he said.

"Oh, yes," she said. "I always get to work on time."

1691. It was mail signing time at the office. As everyone was rushing to get away, the boss stopped his secretary to point out to her several errors she had made in her dictation. Finally, she butted in and said, "Mr. Jones, it's two minutes after five. You're scolding me on my own time."

1692. "That pretty secretary in the front office is leaving," one draftsman said to another.

"You mean she is leaving for good?" the other asked.

"No," said the first, "she is leaving for better or for worse— she is getting married."

417, 444, 475, 534, 760, 1135

Security

1693. One time an Indian came into a bank in Oklahoma and asked about a loan. "Me want $200," he said.

"And what security have you?" the banker asked.

"200 horses," the Indian said.

This seemed to be good security and the loan was made. A month later, the Indian came back with $2,200 in cash, paid off the note, and started to leave with the rest of the money in his pocket.

"Why not let me take care of that money for you?" asked the banker.

He looked the banker straight in the eye and asked, "How many horses you got?"

1694. The reporter was on his first story. A man had been murdered by burglars. The last paragraph of his account read: "The deceased had been very fortunate because only the day before he had put all of his money and negotiable bonds in his safety deposit box at the bank, so that he lost practically nothing but his life."

Security

1695. The theatrical agent was interviewing a man with a pet monkey. "My partner is very clever," the man said, pointing to the monkey. "He can talk, sing and dance, and play the harmonica. He is positively human."

"If he's so smart," asked the agent, "why is he on a leash?"

"Because," said the man, "he owes me 10 bucks!"

460, 501, 684, 767

Self-appraisal

1696. A reporter asked the great man what was the best advice he ever received.

The famous man said, "To marry the girl I did."

"Who gave you that advice?" the reporter asked.

"She did," was the answer.

1697. The Congressman had been out speaking all day and returned home late at night, tired and weary.

"How did your speeches go today?" his wife asked.

"All right, I guess," the Congressman said. "But I'm afraid some of the people in the audience didn't understand some of the things I was saying about our foreign policy."

"What makes you think that?" his wife asked.

"Because," whispered the Congressman, "I don't understand them myself."

168, 266, 269, 424, 728, 824, 1349, 1789

Self-betrayal

1698. At breakfast one morning a man was telling his wife about the meeting of his civic club the night before. "The president of the club," he said, "offered a silk hat to the member who could truthfully say that during his married life he had never kissed any woman but his wife. And not a man stood up."

"Why," his wife asked, "didn't you stand up?"

"Well," he said, "I was going to, but you know how silly I look in a silk hat."

Self-betrayal

1699. The country boy and his girl friend were walking through the woods one Sunday afternoon. Suddenly, he turned to the girl and said, "Honey, will you marry me?"

"Oh, yes," she answered immediately.

They walked along in perfect silence for half an hour. Then she said, "Why don't you say something?"

"It seems to me," he said, "that I've already talked too much as it is."

1700. "Willie," his uncle asked, "do you have a girl friend?"

"Gosh, no," the eight-year-old said as he ran off to the baseball game.

The little girl from next door smiled wisely at Willie's uncle and said, "They're always the last to know, aren't they?"

1701. "With all of the evidence to the contrary," the district attorney said to the defendant, "do you still maintain that your husband died of a broken heart?"

"I certainly do," the woman said. "If he hadn't broken my heart, I wouldn't have shot him."

391, 471, 686, 736, 1027, 1239, 1944

Selfish

1702. Two little boys were in the back yard playing. One was eating a piece of cake. The other was crying. Their mother came out to see what the trouble was.

"What's he crying for?" she asked the first one.

"Because I won't give him any of my cake," he said.

"Is his cake all gone?" his mother asked.

"Yes," he said, "and he cried when I was eating that, too."

1703. The old man was eighty years old and his grandson was trying to get him placed in a nursing home. The place was crowded and the grandson was having difficulty. "Please," he said to the doctor. "You must take him in. He's getting feeble-minded. Why, all day long he sits in the bathtub, playing with a rubber Donald Duck!"

Selfish

"Well," said the psychiatrist, "he may be a bit senile, but he's not doing any harm, is he?" ·

"But," said the man in tears, "it's my Donald Duck."

1704.   The retired machinists pooled their money and bought a tavern in a country town. They immediately closed it and began to paint and fix it up inside and out. A few days after all the repairs had been completed and there was no sign of its opening, a thirsty crowd gathered outside. One of the crowd yelled out, "Say, when you gonna open up?"

"Open up? We're not going to open up," said one of the owners. "We bought this place for ourselves!"

1705.   A Sunday school teacher told her class that people were in the world to help others.

One little boy asked, "Then what are the others here for?"

125, 410, 624, 2016, 2090

Sensation

1706.   A beautiful model was trying on a dress in the cutting room.

"I just don't like that color," said the designer. "If you'd wear a dress to match those stockings, you'd be a sensation."

"I certainly would," said the model. "I'm not wearing stockings."

40

Sense

1707.   An inmate of the asylum was pushing a wheelbarrow upside down. He was stopped by a visitor who said, "What's the idea of wheeling your wheelbarrow upside down?"

"Do you think I'm crazy?" he asked. "Yesterday, I pushed it right side up and they filled it with bricks."

1708.   The young bookkeeper said to his boss, "Sir, I wonder if I can have four days off next week, I am planning to get married."

Sense

"Four days off?" asked the boss. "Why, you just came back from a two week's vacation. Why didn't you get married then?"

"I don't know exactly," the young man said, "except I just didn't want to spoil my vacation."

149, 1091, 1196

Sentimental

1709. A husband was leaving a movie with his wife: "Why do you weep and snuffle," he asked, "in a picture show over the imaginary misfortunes of people you don't even know?"

"For the same reason," she said, "that you scream and cheer when a man you don't know slides into second base."

1710. A little boy said to his mother, "Mom, you know that vase in the living room that's been handed down from generation to generation?"

"Yes," said his mother. "What about it?"

"Well," said the little boy. "This generation just dropped it!"

1711. The prisoner was being booked and all of his possessions were being taken from him. As each item was removed, it was listed and placed in an envelope. Among the articles was a badly tarnished silver dollar.

The prisoner pointed to the dull-looking dollar and said to the desk sergeant, "Would you mind letting me keep that with me?"

"Why?" asked the sergeant.

"Oh, just a sentiment, I suppose," the prisoner said. "It's the first dollar I ever stole."

62, 117, 236, 306, 716, 1581

Service

1712. A man who had been married for ten years consulted a marriage counselor. "When we were first married," he said, "I was very happy. I would come home from a hard day at the office. My little dog would race around barking, and my wife would bring me my slippers. Now after ten years, everything's changed. When I come home, my dog brings me my slippers, and my wife barks at me!"

Service

"I don't know what you're complaining about," said the marriage counselor. "You're still getting the same service."

1713.   A farmer was given a political appointment as postmaster of a backwoods town. As time went on, Washington began getting complaints that no mail was going out from this office. An inspector was sent to investigate. The inspector asked the postmaster why he had not sent out any mail.

The farmer pointed to a large mailbag hanging on a hook and said:

"Because that bag ain't even half full yet."

1714.   A customer in a filling station, waiting to get his car serviced, watched a mechanic change the oil in another car without spilling a drop. He checked the radiator and the battery, cleaned the windshield, wiped away the finger marks. He dusted out the back seat and the floor. He washed his hands and then drove the car slowly and carefully to the parking area.

"Now there's a careful mechanic," the customer said.

"Oh," said the man who was servicing his car, "that's his own car."

110, 197, 514, 690, 803, 928, 1097, 1175, 1705

Sharing

1715.   A schoolteacher asked the little boy: "If your mother gave you a large apple and a small apple and told you to divide with your brother, which apple would you give him?"

Little boy: "Do you mean my little brother or my big brother?"

1716.   A man had a meeting of his creditors and told them that he was about to go into bankruptcy.

"I owe you fellows over a hundred thousand dollars," he said, "and my assets aren't enough to pay five cents on the dollar. I am afraid it will be impossible for you to get anything—unless you want to cut me up and divide me among you."

"I move we do it," said one of his creditors. "I'd like to have his gall."

Sharing

1717.　Two friends were attending a garden party for charity which featured games of chance.

"I just took a one-dollar chance for charity," said one, "and a beautiful blonde gave me a kiss. I hate to say it, but she kisses better than my wife!"

His friend said he was going to try it. Afterwards, the first one asked: "How was it?"

"Swell," said the second, "but no better than your wife."

29, 359, 407, 738, 1124, 1373, 2097

Sheepherder

1718.　A sheepherder finally struck it rich. Among other things, he bought a Rolls Royce limousine. On his next trip to town, the car salesman asked him how he liked his new car.

"Say, fella," said the sheepherder, "that is a real nice car. I sure do like that window that rolls up in back of the front seat."

"I didn't know you had a chauffeur," said the salesman.

"I don't have no chauffeur," said the owner of the Rolls, "but I sure like that window. It keeps the sheep from licking my neck when I'm taking 'em to market."

2008

Shock

1719.　The patient visited the doctor in his office and said, "I'm feeling well again, doctor. I'd like to have your bill."

"Don't be in a hurry," the doctor said. "Be calm and take care of yourself. You're not nearly strong enough yet for that big a shock."

144, 539, 697, 1379, 1535, 1604

Shoes

1720.　A country boy came to town on a rainy day and wandered into the hotel lobby, bringing a lot of mud with him.

"Hey," said the desk clerk, "don't you know enough to wipe the mud off your shoes before you come in here?"

The country boy looked down and around, then said, "Gawsh, mister, what shoes?"

Shoes

1721. A beautiful girl limped past two men standing at a bus stop. "There goes a girl who is willing to suffer for her beliefs," the first one said.

"Why, what belief is that?" asked the other.

"Oh, she believes she can wear a number four shoe on a number six foot," the first said.

92, 837, 1375

Shopper

1722. "Dad," asked a young fellow studying his homework, "what's a counterirritant?"

"A counterirritant?" said his father, who was the manager of a supermarket, "is a woman who picks up and inspects every package of meat in the meat counter before she buys a can of tuna fish."

1723. A woman was shopping in the rug department of a big store. The clerk had been most attentive and had rolled back each rug in the huge pile. He had put himself to great effort and had shown the woman every rug except the last one. He was getting ready to uncover it, when the woman said, "I appreciate you going to all this trouble, but I don't think I'll buy anything. You see, I was really looking for a friend."

"That's all right, lady," the clerk said. "If you think there's any possibility that your friend is underneath that last rug, I'll gladly roll it back, too."

177, 308, 343, 371, 945, 1743, 2101

Shrewd

1724. A lawyer was working on a divorce case. After a preliminary conference with her husband, the lawyer reported back to the man's wife.

"I have succeeded," he told her, "in reaching a settlement with your husband that is fair to both of you."

"Fair to both?" cried the wife. "I could have done that myself. Why do you think I hired a lawyer?"

191, 315, 501, 722, 812

Sick

1725.   A lady returned a ham to the supermarket because she said it was bad.

"Why, that ham's all right," the manager said. "It couldn't be spoiled. It was only cured last week."

"It may have been cured last week," the lady said, "but it's sure had a relapse."

1726.   A little boy was buying a ticket to a movie in the middle of the day, when the girl at the box office said, "Why aren't you in school?"

"Oh, it's all right, lady," said the little boy. "I don't have to go to school today. I've got the measles."

1727.   Two men had been drinking all evening in a bar. One finally passed out and fell to the floor. His friend called a doctor who rushed him to a hospital. When he came to, the doctor asked him, "Do you see any pink elephants or little green men?"

"Nope," groaned the patient.

"No snakes or alligators?" the doctor asked.

"Nope," the drunk said.

"Then just sleep it off and you'll be all right in the morning," said the doctor.

But the drunk's friend was worried. "Look, doctor," he said, "that boy's in bad shape. He said he couldn't see any of them animals, and you and I know the room is full of them."

1728.   The man was suffering from what appeared to be a case of shattered nerves. After a long spell of failing health, he finally called a doctor.

"You are in serious trouble," the doctor said. "You are living with some terrible evil thing; something that is possessing you from morning to night. We must find what it is and destroy it."

"Sssh, doctor," said the man, "you are absolutely right, but don't say it so loud—she's sitting in the next room and she might hear you."

113, 150, 153, 315, 344, 452, 505, 587, 741

Sideline

1729. Every night, the destitute concert violinist shivered in his cold apartment as he enviously watched the daily arrival of a bad neighborhood violinist who played in the street below.

Whenever the bad violinist played his terrible music, windows opened and people threw out wads of money.

Desperate for money, the concert violinist decided to try the same thing. He played beautifully, but all he was tossed was 50 cents.

In utter disbelief, he asked the neighborhood violinist what his trouble was.

"That's easy," said the second-rate player. "You've got to be a bookmaker on the side."

Silence

1730. The woman lecturer was going strong. "For centuries women have been misjudged and mistreated," she shouted. "They have suffered in a thousand ways. Is there any way that women have not suffered?"

As she paused to let that question sink in, it was answered by a voice down front. "Yes, there's one way," the voice said. "They have never suffered in silence."

1731. A man called the doctor for his wife late one night. The doctor arrived, opened his bag, took out a thermometer, and put it in his patient's mouth.

"Hold that in your mouth," he said, "and don't open it for ten minutes."

Later, as the doctor was leaving the house, the man said, "Thanks for looking in on my wife, doctor. But, before you go— how much would you take for that thing you put in her mouth?"

1732. A teen-ager had dented a fender on the family car.

"What did your father say when you told him?" the boy's mother asked.

"Should I leave out the cuss words?" he said.

"Yes, of course," said his mother.

"In that case," said the boy, "he didn't say a word."

Silence

1733. Two young fellows were comparing notes. "Why do you call my girl friend Silent Belle?" the first one asked.

"Because," said the other, "I kissed her the other night, and she never told."

19, 35, 158, 410, 832

Similarity

1734. A man was chatting with an acquaintance at a cocktail party.

"Whenever I see you," he said, "I always think of Joe Wilson."

"That's funny," his acquaintance said, "I'm not at all like Joe Wilson."

"Oh, yes you are," said the man. "You both owe me $100."

64, 287, 303, 532, 679, 752, 792, 1289, 1627

Sin

1735. "Now," said the Sunday school teacher, "can anyone tell me what we must do before we can expect to be forgiven of our sins?"

"Well," said a little boy, "I suppose that first we gotta sin."

1736. The teen-ager's uncle was watching her friends dance at her birthday party.

"I'll bet you never saw any dancing like that," she said, "back when you were a young man."

"Once," said her uncle, "but the place was raided."

1737. A minister on Skid Row approached a man lying in the gutter.

"And so," he asked, "this is the work of whiskey, isn't it?"

"No," said the man. "This is the work of a banana peel."

1738. A farmer came up to an evangelist and told him he had "got religion." "That's fine," said the preacher, "but are you sure you're going to put aside all sin?"

"Yes, sir, I'm through with sin," said the farmer.

Sin

"And are you going to pay up all your debts?" asked the preacher.

"Now wait a minute, preacher," said the farmer, "you ain't talking religion now, you're talking business."

1739. The visiting minister was shouting from the pulpit about the Ten Commandments. His words had a profound effect on the congregation. When the meeting was over, and the people were leaving the church, one feminine voice could be heard. "Well, anyhow," it said, "I never made a graven image."

1740. Two little girls were comparing their progress in catechism. "I've come to original sin," said one proudly. "How far are you?"

"Me?" said the other. "Oh, I'm already away beyond redemption."

1741. The Sunday school teacher was trying to make the little boy behave. "I'm really very much afraid," she said, "that I'm not going to meet you in heaven."

"Gee, that's too bad," said the little boy. "What have you been doing?"

51, 343, 387, 1869

Singer

1742. "It must be terrible," the man said, "for an opera singer to realize she can never sing again."

"Yes," said the critic, "but it's much more terrible if she doesn't realize it."

701, 766, 977, 1354, 1518, 1892

Size

1743. A man went into a department store and stood around, a bit confused.

"May I help you, sir?" asked a salesgirl.

"Yes, I want to buy a corset for my wife," he said.

"What bust, sir?" asked the girl.

"Oh, nothing," he said, "nothing bust. It just wore out."

Size

1744. A man in the restaurant complained to the waiter, "The portions here seem to have shrunk lately."

"That is an optical illusion," the waiter said. "Now that the restaurant has been enlarged, they look smaller."

339, 806, 1197

Sleep

1745. It was the morning after the big party. The man was moaning and holding his head.

"Well, if you hadn't drunk so much last night you wouldn't feel so bad this morning," said his wife.

"Drinking had nothing to do with it," said the man. "I went to bed feeling fine and woke up feeling lousy. It was the sleep that did it."

1746. A man and his wife were camping out in their new portable tent outfit. During the night a terrible storm came up and next morning the camp ground was soaking wet.

"My," said the man's wife, "did it rain during the night?"

"Rain?" he asked. "You never saw such a storm. Thunder and lightning like you never saw."

"You should have wakened me," she said. "You know very well I can't sleep well during a thunderstorm."

19, 432, 510, 857, 1244, 1508, 1796

Sleepwalking

1747. The night clerk in a hotel was surprised to see a guest walking through the lobby in a pair of pajamas.

"Hey, there," he shouted, "What do you think you are doing?"

The guest woke up and apologized. "I beg your pardon," he said. "I'm a somnambulist."

"Well," said the clerk, "you can't walk around here like that, no matter what church you belong to."

1343

Slow train

1748. A lady in a parlor car heard the lady across the aisle ask the porter to open the window. She said to the porter, "If that window is opened, I shall freeze to death."

"And if that window is kept closed," said the other passenger, "I'll suffocate."

The porter didn't know what to do. Finally, he said to a man seated nearby, "What would you do, sir?"

"That's easy," said the man. "I'd open the window and freeze the first lady. Then close it and suffocate the other one."

443, 490, 535

Small town

1749. A small town is a place where a fellow with a black eye doesn't have to explain to people—they know.

1750. A tourist, traveling in the off-season, stopped at a country store in a small town. "I want to buy a toothbrush," he said.

"Sorry," the storekeeper said, "but our line of summer novelties ain't in yet."

169, 666, 970, 1014, 1311

Smoking

1751. "I'm glad my old man is religious," the woman said. "But I do feel sorry for him after every revival meeting until he backslides and starts smoking again."

1752. A man handed a friend a cigar and also lit one himself. "How is it?" the man asked. "These are two for a quarter."

"Is that so?" his friend said. "You must have the twenty-three-cent one."

1753. A rather prim lady was seated on a bus when the man sitting next to her began to stuff his pipe. "Sir," she said, "if you don't mind my saying it, tobacco makes me ill."

"In that case," he said, "I'd give it up if I were you."

Smoking

1754. A fellow who was trying hard to give up smoking was told by his friend that he should join Cigarettes Anonymous.

"How does it work?" his friend asked.

"Well," said the first fellow, "when you reach the point where you think you can't possibly live another minute without a cigarette, you call a certain number. The young lady who answers puts you in touch with someone else in the same fix who has just called in. You in turn call him on the phone and he comes over to your house—and you get drunk together."

1755. The Sunday school teacher was trying to illustrate the difficulty of breaking a bad habit—such as smoking.

"What is it," she asked the children, "that is real easy to get into but very hard to get out of?"

"The bed," said one little girl.

46, 299, 380, 505, 611, 655, 1864

Snake

1756. Big Boy: "Why are you running so fast?"

Little Boy: "I saw a snake, but it wasn't a snake—it was a stick."

Big Boy: "Then why are you shaking?"

Little Boy: "Because the stick I picked up to hit it with was a snake."

1757. "My friend and I," said the cowboy to a dude rancher, "are taking a trip through the mountains next week. He's taking along a gallon of whiskey just in case of rattlesnake bites."

"What are you taking?" asked the dude rancher.

"A sack full of rattlesnakes," the cowboy said.

Snob

1758. First Snob: "I passed by your house yesterday."

Second Snob: "Thanks, we appreciated it."

1759. "Are you going to the White House reception next Thursday night?" asked one Washington society leader to another.

Snob

"No, my husband and I don't think we can make it," the other said. "We have a prior commitment that we cannot cancel."

"I wasn't invited, either," said the other.

601, 627, 948, 1045, 1206, 1262, 1818

Snow storm

1760. The little Florida girl was visiting her grandmother in Pittsburgh. While there, she saw snow for the first time. As it came down she said excitedly, "Oh, Grandma, what is it, what is it?"

"Why," said her grandmother, "that is snow. What did you think it was?"

"Oh," said the little girl, "it looks like popped rain!"

1761. It was a New England blizzard and the man and his wife were hopelessly lost. "Oh, look," she shouted, "there's a chicken. We must be near a farm."

"That's not a chicken," said her husband. "That's the weathervane on top of the county courthouse."

1762. The day after the snowstorm, the little boy in the first grade at school was sound asleep at his desk. The teacher woke him up and asked him why he was sleeping in school.

"It's them folks stealing chickens again," the little boy said.

"Stealing chickens?" the teacher asked. "What has stealing chickens got to do with you sleeping in school?"

"Well," said the little boy, "they've been stealing Pa's chickens for a long time. And he said the next time they come around, he was going to get himself a couple of dead chicken thieves. Then in the middle of the night last night, during the snowstorm, he heard them. Pa jumped up out of bed and ran out as fast as he could go. He didn't even take time to put on his trousers. He ran out in his nightshirt. He grabbed the shotgun as he went through the back door. He loaded both barrels—and he cocked them, too, because he wasn't about to miss them. He tiptoed through that snow and got out to the hen house. He

Snow storm

had both his fingers on those two triggers and he was easing the door open with the barrel of the gun, when that old dog of ours came up behind Pa with his cold nose. And we was up all night long at our house cleaning and picking chickens."

753

Soda fountain

1763.   "I'd like coffee, without cream," the customer said.

"I'm sorry," the waitress said, "You'll have to take it without milk. We're out of cream."

1764.   The local banker was talking to his friend from next door, the druggist.

"Tell me the truth," the banker said. "Do you make much money on your lunch counter?"

"Not really," the druggist said. "We do well to break even. But, look how it stimulates the sale of indigestion medicine."

1765.   The pretty girl customer had ordered a milk shake and when it was set before her she asked the clerk for a straw.

"Hey?" asked the hard-of-hearing clerk.

"No, I said straw," replied the girl.

30

Solution

1766.   "It's being rumored around town," a lady said to her friend, "that you and your husband aren't getting along too well. Is there anything to it?"

"Nonsense," said her friend. "We did have a few words, and I shot him. But that's as far as it went."

1767.   One author was complaining to another about the neglect of his book by the critics.

"There is a complete conspiracy of silence against me," said the man, "an absolute conspiracy of silence. What do you suggest I do about it?"

"Join it," said his friend.

Solution

1768.   A woman sent her son to mail some letters. She asked him later if he had mailed them all right.

"Yes, Mom," the boy said. "But, just as I was about to put them in the mailbox, I noticed you had put the stamps on wrong. The letter to England had the five-cent stamp, and the letter to Baltimore had the twenty-five-cent airmail stamp. But I fixed it."

"But how did you change the stamps?" asked his mother.

"I didn't change the stamps. All I did was change the addresses," said the boy.

42, 298, 399, 442, 661, 1214, 1272, 1494, 1735, 1785

Sorrow

1769.   The lawyer was talking to the insurance man about a friend of theirs who had died.

"So you don't believe his widow is as sorry as she acts?" said the lawyer. "Why is that?"

"Well," said the insurance man, "when I gave her the $50,-000 insurance check, she said she'd cheerfully give $5,000 of it to have him back."

1770.   The word had passed around that Bill's wife had left him. While the news was still fresh, an old friend ran into him.

"I've just heard the bad news that your wife has left you," said the old friend. "I suppose you go home every night now and drown your sorrow in drink?"

"No, I have found that to be impossible," said the man.

"Why is that?" asked his friend. "No drink?"

"No," said the man, "no sorrow."

225, 599, 915

Sound

1771.   "But your story has such a hollow ring," said the lady to the panhandler.

"Yes, lady," he said. "That's on account of I'm speaking on an empty stomach."

Space age

1772. All day the children had been pestiferous and Mother was at the end of her rope. Finally she screamed at them in utter frustration, "Get upstairs to bed this very instant!"

"This time we'd better do it," one of them said. "She's on the countdown and ready to blast off."

1773. Two mellow drunks were staggering through the park together one night, when one looked at his reflection in a puddle of water.

"Say, what's that I see down there?" he asked his friend.

"It's the moon," his friend said.

"Gosh," said the man. "How did I get way up here?"

69, 1088, 1803

Speaker

1774. One time a man shot an after-dinner speaker who talked too long and didn't say anything of interest.

Immediately the man turned himself in to the sheriff, and said, "I just shot an after-dinner speaker."

"You are in the wrong place," the sheriff said. "You should go to the game warden's office. You collect the bounty there."

1775. There was so much disturbance that the speaker couldn't be heard. He finally turned to the chairman and said, "I've been on my feet for over ten minutes and during that time there's been so much noise and interruption that I can scarcely hear myself speak."

"Don't worry," came a voice from the rear, "you ain't missin' much."

1776. The speaker was long-winded and dry. As he went on and on, people gradually slipped out until at last the audience had dwindled down to a single man in the front row.

"I wish to pause here, my friend," the speaker said to this man, "to thank you for your courtesy in remaining to hear all of my speech."

"Oh, that's all right," said the man. "I don't need any thanks —I'm the next speaker."

Speaker

1777. The inexperienced speaker stood up to speak, but was suddenly speechless. The huge audience dazed him. As he stammered and stuttered, a voice from the rear shouted, "Tell 'em all you know, Bill. It won't take long."

"I'll tell 'em all we both know," he shouted as his voice returned. "It won't take any longer."

1778. "Do you know what it is to go before an audience?" a man asked his friend.

"No," said his friend. "Every time I make a speech, the audience goes before I do."

1779. A man was telling his friend about the meeting he missed. "Our speaker sure did make a hit," he told his friend.

"He did? What did he talk about?" asked the friend.

"About five minutes," the man said.

1780. The big speech was over and the program chairman of the civic club handed the speaker a check.

"No, no," he said. "I wouldn't think of accepting payment. I was happy to speak to you. Please contribute my honorarium to some worthy cause."

"Would you mind if we put it in our special fund?" asked the program chairman.

"Of course not," said the speaker. "What's the fund for?"

"To help us get better speakers next year," he said.

1781. It had started to rain during the meeting, so the speaker felt he should cut his talk short. "And now," he said, "I shall conclude my talk for this evening. I'm afraid I've already kept you too long."

"Oh, keep right on," said a voice in the rear. "It's still raining and most of us don't have umbrellas."

1782. After the speech, a man shook hands with the speaker and said he never had a more enjoyable evening.

"You found my remarks interesting, I trust," said the speaker.

"Not exactly," said the man, "but you did cure my insomnia."

Speaker

1783. A minister was asked to address a meeting of the Ladies' Literary Guild. He was asked to speak on China and Chinese art, religion, and philosophy. He spent several weeks in research studying for the lecture. While he was eating his lunch before speaking, he said to the chairman, "Why did you ask me to speak on China?"

"Oh, we wanted the talk to be appropriate," she said. "You see, it's a chop suey luncheon."

1784. After giving his speech, the guest of the evening was standing at the door with the president of the group, shaking hands with the folks as they left the hall.

Compliments were coming right and left, until one fellow shook hands and said, "I thought it stunk."

"What did you say?" asked the surprised speaker.

"I said it stunk. That's the worst speech anybody ever gave around here. Whoever invited you to speak tonight ought to be put out of the club." With that he turned and walked away.

"Don't pay any attention to that man," the president said to the speaker. "He's a nitwit. Why, that man never had an original thought in his life. All he does is listen to what other people say, then he goes around repeating it."

1785. As the speaker was giving the main address, a fellow in the back put his hand to his ear and said, "Louder."

The speaker raised his voice, but the fellow continued to say "Louder."

Finally, a man down front couldn't stand it and yelled at the man in the back, "What's the matter back there, can't you hear him?"

"No," said the fellow in the back.

"Well," said the man down front, "move over, I'm coming back to sit with you."

1786. A man had gone to sleep at a banquet. His wife was embarrassed and tried to kick him under the table and wake him up. But, she couldn't quite reach him with her foot, so she picked up a spoon and tapped him on the head with it.

That woke him. Sitting up, he said in a loud voice, "You're going to have to hit me harder than that, honey, I can still hear him."

1787. A speaker who was given a flowery introduction, said, "It seems to me that the three hardest things in the world to do would be to climb over a barbed-wire fence when it is leaning toward you and kissing a pretty girl when she is leaning away from you—and trying to live up to that very fine introduction."

1788. The luncheon speaker was explaining to his audience that he really didn't have enough time to cover his subject as well as he would like.

"The chairman of today's meeting said I could talk as long as I like," he said, "but that after 1:30 there won't be anybody here but me."

1789. A man was called on to say a few words, but since he was completely surprised by the invitation and was totally unprepared, he stood up and said, "I will stand up to be seen. I will speak up to be heard. And now I will shut up to be appreciated."

1790. A man who had worked hard on his speech was introduced and given his place at the microphone. He stood there for half a minute completely speechless and then said, "The human mind is the most wonderful device in the world. It starts working the instant you are born and never stops working night or day for your entire life—until the moment you stand up to make a speech."

1791. A fellow was telling a friend about a speech he had made in a nearby town.

"They liked my speech so well," he said, "that they gave me this gold watch. Of course, it is only the case. They said that if and when I ever came back, they would then give me the works."

1792. It was the annual 4th of July barbecue. The local radio announcer was the master of ceremonies for the day's events and the principal speaker was the mayor.

Speaker

When it came time to introduce the mayor, the master of ceremonies said to the crowd, "Remember, folks, right after the mayor finishes his speech, the high school band will play and call you all together again."

1793.   During that early part of a speech when the speaker tried to warm up his audience, one man said, "I certainly hope my speech tonight comes out better than one I made last week. I had to stop right in the middle of it because of throat trouble—the program chairman threatened to cut it."

118, 174, 243, 326, 421, 454, 521, 699, 769, 1607, 1699

Speaking

1794.   The lecturer was about to be introduced, when a news photographer was seen moving in close for a close-up shot. The chairman, afraid that the speaker would be annoyed, called the photographer and said:
"Don't take his picture while he is speaking. Try to shoot him before he starts."

1795.   The long-winded speaker had been talking for more than an hour, except for a pause now and then to sip a hasty drink of water. When the meeting was over a fellow told his friend:
"This was the first time I ever saw a windmill run on water."

1796.   The president of the club was chatting with the speaker of the evening.
"What is the hardest part of your work as a public speaker?" he asked.
"The hardest part of my work," the speaker said, "is waking up the audience after the man that introduces me has put them to sleep."

1797.   A newspaper reporter said to a lecturer: "You have a great gift for oratory. How did you develop it?"
"The same way," the speaker said, "I learned to ice-skate. I kept making a fool of myself until I mastered it."

159, 456, 460, 719, 763

Specialist

1798. A friend was having lunch with a dermatologist.

"Was there any special reason," he asked, "why you chose to specialize on diseases of the skin?"

"Yes," said the doctor, "my patients never get me out of bed at night, they never die, and they never get well."

1799. The warden of the prison called in a man who was serving time for fraud. "I understand," he said, "that you're here because of an oil deal in which you wrote a prospectus so glowing that it sold the suckers by the thousands."

"That's right," said the prisoner. "I was a bit glowing in my praises."

"Well," the warden said, "the governor wants a report on conditions in the prison and I'd like you to write it for me."

1800. A man went to a stomach specialist with a severe case of indigestion. "What did you have to eat for dinner last night?" the specialist asked him.

"We started dinner with a fresh fruit cup, then we had sauerkraut and frankfurters with Mexican chili dressing. After that we had a special salad with hot pickles and roquefort dressing. With that we had hot biscuits and honey and gooseberry jam. We had watermelon pickle and brandied peaches on the side and for dessert we had strawberry ice cream and whipped cream."

"After all that," the doctor said, "you shouldn't come to see a stomach specialist, you should go see a brain specialist."

412, 735, 759, 2053

Speech

1801. The speaker had been constantly and rudely interrupted. Finally, he said, "We appear to have a great many fools here tonight. Wouldn't it be better to hear one at a time?"

"Yes," shouted a voice from the rear. "Go ahead and finish your speech."

1802. Another day of hard campaigning was behind the candidate as he and his wife returned to their hotel room.

Speech

"My, am I tired," his wife said. "I'm almost ready to drop."

"You tired!" cried the candidate. "I'm the one to be tired. I made fourteen speeches today."

"I know," his wife said, "but I had to listen to them."

149, 159, 327, 682, 698, 1092

Speed

1803.   A young fellow was doing 95 on the turnpike in his new sports car when he was stopped by a patrolman.

"Was I driving too fast?" he asked innocently.

"Not at all," said the patrolman. "You were just flying too low."

1804.   Airplanes are becoming faster and faster. They have already passed the speed of sound, and it won't be long before they hit the speed of light. It is even conceivable that one day they might even catch up to the speed of the office grapevine.

85, 129, 276, 721, 775, 2099

Spelling

1805.   A young lady was taking a test for employment.

"How do you spell Mississippi?" she was asked.

"The river or the state?" she asked.

1806.   The teacher said to the girl in the second seat, "Joy, you may spell the word neighbor."

"N-e-i-g-h-b-o-r," Joy said.

"That's right," said the teacher. "Now, Joy, can you tell me what a neighbor is?"

"Yes, ma'am," said Joy. "It's a lady who borrows things."

1807.   The teacher was calling out the spelling words to the class. "Spell 'straight,'" she said.

"S-t-r-a-i-g-h-t," spelled the bright little boy in the front seat.

"Correct," she said, "what does it mean?"

"Without ginger ale," he said.

Spelling

1808. "I've got to get a new secretary," a man told a friend. "Everytime I give her any dictation she keeps interrupting me to ask how to spell the words."

"I don't blame you," his friend said. "That would be a great waste of time."

"Oh, I'm not worried about the time," the man said. "I don't like the embarrassment of telling her I don't know."

487, 689, 698, 831, 1038, 1688, 2104

Spend

1809. Two men in a bar were talking about their wives.

"Nearly every night my wife dreams she's married to a millionaire," said one man.

"You're lucky," said the other. "My wife dreams that during the daytime."

1810. The man at the fair was trying to sell a country rube one of those combination gadgets that shred cabbage, cut eggs, and do all sorts of fancy cutting jobs in the kitchen.

"Not me," the country fellow said, "that would be spending money foolishly."

"Okay," said the pitchman, "maybe so. But all of us spend a little money foolishly now and then, don't we?"

"Not me," the man said. "I never spent any money foolishly but once in my life and that was when I paid 25 cents for a pair of socks."

48, 177, 194, 222, 256, 297, 1060

Sports

1811. A vacationing schoolteacher was making her first visit to Brazil and was impressed with everything she saw. She asked a native what the most popular sport was.

"Bullfighting," he replied.

"Isn't it revolting?" she exclaimed.

"No," smiled the Brazilian. "That's the second most popular sport."

Sports

1812. The backwoods couple were visiting the college with the thought of sending their daughter there. In the course of their sightseeing, they came to the tennis courts where a girl and boy were playing.

"This is fine," said the father. "They keep them separated with a net up here."

272, 902, 1229, 1930

Stamp

1813. A young lady bought a postage stamp and said to the clerk, "Must I stick it on myself?"

"No, lady," said the clerk, "it won't do any good unless you stick it on the letter."

638

Statistics

1814. "Do you know," a speaker said, "that every time I breathe, a man dies?"

"Why don't you sterilize your mouth?" a voice in the rear cried out.

1815. The question on the economics examination was: "Give the number of tons of coal shipped out of the United States in any given year."

"1492—none," was one desperate answer.

1816. When people talk statistics, they always like to talk about averages. Average this, and average that. The thing to remember is that the average is exactly halfway between the best and the worst. It is the best of the worst and the worst of the best.

80, 169, 281, 639, 759, 1080, 1152, 1202

Status

1817. A businessman was caught in the rain in a rather run-down neighborhood. He ducked into a cheap, seedy cafe to get out of the weather. He was surprised and shocked to find an old friend of his working there as a waiter.

"Heavens," he said, "you, a waiter in this dump!"

"Yes, I am," said his friend with dignity, "but I don't eat here."

1818.   Three status-minded snobbish women were chatting at a church circle meeting.

"Your husband's a lawyer, isn't he?" asked one.

"No, not exactly," said the other. "He's a barrister."

She turned and asked her other friend, "And your husband sells stocks, doesn't he?"

"Well, not exactly," she said. "He's really a financial consultant."

Then she asked the first woman, "And I understand your husband is a waiter."

"No, he's not a waiter," said the woman. "He's the contact man between the customers and the chef."

1819.   The small resort restaurant had prospered beyond all dreams.

"Guess next season we can afford to have a chef," the owner told his wife.

"What's a chef?" she asked.

"Oh," said the owner, "that's just a cook who knows enough fancy words to give the soup a different name every day for two weeks."

1820.   A fast-talking lawyer was browbeating a meek little witness, unmercifully.

"What do you do for a living?" the lawyer yelled at him.

"I'm a street cleaner," said the man.

"Oh, a street cleaner," sneered the lawyer. "And what do you think your status is in society?"

"Well," the man said, "I know I'm not very highly regarded in the community, but I still feel I'm doing better than my father did."

"What was your father?" the lawyer demanded.

"A shyster lawyer," the little man said.

Status

1821. A farmer yelled at his son and said, "Bring me the ax." But the boy just sat still and ignored the old man.

A stranger, who was visiting the family, said, "Didn't you hear your father speak to you?"

"Oh, sure, I heerd 'im," said the boy, "but I don't pay the old man no mind. Neither does maw or sis, and between us we jest about got the dog so he don't either."

1822. Two little boys were bragging about their fathers.

"My dad is a trustee at Penn State," said the first.

"That's nothing," said the other. "My father is a trusty at the State Pen."

1823. A real estate developer built a fancy subdivision in one of the better neighborhoods. He reserved for himself a lot that faced on a street that was so short that it had room for only one house—his. He named the street Skid Row. He did this, he said, because it immediately eliminated his name from 1,000 mailing lists all over the country and it also stopped insurance salesman from calling him on the phone.

1824. An overdressed dowager entered an exclusive Miami Beach restaurant. "I want some caviar," she said to the waiter, "and make sure it's imported, because I can't tell the difference."

1825. The governor was making his annual inspection visit to the state mental hospital. He wanted to call his office, but was having difficulty in getting an outside connection.

"Look here, my girl," he shouted to the operator, "do you know who I am?"

"No, I don't," she said, "but I know where you are calling from."

1826. Jewelry was the subject of discussion at the ladies' bridge club. "I clean my diamonds with ammonia," said one lady.

"I use Rhine wine for my pearls and emeralds," said another.

"It takes fine brandy to bring out the true sparkle on my star sapphires," said another.

Status

The fourth lady at the table finally spoke up and said, "Do you really bother to clean your jewelry? I just throw mine away when it gets dirty."

195, 1024

Steadfast

1827.   A girl was chatting with her friend. "Our engagement is over," she said. "My feelings have changed completely from what they were when I accepted him."

"If that's true," her friend said, "why do you still wear his ring?"

"Oh," said the girl, "my feelings toward the ring are just the same."

1828.   The young lover was in tears. He was pleading with the young lady. "Why did you flirt with me?" he asked. "Why did you let me take you on picnics? Why did you let me take you to the drive-in movie every night? Why did you lead me on when you were already engaged?"

The girl was a little ashamed, but said, "I just wanted to test my love for David."

1721

Steak

1829.   A man said to a waiter in the restaurant, "I was here yesterday and had a steak."

"Yes, sir," said the waiter. "Will you have the same today?"

"Yes," said the man. "I think I'll try it again, if no one else is using it."

1477, 1615, 2041

Stealing

1830.   Judge to defendant: "You have been accused of stealing chickens and you say you have an alibi. Do you know what an alibi is?"

Stealing

Defendant: "Yes, your honor. I know what an alibi is. An alibi is proving I was at prayer meeting where I wasn't and not in somebody's chicken coop where I was."

1831.   The judge said to the man accused of stealing chickens, "Guilty or not guilty?"

"Well, Judge, I might be guilty," said the man, "but I'd rather be tried to make sure."

60, 171, 255, 396, 663, 725, 983

Stewardess

1832.   At 35,000 feet an airline hostess passed out chewing gum to the passengers.

"It will keep your ears from popping at high altitudes," she explained.

After the plane had come to a stop and the passengers were leaving, a timid-looking man said to the hostess, "I had a most pleasant flight, but how do I get the chewing gum out of my ears?"

81, 238, 473, 767

Story

1833.   Once upon a time, about 2:30 A.M., a little girl woke up and crawled into bed with her mother.

"Tell me a fairy story, Mamma," she said.

"Hush, dear," said her mother. "Lie still for a little while. Daddy ought to be along pretty soon now, and he'll tell us both one."

85, 361, 672, 941, 1044

Stranger

1834.   The doctor checked the young man's badly swollen lips. The diagnosis was a bit puzzling and the doctor asked, "Kissed anybody lately?"

"Yes," the young man said. "Last night."

Stranger

"This is undoubtedly a case of lipstick allergy," the doctor said. "Before I can treat you properly, you must ask the girl what brand of lipstick she uses."

"But I couldn't do that, Doctor," said the young man. "I don't know her well enough to ask her such a thing."

1835. The famous Civil War general's great-grandson was visiting the small town in which his famous ancestor was born and raised. Strangers were scarce in the town, and as he walked down the street, several people were staring at him.

"I wonder who that fellow is," one of them asked.

"You don't know who he is?" the other said. "He's the great-grandson of that statue down in the city park."

33, 654, 1157

Strategy

1836. The little boy came home with a black eye.

"You have been fighting again," said his mother. "Didn't I tell you that when you get angry you should count to a hundred before you do anything?"

"I did," said the little boy, "but the other boy's mother told him to count only to fifty."

1837. The lawyer was giving some advice to his son who was going into business.

"Always remember, son," said the lawyer, "that in business, honesty is the best policy."

"Yes," said the boy.

"And you'd better study up a bit on corporation law," continued his father. "You will be surprised to find how many things you can do in business and still be honest."

55, 279, 1003, 1241, 1401

Strength

1838. "There just isn't any justice in this world," a man said to a friend. "I used to be a 97-pound weakling, and whenever I went to the beach with my girl, this big 197-pound bully came over and kicked sand in my face. I decided to do something

416

Strength

about it, so I took a weight-lifting course and after a while I weighed 197 pounds."

"So what happened?" his friend asked.

"Well, after that," the man said, "whenever I went to the beach with my girl, a 257-pound bully kicked sand in my face."

291, 741, 988

Student

1839.   The old barber was showing the young barber the ropes. Then, the young fellow's first customer came in for a shave. The older barber whispered a few last-minute instructions and then said, "All right, you try it and see how you do. But be careful and don't cut yourself."

1840.   The professor had returned the student's paper with a notation in the margin. Not being able to read the professor's handwriting, the student showed his paper to the professor and asked what the notation meant.

After several minutes of careful scrutiny, the professor said, "Oh, yes, I remember now. This is a note asking you to write more legibly."

206, 369, 373, 542, 543, 757, 1815

Stupid

1841.   One nice thing about being stupid is you get out of a lot of time-consuming committee work.

1842.   The woman's husband had fallen out of a cherry tree and had broken his arm. He was rushed to the hospital where the doctor put him in the emergency room to set the broken bone. As the doctor was placing a white cone over his face, the man's wife said, "What is that for?"

"I am going to give him an anesthetic," said the doctor. "Then he won't know anything."

"No need to do that," she said. "He don't know nothing already."

345, 503, 550, 1713

Stylish

1843.   The judge was questioning the defendent in a traffic case.

"Tell me, young lady," the judge said, "what gear were you in at the time of the accident?"

"Oh, I had on a black hat," she said, "with brown shoes, and a tweed suit."

1844.   One woman pointed to another across the street, and said to her friend, "Look at that! She looks like she'd been poured into that dress.

"Yes," said her friend, "and she forgot to say when."

1845.   A young lady was showing off her new outfit to her boy friend. "Don't you think this blue sweater brings out my eyes?" she said.

"Yes, it certainly does," he said, "and it also brings out mine."

1846.   It was at a cocktail party, where all of the ladies were dressed in their finest. One of them cornered a famous judge. "I hear that you have a reputation," she said, "for being able to judge a woman's character from her clothing. What would be your opinion of my daughter, the one in the white strapless gown over there?"

The judge took a good look. "Insufficient evidence," he said.

1847.   Two elderly grandmothers were talking about their grandchildren. "And how is your oldest one coming with her golfing?" asked one. "My granddaughter tells me she's going around in less and less every week."

"I know," said the other. "I think it's disgraceful. They would have put us in jail if we had run around like that, wouldn't they?"

1848.   A sign in the window of the small-town store read: Ladies Ready to Wear Clothes.

"Well, it's about time," said the farmer.

1849.   The long-suffering husband said to his spendthrift wife, "Darling, you promised not to buy any new clothes this month. What made you do it?"

"I'm sorry," she said, "but the devil tempted me."

Stylish

"Why didn't you say, 'Get thee behind me, Satan'?" her husband asked.

"I did," his wife said, "and he whispered over my shoulder, 'Honey chile, it fits you beautifully in the back.'"

1850. A man and his wife were attending a fashion show. The man sat bug-eyed as the girls paraded across the stage in all of their finery. He became most attentive when a young lady came out wearing a huge red, white, and blue bow across her back—rather low down.

Watching her husband out of the corner of her eye, the woman said, "Quit staring like that. Haven't you ever seen anything like that before?"

"Yes, honey," her husband said, "but it's the first time I ever saw one of them gift wrapped."

188, 355, 366, 389, 547, 829, 1528

Substitute

1851. A motorist jammed on his brakes but didn't stop in time. Meekly he approached the door of the house nearest the accident. "I am terribly sorry," he said to the lady who opened the door, "but I just ran over your cat." Seeing the shocked look on her face, he added quickly, "But I want to replace him."

The lady opened the door wider and said, "Come in and get busy, there's a mouse in the kitchen."

1852. A schoolteacher substituted for a friend who was taking a week's honeymoon. Later, at a party, someone started to introduce her friend's husband to her.

"Oh," the husband said, "I know Miss Jones. In fact, she's the young lady who substituted for my wife on our honeymoon."

1853. The man tossed a quarter at the blind man's tin cup. The quarter missed the cup and started rolling along the sidewalk. But the beggar quickly put his foot on it.

"Hey, I thought you were blind," said the man who had tossed him the quarter.

Substitute

"Oh, I'm not the regular blind man," said the man with the tin cup. "I'm just taking his place today. This is his day off. He's at the movies."

1854. The local little theater group was having tough going with a bit of Shakespeare.

"A horse! A horse! My kingdom for a horse!" cried the actor.

"Would an ass do?" shouted a smart aleck from the rear.

"Sure, come on down," said the actor.

1855. A salesman called the head of a company on the phone and said to him, "I've been trying all week to see you. May I have an appointment?"

"Make a date with my secretary," said the businessman.

"I did and she's a cute girl," said the salesman, "but I still want to see you."

24, 243, 584, 703

Success

1856. During the question-and-answer period of the big oil company's annual stockholders' meeting, a little lady near the back raised her hand. She was invited to the nearest microphone and asked: "Mr. Chairman, one thing has worried me ever since I bought stock in this company. When you build a new gas station on a street corner, how do you know you'll find oil?"

1857. A new vacuum cleaner salesman was looking downcast.

"Come, come!" said the boss. "Don't look so down-in-the-dumps. It's not easy at first, but you'll soon catch on. With a little experience you'll do all right."

"Oh, it isn't that," said the salesman. "When I got home last night, I practiced my sales talk on my wife, and now I've got to buy her a vacuum cleaner."

1858. A wealthy soap tycoon was being interviewed for a typical trade-magazine success story.

The reporter said: "To what one thing, sir, do you attribute your great success?"

Success

"To clean living, my boy, just clean living," the soap manufacturer said.

1859. "I have a friend," the young fellow said, "who is a ghost writer. And he has finally reached the peak of his success."

"And what is that?" his friend asked.

"He is ghost-writing for another ghost writer."

1860. A tramp was bragging to his friends in the railroad jungle.

"Thirty years ago," he said, "I started out, alone, unaided, and without friends to help, with the intention of making the world pay me the living that it owes me. All I had was a dollar bill and the determination to make a million more. Today, I still have the determination and fifty cents in change."

1861. During the interview for the trade journal, a businessman said, "I owe my success and wealth wholly to my wife."

"Oh," said the reporter, "her loyal help, her faith in you . . ."

"No," said the businessman. "I was just curious to know if there was any income she couldn't live beyond."

1862. They were having a testimonial dinner for the richest and most successful man in town.

"Friends," said the toastmaster, "when this man walked into our town 40 years ago, it was nothing but a few shacks along a dirty, muddy road. The only earthly possessions he had were the clothes on his back, the shoes on his feet, and a few things wrapped in a handkerchief over his shoulder."

"And look how he has prospered," the toastmaster continued. "He now owns businesses with branches all over the country. He owns apartment houses and office buildings. He is on the boards of clubs and banks. Yes, our honored guest has come a long way since that first dusty walk into town."

After the dinner, an old friend said to the famous man, "I've known you for years, and have often wondered what did you have in that handkerchief 40 years ago?"

"Well, sir," said the old man, "it was a toothbrush, a razor, and $500,000 in negotiable bonds.

35, 95, 266, 293, 402, 736, 865, 1245, 1288, 1366, 2112

Suffer

1863.   Two friends were talking. "You look sad," said the first. "What's the matter?"

"I had an argument with my wife," the other said, "and she swore she wouldn't talk to me for 30 days."

"Well, you should be very happy," said the first.

"Happy?" said his friend. "This is the 30th day."

1864.   "Doctor," the man said, "I have been reading all those reports about cigarettes. Do you really think that cigarette smoking will shorten your days?"

"I certainly do," the doctor said. "I tried to stop smoking last summer and each of my days seemed as long as a month."

333, 614, 697, 756, 1730

Suggestion

1865.   An employer was proud that his men worked under the best conditions. "Whenever I enter the workshop," he said, "I want to see every man working cheerfully. Therefore I invite you to place in the suggestion box any ideas you might have as to how that can be brought about."

When the box was opened, there was only one suggestion in it: "Don't wear rubber heels."

1866.   The man had moved from the city to the suburbs and had spent a lot of time and money on his lawn. Then, up came a crop of dandelions. He tried everything he could think of to get rid of them, but nothing helped.

Finally in desperation he wrote to the Department of Agriculture and asked them what they thought he should do.

Two weeks later he received this reply. "We suggest," said the letter, "that you learn to love them."

122, 630, 683, 737, 1286, 1468, 1840

Suicide

1867.   A man had been pulled from the river in what the police suspected was a suicide attempt. When they were questioning him at headquarters, he admitted that he had tried to kill himself. This is the story he told:

Suicide

"Yes, I tried to kill myself. The world is against me and I wanted to end it all. I was determined not to do a halfway job of it, so I bought a piece of rope, some matches, some kerosene, and a pistol. Just in case none of those worked, I went down by the river. I threw the rope over a limb hanging out over the water, tied that rope around my neck, poured kerosene all over myself and lit that match. I jumped off the river bank and put that pistol to my head and pulled the trigger. And guess what happened? I missed. The bullet hit the rope before I could hang myself and I fell in the river and the water put out the fire before I could burn myself. And you know, if I hadn't been a good swimmer, I'd have ended up drowning my fool self."

Summer

1868.   A man had a house right on the United States-Canadian border. No one knew whether the house was in the United States or Canada. It was decided to appoint a committee to solve the problem.

After deciding it was in the United States, the fellow leaped with joy. "Hurrah!" he shouted, "now I don't have to suffer from those terrible Canadian winters!"

230

Sunday school

1869.   The minister was visiting the junior department in the Sunday school. He paused to question one little girl.

"Can you tell me," he asked, "what are the sins of omission?"

The little girl thought a moment, then said, "Aren't they the sins we should have committed, but didn't?"

1870.   The Sunday school teacher was telling her class the story of the prodigal son. "But even with all this joy and celebration," she said, "there was one who was not happy with the preparation of the feast for the return of the son, who felt only bitterness and did not wish to attend the feast. Who was it?"

After a moment's silence, a small voice said, "It must have been the fatted calf."

Sunday school

1871. The little boy's uncle had taken him to see his first circus. When he came home, his mother asked, "Well, how did you like it?"

"Gee, Mom," said the little fellow, "if you'd only go to the circus one time, you'd never go to church again as long as you lived!"

1872. The Sunday school teacher had just read the story of Genesis to her young pupils. "Are there any questions?" she asked.

"Yes," said a smart little boy. "My father says that we didn't come from Adam. He says we are descended from apes. What about that?"

"We did not come here," the teacher said, "to discuss your private family matters."

1873. In an effort to teach the little boy a lesson in giving, his father gave him a dime and a quarter and told him that one was for Sunday school and one was for him to spend. He said that he would leave the decision up to the little boy.

When his son came home, his father asked him which coin he had put in the collection plate.

"Well, I started to put in the quarter," he said, "but the teacher said that the Lord loves a cheerful giver and I knew I would feel more cheerful if I put in the dime—so I did."

1874. For four or five weeks, the Sunday school teacher had been telling the story of Moses. Every Sunday her most eager listener was a little girl who sat on the front row. Then, one Sunday morning when it was time to go to Sunday school, the little girl refused to move.

"What in the world is the matter with you?" her mother asked. "I thought you liked Sunday school."

"I don't like it any more," the little girl said. "Not since Moses died."

258, 379, 387, 511, 631, 737, 1617, 1741

Surprise

1875. A rich uncle was talking to his teen-age nephew. "The boys of today want too much money," he said. "Do you know what I was getting when I married your aunt?"

"No," said the nephew, "and I'll bet you didn't either."

1876. The high-pressure vacuum cleaner salesman was out to make a quick sale. The moment the lady of the house opened the door, he rushed in. He took a handful of soot from the chimney and threw it all over the living-room rug. Then he grabbed a handful of ashes and scattered them all over the soot. Then he turned to the lady of the house and said: "You're going to be surprised when you see how quickly I clean this up. Now tell me, where's the electric socket so I can plug it in?"

"You're the one who is going to be surprised," said the lady. "We don't have electricity in this house."

1877. Two men were chatting about their wives.

"What would your wife say if you bought a new car?" the first asked.

"Look out for that traffic light. Be careful now. Don't hit that truck. Watch where you're going. Won't you never learn to drive? And a lot of other stuff like that."

1878. After the accident, the lady driver said, "I turned the way I signaled."

"I know it," said the man. "That's what fooled me."

1879. "There has been a terrible mistake," the railroad conductor told the inebriated passenger. "Your ticket is for Cincinnati, and this train is on the Chicago line. It doesn't go through Cincinnati."

"Good gracious," said the drunk. "Have you told the engineer?"

236, 260, 320, 370

Suspicion

1880. A visitor to the prison asked the convicted burglar, "You always did your burglaries single-handed. Why didn't you have an accomplice?"

Suspicion

"Well," the prisoner said. "I was always afraid he might turn out to be dishonest."

1881.   "Why did you ask your boarder to leave?" a lady asked her neighbor.

"Well, I am not the suspicious type and I don't distrust people," said the lady. "But when a man always hangs his hat over the keyhole, there must be something going on that isn't right."

1882.   A city man was visiting the family of his sister who had moved to a small southern town. "I've never been to a small town before," he said to her one evening at dinner. "It certainly is true that half the world is ignorant of how the other half lives."

"Not in this town, it isn't," his sister said.

26, 375, 620

Swim

1883.   A hard-to-handle little boy was sent to the country to spend the summer with an uncle his parents figured could straighten him out. At the end of the first week his mother visited him. She asked how he got along with his uncle.

"Real swell. Every day he rows me out to the middle of the lake and lets me swim back."

"My goodness, isn't that a hard swim for a boy your age?"

"Oh, no. The only hard part is getting out of the bag."

1884.   A lady dropped her three-year-old boy off at a birthday party. Later, when she picked him up, he said excitedly, "Well, we all went swimming in the pool."

"How nice!" said his mother. "But you don't have a bathing suit."

"We went in naked," the little boy said.

"Oh," said his mother. "Did the little girls go in naked, too?"

"Goodness, no," the little boy said. "They wore bathing caps."

1885.   "You've been swimming in the creek again," the little boy's mother shouted at him. "I can tell by your wet hair. I told you not to go in and now you are going to get a whipping."

Swim

"I couldn't help it," the little fellow said. "I was tempted and just couldn't resist the temptation."

"That's a likely story," his mother said. "How come you had your bathing suit with you?"

"Oh," he said, "I took it along just in case I got tempted."

278, 536, 781, 1646, 1889, 1929

Sympathy

1886. The minister was preaching on temperance. "I have no sympathy," he said, "for a man who gets drunk every night."

"A man who gets drunk every night doesn't need sympathy," came a whisper from the congregation.

1887. A charitable lady was visiting the veterans' hospital and stepped into a convalescent ward where the patients were allowed to sit up. One young fellow's head was completely covered with bandages except for two small holes for his eyes. The lady rushed up to him and said, "My, how terrible, were you injured in the head?"

"No, lady," the young man said. "I was shot in the ankle, but my bandages just slipped a bit."

18, 446, 502, 708

System

1888. A little boy began to throw a tantrum in the dime store.

"My mama won't buy me a cap pistol!" he screamed.

"Well, now," said the manager, "does your mother always buy what you want when you act like that?"

"No," said the boy. "Sometimes she does, sometimes she doesn't. But it isn't any trouble to scream."

1889. Two lifeguards were talking. "What's the best way to teach a girl to swim?" the first asked.

"First you put your left arm around her waist," his friend said. "Then you gently take her left hand and . . ."

"She's my sister," the first lifeguard interrupted.

"Oh, push her off the dock," his friend said.

System

1890. Two mothers were comparing notes about how to manage their children. "How do you keep your children out of the cookie jar?" the first one asked.

"Oh, that's an easy one," the other said. "I just lock the pantry door and hide the key under the cake of soap in the bathroom."

237, 394, 445, 656, 1101, 1686

Tact

1891. A lady at a cocktail party asked her new acquaintance to guess her age. After he hesitated, she said, "Come on, guess. You must have some idea."

"I have several ideas," he said. "The trouble is I don't know whether to make you ten years younger on account of your looks, or ten years older on account of your intelligence."

572

Talent

1892. A matronly sort was singing for the first time with a new accompanist.

"How do you like my voice?" she asked.

"Lady," he said, "I've played the white keys and I've played the black keys. But never before have I heard anyone who could sing in between."

1893. A street cleaner let out a burst of profanity which shocked a lady social worker who was passing by. She looked at him critically and said: "My, where did you learn such awful language?"

"Where did I learn it?" the street cleaner said. "Lady, I didn't learn it, it's a gift."

1894. A college professor appeared one day before his class with his face badly cut and patched here and there with adhesive tape.

Talent

"What happened to you?" a student asked.

"I was shaved today," the professor said, "by a man who took highest honors at Harvard in scholarship, speaks several languages, and is an outstanding authority on French literature."

"My," said the student, "if he is so highly educated, how come he's a barber?"

"He isn't," said the professor. "I shaved myself today for the first time."

1895.   The successful businessman had been talking to the high school students about their careers and the possibilities in the world of business. Throughout his talk he had spoken about how talent was bound to pay off and also he paid high tribute to the genius of the American businessman.

During the question-and-answer period, a young man asked, "Sir, just what would you say is the difference between talent and genius?"

"I would say that the most important difference," said the speaker, "is that talent gets a check regularly every payday."

37, 144, 412

Talk

1896.   "This is some world we live in today," the man said to a friend. "What changes we have seen! I was at a party the other night and the women were all talking politics while the men got off in a corner and exchanged recipes and household hints."

1897.   Two women were gossiping over the back fence.

"That woman," said the first, "is the talkingest person in the world. And she can't be telling the truth all the time. There just isn't that much truth."

1898.   A woman said to her husband, "Why do you always refer to the folding bed as 'he'?"

"Because," he said, "you can shut it up once in a while."

Talk

1899.   "My wife talks to herself," the man told his friend.

"So does mine," his friend said, "but she doesn't realize it. She thinks I'm listening."

1900.   "I sure was outspoken," said a housewife to her husband at supper as she reported on her activities at her club that afternoon.

"I don't believe it," her husband said. "Who in the world ever outspoke you?"

2, 51, 156, 205, 405, 438, 473, 596, 1447, 1503, 2078

Taste

1901.   A man in a restaurant said to the waitress, "What do you call this stuff—coffee or tea? It tastes like kerosene!"

"If it tastes like kerosene," she said, "it must be coffee. The tea tastes like paint."

78, 363, 394, 408, 479, 557, 631 1377

Tavern

1902.   The judge was questioning the man who had been arrested for drunkenness. "What did you get drunk for, in the first place?" the judge asked.

"I didn't get drunk in the first place," the man said. "I got drunk in the last place."

636, 762, 971, 1515

Taxes

1903.   A passing motorist heard a woman's screams for help. He rushed into the house to find that her little boy had swallowed a dime. The man grabbed the little fellow by the feet and shook him upside down until the dime fell to the floor.

"Oh, doctor," the lady said, "it certainly was lucky you happened by. You knew just how to get the dime out of him."

"I'm not a doctor, lady," the man said. "I work for the Income Tax Department."

Taxes

1904. A man stormed into the Postmaster General's office in Washington and shouted, "I'm being pestered by threatening letters, and I want somebody to do something about it."

"I'm sure we can help," said the Postmaster General. "That's a federal offense. Do you have any idea who is sending you these letters?"

"I certainly do," said the man. "It's those income-tax people."

1905. A minister received a phone call from the income-tax man inquiring about a $400 contribution to the church, listed as a deduction by a parishioner.

"Did he make this donation?" the tax man asked the minister.

The minister hesitated a moment and then said, "No, but he will. I'm sure he will now!"

1906. A man opened his pay envelope one Friday, only to find it empty. He wrote a note to the accounting department: "What happened? Did my deductions finally catch up with my salary?"

1907. The pretty young secretary was complaining about the amount of income tax that was being withheld from her pay check.

"Well," said the accountant, "we must all learn to pay our taxes with a smile."

"I wish I could," said the secretary, "but the tax people insist on money."

146, 264, 803, 1049

Taxi

1908. A woman visitor to Washington entered a taxi. As soon as the door closed, the car leaped forward violently. It then went racing wildly down the street, narrowly missing car after car. The lady was scared to death and cried to the taxi driver, "Please be careful. I'm nervous. This is the first time I ever rode in a taxi."

The driver yelled back, "That's all right, lady. It's the first time I ever drove one!"

Taxi

1909.   A man was hit by a taxi and thrown all the way across the sidewalk into a huge hedge. As he picked himself up and stretched his arms and legs to see if he was hurt, the taxi driver rushed over to him.

"Are you hurt?" the taxi driver shouted.

"Well," said the victim, "it sure didn't do me any good."

449, 770, 1236

Tea

1910.   It was the seventh inning of the ball game and everyone stood up to stretch. The Englishman, experiencing his first baseball game, said, "I say, old fellow, is this when they serve tea?"

"Tea!" said an American. "They don't serve tea at a ball game."

"They don't?" said the Englishman. "Then what's the point of the game?"

1911.   "A cheese omelet and a cup of tea," the customer said to the waitress. "And please make the tea weak."

Later, when the food was set before him, the customer looked at the tea, called the girl and said, "I said I wanted my tea weak—not helpless."

537, 851, 1901

Teacher

1912.   Mathematics teacher: "What do we mean when we say that the whole is greater than any of its parts?"

Student: "A restaurant doughnut."

1913.   A schoolteacher was teaching the second grade. "What's the opposite of misery?" she asked a little girl.

"Joy," the girl said quickly.

"That's right," the teacher said. "Now what's the opposite of sorrow?" she asked another little girl.

"Happiness," she said.

432

Teacher

"Right," the teacher said. "Now what's the opposite of woe?" she asked a little boy.

"Giddyap!" he said.

1914. A teacher said to a little boy in her class, "Give me a brief biography of Benjamin Franklin."

"Well," said the boy. "Benjamin Franklin was born in Boston. He traveled to Philadelphia. He met a lady who smiled at him. He got married and discovered electricity."

1915. The Sunday school teacher was testing her pupil's knowledge of proverbs. "Cleanliness is next to what?" she asked a little boy.

"Impossible," he said.

1916. It was the first day at school and the teacher asked the little boy, "And do you know your A, B, C's?"

"Shucks, no," he said, "I've only been here ten minutes."

1917. A Sunday school teacher had been talking about the Ten Commandments. When it came time for questions, she asked, "Can anyone tell me a commandment that has only four words?"

"I can," said a little boy. "Keep off the grass."

24, 125, 129, 212, 228, 336, 346, 367, 788, 1438, 1653

Teamwork

1918. A husband and wife had just been fighting. The husband felt a bit ashamed and was standing looking out of the window. Suddenly, something caught his attention.

"Honey," he called. "Come here, I want to show you something."

As she came to the window to see, he said, "Look at those two horses pulling that load of hay up the hill. Why can't we pull together like that, up the hill of life?"

"The reason we can't pull up the hill like a couple of horses," his wife said, "is because one of us is a jackass!"

471, 1000, 1431

Tears

1919. The movie had brought tears of sadness to the girl's eyes, but even after her boyfriend was driving her home, they continued to flow.

"There, there, honey," he said. "I'll kiss those tears away."

He tried to fulfill his promise for half an hour without success. "Will nothing stop them?" he asked.

"I'm afraid not," she said. "It's asthma. But please go right ahead with the treatment."

130, 750

Technique

1920. An attractive young lady had set a record in the house-to-house sale of vacuum cleaners. Asked the secret of her success, she explained to her boss.

"I always direct my sales talk to the husband—in tones so low that the wife doesn't dare miss a single word."

1921. An aspiring young actor was telling how he met a big producer. "He just put out his hand," said the actor, "and I went right up and shook it."

"Shook it!" said a veteran in the business. "You're done for. You should have licked it!"

1922. The henpecked husband visited the police station and said he would like to speak to the burglar who had robbed his home the night before.

"What do you want to see him for?" the jailer asked. "He's already confessed."

"You don't understand," the man said. "I just want to ask him how he got in the house without waking up my wife."

1923. The little boy saw his grandfather milking a cow for the first time. He watched fascinated.

"Now you know where the milk comes from, don't you?" his grandfather said.

Technique

"Sure," said the boy. "You feed the cow some breakfast food and water and then drain the crankcase."

390, 396, 735, 753, 903, 1081

Telephone

1924. The telephone operator said, "Special Operator, may I help you, please?"

The voice on the other end said, "Dustin."

"Dustin?" asked the operator. "What number in Dustin?"

"No number. Just Dustin," said the voice. "Just dustin' the telephone."

1925. The army psychiatric board was testing the mentality of a hillbilly draftee. "Did you ever hear voices without being able to tell who is speaking or where the sound comes from?"

"Yes, sir," said the hillbilly.

"When does this happen?" the doctor asked.

"Every time I talk over the telephone," the hillbilly said.

99, 159, 423, 649, 1074, 1125, 1131, 1583, 1628

Television

1926. In the midst of a bad electrical storm, a mother thought her young son might be frightened. She tiptoed into his room to look after him.

The little boy opened his eyes and said, "What's Daddy doing to the television set?"

307, 554, 1041, 1043, 1266

Temperance

1927. The political candidate had finished his speech and was answering questions.

"One question, sir, if I may," said a man down front, "do you ever drink alcoholic beverages?"

"Before I answer that," said the politician, "I'd like to know if it's in the nature of an inquiry or an invitation."

Temperance

1928. The temperance lecturer was nearing the close of his speech.

"I have lived in this town all my life," he said. "There are sixty-four cocktail bars in this town and I am proud to say that I have never been in one of them."

"Which one is that?" asked a voice from the rear.

1929. The man's wife was always after him to stop drinking. This time, she waved a newspaper in his face and said, "Here is another powerful temperance moral: 'Young Wilson got into a boat and shoved out into the river, and as he was intoxicated, he upset the boat, fell into the river and was drowned.' See, that's the way it is, if he had not drunk whiskey he would not have lost his life."

"Let me see," said her husband. "He fell into the river, didn't he?"

"That's right," his wife said.

"He didn't die until he fell in, is that right?" he asked.

"That's true," his wife said.

"Then it was the water that killed him," the man said, "not whiskey."

187, 617, 646, 1886, 1933

Test

1930. This question was on an I.Q. test: "Name two ancient sports."

The answer the student gave was: "Anthony and Cleopatra."

1931. A man bet ten dollars that he could ride the flywheel in a sawmill. As his widow paid off the bet, she said, "Bill was a kind and loving husband, but he didn't know much about flywheels."

1932. "What happened to Joe?" a fellow asked a friend. "How did he lose his fingers?"

"He put them in a horse's mouth to see how many teeth he had," his friend said.

Test

"And then what happened?" the first asked.

"The horse shut his mouth to see how many fingers Joe had," his friend said.

418, 682, 1195, 1432, 1727

Testimonial

1933.   A temperance organization was holding a meeting in the same hotel where a group of salesmen were gathered for a convention. The salesmen planned to have a big dinner with spiked watermelon for dessert. Somehow, the waiters got a bit mixed up and served the whiskey-flavored watermelon to the temperance organization by mistake. The hotel manager was frantic when he heard of the mix-up.

"That watermelon is soaked in whiskey," he shouted. "Get it away from those teetotalers before they run me out of town."

The waiters said it was too late. The dinner was over.

"What did they say?" asked the hotel manager. "How did they like it?"

"I don't know how they liked it," said the headwaiter, "but they're all putting the seeds in their pockets."

1934.   The bailiff was calling the roll of the witnesses for the defense in a personal damage suit. As their names were called, the lawyer for the plaintiff began to look worried. Finally, he leaned over to the lawyer for the defense and said, "Are all those witnesses really on your side?"

"They sure are," the defense attorney said.

"Okay," said the lawyer. "I'll drop the case. Because I've used those same witnesses in two of my cases—and they are sure winners every time."

84, 281, 326, 398, 595, 614, 677, 733, 821, 1256, 1347, 1862

Texas

1935.   A man from Kentucky was trying to brag to a Texan. "In Kentucky," he said, "we have Fort Knox. There is enough gold there to build a fence three feet high completely around Texas."

"Go ahead and build it," the Texan said. "If I like it, I'll buy it."

1936. A woman met a Texan who was on a visit to Philadelphia. Curious about his wealth, she said, "I suppose you own a lot of oil wells?"

"No," said the Texan, "not a one."

"Oh, you go in for cattle, then?" she asked.

"No," he said, "no cattle."

"Real estate, maybe? How much land do you own?" she said.

"Oh, about thirty-five acres, I reckon," he said.

"That's not much of a ranch," she said, "but what do they call it?"

"Right now, lady," the Texan said, "they call it downtown Dallas."

1937. A traveling salesman from New England made his first trip to Texas. When he returned home, he brought his wife a mink coat, a Cadillac, a portable television set, and half a dozen bracelets.

"How did you ever get all those things?" his wife wanted to know.

"Nothing to it, darling," he said. "I was in Houston during Halloween and went out playing trick or treat."

1938. Two Texans were hailed into court before a judge who knew them. "You fellows should be ashamed of yourselves," the judge said, "for being brought into court to settle a fence boundary. Why can't you be sensible and settle this matter out of court?"

"That's what we were doing," said the first one, "until the sheriff butted in and took our guns away!"

1939. A Texan was visiting in the Alps. A native, wishing to show off his country, took him to a certain spot, gave a loud cry, and waited. After about six minutes, the echo came back clearly. "I'll bet you don't have anything like that in your country!" he said triumphantly.

Texas

"Oh, I wouldn't say that," said the Texan. "At our summer place in the hills, I just lean out the window before going to bed and yell, 'Hey, wake up' and eight hours later the echo wakes me."

265, 275, 871

Theater

1940. It was after the intermission at the theatre, and the fat man and his wife were returning to their seats.

"Did I step on your feet as I went out?" he asked a man at the end of the row.

"You certainly did," said the man awaiting an apology.

The fat man turned to his wife. "It's all right, darling," he said. "This is our row."

36, 1854

Thief

1941. A wife was reading the newspaper and said to her husband, "It says here that they have just caught the biggest hotel thief in Miami Beach."

"Is that so," her husband said, "what hotel did he run?"

1942. "Where's Harry been lately?" a man asked a friend. "I haven't seen him for months."

"Haven't you heard?" the friend said. "He got sent up for three years for stealing a car."

"Why in the world did he steal a car?" asked the man. "Why didn't he buy one and not pay for it, like any other gentleman?"

1943. A man's wife was storming mad and said to her husband, "That new cleaning woman must have stolen two of our towels."

"Well, some people are like that," her husband said. "Which towels were they?"

"The new ones," she said. "The ones we brought back from the hotel in Miami Beach."

Thief

1944. A rather ignorant man accused of car theft had just taken the witness stand in court. The judge said to him, "Are you the defendant in this case?"

"No, sir, your honor," the man said, "I ain't defended nobody. I'se just the man what stole the car."

60, 151, 171, 185, 248, 303, 393, 455, 573, 1681

Think

1945. A Congressman was on his way to address a meeting. He was late and was rushing to get there, when he was stopped by a reporter.

"Sir, what do you think of our foreign policy?" asked the reporter.

"Please don't bother me now," the Congressman said. "I've got to make a speech. This is no time for me to think."

503, 535, 1146, 1633

Thirst

1946. The platoon was marching through the desert. It was hot and dry with not a drop of water anywhere. One soldier fell to the ground and moaned.

"What's the matter with him?" asked the sergeant.

"He's just homesick," said his buddy.

"Homesick? We're all homesick," said the sergeant.

"Yes," said the fellow's buddy, "but his is worse. His father owns a tavern."

1947. "Good morning," the doctor said to the woman. "How is your husband feeling this morning? Did you do as I said and take his temperature?"

"Yes, just as you said, doctor," the woman said. "I put a barometer on his chest and it said dry, so he took two shots of whiskey and got out of bed and went to work this morning."

78, 129, 644, 822, 886, 2066

Thrift

1948. Two little girls were discussing the subject of saving money in piggy banks.

"I think it's childish to save money that way," the first little girl said.

"I do, too," said the other. "And besides, I believe it encourages children to become misers."

"That's not the worst of it," said her friend. "It also turns parents into bank robbers."

1949. A hillbilly was visiting the small town dentist to get some advance prices on his work.

"The price for pulling a tooth is four dollars each," the dentist told him. "But in order to make it painless we'll have to give gas and that will be three dollars extra."

"Oh, don't worry about giving gas," the man said. "That won't be necessary. We can save the three dollars."

"That's all right with me," said the dentist. "I have heard that you mountain people are strong and tough. All I can say is that you are a brave man."

"It isn't me that's having my tooth pulled," the man said. "It's my wife."

191, 237, 298, 671

Ticket

1950. A patrolman was about to write a speeding ticket, when a woman in the back seat began shouting at the driver, "There! I told you to watch out. But you kept right on. Getting out of line, not blowing your horn, passing stop streets, speeding, and everything else. Didn't I tell you you'd get caught? Didn't I? Didn't I?"

"Who is that woman?" the patrolman asked.

"My wife," said the driver.

"Drive on," the patrolman said. "You have been punished enough."

1951. A missionary from Africa was visiting the Sunday school and telling about conditions on that faraway continent.

Ticket

"And just think," she told the children, "there isn't a Sunday school for two thousand miles. Now, you know what you should save your pennies for, don't you?"

"Yes," said a little boy, "to buy a ticket to Africa."

310, 1376, 1587

Tightwad

1952. The stingy businessman, on an out-of-town-trip, sent his wife a check for a million kisses for her anniversary present.

The wife was burned up and sent back a telegram: "Darling, thanks for the anniversary check. The man at the supermarket cashed it for me last night."

1953. "I wonder what women will wear in heaven?" a woman said to her husband.

"I don't know," her husband said, "but I suppose you'd want to buy the most expensive clothes, just as you do here."

"That's something you won't have to worry about," she said. "You won't be up there to pay for them."

1954. A young man asked his uncle how he had become so rich. "It's a long story," said his uncle, "and while I am telling it we might as well save the electricity." And he turned out the lights.

"No need to tell the story," said his nephew. "I get the message."

1955. The stingiest man in the world was the owner of a small hotel in New England. He kept everything locked up. He fixed it so none of the loafers around the place could get his hands on a newspaper or a piece of stationery, a book of matches, or even a chance to wash up in the men's room. He left only enough chairs in the lobby to seat his paying guests.

One day he had another inspiration and put a small sign over the clock in the lobby that read "for use of hotel guests only."

442

Tightwad

1956. A man went to the doctor with a stomachache. The doctor examined him carefully and couldn't find anything wrong with him.

"We have checked you over carefully," the doctor said to him, "and we can't find a thing organically wrong with you. We can't figure out what is causing your stomach trouble unless it is some sort of occupational disease. What sort of work do you do?"

"Oh, I'm a truck driver," the man said. "I work for John Henderson at the cement plant."

"You work for John Henderson," the doctor said. "Why in the world didn't you say so when you first came in? Here's a dollar, go get something to eat."

1957. The professional money raiser called upon the stingiest man in town. "I am seeking contributions for a worthy charity," he said. "Our goal is $100,000 and a well-known philanthropist has already donated a quarter of that."

"Wonderful," said the tightwad. "And I'll give another quarter. Have you got change for a dollar?"

226, 670, 1059, 2063

Time

1958. A man died and was greeted at the pearly gates by St. Peter. The man said: "You've had this job a long time, haven't you?"

"Well," said St. Peter, "here we count a million years as a minute and a million dollars as a cent."

"Wonderful," said the man. "I need a little cash. Lend me a cent."

"Sure," said St. Peter, "just wait a minute."

1959. The clerk in the jewelry store was trying to sell a lady an eight-day clock. He told her about the reliability of the manufacturer, then said, "And this remarkable clock will run for eight days without winding."

The lady's eyes popped in amazement. "You don't say," she said. "And how long will it run if you wind it?"

Time

1960.   Two girls were talking about a friend. "She got an idea no man's good enough for her," the first said.

"Well, she may be right," said the second.

"And on the other hand, she may be left, too," the first one said.

1961.   The county agricultural agent was driving down a country road and saw a farmer dumping a bucket of fruit and vegetable scraps to the hogs.

"You should cook those," said the county agent, "and your hogs could digest them in half the time."

The farmer thought about it for a moment. "What if they could," he said, "time don't mean nothing to a hog."

65, 174, 312, 322, 485, 544, 1133, 1205, 1333, 1353, 1779, 1836, 1863, 2098

Timely

1962.   The used-car salesman was trying hard. "Just look at those beautiful lines and that attractive upholstery. Besides, its purchase would be a most timely one."

"Timely?" asked the customer. "What do you mean it would be timely?"

"Because," said the salesman, "if I don't make this sale, my boss will fire me."

1963.   The man climbed on the stool at a little lunch counter for breakfast. "Quite a rainy spell, isn't it?" he said to the man next to him. "Almost like the flood."

"Flood? What flood?" said the man.

"Why, the flood," the first man said, "you know, Noah and the Ark and Mount Ararat."

"Nope," said the man, "I haven't read the morning paper yet."

1964.   A fellow met a friend who was pretty badly beaten up. "What happened to you?" he asked. "How did you get that black eye and cut lip?"

444

Timely

"Aw," his friend said, "just because I kissed the bride after the ceremony, this fellow took a poke at me."

"Why, that's a respectable custom around here," the man said. "Why should he object to that?"

"I don't know," said his friend, "unless because it was three years after the ceremony."

1965.   A man had ordered three fine suits from a tailor but had never received a bill. Thinking that the tailor might have over-looked sending him a statement, the man dropped by the tailor's shop.

"You never sent me a bill," the man said.

"Oh," said the tailor, "I never send out bills. I figure that all of my customers are gentlemen and they will come by and pay me."

"That's a funny way to do business," the man said. "Suppose a customer never comes by. You end up never getting your money."

"Not exactly," the tailor said. "You see, after a certain length of time I realize he is no gentleman—and so I sue him."

197, 212, 587, 666, 773

Tobacco

1966.   "My husband smoked a pack a day when we were mar-ried," said a lady to her neighbor. "Today he never touches cigarettes."

"That's wonderful!" her neighbor said. "To break a habit of a lifetime like that certainly requires a lot of will power."

"It certainly does," said the man's wife, "and that's just what I've got."

1967.   A farmer asked his friend, "Did you make any money on your tobacco crop this year?"

"We made just about enough to keep my wife and daughter in cigarettes for another year," the farmer said.

1475, 1527, 1753

Tourists

1968. A farmer was putting up a building on the lower forty. "What are you building?" asked a neighbor.

"Well," the farmer said. "If I can rent it, it's a rustic cottage nestled 'neath two tall pines. If I can't rent it, it's a cow shed."

1969. A tourist asked the hotel clerk, "May I have some stationery?"

"Are you a guest of the house?" the clerk asked.

"I certainly am not," he said, "I'm paying thirty-five dollars a day."

1970. After a thirty-minute wait, the bellhop knocked on the door and said, "Did you ring, sir?"

"No," said the guest, "I was tolling. I thought you were dead."

1971. A man who took his two little girls to the amusement park noticed that a rather well-dressed man kept riding the merry-go-round all afternoon. Once when the merry-go-round stopped, the man rushed off, took a drink of water and headed back again. As he passed near the little girls, their father said to him, "You certainly do like to ride on the merry-go-round, don't you?"

"No, I don't," the man said. "But, the fellow who owns this thing owes me $80 and taking it out in trade is the only way I'll ever collect from him."

77, 121, 256, 488, 541, 745, 1281, 1750

Traffic

1972. A wife said to her husband as they sat in their car in bumper-to-bumper traffic, "I told you it was too nice a day to go to the beach."

20, 1004, 1609, 1843

Trained

1973. A woman of experience was advising a class of young ladies. "Marry an army man," she said. "He can cook, make

Trained

beds, sew, is in perfect health, and already knows how to take orders."

445, 549, 583, 626, 694

Tramp

1974. The mild-mannered tramp had his usual hard-luck story all ready when he knocked on the back door. But he was not ready for the angry woman who opened the door and shouted:

"Well, did you wish to see me?"

The poor tramp was speechless for a moment, and then said meekly, "I-I ain't s-sure, but if I d-did, I sure got my wish."

1975. A tramp went to a free soup kitchen for a handout. He was quickly handed a bowl of soup.

"What, no menu?" he asked. "Don't I get a choice?"

"You get two choices, here, Bud," said the attendant, "take it or leave it!"

1976. A tramp knocked on the door and when the lady of the house opened it, he said:

"I wonder if you could give me a drink of water, please, because I'm so hungry that I don't know where I'm gonna sleep tonight."

1977. The tramp knocked on the back door and the lady who appeared said to him, "Has not Fortune ever knocked at your door?"

"He did once," said the tramp, "but I was out. Ever since then he has sent his daughter instead."

"His daughter," asked the lady. "Who is she?"

"Oh, her name is Miss Fortune," the tramp said.

1978. A tramp hit a man for a handout, but the man said, "Sorry, I'm in too big a hurry now, but I'll give you something on my way back."

Tramp

"You can't do that," said the tramp. "You just don't know how much money I've lost by giving credit to people I don't know."

1979.   The panhandler stopped a man on the street and asked him for a dime for a cup of coffee.

"What's the idea?" the man said. "What's the idea of stopping people on the street asking for money?"

"What do you want me to do," said the panhandler, "open an office?"

1980.   The lady of the house made the mistake of feeding the tramp before he did any work. Now, all she could do was hint. "The woodpile is in the backyard," she said.

"That's fine," he said. "What a wonderful place for a woodpile!"

112, 132, 218, 360

Trap

1981.   A boy said to his father: "Dad, how do you catch lunatics?"

"With face powder," his father said, "and fancy dresses and pretty smiles."

711

Travel

1982.   Two friends were talking about plans for the summer.

"Where are you going on your vacation?" the first man asked.

"We haven't decided yet," his friend said. "I want to take a trip around the world, but my wife wants to go someplace else."

1983.   "When I take a trip overseas, I'm going on one of those stabilized ships," a man told his friend.

"Those ships are all right," his friend said, "but it will cost you more."

"Maybe so," said the man, "but expenses are not what I have to keep down when I take a trip over seas."

Travel

1984. A lady wanted to be sure she was on the right train, and asked the conductor where it went.

"This train goes to Philadelphia and points west," he said.

"Well," she said, "I want a train that goes to Altoona and I don't care which way it points."

1985. An Eskimo was being tried for bigamy. He had a wife in Nome, another in Fairbanks, and still another in Juneau.

The judge looked at him severely and asked, "How could you do such a thing?"

"Fast dog team," the Eskimo said.

385, 490, 592, 717, 1014, 1276

Traveling salesman

1986. One traveling man to another: "I see you keep copies of all the letters you write to your wife. Do you do that to avoid repeating yourself?"

The other: "Nope, to avoid contradicting myself."

1987. A traveling salesman was riding a bus late one night, when the young man next to him said, "Excuse me, sir, but do you have a light?"

"Yes, I have a light," the salesman said, "but I'm not going to let you have it. Because if I give you a light, we'll get to talking. I'll ask what you do for a living and you say you are a salesman. You'll ask me where I'm from and I'll tell you Washington. Then, I'll ask you if you were ever there and you will say you get there now and then. Then, I'll suggest that the next time you are there, you should call us on the phone and come by for dinner. And the trouble is you will do it. And in that way you'll meet my attractive teen-age daughter and you will start going together and fall in love and get married. And I don't want it to happen. I don't want my daughter married to a traveling salesman. And I'm not going to give you a light."

1988. A salesman, with his car loaded with samples, became lost on a back country road. When he tried to turn around and

Traveling salesman

head back the way he had come, his car slipped off the black-top and became stuck in the mud.

He finally located a farmer with a mule who agreed to help him. After three hours of hard work, the farmer and the mule succeeded in getting his car back on the road and the salesman was sent on his way.

When he returned home, the farmer's wife asked him, "Well, that was some job. How much did you charge the man?"

"Two dollars," the farmer said.

"My," said his wife, "sometimes I think you should do the work and let that mule of yours handle the administrative end of the business."

770, 873, 1476, 1613, 1656, 1937, 2014

Treasurer

1989. The treasurer of the woman's civic club had just given her annual report and the president had called on a motion to approve it.

"I move we approve the report," one of the members said. "And I also move that since we have so much money in the treasury, that we do some good with it. I move we give one third of it to the school library, and one third of it to our building fund, and a third of it to the playground fund. And if we have any left over, I think we should give it to the Girl Scouts."

1990. After much protesting, a woman's husband finally agreed to go with her to "husbands' night" at her club meeting. Strangely enough, he seemed to enjoy himself immensely. But, on the way home his wife acted extremely peeved with him.

"What's the matter, honey," he said to her. "I went with you, didn't I? And I had a wonderful time. I tried to be real polite and I laughed every time one of the ladies said anything funny."

"That's just it," his wife said. "That last funny story you laughed at so hard was the treasurer's report."

450

Truck driver

1991. A truck driver was busy working with a shovel in the mud trying to free his truck, when a car stopped and a man yelled at him:

"Stuck in the mud?"

"Oh, no," the truck driver said gaily, "My truck just died and I'm digging a grave for it."

20, 75

True love

1992. A man had lost all of his money in a business deal and was flat broke. He told his girl friend about it and asked, "Darling, in spite of the fact that I'm not rich any more will you still love me?"

"Certainly, honey," she said, "I'll love you always—even though I'll probably never see you again."

1993. "Have you ever kissed a man before?" the young man asked the first girl he had ever kissed.

"Yes," admitted the girl.

"Tell me his name so that I can whip him," the boy said.

"But—but," she said, "he might be too many for you."

1994. The young man-of-the-world had just asked his newest girl friend to marry him. But she seemed undecided.

"If I should say no to you," she said, "would you commit suicide?"

"That," he said gallantly, "has been my usual procedure."

1995. Two fellows were talking about their girl friends. "Why do you go with Jean?" the first asked. "She's not really very pretty."

"Oh," said his friend, "she's different from the other girls I've met."

"Different?" asked the first. "How is she different?"

"Because," said the first, "she's the only girl who will go out with me."

True love

1996.   The college boy's father was visiting his son at school on homecoming day. After the big luncheon for visiting parents, they headed for the football game.

"This is going to be some game," the boy told his father. "You are going to see more excitement for four dollars than you ever saw for four dollars in all your life."

"Oh, I don't know about that," the boy's father said. "After all, that is all I paid for my marriage license."

78, 159, 198, 245, 496, 559, 1501, 2075

Trust

1997.   A man told his little boy to climb to the top of the step-ladder. He then held his arms open and told the little fellow to jump. As the little boy jumped, his father stepped back and the boy fell flat on his face.

"That's to teach you a lesson, son," the man said. "Don't ever trust anybody, even if he is your own father."

534, 1824

Truth

1998.   The boss caught the office boy in a lie. "Son," he said, "I'm surprised at you. Do you know what happens to boys who tell lies?"

"Yes, sir," he said. "When they get old enough, the company sends them out as salesmen."

1999.   An executive has given up trying to get neat, clean, correctly spelled letters from his secretary. Instead, he merely rubber stamps an explanation on each letter: "She can't type—but she's beautiful!"

2000.   First Wife: "Does your husband always lie to you?"

Second wife: "No, some nights I'm too tired to ask him any questions."

Truth

2001. A man had been fishing, and was telling a friend how big a fish he had caught.

"It was this long," he said, spreading his hands apart. "I never saw such a fish."

"I am sure you didn't," said his friend.

2002. "Surely you don't believe your husband's story about going fishing with his friends," the nosy neighbor said. "I notice he didn't bring any fish home."

"That's what makes me believe he was fishing," said the man's wife.

2003. A patent medicine salesman at the fair was shouting his claims for his Rejuvenation Elixir. "If you don't believe the label, just look at me," he shouted. "I take it and I'm 250 years old."

"Is he really that old?" asked a farmer of the salesman's young assistant.

"I really don't know," said the young man. "You see, I've only been with him for 120 years."

144, 235, 270, 363, 404, 421, 434, 569, 815, 1171, 1561

Twins

2004. A man went to his boss and asked for a raise.

"Can you give me two good reasons why you should get a raise?" asked his boss.

"Sure," said the man. "Twins!"

2005. There were two grown men—twins—living in the same town. One was a minister and the other was a doctor. People were always getting them confused.

One day a man stopped the doctor on the street and said, "Sir, I want to compliment you on the inspiring sermon you preached last Sunday."

"You have us mixed up," the doctor said. "I'm not the brother who preaches, I'm the one who practices."

58, 172, 1674

Umbrella

2006.   A customer said to the waiter, "Did I by any chance, leave an umbrella here yesterday?"

"What kind of umbrella?" the waiter asked.

"Oh, any old kind," the customer said. "I'm not a bit fussy."

255

Understanding

2007.   A strong masterful type fellow was blowing off steam in a bar.

"I say a man should be head of his own house, or know the reason why," he said.

"You're right, and most men do know the reason," said his friend.

2008.   It was arithmetic time, and the teacher asked the class: "If there were eleven sheep in a field and six jumped the fence, how many would there be left?"

"None," said the little boy in the front seat.

"Oh, yes, there would," said the teacher, "there would be five left."

"No, ma'am, there wouldn't," said the little boy. "You may know arithmetic, but you don't know sheep."

2009.   "You just can't imagine what things are like up in the arctic regions," the explorer was telling a group of friends, "until you've stood there, a small, insignificant speck, surrounded by vast stretches of white."

"Yes, I know," one of his friends said. "I've been like that."

"You have?" the explorer asked. "Where was that?"

"Once," his friend said, "when I appeared at a formal dinner in a sports jacket."

2010.   A lady who suffered occasionally from arthritis, said to her new maid: "Sometimes it will be necessary for you to help me upstairs."

"I understand, ma'am," said the maid. "I drink a little now and then myself."

454

Understanding

2011. "I wish I knew where Wilbur was," the young bride said to her mother.

"I am sure," said her mother, "that you mean you wish you knew where Wilbur is."

"Oh, no," her daughter said. "I knew where he is. He's in bed with a black eye and a headache. I would like to know where he was."

2012. It is easy to understand the truth of the recent report that says that the children of today cry more and behave worse than the children of a generation ago. Because those weren't children—they were us.

2013. An Italian was trying to learn the English language, but was having his difficulties. He asked an American friend of his, "What is a polar bear?"

"A polar bear?" the friend asked. "He lives up North."

"But what does he do?" asked the Italian.

"Oh, he sits on a cake of ice and eats fish," the American said.

"That settles it," said the Italian. "I will not accept!"

"What in the world are you talking about, you won't accept?" asked his friend.

"Ah," said the Italian. "I was invited to be a polar bear at a funeral."

94, 295, 357, 446, 472, 531, 681, 1439, 1751, 1765, 1898

University

2014. A book salesman, trying to find a certain university, got on the wrong road and ended up at a mental hospital. He discovered his mistake right away and the guard told him how to find the university.

"Well," he said as he left, "I suppose there isn't much difference between the two institutions, anyway."

"That's where you are wrong," said the guard. "In this place, you've got to show improvement to get out."

619, 1082

Unreasonable

2015.   A young fellow was talking to his friend.

"Why did you break your engagement?" he asked.

"Because she wanted to get married," he said.

2016.   A fellow complained to the health department about his brothers.

"I've got six brothers," he said. "We all live in one room. They have too many pets. One has twelve monkeys and another has twelve dogs. There's no air in the room and it's terrible! You've got to do something about it."

"Have you got windows?" asked the man at the health department.

"Yes," said the man.

"Why don't you open them?" he suggested.

"What?" yelled the man, "and lose all my pigeons?"

2017.   The poker party was still going on at 3 A.M. in the hotel room. By that time, it was pretty noisy. Finally, a weary guest in the next room started to pound on the wall.

"Well, I must say," said one of the players, "this is certainly an unreasonable hour to be hanging pictures."

534

Used car

2018.   The farmer in the old, broken-down wreck drove up to the toll booth.

"Two dollars," said the toll collector.

"Sold," said the owner.

2019.   A preacher drove into the used-car lot and crawled out of his beat-up old car.

"You sold me this car last week," he told the dealer, "but I've decided to bring it back."

"What's the matter?" asked the dealer. "Can't you run it?"

"Not and stay in the ministry," the preacher said.

2020.   The salesman was trying to close the deal.

"This car is absolutely the very last word," he said.

Used car

"Wonderful, I'll take it," said the man. "My wife will love it."

2021.   "You sold me a car two weeks ago," the man said to the used-car salesman.

"Yes, sir, I remember," the salesman said.

"Well, tell me again all you said about it then," the man said. "I'm getting discouraged."

935, 965, 1351, 1657, 1962

Vacancy

2022.   One day Joe didn't show up for work as handy man around the store. A customer missed seeing him and asked, "Where is Joe? He's not sick, is he?"

"No," said the manager, "he doesn't work here any more."

"Oh," said the customer. "Have you got anybody in mind for the vacancy?"

"No, I haven't," he said, "because Joe didn't leave no vacancy."

Vacation

2023.   A guest at a summer boardinghouse had been complaining constantly since her arrival. Finally, the manager told her, "I didn't mind moving your bureau, changing the position of your bed, letting you have an extra blanket, and giving you some wedges to keep the windows from rattling, and letting you sit at a table by the window, but you've got to take the weather as you find it."

2024.   "Well," said an office worker to his friend down the hall, "what kind of vacation did you have?"

"I took a honeydew vacation this year," the fellow said. "You know, that's where you stay at home and your wife keeps saying, 'Honey, do this' or 'Honey, do that.' "

2025.   "Hi, Joe," said a fellow to his friend. "I haven't seen you around lately. Where have you been?"

Vacation

"I've been to the mountains for a change and a rest," his friend said.

"How did it go?" asked the first fellow.

"Okay, I guess," said his friend, "except it was the bell captain who got the change and the hotel that got the rest."

32, 541, 560, 827, 1590, 1708, 1972, 1982

Value

2026. "All that I am worth today I owe to my mother," said the speaker.

A voice in the back said, "Why don't you send her 30 cents and settle the bill?"

2027. A man was seriously ill and was advised by his family doctor to consult a famous specialist. Arrangements were made with the famous doctor for an operation. As the man was leaving the doctor's office he asked what the fee would be.

"This is a most delicate operation," the doctor said, "and the fee will be $2,000."

"What?" cried the man, "$2,000? That's an outrage. Why, the doctor in my home town would do that same operation for only $200."

"My advice to you," said the specialist, "is to let him do the operation. And if you do, you won't even have to pay the $200 —your heirs will pay it for you."

43, 198, 404, 558, 563, 766, 1052, 1274

Versatile

2028. A sign in the window of a restaurant read: "$500 to any person who orders something we can't serve."

A smart college boy said to the waitress, "Bring me an elephant ear sandwich."

Going to the manager, she said: "We've got to pay out $500. There's a college boy who wants an elephant ear sandwich."

"What!" cried the manager. "Do you mean to tell me we're out of elephant ears?"

Versatile

"No, we're not out of elephant ears," the waitress said, "but we don't have any more of those big buns."

2029. "The most adaptable and versatile man I've ever met," said a fellow, "was a piano tuner I once knew in the cattle-raising section of Texas.

" 'You certainly can't make much of a living at piano tuning out here,' I said to him. 'There's not a dozen pianos within a hundred miles.'

" 'That's right,' the fellow said, 'but I make out all right by tightening up barbed-wire fences.' "

355, 1559, 1685

Veteran

2030. A young recruit was talking to a battle-scarred old-timer.

"Did you participate in many engagements in the Pacific?" he asked.

"Only five," said the old-timer.

"And you came through all of them without injury?" he asked.

"Not exactly," the old-timer said. "I married the fifth."

463, 1629

Vice

2031. The young lady had said she would marry him, and he was holding her tenderly. "I wonder what your folks will think," he said. "Do they know that I write poetry?"

"Not yet, honey," she said. "I've told them about your drinking and gambling, but I thought I'd better not tell them everything at once."

459, 939

View

2032. As the guest was checking out of the hotel, the manager offered him a number of picture postcards. "Here are a few views of our hotel for you to take with you."

View

"Thanks," said the guest, "but I have my own views of this hotel."

2033.   An artist was hunting a spot where he could spend a week or two and do some work in peace and quiet. He had stopped at the village store in a small mountain community and was talking to one of the customers about staying at his farm.

"I think I'd like to stay up at your farm," the artist said, "provided there is some good scenery. Is there very much to see up there?"

"I'm afraid not," said the farmer. "Of course, if you look out the front door you can see the barn across the road, but if you look out the back door, you can't see anything but mountains for the next forty miles."

146, 1429

Violin

2034.   The little boy was practicing his violin lessons, while his sister played with her dog. As the boy scraped back and forth with the bow, the dog set up a heartbreaking wail.

Finally, his sister yelled at her brother, "For goodness' sakes, can't you play something the dog doesn't know?"

1293, 1415, 1729

Virtue

2035.   "My grandfather," bragged the man from Kentucky, "lived to be ninety-nine and never used glasses."

"Well," said his friend, "lots of people would rather drink from the bottle."

2036.   The man went to the doctor with a severe headache. The doctor examined him carefully and at great length.

"I don't know exactly what is causing your headaches," the doctor said, "but I would advise you to give up smoking and drinking and to go to bed earlier at night and get more rest."

Virtue

"But," cried the patient, "I don't smoke or drink and I'm always in bed by ten o'clock. I never fail to get at least nine hours' sleep a night."

"In that case," the doctor said, "I know what is causing the headaches. Your halo is on too tight."

982

Visitors

2037. The new Baptist preacher had been invited to join the local Kiwanis Club. He made friends rapidly and became one of the most popular members of the club. After a few weeks, several of the members suggested that they pay a surprise visit to hear their new member preach. Only three of them showed up at the church, and they were a few minutes late. They came in just as the deacons were preparing to receive the morning offering. The church was absolutely full—not a vacant seat in the entire sanctuary. The three men had to stand in the back.

As they entered, the preacher saw them and leaned over and whispered to one of the deacons: "As soon as you have taken up the offering, how about three chairs for those Kiwanians."

After the offering had been received and brought to the altar, the deacon turned to the congregation and said in his most solemn tones, "I don't know exactly what this is all about, but the minister wants all of us to stand and give three cheers for the Kiwanis Club."

121, 229, 304, 483, 496, 1099

Vote

2038. An irate voter said to the man running for office: "I wouldn't vote for you if you were St. Peter himself."

"If I were St. Peter," said the candidate, "you couldn't vote for me. You wouldn't be in my district."

2039. It was late at night on election day. Two loyal party workers were watching the returns on television. As their man continued to fall behind in the count, one of them said to the other, "That election was crooked. We were robbed."

Vote

"What makes you say that?" his friend asked.

"For one thing," the first man said, "when I was voting this morning, I saw our opponent's campaign chairman and his publicity man stuffing the ballot box."

"Why," said his friend, "I was with you when you voted, and I didn't even see them at the polls."

"Oh," said the first man, "that was the first time I voted. I saw them on the second time around."

284, 325, 328, 448, 1454

Wager

2040. The draftee asked the sergeant, "What must a man be, Sergeant, in order to be buried in Arlington Cemetery?"

"He must be a veteran, or else serving in the Armed Forces," said the Sergeant.

"Shucks!" said the draftee, "Then I lose my bet."

"Why, what did you bet?" asked the Sergeant.

"I bet that he had to be dead," said the draftee.

2041. The waiter suggested to the customer the steak smothered with mushrooms.

"No," said the customer, "I don't want any mushrooms. I ate some here last week and was almost poisoned."

"Is that a fact, sir?" the waiter said gaily. "Then I did win my bet with the chef."

2042. Two men in a bar were arguing about such things as names and spelling. "I'll bet you a dollar that I've got the hardest name of anybody here," said the first.

"I'll take that bet," said the other. "What's your name?"

"Stone," said the first triumphantly.

"Pay me," said the second. "My name's Harder."

1555, 1931

Waiter

2043. "Look here," said the customer, "I just found a collar button in my soup."

Waiter

"Oh, thank you, sir," said the waiter. "I have been looking all over for it."

352, 472, 683, 1218, 1303, 1361, 1464, 1536

Waitress

2044. The owner of the restaurant was complaining to a waitress:

"Each week you break more things than your wages amount to. What can we do about it?"

The waitress shrugged her shoulders and said, "I don't know, unless you raise my wages."

2045. A waitress was trying to look after her customer.

"How did you find your steak?" she asked.

"Oh," he said, "without too much trouble. I moved a piece of potato and there it was."

2046. A grouchy-looking man went into a seafood restaurant and asked the waitress, "Do you serve crabs here?"

"We serve anybody," she said. "Come in and sit down."

2047. The restaurant manager asked his head waitress, "Have the customers found something fresh to complain about this morning?"

"No," said the waitress, "it's the eggs."

110, 322, 364, 416, 1118, 1430, 1570

Warning

2048. A little boy in school raised his hand, and the teacher asked, "Yes, Johnny, what is it?"

"I don't want to scare you," Johnny said, "but Dad said if I don't get better grades someone is going to get in serious trouble."

2049. A man and his wife were sitting on a bench in the park one evening just at dusk. Without knowing that they were close

Warning

by, a young man and his girl friend sat down at a bench on the other side of a hedge.

Almost immediately, the young man began to talk in the most loving manner imaginable.

"He doesn't know we are sitting here," the woman whispered to her husband. "It sounds like he is going to propose to her. I think you should cough or something and warn him."

"Why should I warn him?" her husband asked. "Nobody warned me."

568, 589, 944

Washington

2050.   Two partners with a small store down a side street in a poor neighborhood were going broke.

"I think we'd better quit the store," the first one said. "Business is terrible. We haven't made a dime in a whole month. I think we ought to close up and look for a job."

"I can't understand it," said the other. "We're not doing any business at all, and here in the paper, the President says business is wonderful!"

"Well," said his partner, "maybe he's got a better location."

2051.   After a full day of being shown from clerk to clerk, a little lady was finally shown into the office of the Assistant Secretary of the Department of Agriculture in Washington.

"But you won't do," she said. "I want to see the Secretary of Agriculture himself."

"He's out of town just now," said his assistant. "Can't you tell me what you want?"

"Well, maybe," said the little lady. "I wanted to ask him about a geranium I have that isn't doing so well."

2052.   The local chairman had just given a glowing biographical sketch of the distinguished government official who had flown down from Washington to address their annual meeting.

He wound up his introduction by saying, "And now, ladies and gentlemen, you will hear the dope from Washington."

Washington

2053. The chicken farmer was losing a lot of his flock, and wrote to the Department of Agriculture: "Gentlemen, Something is wrong with my chickens. Every morning when I come out, I find two or three lying on the ground cold and stiff with their feet in the air. Can you tell me what is the matter?"

Eight weeks later he received this letter from Washington: "Dear Sir, Your chickens are dead."

2054. A little fellow asked his father, "Dad, what is money?"

"Money," said his father, "is something that rubs against you on its way to Washington."

2055. A little boy who had been visiting his uncle all summer in Washington, had to return home. Before he left, he said he wanted to say goodbye to his favorite statue. It was a regal pose of General Lafayette on his horse. "Goodbye, Lafayette," the little boy said. Then, as they turned away, he asked his uncle, "Who's that man on Lafayette?"

2056. The family was visiting Washington and the boy's father had taken him to see the Senate in session. The Senate was opened by a prayer, offered by the chaplain.

"Who is that man?" asked the boy.

"That is the chaplain," said his father.

"Does he pray for the Senators, Dad?" asked the boy.

"No, son," his father said. "When he gets up there and looks out over the Senate, he prays for the country."

403, 447, 1759, 1904

Weather

2057. Meteorologist: "Do you know why hurricanes are named after women?"

Secretary: "No, why?"

Meteorologist: "Because they are 'her'-icanes—not 'him'-icanes."

2058. A fierce sleet storm was sweeping through Los Angeles. The loyal member of the Chamber of Commerce said to a friend, "My, some pretty rough weather blows in from Nevada, doesn't it?"

2059.   "The forecast for this afternoon will be rain," said the weatherman to his assistant.

"But what makes you so sure?" said the assistant. "There isn't a cloud in the sky."

"It's a cinch," said the weatherman. "I've got a date for golf, I've lost my umbrella, my kids are going on a picnic, and my wife is giving a lawn party."

2060.   The local weatherman was wrong so much of the time, that he became the laughing stock of the town. Finally, he asked for a transfer.

"Why," asked Washington, "do you wish to be transferred?"

"Because," the weatherman wrote back, "the climate here doesn't agree with me."

398, 409, 419, 695, 1650, 2023

Wedding

2061.   A salesman traveling through the mountains stopped for the night in a small town. He managed to make a date with one of the local belles. Late that night they were parked cozily on a lonely road. Snuggled up close to him in a tight embrace she said: "Papa is the best rifle shot in the state."

"So," he said. "Your old man's the best shot in the state. And just what does that make you?" the salesman said with a touch of sarcasm in his voice.

She snuggled closer and whispered, "It's gonna make me your bride."

2062.   A woman arrived late for the wedding. As she rushed up to the door, an usher asked her to show her invitation.

"I have none," she growled.

"Are you a friend of the groom?" asked the usher.

"I certainly am not," the woman said. "I'm the bride's mother."

Wedding

2063. "Oh, Mother," said the bride-to-be, "look at the silver tray Aunt Millie sent me."

"It isn't silver," said her mother.

"Do you know silver that well?" the girl asked.

"No," her mother said, "but I know your Aunt Millie."

28, 101, 277, 288, 368, 414, 536, 936, 1360

Weeds

2064. A man who had just moved into the suburbs said to his next-door neighbor, "I want to start a garden, but how do you tell the weeds from the garden plants?"

"There is only one way," said the experienced neighbor. "Pull them up. If they come up again, they're weeds."

1465, 1567

Whiskey

2065. A little boy's father died from alcoholism. After the funeral, the little boy asked his mother, "Mama, when I go to heaven, how will I know Papa?"

"Just look for an angel with a red nose and bleary eyes," she said.

2066. One of the town's leading drinkers was called as a witness in a bootleg case.

"Did you ever buy any bootleg whiskey from the defendant?" the judge asked.

"Well, your honor, I don't exactly know what you mean by bootleg whiskey," the witness said.

"You certainly can tell the difference between good whiskey and bad whiskey, can't you?" asked the judge.

"To tell the truth, judge," the man of experience said, "I don't reckon I ever tasted any really bad whiskey."

2067. The county agent was traveling in the mountains of Kentucky and was talking to a backwoods farmer. "Are you folks around here ever troubled with bugs getting into your corn?" he asked.

"Sure, all the time, mister," the farmer said. "But we just dip them out and drink it down anyway."

2068.   A visitor from New England asked the Texan, "Is there any other cure for snake bites besides whiskey?"

"Who cares?" said the Texan.

2069.   The man hated the thought of seeing a doctor, but his symptoms were serious enough to make him overcome his dread. He made an appointment for an examination but before keeping his appointment, he fortified himself rather strongly with a few shots of bourbon.

After the examination, he asked the doctor, "Well, doctor, what does the report show?"

"According to the analysis from the laboratory, there seems to be an indication of a small amount of blood flowing through your alcohol stream," the doctor said.

2070.   The farmhand had been in town all afternoon and had finished his Christmas shopping. With his arms full of bundles, he stood waiting for the bus. As the door of the bus opened and he stepped up, one of the packages in his arms fell to the ground with the unmistakeable sound of broken glass.

As the man stood watching the brown liquid flowing toward the gutter, he said, "Christmas sure did come and go in a hurry this year."

2071.   A man at the race track rushed into the clubhouse section. "A lady has fainted in the corridor," he shouted. "Has anybody got any whiskey?"

Immediately, a half-dozen bottles were handed to him. He took the nearest one, turned it up, and took a big drink. Handing the bottle back, he said, "Thank you. It always did make me feel sick to see a lady faint."

13, 65, 187, 202, 319, 360, 408, 490, 617, 817, 1057, 1192, 1543, 1737, 1757

Whistle

2072. The bellboy was whistling as he went about his work.

"Young fellow," said the hotel manager, "you know better than to whistle while you are on duty."

"Oh, I'm not whistling, sir," said the bellboy. "I'm paging a lady's dog."

2073. "How many times have I told you not to whistle at your work," the boss shouted at the mail-room clerk.

"Oh, that's all right," said the young man, "I wasn't working."

441, 845, 1053, 1663

Wholesale

2074. Surprised at what she had just heard, a young girl said to her friend: "Do you mean to tell me that you are engaged to five boys at once?"

"Yes," her friend said, "and I can hardly wait until after Christmas to get things straightened out."

2075. A young lady was looking over greeting cards. The salesman said, "Here's a nice one—'To the Only Boy I Ever Loved.'"

"Wonderful," said the young lady, "I'll take six."

172

Widow

2076. "So our friend finally got married," a man said to his buddy. "I thought he was a confirmed bachelor looking out for number one."

"Oh, he was," said the other, "but he met a widow who was out looking for number two."

2077. "Tell us about the widow getting married," the girls at the bridge club said to their friend who had just come from the wedding.

Widow

"It was beautiful," she said, "only the strangest thing happened. Just as she and the bridegroom were walking down the aisle, the lights in the church went out."

"What did they do?" asked one of the ladies.

"Oh, they kept right on," the wedding guest said. "The widow knew the way."

72, 361, 371, 411, 558, 1087, 1498, 1769, 2084

Wife

2078.   A man sitting on a bus said to his friend, "They say your wife is outspoken."

"By whom?" asked the husband.

2079.   Two men were talking about their vacations. "I'm going to Yellowstone Park," said one.

"That's great," said the other. "Don't forget to see Old Faithful."

"See her?" said the first one. "She's going with me."

2080.   "How is your cold?" a fellow asked his friend.

"It's pretty stubborn," the man said.

"And how's your wife these days?" the friend asked.

"Oh, she's about the same," the man said.

2081.   "You have been charged with vagrancy," the judge said to the prisoner before him. "And I'm going to sentence you to sixty days in the workhouse because you have no visible means of support."

"Oh, yes I have, judge," the man said. "Honey, come stand up here where the judge can see you."

2082.   "You look mighty dressed up," a fellow said to his friend. "What's going on, something special?"

"Yes," his friend said, "I'm celebrating tonight with my wife. I'm taking her to dinner in honor of seven years of perfect married happiness."

"Seven years of married happiness," the fellow said. "Why, man, I think that's wonderful."

Wife

"I think it's pretty good myself," his friend said, "seven out of thirty."

10, 11, 49, 111, 139, 151, 164, 241, 249, 256, 331, 335, 415, 518, 764, 1568, 1728

Will power

2083. The little boy wouldn't take his medicine. His father was trying to persuade him.

"Come on," said his father. "I don't like medicine any better than you, but I just make up my mind that I'll take it, and I do. It's just a question of will power."

"Well, when I've got medicine to take," said the little boy, "I just make up my mind that I won't take it, and I don't."

282, 1966

Wine

2084. A little old widow was visiting her son's home for the first time in years. At dinner, they served wine and the little lady tasted her first glass.

After a minute or two she said, "How strange. It tastes exactly like the medicine your father had been taking every night for the past thirty years."

333, 391, 418, 1039

Winner

2085. The man having dinner said to the waiter, "My lobster doesn't have a claw. Why is that?"

"Well, sir," the waiter said. "They are so fresh that they fight with each other in the tank in the kitchen."

"Well," said the customer, "take this one away, and bring me the winner."

2086. "I hear your little brother broke his arm," a neighbor said to the little girl next door. "How did it happen?"

Winner

"Oh," the little girl said, "we were playing a game. We were trying to see who could lean out of the window the farthest, and he won."

95, 556, 801, 873, 2028

Wishes

2087. A young lady asked her girl friend, "If you could have two wishes, what would they be?"

"Well," said the second. "I'd wish for a husband."

"That's one wish," said the first. "What's the second?"

"I don't know right now," said her friend. "I'd save the other until I saw how he turned out."

91, 261, 377, 412, 754, 1388, 1526

Witness

2088. A farmer was testifying in court. He noticed that everything he was saying was being taken down by the court reporter. As he went along, he began talking faster and still faster. Finally, the reporter was frantic to keep up with him.

Suddenly, the farmer said, "Good gracious, mister, don't write so fast, I can't keep up with you!"

2089. The little lady in the witness box had been getting the best of the lawyer.

"You claim to have had no education," he said sarcastically, "yet you have been able to answer my questions all right."

"You don't have to be educated," she said, "to answer a lot of silly questions."

437, 569, 595, 799, 878, 1820, 1934

Woman

2090. A lady's maid rushed into the room and cried, "Hurry, your husband's lying unconscious in the hall beside a large round box with a piece of paper clutched in his hand."

"How exciting," the lady said, "my fur coat's come."

Woman

2091. Two fellows at a cocktail party were talking about a friend of theirs who also was there.

"Look at him," the first friend said, "over there in the corner with all those girls standing around listening to him tell big stories and bragging. I thought he was supposed to be a woman hater."

"He is," said the second friend, "only he left her at home tonight."

122, 298, 336, 405, 713, 1318, 1722

Woman driver

2092. A woman trying to pull her car out of a parking space banged into the car ahead. Then she backed into the car behind. Finally, after pulling into the street, she hit a beer truck. When the police arrived, the patrolman said, "Let's see your license, lady."

"Don't be silly," she said. "Who do you think would give me a license?"

2093. Remember, if your wife wants to learn to drive the car, don't stand in her way.

2094. Two men were in a car following a woman driver.

"She's got her hand out," said the driver. "What does that mean?"

"It only means one thing for sure," said his friend, "the window is open."

2095. A lady had just squeezed her car into the only parking place on the street.

"What do you think you are doing?" asked a policeman.

"I'm just parking my car," she said. "This looks like a good place. The sign there says, 'Safety Zone.' "

2096. "You saw this lady driving toward you," the officer said. "Why didn't you move over and give her half the road?"

"I was going to," said the man, "as soon as I could tell which half she wanted."

Woman driver

2097. "Lady," said the patrolman, "how long do you expect to be out this morning?"

"What do you mean by that question?" she said sourly.

"Well," he said, "there are several thousand other drivers who would like to use this street after you get through with it."

2098. One man asked another, "How long did it take your wife to learn to drive?"

"It will be ten years in September," he said.

2099. The officer was questioning a woman he had stopped. "How do you get along without a speedometer on your car?" he asked.

"Well," she said, "when I drive fifteen miles an hour, my fender starts to rattle. At twenty-five the windows rattle. At thirty, the motor starts smoking, and besides that's as fast as it goes anyway."

2100. A woman parked downtown on a crowded street in a tight parking place. She backed in until she hit the car in back of her with a loud bang. Then she pulled forward and banged the car ahead. The noise drew the attention of the policeman at the corner.

Noticing that he was watching, the lady called to him and said, "Did I make it all right, officer?"

"Yes, lady, you made it all right," he said, "but do you always park by ear?"

16, 51, 66, 147, 239, 345, 442, 1878

Women's hats

2101. A husband was shopping for a hat with his wife. She tried on a wide-brimmed model, and said: "Do you like this turned down, dear?"

"How much is it?" he asked.

"Twenty-five dollars," she said.

"Yes," her husband said, "turn it down."

Women's hats

2102. The minister was chatting with a member of his congregation on the street one day.

"I felt so sorry for your wife in church last Sunday," he said, "when she had that terrible spell of coughing and everyone turned to look at her."

"Don't worry about that," the man said. "She had on her new spring hat."

66, 90, 668, 1846

Words

2103. "Those words mean fight where I come from," the man at the bar said.

"Well," said the man sitting next to him, "why don't you fight?"

"'Cause I ain't where I come from," the first man said.

2104. "What is a synonym?" asked the teacher.

"A synonym," said the young man in the back, "is a word you use in place of another when you can't spell the first one."

2105. Two boys who lived on a farm were arguing about what they had learned in school. "I'll bet it's right to say a hen is sitting," said the first.

"You are wrong," said the other. "It should be setting."

Their father finally got into the argument and said, "That's not important, boys. All I want to know is, when a hen cackles be she layin' or lyin'."

229, 252, 363, 640, 958, 1002, 2020

Workman

2106. The businessman fired an employee by writing him a letter. He was absent for four days, but on the fifth he was back on the job.

"Didn't I send you a letter telling you that you were fired?" the boss asked him.

"Yes, sir," said the man, "the letter said I was fired, but on the envelope it said, 'Return in five days.'"

Workman

2107. The president of the company was walking down the loading platform when he noticed a young man sitting on a box reading a comic book.

"How much do you get paid?" he asked.

"Forty dollars a week," the young man said.

"Okay," said the president, "here's a week's pay. Now get out. You're fired."

Later, he saw the foreman and asked, "How long have we had that fellow working here?"

"Oh, he didn't work here," said the foreman. "He was just picking up a package for a customer across town."

71, 497, 1608, 1668

Works

2108. Two ministers were rushing to catch a train. Afraid they were late, one looked at his watch but found it had stopped.

"This is awful," he said. "I've always put such faith in this watch."

"This is once," said the other, "when good works would probably have served better."

460, 1791

Worry

2109. "I'm terribly worried," said a woman to the psychiatrist. "My husband thinks he's a horse."

"We should be able to cure him," said the psychiatrist. "But it will take a long time and quite a lot of money."

"Oh, money is no object," the woman said. "He just won the Pimlico Sweepstakes."

2110. "You sure look depressed," a fellow said to his friend. "What's the trouble?"

"Well," the man said, "you remember my aunt who just died. I was the one who had her confined to the mental hospital for the last five years of her life. When she died, she left me all her money. Now I've got to prove that she was of sound mind when she made her will six weeks ago."

2111. The barber asked the man in his chair, "How did you lose your hair?"

"Worry," his customer said.

"What did you worry about?" asked the barber.

"About losing my hair," the man said.

105, 107, 190, 335, 385, 444, 467, 516, 638

Writer

2112. Two friends were chatting in a bar.

"Did you know that I had taken up writing as a career?" asked the first.

"Congratulations," said his friend. "Sold anything yet?"

"Yes," said the writer, "my watch, my violin, and a shotgun."

2113. The editor said to the writer as he turned down his manuscript, "Your style of writing must be very hard work."

"Yes, it is," said the writer. "But how did you know?"

"Why," said the editor, "it makes me tired to read it."

2114. A young lady in Chicago was trying to sell a short story to a magazine editor.

"Did you ever write anything before?" asked the editor.

"Oh, yes," she said. "I wrote a confession story once."

"Was it published? he asked.

"No, it wasn't published," she answered, "but the editor came all the way from New York to meet me."

2115. A fellow was talking to an aspiring author.

"Don't you find writing a thankless job?" he asked.

"Oh, no," the writer said, "everything I write is returned with thanks."

2116. A would-be writer called on a publisher about a manuscript he had submitted.

Writer

"It is well written," the publisher said, "but we publish only works by writers with well-known names."

"That's good," said the author. "My name is Smith."

2117. A friend asked the young author about his first and only novel.

"How is it going?" he asked.

"Well," said the author, "it certainly isn't one of those trashy best-sellers."

88, 163, 327, 351, 510, 673, 771, 1108, 1488, 1767, 1859

Younger generation

2118. A newspaper reporter was interviewing a man on the occasion of his 99th birthday.

"Tell me," he said, "do you believe the younger generation is on the road to perdition?"

"Yes, sir," said the old man. "And I've believed it for more than eighty years."

69, 99, 107, 136, 174, 194, 251, 376, 1161, 1179, 1875, 2012

Zoo

2119. Two little boys were visiting the zoo. When they came to the ostrich cage, the first one said: "That's the biggest living bird, did you know that?"

"It ain't only the biggest living bird," said the other, "it's the biggest bird when it's dead, too!"

2120. This conversation went on not long ago at the zoo.

"Look at that one, the one staring at us through the bars. Doesn't he look intelligent?"

"Yes, there's something uncanny about it. He looks as if he understood every word we are saying."

"Look at the way he walks on his hind legs and how he swings his arms, too. There! He's got a peanut . . . and he knows he has to remove the shell just like us."

"That must be a female beside him. Listen to her talk. He doesn't seem to be paying much attention to her. She must be his mate. They look rather sad, don't they?"

"Yes, I bet they wish they were in here with us monkeys."

2121. A schoolteacher who was escorting her class of little ones through the zoo, noticed two of the keepers standing near one of the big barless cages crying as though their hearts were broken.

"What in the world is the matter?" she asked. "Is there anything I can do?"

"Nothing you can do, lady," one of the men said. "The elephant died this morning."

"Oh," said the schoolteacher, "I can understand how heartbroken you must be. You must have loved that elephant deeply."

"That isn't it, lady," said the other man. "It's just that the manager of the zoo told us we had to dig her grave."

171, 741, 1066, 1194, 1412, 1578